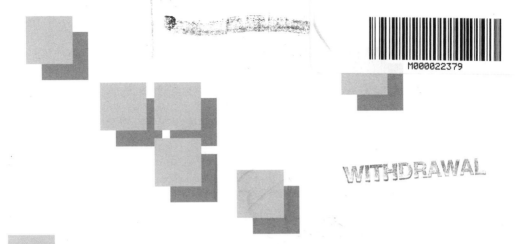

Understanding and Implementing Successful Data Marts

 # Douglas Hackney

▲
▼▼

Addison-Wesley Developers Press
An Imprint of Addison Wesley Longman, Inc.

Reading, Massachusetts • Harlow, England • Menlo Park, California
Berkeley, California • Don Mills, Ontario • Sydney • Bonn
Amsterdam • Tokyo • Mexico City

Library of Congress Cataloging-in-Publication Data

Hackney, Douglas.
    Understanding and implementing successful data marts / Douglas Hackney.
        p.   cm.
    Includes bibliographical references and index.
    ISBN 0-201-18380-3
    1. Data marts.   I. Title.
  QA76.9.D34H33   1997
  005.74—dc21   97-22448
                                           CIP

Sponsoring Editor: Mary Treseler
Project Manager: John Fuller
Production Coordinator: Melissa Lima
Cover design: Eileen Hoff
Text design: David Kelley
Set in 10-point Sabon by NK Graphics

1 2 3 4 5 6 7 8 9—MA—0100999897
First printing, August 1997

This book is dedicated to my grandfather,

Clarence Hackney,

who instilled in me that most precious gift,

a sense of wonder.

Table of Contents

Contents

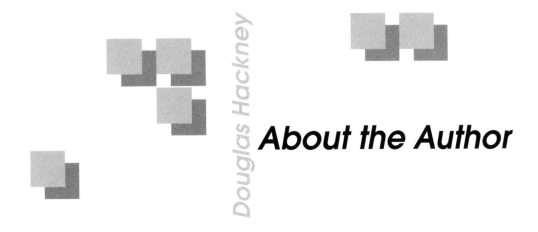

About the Author

Douglas Hackney is president of Enterprise Group Ltd., a consulting and knowledge transfer company specializing in data warehousing and data marts. Enterprise Group Ltd. helps organizations understand, plan, and implement data warehousing and data mart solutions to better manage and use business information. Hackney is an author, lecturer, industry analyst, and practicing data warehousing consultant.

Hackney has over seventeen years of experience in business management and designing and implementing data warehouse and information delivery system solutions for Fortune 500 organizations. He offers clients practical knowledge of the challenges and critical success factors involved in building and managing data warehouses across a variety of industries and business applications. His approach is distinguished by his ability to discover and understand the business needs of the organization, and then answer those needs with information technology solutions.

Hackney is a frequent speaker at data warehouse industry conferences, including DCI's Data Warehousing Conferences and The Data Warehouse Institute, where he is a master instructor and the primary instructor for data mart initiatives. He also speaks at industry user conferences and at educational and product seminars around the globe. He is a founding board member of the International Data Warehouse Association. Hackney served as one of three judges for the 1996 and 1997 Excellence in Business Information award, an industry competition recognizing outstanding implementations of information technology. He also served as a judge for the 1997 RealWare data warehousing award.

Hackney is the author of the forthcoming book *The Seven Deadly Sins of Data Warehousing*. He is also the author of "Data Warehouse Delivery," a monthly column for *Data Management Review,* where he draws on real-world case studies to discuss solutions to common data warehouse and data mart implementation issues and challenges, and has contributed to other industry publications.

Hackney can be reached via e-mail at: doug@egltd.com or www.egltd.com.

Acknowledgments

A book of this style and scope is not possible without the contributions of a great many people, without whose generous contribution of ideas, feedback, encouragement, and support this work would not have been possible.

I would like to express my special gratitude to Tim Harmon of Meta Group for his encouragement for the effort and his thoughts on the data mart market space. I would also like to thank Nagraj Alur of Database Associates International and Wayne Eckerson of the Patricia Seybold Group for their input on the trends and issues in the data mart segment.

Many thanks go out to all the vendors participating in the data warehouse and data mart market segment for their gracious contribution of time and resources in briefing me on their current and future product plans. Special thanks in this regard to the entire team at Informatica for sharing their thoughts, plans, and resources on the data mart segment.

From my publisher, Addison Wesley Longman, I would like to first thank Jo Hoppe, CIO, without whom none of this would have been possible; second, my editors, Kathleen Tibbetts, Mary Treseler, Elizabeth Spainhour, and Lana Langlois, for their support and undying patience; also, Carol Nelson and Shannon Patti for their help in preparing and executing the marketing plans for the title; and finally, John Fuller, Melissa Lima, and the entire design and production team whose talents you will see reflected throughout this book.

The illustrations in the book are the work of Heidi Setaro of Setaro Graphic Design. I thank Heidi for her patience, fortitude, and especially her talents.

Great thanks are due to the members of our industry who invested much time and energy in reviewing this title during its development. The factual validity of this work is due in large measure to their efforts; any errors or omissions are purely my responsibility.

Last, I thank my wife Stephanie and our children, Chari, Adam, Shaun, and Amber, for their support, encouragement, understanding, and endless patience during the development and production of this work.

Introduction

Purpose

This book is intended to serve as a guide to the understanding, design, development, implementation, and sustenance of data marts as high-value, mission-critical information resources. In reading this book, you will learn the history and value of data marts in the enterprise. Design fundamentals, "land mines" to avoid, keys to success, and industry trends will also be revealed in this text.

Due to the scope and design of the book, it is impossible to deal with each subject in as much detail as I would have liked, and I'm sure there will be times when you feel the same. However, I have attempted to cover the breadth of issues, dangers, opportunities, and technologies in the data mart area in sufficient depth to provide you with all the tools and understanding you and your team need to deliver valuable and sustainable data marts to your organization.

Intended Audience

This book is intended to deliver a broad scope of data mart information to a wide range of readers.

- *Business executives and managers*
  Successful and sustainable data marts are built solely to serve the needs of the business user community. These readers will be able to understand what the data mart can provide and what key features will deliver true user value. The business community provides the business driver, the business pain, and the funding to give life to the data mart system. This book will help this community understand how the data mart system can relieve their pain, and how the data mart system must be measured to gauge ROI (return on investment).

- *CIOs (Chief Information Officers) and IT (Information Technology) managers*
  CIOs and IT managers are tasked with understanding the available technological solutions to the business challenges they are faced with solving. This book provides the necessary foundation to understand the prerequisites for a successful data mart

system implementation in an enterprise context. Proper tactical and strategic use of data marts is mandatory to achieve the goals of effective information delivery in today's corporate environment. This book provides all the tools a CIO and IT manager need to meet this challenge.

- *Data mart project leaders*
  Data mart project leaders are faced with the daunting task of designing, building, and implementing quick-hitting, high-impact, low-cost data mart solutions to tactical and strategic needs of the business. This work provides specific methodologies and the design, project, and team criteria necessary to ensure success. It functions as a guide book through the maze of organizational, cultural, and technological challenges that lie before every data mart project.

- *Data mart team members*
  This book provides the data mart team with both high-level and detailed understanding of the data mart system. It provides the entire context of the data mart project, where it fits in politically, organizationally, and technically. Team members will learn about the specific challenges that lie ahead and where the best rewards for their efforts can be found.

- *Network team leaders and members*
  Data marts are entirely dependent on the underlying computer networks of the organization to survive. They also can place tremendous strain on existing networks. It is extremely important for network team leaders and members to be aware of the potential bandwidth demand sources that are inherent in data mart systems, and of the network implications of specific technological choices. This book specifically highlights potential network trouble spots and provides the insight required to head off implementation problems.

- *Support team leaders and members*
  Support teams have a host of new and unique challenges from data mart systems. This book targets the specific areas of need for support teams. Team leaders and members can learn about the multiple areas of support required in a data mart system and the necessary resource and skill requirements.

Structure

This book is designed in a "random access" format. This design acknowledges the fact that few readers of technical publications read them in a linear manner, from beginning to end. Most readers directly access the portions of this book that they feel are most relevant to their role or the specific challenge that confronts them. To answer their needs and reflect this reality, I have chosen to build the book in a modular format, where nearly every chapter can stand on its own. Although the reader would certainly enjoy a sense of continuity by an "alpha to omega" approach, I believe that any combination of random access will also supply you with full understanding of the specific issues that you seek.

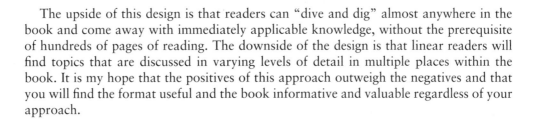

The upside of this design is that readers can "dive and dig" almost anywhere in the book and come away with immediately applicable knowledge, without the prerequisite of hundreds of pages of reading. The downside of the design is that linear readers will find topics that are discussed in varying levels of detail in multiple places within the book. It is my hope that the positives of this approach outweigh the negatives and that you will find the format useful and the book informative and valuable regardless of your approach.

Chapter Guidelines

To help you understand what parts of this book are most applicable to you, I've prepared the guidelines found on page xxvi for various roles.

Where Do I?

As you'll learn in Chapter 7, one of the two critical user meta data questions that a data mart system must easily answer is "where do I?" Although the delivery medium of this book doesn't allow me the opportunity to offer hyperlinked answers to that question, I have provided some quick answers to what I believe will be common questions. You could consider this the FAQ (Frequently Asked Questions) section for this book. For an electronic resource for some of the processes and techniques mentioned in the book, refer to the book's web site at: http://www.datasmarts.com.

Where do I . . .

- *Learn what a data mart is?*
  The beginning of Chapter 3 is devoted to the overall definition of data marts. Chapter 8 is also devoted to defining the two types of data marts.

- *Learn about picking a data mart tool?*
  Chapter 3 has valuable background on the evolution of data mart tools. Chapter 13 has a detailed discussion of data mart tools.

- *Learn about the different types of user access tools?*
  Chapter 3 has basic background information on the categories of end-user tools.

- *Find an overview of data mart design?*
  The basics of data warehouse and data mart design are discussed in Chapter 3.

- *Get information about detailed design issues?*
  The details of data mart design are covered in Chapter 12.

- *Learn about integrating my existing data marts into a coherent system?*
  This is covered in Chapter 13.

- *Learn about the steps to create a data mart?*
  The steps of a data mart project are described in detail in Chapter 6.

- *Determine if a data mart is what we really need?*
  Chapter 4 will help you establish if a data mart is suitable for your site.

Chapter	Executive	IT Manager	DM Team	Network Team	Support Team
Section One: Background and Evolution					
1 - The Data Mart Trend	X	X	X		X
2 - Data Mart Drivers	X	X	X		X
3 - Definition and Evolution of Data Marts	X	X	X	X	X
Section Two: Preparation and Planning					
4 -Site and Team Assessment		X	X	X	X
5 - Development and Communication Methodology		X	X		
6 - Project and Process Flow		X	X		
7 - Understanding and Implementing Meta Data		X	X		X
Section Three: Development and Implementation					
8 - Understanding the Two Types of Data Marts	X	X	X		X
9 - Successful Subset Data Marts			X		
10 - Subset Data Mart Implementation			X		
11 - Successful Incremental Data Marts			X		
12 - Incremental Data Mart Design			X		
13 - Incremental Data Mart Construction and Integration Options			X		
14 - Critical Implementation Issues	X	X	X	X	X
15 - Maintenance and Sustenance	X	X	X	X	X

- *Find out about the potential hazards of data mart development and implementation?*
  I have included the major "red flags" throughout the book, but a detailed discussion of the most significant issues is in Chapter 14.

- *Learn how to construct an enterprise data mart architecture?*
  The enterprise data mart architecture is discussed in Chapters 3, 6, 8, 11, and 12.

- *Learn how to conduct user interviews?*
  Chapter 6 contains a detailed user interview structure in the section "Survey User Needs."

- *Determine roles and responsibilities for my data mart project?*
  Chapter 4 contains a listing of responsibilities that must be assigned in a data mart project.

- *Learn about the basics of thin clients and NCs (Network Computers)?*
  Chapter 3 has an overview of thin clients and thick clients and the pros and cons of thin client solutions.

- *Determine how much technical meta data I need?*
  Chapter 7 examines technical meta data in detail.

Weights, Measures, and Cultural Bias

You will quickly notice that throughout this book I have used measures and formatting that reflect the U.S. marketplace. This is not intended as a slight on other cultures, nor as yet another example of U.S. culture being imposed on other peoples and cultures of our world. It is primarily a reflection of my own history of growing up in and working primarily in the United States. Insert relevant measures and formatting appropriate for your customs and culture where appropriate.

Reality Check

Throughout the book, you will find special sections labeled "Reality Check." These sections contain observations gleaned from my real-world experience designing, developing, implementing, and maintaining data warehouse, data mart, and information delivery systems at scores of sites across all industry segments. These comments are intended to reflect a "real world" viewpoint, where things do not always run like the demo, where sponsors disappear, where budgets evaporate, where requirements change mid stream, where the answers are not always known, and where compromise of rarefied ideals expressed by pundits and visionaries in order to deliver the solution is an everyday occurrence. In short, the reality checks are just that. A way to compare the ideals and principles so often expressed in these books to practical, everyday reality.

REALITY CHECK If you read this book from start to finish, you will see several repeated themes that consistently appear in many chapters. These are not repeated to simply drive you batty or to insult your intelligence. These themes are repeated because I have seen them neglected at site after site, to the detriment of the team and the project. If I am successful, by the end of the book you may be tired of hearing about solving specific business pain, sustainable political will, user-focused design, and meta data, but the message will also stick with you and your team. If I am successful, you will never experience failure due to any of these factors.

A Word About Vendors and Tools

This book does not contain a section or chapter on the currently available tools and technologies for the data mart segment. The reasons for this are twofold. First, my discussions with the new and existing vendors who sell data mart products have made it clear that whatever I could include now will be out of date by the time this book is published. I felt it would do you as a reader little good to list products and features that would not reflect the vendors' current offerings in just a few months. Second, I believe that the book's web site, http://www.datasmarts.com, is a more appropriate medium to present a listing of the solutions available in the market today. It is possible for me to maintain and update the web site to reflect the dynamic and fast-changing landscape in the data mart tools world. It would not be possible to publish a new edition of this book every three months in order to attempt the same feat.

I encourage you to visit the site, where you can use resources from this book, link to other data mart and data warehousing sites, link to vendors' sites, and view up-to-date product and technology listings pertinent to the data mart market segment.

Summary

I have greatly enjoyed the process of creating this book based on my experiences in designing, building, and implementing data warehouses, data marts, and information delivery systems for a wide variety of clients around the world. I hope that you find it valuable, and enjoy your experiences bringing successful and sustainable information assets to your organizations.

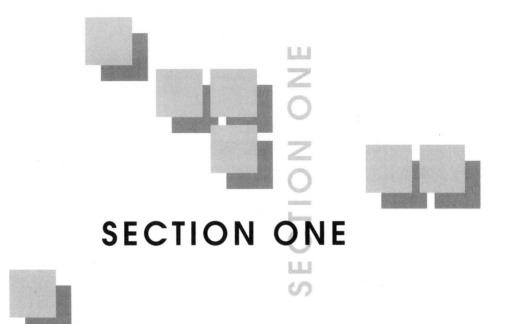

SECTION ONE

▶ ***Background
and Evolution***

The Data Mart Trend

Data marts have recently gained prominence in the area of DSS (Decision Support Systems). To understand this trend, and the position of data marts in the overall context of DSS, we must look first to the burgeoning overall data warehouse market segment.

Data Warehouse Overview

Data warehousing has quickly evolved from a small market segment to what is projected to be up to a $17 billion dollar market segment by 2000. What began as a relatively simple concept first noted by B. Devlin and P. T. Murphy in the *IBM Systems Journal* in 1988 and popularized by Bill Inmon in his 1992 book *Building the Data Warehouse* (John Wiley & Sons) has exploded into a major market segment in information technology. Where once there were no vendors who even knew what data warehousing meant, there are now dozens of vendors selling purpose-built data warehousing tools. Where once there were only a few scattered presentations at information technology industry conferences, there are now dozens of data warehousing conferences worldwide, each attracting thousands of attendees. Where once there was Bill's lone volume, there are now over twenty data warehousing books available, with more being added monthly. Where once the concepts and terms of data warehousing were arcane and obscure, there are now multiple data warehousing industry trade associations, user groups, and internet mailing lists.

And perhaps most telling of all, where there were once only a handful of organizations tentatively testing the waters of implementing data warehousing, there are now over 96% of companies in a recent Meta Group survey using, building, or planning data warehouses. Clearly data warehousing is a mainstream concept in today's world of information storage and delivery. CEOs (Chief Executive Officers) discuss it at retreats, business weeklies feature it in cover stories, analysts employ dedicated teams to research it, CIOs (Chief Information Officers) consider it a prime weapon, and practical knowledge of it is a prerequisite for information technology professionals.

All of these corporations are in search of the same high rates of ROI (Return On Investment) that early adopters have enjoyed. An IDC (International Data Corporation) survey revealed that successful data warehouses demonstrate ROIs of over 400%. These numbers would attract even the most obstinate board of directors.

As data warehousing has moved into the mainstream and businesses everywhere have begun to build and implement them, two developments have emerged: challenges to data warehousing and a move to data marts.

Data Warehouse Challenges

The first development is described by the following wide-ranging set of challenges that are inherent in an enterprise data warehouse project:

- Data warehouses take a very long time to build, usually two or more years.
- Data warehouses are very expensive, usually $2 to 5 million dollars.
- Data warehouses are inherently cross-functional, requiring widespread sustained cooperation and communication across the business.
- Data warehouses are very high risk; if they fail, individuals usually pay the price.
- Data warehouses require very high levels of sponsorship, usually CEO and/or board level.
- Data warehouses require very high levels of long-term political will, usually for 8 to 12 consecutive quarters.
- Data warehouses require new management skills from all concerned, both business and technical.
- Data warehouses require a very specialized set of skills to design and construct, skills that are not widely available.

The Data Mart Move

The second development is the move to data marts as both their traditional role as a complement to the data warehouse and as an alternative route to information delivery. Data marts are highly focused sets of information that are designed in the same way as data warehouses, but are implemented to address the specific needs of a defined set of users who share common characteristics. Data marts are specific solutions to specific pain in the business. As such, they offer immediate relief to business divisions, functions, and departments.

Data marts originated at the same time as data warehouses, but at that time they were defined exclusively as moderately to highly summarized subsets of data warehouses. They generally were used to address the data storage needs of specialized analytical applications and management reporting systems. As they have matured, data marts have evolved to represent much more than this small and confining definition. Today's data marts offer the enterprise the opportunity to build and deploy robust information resources that quickly address the needs of specific groups within the organization, regardless of role, function, or mission. Data marts have the following characteristics:

- Data marts take a much shorter time to build, usually two to nine months.
- Data marts cost much less, usually $100,000 to $2 million.
- Data marts are usually single-purpose, solving a problem for a specific group of users, minimizing the need for extensive and sustained cross-functional, cross-department, or cross-divisional communication and cooperation.
- Data marts are low risk, technically and politically.
- Data marts require low levels of sponsorship, usually manager level.
- Data marts require low levels of political will for very short time periods.
- Data marts are the ideal environment to learn the management and technical skills required for data mart and data warehouse success.

Today's data marts are not only being used as decision support solutions, as they were originally defined, but they are also being used as a learning laboratory for development teams to enable them to incrementally build an enterprise data warehouse step by step.

Data Mart Segment Growth vs. Data Warehouses

Data marts are less complex, less expensive, take less time, and they provide a very targeted solution to specific business pain. It seems clear that the trend toward their use will continue for the foreseeable future. (See Figure 1.1.)

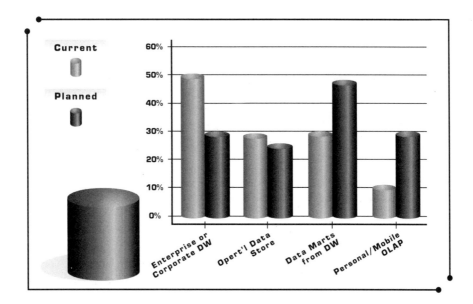

Figure 1.1 Implementation Trends   *Source: Meta Group*

REALITY CHECK   Let's be clear. Data warehouses are not going to go away. Just as the dire predictions that mainframes would be erased from the surface of the earth were proved ludicrous, sweeping predictions about the eminent demise of data warehouses are delusional at best. Data marts are a complement to a data warehouse effort, not a replacement. If you want to enjoy the benefits of an enterprise view, data marts will get you no closer than a "virtual" data warehouse. A full-scale enterprise data warehouse, be it physical or virtual, will always be required for a true "top down" look at an enterprise.

It comes as little surprise then that a recent Meta Group survey of DCI (Digital Consulting Incorporated) Data Warehousing conference attendees revealed that:

- Data marts comprise 50% of the demand for planned data warehouse solutions.
- Data marts are growing from 31–48% of planned IT (Information Technology) projects.
- Data warehouses are decreasing from 50–30% of planned IT projects.

Summary

Data warehouses have proven to be very rewarding when successfully implemented. Their ability to deliver a source of integrated, scrubbed, historical information is unprecedented in its impact and ROI. At the same time, organizations are increasingly turning to data marts as an alternative means to deliver information due to their quicker delivery, lower risk, and lower costs. Data marts will continue to grow in use as an incremental development route to the end goal of an enterprise data warehouse and as stand-alone information delivery systems.

Data Mart Drivers

The rapid rise of the data mart market segment has been due to several factors, including time to market, cost, risk, iterative development, speed of decision making, politics, and vendors.

Time to Market

A primary driver for data marts in the enterprise has been the much faster turnaround time for a data mart solution as opposed to an enterprise data warehouse. An enterprise data warehouse project lasts from 12 to 36 months, with the average over 24 months, from inception to production. This is a very long period of time in today's fast moving competitive marketplace. It is challenging to maintain 24 months of very significant outflows before you can demonstrate any ROI (Return On Investment) from the enterprise data warehouse system. In addition, it is challenging to retain a consistent development team over such a long period of time. Turnover, transfers, and other forms of attrition conspire to make team continuity an elusive goal.

Such long timeframes also make it very challenging to retain the high levels of sustained political will required for an enterprise data warehouse implementation. The high-level executives who must supply this high-level sponsorship are measured in a fiscal year quarter to fiscal year quarter time frame. An average data warehouse will span eight to twelve quarterly measurement periods for this executive team. During this time, new challenges and crises will arise and take the spotlight of rich potential and promise from the data warehouse project. In a two-to-three year time span, it is also very unlikely that the executive management team will stay static. The inevitable turnover will give new personalities opportunities to establish new priorities for the business. Consequently the data warehouse project must be continuously, endlessly, "sold" to executive management. Meanwhile, the new assortment of challenges and crises will be attempting to pull resources from the data warehouse team.

All the while, the data warehouse team will be fighting off the dragons of scope creep, underperforming technologies, unfulfilled vendor promises, missed deadlines, blown budgets, and continually compromised project goals. On the one hand will be the business screaming for relief and on the other will be the development team screaming for fewer deliverables and longer time lines. Pity the poor data warehouse project manager.

> **REALITY CHECK**   Has your organization been entirely static at the upper two executive bands for the last two to three years? Have there been no market redefining events for your business in the last two to three years? Have you faced no acquisitions, mergers, or reorganizations in the last two to three years? It's most likely that most of these have happened in the recent past. The past is preview to the future. There is no reason to believe that these factors will not be a part of *your* future.

Given these challenges, it is little wonder that many organizations turn to data marts to provide nearly instant relief. Data mart projects can be accomplished in as little as eight weeks, with most projects taking no longer than six to nine months. The quick turnaround not only provides quick relief to business pain, but also provides demonstrable ROI (Return On Investment) to the business within one to three quarterly periods. This is a short enough period for almost any required political will.

Data marts, because of their short duration, do not require the height nor length of political will that an enterprise data warehouse does. This allows data mart teams to avoid long entanglements with high levels of the organization in order to win and sustain sponsorship. Data marts are quick, focused, high-impact solutions to specific points of business need. Data marts provide a well-packaged and quantifiable solution to specific business problems. Their tightly focused challenge leads directly to a tightly focused development team.

A tightly focused team is relatively easy to manage and to keep together for the short time lines associated with a data mart project. Deliverable dates happen quickly and often in a data mart project, with little time for team members to become distracted or be recruited by rival teams in the business.

Cost

Another primary driver for data marts in the marketplace is their much lower cost compared with an enterprise data warehouse solution. Surveys conducted at recent DCI (Digital Consulting Incorporated) Data Warehousing industry conferences reveal that enterprise data warehouses projects cost from $2 to 5 million, whereas data mart projects ranged from as little as $200,000 to $2 million. (See Figure 2.1.)

Since the time that these surveys were taken in 1995 and 1996, total costs to deliver a data mart project have continued to fall dramatically. (See Figure 2.2.) For instance, the basic EMT (Extract, Mapping, and Transformation) capabilities required for a data mart project cost up to and over $400,000 for early tool solutions. In the last year, new products have brought down that price dramatically, to the point that today less than $50,000 will purchase a solution that has significantly more capabilities than early technologies.

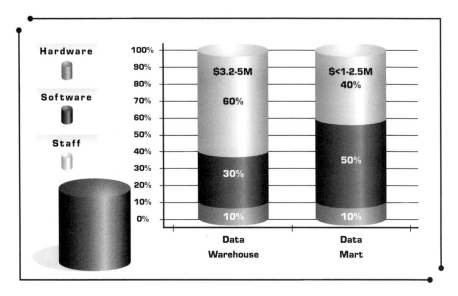

Figure 2.1   Average cost to deliver DW versus DM   *Source: Meta Group*

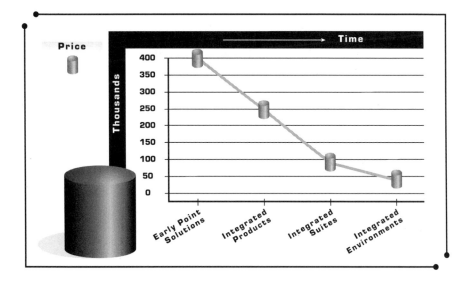

Figure 2.2   Decreasing cost of data mart solution

These low costs allow data mart projects to be developed at the department level, with department level funding sources. This allows data mart projects to stay off the radar screens of most CFOs (Chief Financial Officer) and CEOs (Chief Executive Officer), which minimizes political exposure.

Risk

Staying off the radar screen of high-level executives is impossible for an enterprise data warehouse project, which requires very high levels of commitment and sponsorship. With this high-level exposure come very high risks. An enterprise data warehouse requires board of directors level approval for the $2 to 5 million dollar commitment. Any enterprise data warehouse project manager can tell you that this level of exposure equates to maximum political risk.

Given the historically high failure rate for initial enterprise data warehouse projects, which range from 40–60% depending on the source, the fact that your career is essentially on the line does nothing to relieve the pressure on the typical enterprise data warehouse team. This stress is added to the huge, unmanageable scope; ballooning budget; and cultural challenges that are among the many factors that often underlie the high failure rates of initial enterprise data warehouse projects.

Data marts, in contrast, are in the "test and toss" category for most organizations. Failure of a data mart project does not represent a maximum level CLM (Career Limiting Move). Data marts are exceedingly low risk compared with an enterprise data warehouse. They usually require only divisional or at most vice president level of approval, and they are often carried out in a complete "skunk works" scenario.

Data marts also enjoy a much higher initial success rate than their larger brethren. Data marts are by nature very targeted toward specific business pain. This greatly increases their chances of delivering value to the enterprise and bringing resulting success to the team. Data marts have smaller, more manageable scope and operate at budget levels well below the field of view of executive management. Even if a data mart fails completely, it remains in the "flush and forget" category.

> **REALITY CHECK** Where do these 40–60% initial failure rate numbers come from? Well, you won't find any industry surveys touting them. There are many data warehouse failures, but almost nobody is talking about them. The reasons are pretty clear. The organizations don't want to admit that they failed to achieve the success their competitors have and have managed to flush several million dollars in the process. The vendors don't want to talk about failure—they sell products based on success. The industry associations don't want to feature failure—they are attempting to grow the segment and their membership and participants. These failure rates are based on informal surveys I have conducted among my peers in the industry and my direct experience and observation. Note especially that most organizations who fail try again, until they succeed. The ROI of a successful data warehouse is just too great to walk away from.

Iterative Development

Many organizations have developed a conscious methodology that purposely uses data marts to test failure and success points. Along the way, they will "test and toss" many tools, processes, designs, and approaches. But each step—success or failure—brings them one step closer to their goal. These organizations use data marts as part of an iterative development process toward their goal of an enterprise data warehouse.

Rather than start out with a stated goal of a "galactic" enterprise data warehouse that would expose them to the upper reaches of executive management and its attendant risk, many organizations start out by constructing a series of architected data marts. Step by low-budget step, they test tools and technologies. Step by low-risk step, they test designs and infrastructure elements. With each success, they can demonstrate the validity of fundamental data warehouse concepts and designs. With each failure, they can learn lessons and do it better in the next iteration.

The iterative development model of data warehouse construction using incremental data marts has evolved into the optimum model of data warehouse implementation for many organizations. It allows them to start small, prototype solutions, and to test vendors, methodologies, tools, consultants, technologies, topologies, and designs. The iterative development model is the optimum way to grow an internal skill set among team members at low cost and low risk. It offers a safe growth environment for the internal staff, relationships with vendors, and tools and technologies.

Speed of Decision Making

Another primary driver for data marts in the business is the speed of decision making in today's enterprise. Knowledge, information, and data are integral parts of fundamental business processes today. Very few organizations can afford to proceed at the levels of information access they have currently for another two to three years until the enterprise data warehouse is available. Information driven processes such as sales, marketing, manufacturing, and finance require information solutions now, not as a distant promise somewhere over the horizon.

Vice presidents, managers, and analysts need quick hit solutions now to their business challenges. They do not have the time to wait two weeks for a mainframe-based report, much less two years for an enterprise data warehouse. These users form the primary audience for the data marts' tightly focused data sets and packaged solutions.

Political Factors

Political factors also influence the move to data mart solutions. A well-placed data mart can enable entire departments, functional areas, and divisions to achieve significant short-term impact on the enterprise. Data marts specialize in delivering high-impact tactical solutions to specific business areas. Consequently they can directly drive success of programs, initiatives, and individuals.

When used to drive revenue, a single data mart can have significant impact on the top line revenues. When used to control costs, a single data mart can have major direct impact on the bottom-line profits of the organization. Many astute individuals and groups will personally fund and drive the development of data marts to enable these initiatives. Their resulting success has a notable positive halo effect on the careers of those associated with the program.

Vendors

The vendors in the data mart segment continue to make data marts incredibly easy and low-cost projects. Data marts have become the latest rage, and it is a lonely vendor indeed that doesn't offer a prepackaged data mart bundle solution. From the database vendors to the data access vendors, everyone is on board with a turn-key solution at very attractive price points.

Where it once could cost well over $800,000 to assemble the hardware, software, and consulting elements of a data mart solution, multiple vendors now offer packaged solutions containing all of these elements at price points under $200,000. These packaged solutions allow data mart teams to simply make one call and have a solution show up on their door step, complete with the consulting expertise to ensure success. Although not the panacea that the vendors would like us to believe they are, these packaged offerings are appropriate solutions to many common business challenges.

If your business pain is not appropriate for a bundled solution, you are still in luck. The emergence of comprehensive data extraction, transformation, loading, monitoring, and management application suites for the data mart market has allowed organizations to implement "end to end" solutions for their unique problems for very attractive price points. What is even more significant than the $35,000–100,000 price points for these tools is the speed they bring to the design, development, and implementation process. These integrated environments allow organizations to design, build, and use the data mart system all within one common, shared, consistent user environment. The elimination of the requirement to spend person-years in fruitless efforts to get disparate tools from multiple vendors to play well together has freed development teams to concentrate on delivering timely solutions to business challenges to the enterprise.

In the end, businesses rely on vendors to invent and market technological solutions to enable development teams to address and solve business challenges. Fortunately for us, the vendors have jumped on the data mart bandwagon with a vengeance. The result is rapidly dropping prices and rapidly expanding capabilities.

> **REALITY CHECK** Politics are the wildcard driver for data marts. If you are going to play with the fire of a politically-driven data mart project, be aware of the potential risks. It's very easy to come out a crisp cinder.

Summary

The benefits of an enterprise data warehouse are undeniable. An enterprisewide store of integrated, scrubbed, historical information is essentially invaluable, and it is a worthy goal for those who can afford the time and expense to achieve it. Many organizations do not have the time to wait for that galactic solution; they choose instead to build immediate data mart solutions that can be used as building blocks to create the enterprise data warehouse solution.

Historically, data warehouses represented the only path to access to integrated, scrubbed historical detail. Many organizations viewed data marts strictly as replacements for existing reporting functionality, and as very limited single-purpose data resources. In today's incremental data mart approach to the ultimate goal of an enterprise data warehouse, these occluded views are being tossed aside as all types of data marts, from single-source to widely cross-functional, are being used to provide easy access to targeted data sets consisting of whatever information is required to solve the needs of the user audience.

The data mart is the ideal path to information delivery for many organizations. The following chapters point out the potholes and the route to success on this path.

Definition and Evolution of Data Marts

What Is a Data Mart?

As the marketing and product spotlight has focused on data marts, and they have emerged from the shadow of the overwhelming attention paid to enterprise data warehouses, a plethora of definitions and criteria have emerged as litmus tests to qualify data sets as a legitimate "data mart."

The Meta Group defines a data mart as a subject-oriented equivalent of a data warehouse, typically a single functional area, which is tied to one or more specific applications. Data Base Associates International defines a data mart as an application-oriented subset of corporatewide information that departmental users use to make better informed decisions. The Patricia Seybold Group defines a data mart as a highly focused information resource used to address a single business problem.

As you can see, almost everyone has a cut at what defines a data mart. Each has a unique perspective, with unique criteria for establishing legitimacy. All assume that the data mart is designed using the basic principles of data warehousing that we will examine in detail later in this chapter. Beyond that, considerable debate remains as to what, exactly, defines a data mart.

The various definitions of data marts usually revolve around the following criteria:

- Target application(s)
- Size
- Number of users
- Level of aggregation
- Location/topology
- Audience

Target Application(s)

The term "data mart" was primarily driven into legitimacy through the efforts of application vendors who needed a valid platform to host their three-tier applications. The initial drivers were the MOLAP (Multidimensional On-Line Analytical Processing) vendors who needed a

15

legitimate discrete location for their MDDBMS (Multi-Dimensional Data Base Management System) and its associated analytical processing engines.

Because of this heritage, some analysts are still application focused in their criteria for data mart legitimacy. In their view, if a data mart does not have a dedicated application for its data set, it does not qualify.

In the quickly evolving world of data marts, the criterion of target applications is losing its relevancy. As data marts become a general-purpose DSS (Decision Support System) information repository, assigning specific dedicated applications to specific dedicated data sets becomes increasingly difficult.

Size

It has been popular historically to segment data marts by size. "Less than 20 gigabytes" was a common breakpoint for some time. Today, however, you don't have to look far to find data marts of all sizes, from the classic 2–20 gigabytes up to 250 gigabytes and well beyond. Clearly it is not possible to identify and segment data marts by size alone.

Number of Users

It has also been popular to attempt to attach a segmentation based on the number of users of a data set to qualify it as a legitimate data mart. When data marts were primarily used to host specific MOLAP applications, with tightly segmented knowledge worker constituencies, this was somewhat appropriate.

Today's data mart, however, is a vital information resource for everyone, from work groups of five to functional divisions of thousands. As the data mart has evolved away from the application centric definition, the number of users criterion has lost its validity and relevancy.

Level of Aggregation

Bill Inmon's *Building the Data Warehouse* (1992, John Wiley & Sons) defined a data mart as being composed of summarized information derived from the detail in the parent enterprise data warehouse. This provided a natural starting point for the MOLAP application vendors who soon followed with their aggregate dependent solutions.

As we shall see, however, a criterion that excludes detail in the data mart does not last long in the realm of real-world requirements, where myriad business needs for detail exist among data mart users. The quickly evolving world of distributed and virtual data warehouses composed of multiple data marts demands detail resident in the data mart. As a result, criteria based on aggregation level are no longer applicable to defining a data mart.

Location/Topology

Another popular criterion, especially among RDBMS (Relational Data Base Management System) and server vendors, is physical location or topology of the data set. In this view, any data set that is physically separate from the enterprise data warehouse or central location is a data mart.

Although this criterion makes the labeling of topology diagrams much easier and is an easily understandable criteria for nontechnical audiences, it ignores the prerequisite of a valid design and architecture to the data set. This criterion allows any subset of data, regardless of architecture and level of integration to inherit the mantle of "data mart." We shall see later in this chapter that this is a dangerous precedent.

Audience

The last, and perhaps only valid criterion, is audience. To succeed, data marts must be driven by a clear business need, as you will see in detail in Chapter 5. Thus the only valid segmentation and qualification of "data marts" is based on the business user.

Data marts are defined by users that share one or more of the following traits:

- Common business problems
- Common semantics
- Common metrics (how the users are measured for performance, or how their business activity is measured, that is, units or turnover rates)
- Common roles/levels
- Common mission
- Common domain (a common area of influence, for instance, all shipping dock managers in all locations)
- Common geography

You undoubtedly have many data sets with users that pass one or more of these criteria. However, the data set is not architected, is not integrated, or does not reflect the design criteria covered in detail in Chapter 12. In this case, you are the proud owner of a classic nonarchitected LegaMart, which we will categorize later in this chapter.

Any data set that reflects a valid design, is integrated, and/or is developed under a valid enterprise data mart architecture, and has users that meet these criteria can legitimately be called a data mart.

Data marts may be of two distinct types: subset or incremental. A subset data mart is a "child" of a parent enterprise data warehouse or a parent data mart. There may be an unlimited number of "generations" of subset data marts, each directly derived from a parent. A subset data mart directly inherits its parent's architecture, thereby ensuring that all subset data marts share common sources, business dimensions, business metrics, semantics, and business rules. The subset data mart is the classic data mart reflected in traditional enterprise data warehouse design. Subset data marts are covered in detail in Chapters 8, 9, and 10.

The incremental data mart is an independent, "bottom up" collection of data that is designed and implemented to satisfy the needs of a specific set of users sharing a common business challenge. Incremental data marts have gained popularity in recent years as the challenges of full-scale enterprise data warehouse projects have driven organizations to find faster and less expensive solutions to their information needs. The introduction of data mart specific products such as Informatica's PowerMart, which was the first tool of this type, legitimized this market segment and led to the widespread adoption of the incremental data mart as the preferred method of providing information resources and demonstrating data warehouse design principles. Incremental data marts are commonly used to illustrate the advantages and capabilities of the concept of data warehousing, and to prove methodologies, processes, and technologies prior to the commencement of full-scale enterprise data warehouse projects. The recent advent of new technologies and approaches allows architected incremental data marts to be joined to form "virtual" enterprise data warehouses.

The greatest danger that has arisen with the widespread popularity of incremental data marts is the proliferation of nonarchitected, nonintegrated data marts throughout organizations around the globe. These "quick fix" collections of data will inevitably lead to disaster as the multiple versions of "the truth" inherent in their unique data preparation processes and the inescapable eventual need to integrate them will overwhelm the teams responsible for them.

Incremental data marts are examined in detail in Chapters 8, 11, 12, and 13.

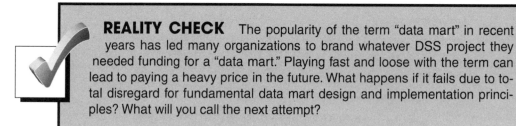

REALITY CHECK   The popularity of the term "data mart" in recent years has led many organizations to brand whatever DSS project they needed funding for a "data mart." Playing fast and loose with the term can lead to paying a heavy price in the future. What happens if it fails due to total disregard for fundamental data mart design and implementation principles? What will you call the next attempt?

Historical DSS (Decision Support System)

To fully understand data marts and where they fit into the information universe, it is necessary to review the history and evolution of DSS (Decision Support Systems).

OLTP (On-Line Transaction Processing System) History

Businesses have spent most of the last 40 years automating the operational aspects of their business processes. This has included every aspect of the business operations, beginning with such basics as order entry, inventory, and accounting and proceeding through every functional area of the business. It is a rare business in today's world that has not automated every possible function of the enterprise.

Early systems were batch oriented, meaning that they would capture the transactions throughout a time period, typically the business day, and then update the system's records with all of the queued transactions in one large job, or "batch." These systems were huge improvements over keeping transaction records by hand, but they had the disadvantage of not being able to display in real time the status of an account or order.

Users were forced to wait until the batch process had completed before being able to check on an updated account balance or order status.

The next stage of evolution for business processing systems were on-line, or live, systems that updated the systems records in real time, as the users entered or edited the data. These operational computer systems are called OLTP (On-Line Transaction Processing) systems. They allow users to interact with a computer program to input, update, delete, and monitor transactional activity in real time. A surprising number of batch systems are still running in today's business world, although the trend has been toward OLTP for many years.

Both batch and OLTP systems were first hosted, or executed, on large mainframe computers. These systems consisted of very fast, proprietary processors (calculation engines), along with memory and physical storage devices to store the operational information. Data was stored on hard disk drives, which provided relatively fast 'on-line' storage, and magnetic tape, which provided high capacity and lower cost 'off-line' storage.

It is sobering to note that the computing power of early mainframe systems, which cost many hundreds of thousands of dollars at the time, is easily surpassed by common desktop systems of today. This rapid evolution of computing power has allowed modern OLTP systems to be deployed on much lower cost platforms, using new technologies.

Platforms

Today's computing environment consists of new generations of mainframe computers, many much more open, or able to interact and communicate with other computing systems, than their forefathers. These much more powerful mainframes are joined by a variety of servers that provide printer sharing, file storage, and application services to users. Servers store and execute application programs and also store data files and drive printers. The servers are usually connected to the users via a physical network that uses some form of physical medium such as copper wire to pass data back and forth between the server and the user's system. A less common method uses wireless technology to connect servers and users. The business users of today use high-powered desktop computers with easy-to-use GUIs (Graphical User Interfaces) that use visual images and icons to intuitively interact with users. A recent trend has been toward "thin client" user platforms that still provide the powerful GUI, but do most or all of the application processing on the servers hosting the application. We will examine thin client platforms in detail later in this chapter.

Processors

Server platforms consist of a variety of systems using proprietary and nonproprietary microprocessors. Most servers use a type of microprocessor known as RISC (Reduced Instruction Set Computer). This type of processor uses a very small library of instructions to accomplish its work, but it processes these instructions very quickly. Desktop computers, in contrast, primarily use a type of microprocessor called CISC (Complex Instruction Set Computer). CISC chips have a large variety of complex instructions available to programmers that allow very complex tasks to be accomplished in one cycle, or step, of the microprocessor.

The trade-off between the two designs is that CISC chips generally run slower than RISC chips. RISC chips are also commonly optimized for specific tasks, such as rendering 3D (three-dimensional) graphics, so they are more often used for high-end engineering and graphical workstations, as well as for high-demand file and application servers.

Parallel Servers

Both types of processors, RISC and CISC, are being used in parallel servers. These systems employ two to 32 and more processors to share the workload. The most popular type of parallel system is called SMP (Symmetrical Multi-Processing). These systems usually share common memory, I/O (Input/Output), and hard disk drive resources between all the processors. (See Figure 3.1.) Another type of parallel system is called MPP (Massively Parallel Processing). MPP systems are usually of a "shared nothing" design, where each processor has dedicated memory, I/O, and hard disk storage resources. (See Figure 3.2.)

SMP systems are generally lower cost and more popular than MPP systems. MPP systems are usually reserved for the extreme high end of computing problem solutions, although the use of commodity priced CISC microprocessors has allowed MPP vendors to penetrate the lower echelons of the market.

Both types of parallel systems split up applications and spread the work out among the available processors and components. Because SMP systems share memory and disk space, any one of the processors can stall the others by tying up the disk drives or large

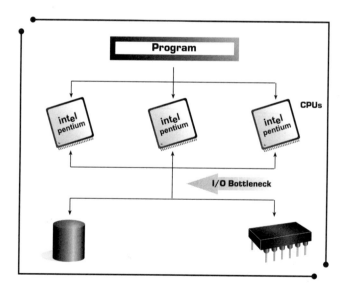

Figure 3.1   SMP shared design

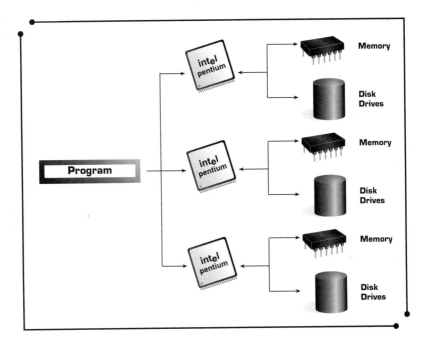

Figure 3.2 MPP shared nothing design

amounts of memory. MPP systems avoid this problem by allowing each processor to primarily access only its dedicated memory and disk drive resources. MPP systems face challenges in effectively and efficiently partitioning the work and the data among the processors and their memory and disk subsystems.

A key feature of both types of designs is scaleability. Performance can be greatly increased by adding more processors, I/O channels, and memory to a parallel system. Because of the critical prerequisite of scaleability for data mart systems, which we will review in detail later in this chapter, parallel systems are extremely popular for data mart solutions.

Networks, Tiering, and the Internet

Mainframes, servers, and desktop computers are linked together by networks that allow each system to share information and messages easily. The rise in LAN (Local Area Network) and WAN (Wide Area Network) technology and capability has allowed the development and deployment of multi-tier applications. These applications split up the work of an application and share it across the multiple systems connected by the network.

In a multi-tier application, some of the work is done on the server, some is done on the client or desktop, and the data may be stored in an entirely different system. Multi-tier data mart architectures are described in detail later in this chapter.

The common protocols of the Internet, which is simply a connection of multiple WANs and LANs, have facilitated the evolution of widely dispersed, seamlessly distributed applications. In a distributed application, the application itself is broken into a variety of components, and each component is processed on different systems. This allows a variety of servers to be specifically configured and tuned for optimum performance for a particular task, and each element of the application processing to take place in an optimized environment.

For instance, an Internet application might consist of a WWW (World Wide Web) form that allows a customer to request information on a product. The distributed application architecture of the Internet, enabled by its low-level protocols such as FTP (File Transfer Protocol) and HTTP (Hyper Text Transfer Protocol), allows the form to be generated and distributed by an optimized WWW server, while the product information is stored and retrieved by an optimized RDBMS (Relational Data Base Management System) server, and the dynamically generated product information form is displayed on an optimized desktop thin client.

The wide-scale interconnection of the Internet has also given new life to object standards that enable application developers to easily partition business applications across multiple server platforms. These standards promise to deliver a new generation of applications that will easily share components and features, and seamlessly and dynamically partition themselves across the optimum platforms available.

DSS Architectures

Automation of business processes was quickly followed by the need to understand the operations of the business, which required some decision support functionality. These early systems consisted primarily of reporting systems that directly accessed the OLTP systems.

Direct to OLTP

The primary problem that arose with the direct to OLTP approach is one of metrics. The people tasked with the maintenance of OLTP systems are measured on the response time of the system. Their goal is subsecond response to user input and edits. Unfortunately OLTP systems use database designs that are highly normalized. Normalized design is fantastic for quick response time for OLTP operations, but it is dismally slow and resource intensive for answering decision support questions. Asking a typical decision support question such as "what was the average sale on weekend days by product line" of a normalized OLTP database would quickly bring the system to its knees, dramatically slowing response times or bogging down the system entirely. (See Figure 3.3.)

OLTP systems have long been held in ultimate esteem, being seen as the heartbeat of the entire enterprise. Indeed, if an OLTP system is down, the business cannot function in that specific area. A business that cannot process orders or run its manufacturing lines is in a seriously precarious position. Correspondingly negative effects are evident on the careers of those responsible for OLTP systems if the OLTP systems are consistently being slowed or stopped by pesky decision support users.

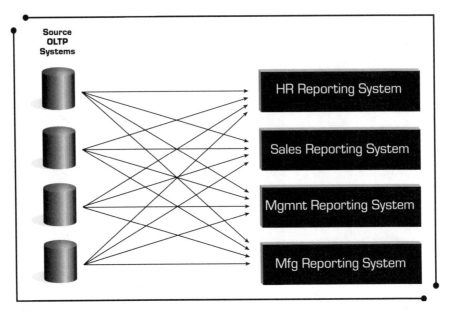

Figure 3.3 Direct to OLTP architecture

OLTP Extracts/Replications

The resulting hue and cry from the OLTP system administrators led to the creation of duplicate data sets, which could be used for decision support, without the crippling effects of direct access to the OLTP system database itself. (See Figure 3.4.) These duplicate sets are commonly snapshots taken periodically of the master OLTP system database tables. The frequency with which these replicated tables are updated varies depending on users' needs, but many are snapshotted daily.

Decision support users still experienced the excruciatingly slow response times of the normalized database design, but at least they were out of the hair of the OLTP system administrators. The users, however, continued to be hampered by the fact that these OLTP extracts were limited to the data normally stored in the OLTP systems. This data was often "dirty," or filled with entry and processing errors. The data also lacked historical transactions. Most OLTP systems retain only a short section of historical data, 30 to 90 days. This is of no help to analysts attempting to examine activity over several years. Also, no summarized data was available. Users who wanted to see total sales by region were forced to slowly add up all the detail transactions to arrive at the total. These inherent shortcomings drove business users in their search for responsive and flexible decision support resources.

End User-Developed DSS

What followed was an evolution of end user–developed decision support systems. Using tools like Focus and SAS, they replicated, distributed, massaged, duplicated, modified,

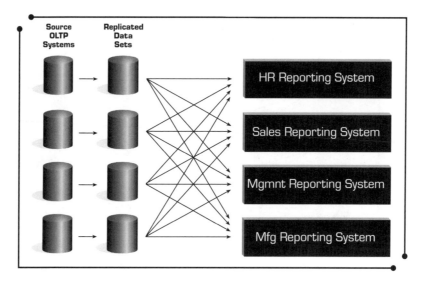

Figure 3.4   Replicated data sets architecture

distributed, summarized, and leveraged the replicated OLTP data sets. What resulted was a spider web of extract and replication jobs, feeding multiple home-grown reporting and analysis systems. (See Figure 3.5.) Because each user group developed its own systems, using its own semantics and business rules, huge disparities in aggregations and metrics resulted.

Of course, this situation was viewed as absolute anarchy by the central IS (Information Systems) organization. Most considered it a cancer that would consume the organization straight away if Focus was not deleted from the mainframe immediately. Although generally recognizing that the extract jobs had grown like kudzu, users were more concerned that these systems be:

- Independent of IS control
- Focused, tactical solutions to business problems
- Flexible
- Quickly developed
- Reasonably priced
- Localized
- Able to integrate business terms and semantics
- Denormalized where appropriate
- Responsive

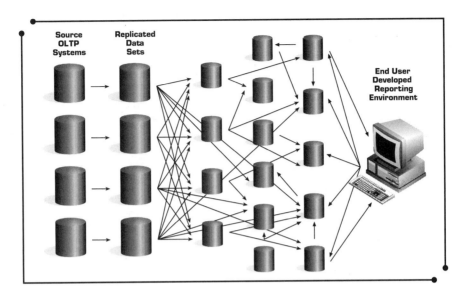

Figure 3.5   Spider web DSS systems

Obviously yet another chasm was developing between the business user and IS communities. IS was drowning under extract jobs, yet unable to answer the decision support needs of the business in any other way.

Meanwhile, the strategic importance of timely and flexible decision support was changing the historical pecking order of systems in the organization. The OLTP system's days of uncontested supremacy were drawing to a close as organizations discovered that the pace of global business demanded instant analysis and decision making capability. A business no longer had the luxury of waiting for three weeks for a developer to generate a report. By then, the questions had all changed and the report's answers were meaningless. Business managers needed answers now, and IS was sorely challenged to provide them.

Data Warehouse Architecture

To meet these changing demands of the enterprise, an architecture evolved. Codified by Bill Inmon in his groundbreaking books, the architecture has since been known by its ubiquitous moniker "Data Warehousing."

It is critically important to understand that data warehousing is not a product, or hardware, or software. It is fundamentally an architecture. You use the data warehouse architecture to build data warehouse systems. Data warehouse systems are not defined by their components, such as databases, access tools, or the data itself. A data warehouse is a holistic system that comprises processes, products, data, personnel, and most importantly, service.

Fundamentally simple, data warehousing architecture answers the needs of the business organization seeking flexible and scaleable decision support resources. A data warehouse integrates data from a variety of OLTP and third-party sources into a common environment that business users can easily access. The data is scrubbed to remove the errors and omissions in the source systems as it is fed into the data warehouse, so users can have confidence in the information they extract from the system. The data warehouse system contains historical data, so users can examine trends and explore detailed historical data for hidden patterns. Data warehouse data is read only, so users can have confidence that what they report today will match what they report next month. And most importantly, the data warehouse system's information is integrated, reflecting a common view of all the information in the business from all the OLTP systems.

Classic data warehouse (DW) architecture is defined by the following series of fundamental characteristics:

- Separate DSS database from OLTP systems
- Storage of data only; no data is created, but it may be derived
- Integrated data
- Scrubbed data
- Historical data
- Read only
- Various levels of summarization
- Meta data
- Subject oriented
- Easily accessible

Separate DSS Database

As we have seen, it is impossible to maintain acceptable OLTP system performance or to have acceptable DSS performance by having the DSS system access the normalized OLTP database. The data warehouse is always resident in a separate database from the OLTP system in the classic data warehouse architecture. (See Figure 3.6.) This allows separate environments for both the OLTP system and the data warehouse DSS system. Because the data warehouse is commonly hosted on a dedicated server, it allows the server and the database to be individually optimized, or tuned, for the highest possible levels of performance in this dedicated DSS implementation. OLTP implementations require completely different tuning parameters than DSS applications.

Because the OLTP system and the data warehouse system are resident on completely separate physical devices, data warehouse users will have no impact on OLTP system performance.

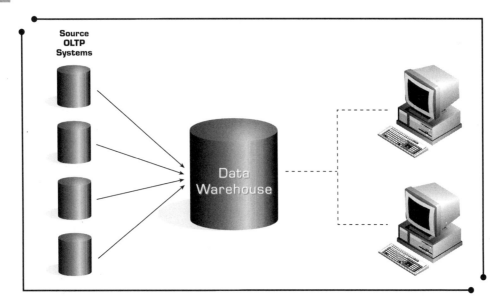

Figure 3.6 Basic DW design

Storage of Data Only

The data warehouse functions only as a repository of information. No data is created in the data warehouse. Although new data points may be derived from the source data, no inherently unique or new data is created in the data warehouse system.

Integrated Data

One of the primary missions of the data warehouse is to integrate data from disparate OLTP systems. The data warehouse contains information from all OLTP systems in the business. This allows users to access transactional and descriptive information from the entire set of available enterprise information resources. Obviously this is the core of the value of the data warehouse system. The ability of the data warehouse system to open a window into the entire range of data from the entire enterprise is incredibly empowering for the enterprise. Integrated data makes possible what was only dreamed of in the past. Integration is the fundamental enabler upon which the 400% ROIs of data warehouse systems are built.

Scrubbed Data

As the data is loaded into the data warehouse from the source OLTP systems, it is scrubbed of all errors, irregularities, and other anomalies. This critical step creates an environment that users can access with confidence. No effective use of the system is possible unless the OLTP source system data is scrubbed before being loaded into the warehouse.

Historical Data

Data warehouses contain historical data to allow users to examine trends and historical performance. The length of history is completely dependent on business needs and can range from as few as 30 days (very rare) to over 20 years (a major scrubbing and integration challenge). History can be kept for summary level data only, or for detail and summary data. Often, the presence of integrated, scrubbed historical data is a key driver for sponsorship and construction of data warehouses.

Read Only

The transaction information contained in a data warehouse is inviolate. Once the transaction detail data is written to the data warehouse, it is never altered, recast, or modified. This key feature enables users to have complete confidence that what they report today will be what they will report a month from now or a year from now. The data warehouse becomes a central repository for corporate memory of all OLTP systems.

Various Levels of Summarization

The data warehouse contains various levels of summarization or aggregation for the various users of the system. Product managers require access to very detailed transactional data about their products. Executive level users, however, require only highly summarized data about divisional or corporate performance. The data warehouse provides appropriate levels of summarization for all audiences.

Meta Data

No data warehouse can be successful without a complete, accurate, and easily accessible set of meta data. Meta data provides information about the content, operation, structure, and management of the data warehouse system. It allows users to quickly identify and share information resources, and it allows the tools used to create, maintain, and use the data warehouse to share information.

Subject Oriented

The data warehouse is designed around business terms and areas of interest. This is referred to as "subject oriented" design. For instance, data objects in a data warehouse contain information about Human Resources, Sales, and Manufacturing. This organization of data is radically different than OLTP systems, where the data is organized to best fit the operational needs of the OLTP system itself.

Subject-oriented design is entirely user driven. The elements of the data warehouse system are optimized to provide a flexible, easy to understand, and easy to use system.

Easily Accessible

The data warehouse must be easily accessible by all users. Intuitive, easily used tools to access and leverage the data warehouse asset are a fundamental prerequisite for every data warehouse system.

Data Warehouse Process

As J. D. Welch of Data Wing Consulting has said, "Data warehousing is a journey, not a destination." Data warehousing consists of a set of processes executed within the data warehouse architecture. (See Figure 3.7.)

The data warehouse is typically designed and undergoes an initial loading process, which may be quite lengthy. After this initial load, only the incremental transactions processed since the last data warehouse extraction are captured and processed. This is commonly known as CDC (Change Data Capture). CDC is a prerequisite capability of EMT (Extract, Mapping, and Transformation) tools that are used to automate portions of this extraction and population process. It is not sustainable to replicate and process

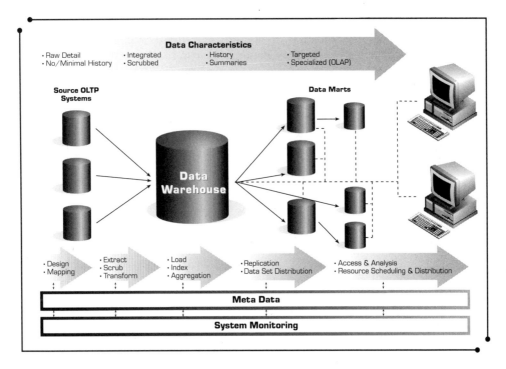

Figure 3.7   DW design with processes and meta data feeds

the entire available set of detail transactions every night in order to update the data warehouse or data mart.

The standard operational processes of data warehousing consist of:

- Mapping
- Extracts
- Scrubbing
- Transformations
- Field aggregation
- Loading
- Table summarization/aggregation
- Replication/distribution
- Populating and maintaining meta data

Mapping

Mapping is the design process of identifying the source of the data and the target, or place in the data warehouse where you want to put it. The initial design phase consists of identifying the "system of record"—the optimum OLTP system to extract any given data point from—for the source information. For example, the system of record for customer information might be the order entry OLTP system. This source data point is then mapped to a target location in the data warehouse system. For example, Customer name would be mapped to the Customer table in the data warehouse.

Extracts

Extracting data from the source OLTP systems is the fundamental starting point of the operational data warehouse process. Once the source system of record has been identified, individual data points, or fields, are extracted from the source system and passed to the data warehouse target fields. Because source systems run on a variety of platforms, using a wide variety of database formats, a database gateway must often be used to access the source OLTP data or a copy of the OLTP data must first be replicated in a format that the tools or technologies used for the extract process can access.

Scrubbing

After the data is extracted and before it is loaded into the data warehouse, it is scrubbed to correct any errors, omissions, or inaccuracies. For instance, a scrubbing process might verify that the zip codes of addresses are correct for the state and city in the address.

Transformations

The transformation operation restructures, reformats, or modifies the scrubbed data to make it ready for use in the data warehouse. Examples include adding formatting characters to part numbers, breaking customer codes into separate fields, or looking up descriptions for codes (e.g., looking up the description "blue" for the code BL).

Field Aggregation

Data is often aggregated prior to loading into the data warehouse. Multiple transactions may be combined into a single field, or a range of transactions can be summed or averaged.

Loading

The data now must be loaded into the data warehouse database. Traditionally, flat files of the integrated, scrubbed, transformed, and aggregated data are prepared and then loaded into the database using a high-performance parallel loader.

Table Summarization/Aggregation

To meet the needs of various user groups, the detail data is "rolled up," or aggregated, into various summary data sets. These summary sets consist solely of aggregations that can be created from the base elements contained within the data warehouse. Non–data warehouse resident aggregation elements are forbidden, as it is essential that the data warehouse "roll up" and audit to itself. These summary data sets can be simple one- or two-dimensional summaries, such as sales of product by week, or very large and complex multidimensional data sets to support MOLAP (Multidimensional On-Line Analytical Processing) applications (described in detail later in this chapter).

A large selection of summary data sets targeted toward various users is very common in the data warehouse. In a classical enterprise data warehouse design, data marts existed solely within this summarization/aggregation space. In a well-designed and targeted data warehouse, the vast majority of ongoing changes and 80% of the usage occurs in the summary data sets.

Table aggregations are accomplished by simple script driven SQL (Structured Query Language) commands and by dedicated EMT (Extract, Mapping, and Transformation) tools.

Replication/Distribution

Once the data warehouse is populated and updated, data sets must be replicated and distributed out to various user constituencies. In a classic enterprise or galactic data warehouse, subset data marts are sliced out of the summarization data sets and distributed out to the targeted users groups. In this scenario, data mart users are restricted to summary data only. They must drill through to the corporate data warehouse to access detail transaction data.

Actual implementations of data warehouses and subsetted data marts have demonstrated that the pertinent detail transaction data must often be replicated out to the subset data mart along with the summary data because business users need to be able to seamlessly drill up and down in the information. Remotely located detail information presents operational challenges for tools to seamlessly drill into the remote galactic data warehouse detail, as well as network traffic implications with large detail answer sets moving over the network at peak mid-day traffic levels.

Replication and distribution to data marts is accomplished in various ways, from manually transferring and loading magnetic media such as tape, to simple FTP (File Transfer Protocol) batch jobs, to native database replication tools, to sophisticated, dedicated replication management tools.

Populating and Maintaining Meta Data

A very critical aspect of the data warehousing process is the ongoing population and maintenance of the meta data. Frequently neglected or ignored, meta data is an absolute prerequisite for successful implementation and utilization. Although the vast majority of meta data is manually populated and maintained, a very meaningful portion of this ongoing population and maintenance can be "electrified," or automated using EMT (Extract, Mapping, and Transformation) tools, suites, and environments. A growing number of data access tools can also access and populate open meta data repositories.

As you will learn in Chapter 7, meta data is the core foundation upon which all data warehousing and data mart success is built. Ignore or minimize it at your peril.

Process Vision versus Reality

In the beginning, all data warehouses were built, monitored, and managed manually. Several years ago, the first generation of data warehousing tools appeared in the EMT (Extract, Mapping, and Transformation) market segment.

These tools were all code generators, in that they produced COBOL or C program source code and assisted in the data warehousing effort by automating some aspects of the EMT processes. They each allowed the users to map source to target, and to generate program code for extract programs and JCL (Job Control Language) and other sequencing and scheduling scripts. (See Figure 3.8.) To an extent, they populated meta data, although the number of required meta data fields were few (usually only source, target, and transformation algorithms, which were implicit in their process and function), and consequently the vast majority of valuable meta was still manually populated.

The code generators were valuable tools because generally 80% of the work of data warehousing is in the mapping, extract, integration, scrubbing, and transformation processes, but they were hampered by:

- High cost (Average deal prices were in the $250–400K range.)
- Long learning curves for some tools

- Perceived value (Most teams felt they could write better code.)
- Cultural challenges (As they would with a CASE tool, the team must use the code generator for all creation and changes, no matter how minor.)
- Core capabilities (Complex transformations still required manual code.)
- Management requirements (Teams still had to manage all the code, files, programs, and scripts generated.)
- Performance issues (The resulting programs were single threaded applications and could not internally leverage parallelism.)

The next step was the appearance of meta data repositories and browsers that were sold along with the code generators. These repositories stored the meta data generated by the code generators and usually could store meta data generated by a limited number of access tools that were tightly bound to the proprietary meta data repositories. These "pairing" meta data standards typically consisted of one EMT tool vendor and one or two other vendors. The "pairing" meta data standards did not take hold in the marketplace, so customers were unable to fully leverage these repositories unless the specific vendors participating in the proprietary solution happened to be the vendors selected for the data warehousing project.

The second generation of data warehousing tools consisted of much lower cost suites and environments that allowed not only EMT (Extract, Mapping, and Transformation) but also design, monitoring, and management of the data warehouse and data marts.

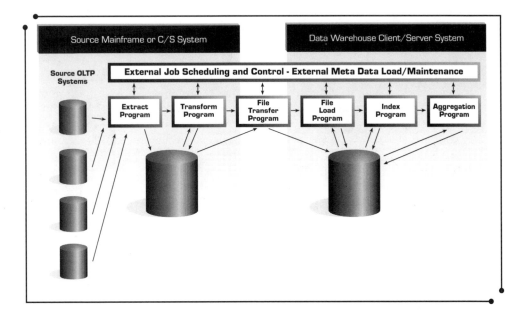

Figure 3.8 First-generation code generator process map

This class of tools is referred to as DTEMM (Design, Transformation, Extract, Monitoring, and Management) suites. They typically consist of multiple programs or modules that coordinate the processes and activities associated with these tasks.

These second-generation DTEMM products also move beyond the code generator paradigm into a "transformation engine" model. In this design, the data is extracted directly from relational or flat file sources and fed to a transformation engine application running on a server platform. The data is manipulated in memory and written directly to the database target. Because the engine is a general-purpose transformation engine, it is fully capable of both internal and external multithreading and other parallel tasks that fully leverage today's powerful parallel server technologies. Also, and most important from the throughput performance standpoint, in a relational source to relational target scenario, the data is not being written to and read from various files throughout the extract, scrubbing, transformation, and load process. This results in savings in I/O (Input/Output) management, time, and resource overhead. (See Figure 3.9.)

In an optimum scenario—where the transformation engine uses no intermediate files or temporary database tables, the source and target are relational databases, and the target database has a parallel loader API (Application Programming Interface)—performance throughputs are many times faster than a code generator scenario.

In addition, these second-generation DTEMM suites provided integrated environments in which all the various elements use the same GUI (Graphical User Interface) design, and all the elements populate and maintain the pertinent meta data in a logically

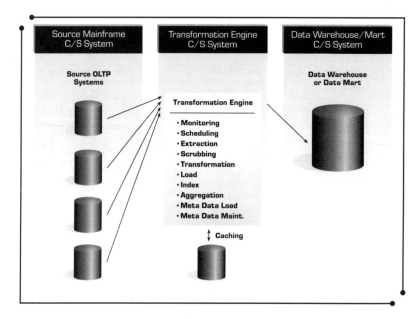

Figure 3.9   Second-generation transformation engine process map

common, open, and extensible meta data repository. This allows both technical and business users to easily access and leverage meta data. It also significantly reduces the manual meta data population and maintenance overhead of the technical team. (See Figure 3.10.)

Second-generation DTEMM tools built on the foundation of the capabilities of the early first-generation code generator products. Organizations considering these tools should insist that any product they select include the following features:

- Transformation engine design
- Ability to fully leverage parallel server technology
- CDC (Change Data Capture, which allows only the new data to be extracted)
- Incremental aggregation (ability to add CDC incremental data to existing aggregations)
- Limited or no use of temporary files or database tables (virtual caching only)
- Logically common, open, and extensible meta data repository
- Common UI (User Interface) across all processes
- Extensive selection of transformation algorithms
- Easily extensible scrub and transform algorithm library
- Extensive heterogeneous source and target support

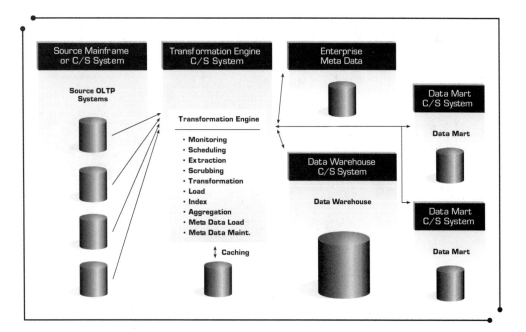

Figure 3.10   DTEMM suite process map

- Native OLAP data set target support
- System management
- System monitoring
- Star schema support and optimization

The next evolutionary step along the path was to provide true enterprise-scale capabilities in these DTEMM (Design, Transformation, Extraction, Mapping, and Management) suites along with integrated information access, analysis, scheduling, and delivery. An integrated environment centered around a logically common, open, and extensible meta data repository allows the efficient creation, utilization, maintenance, and management of data warehouse and data mart systems. These inclusive environments are called DTEAMM (Design, Transformation, Extract, Access, Monitoring, and Management) environments. They combine the technical operations of designing, populating, and managing a data warehouse or data mart system with the ability to access the information resource and to share and schedule delivery of such information resources as queries, reports, and analysis data sets among users. (See Figure 3.11.)

Key capabilities of enterprise-scale DTEAMM suites and environments are:

- A logically common, open, and extensible enterprise meta data repository (content, resources, structure, etc.)

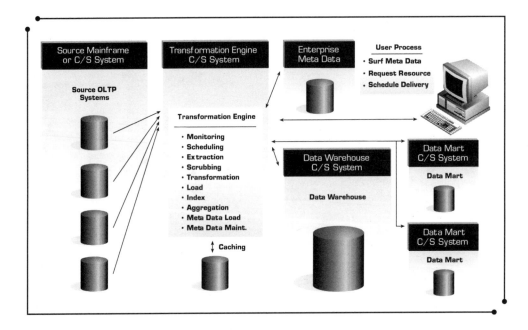

Figure 3.11 DTEAMM environment process map

- Ability to schedule delivery of user-created reports and analysis data sets in a variety of formats
- Extensible library of transformations and business rules
- Object oriented/building block scrub and transformation algorithms
- Transform once, populate many (populate multiple targets with a single transformation output)
- Integrated enterprise-scale scrubbing capabilities
- Seamless interoperability with external point solution tools
- Integrated information access, analysis, scheduling, and delivery
- Shared repository of information assets (queries, reports, analysis data sets, etc.)
- Aggregate aware information request broker (enables virtual data warehouse)
- Ad hoc aggregation management and monitoring

The industry has rapidly made the transition from second-generation DTEMM suites to enterprise-scale DTEAMM environments, which can be described by two basic approaches: integrated DTEAMM environments and segregated DTEAMM environments.

In an integrated environment, all aspects of DTEAMM functionality, including business user access, are carried out in one environment sharing a common UI and a logically common meta data repository. This allows seamless meta data population and sharing across all processes and functions. In an integrated environment, all meta data is available to all process elements and functions. This allows all users of all data access functions, be it simple reporting or advanced analysis, to share all available prebuilt information assets such as queries, reports, and analysis data sets.

In a segregated environment, the information access functions are handled by dedicated, separate, disparate data access products, which have their own unique GUI and their own proprietary meta data repositories. In the segregated environment, the access tools use an API or a specific view into the separate technical meta data repository to provide users with access to the technical information regarding sources and transformations. The segregated approach provides all of the functions of a DTEAMM environment, but it is challenged by the multiple, fragmented meta data repositories of each access tool. This prevents users from having one common repository of information assets to share among all users.

In the future, information access functions will evolve into small "applets" that perform specific functions and will either reside on application servers in a server-centric "thin client" architecture or be bound to the data itself. If a common industry meta data standard evolves for these applets to store and share their meta data, the fragmented segregated environments will fade away, along with their challenges.

The segregated DTEAMM approach is popular among vendors who do not want to re-create the wheel and waste needless development resources duplicating the capabilities of well-known and deeply entrenched business user access tools. It is more expedient and a better tactical solution to build a bridge from the technical meta data into the business user access tools to allow simple viewing of the technical meta data repository.

Vendors who construct purpose-built DTEAMM environments from the ground up are more likely to provide truly seamless business user access with full GUI compatibility and utilization of a logically common meta data repository, thereby enabling information asset sharing across all users.

Data Warehouse Design

Data warehouse design is driven by the business user focus of the solution set and the required processes. Fundamentally the data warehouse requires extraction from existing OLTP systems to a separate, common database that hosts the data warehouse. In a classic enterprise data warehouse design, "child" data marts are then subsetted from this enterprise collection of information.

This section provides an overview of enterprise data warehouse and incremental data mart design principles. A more detailed examination of design can be found in Chapter 12.

Denormalization

At the physical level, data is highly denormalized and heavily replicated across the data warehouse and data mart systems. Normalization and denormalization can be thought of as two different ways to deliver information to users. If you think of information as a sandwich, you can compare denormalized and normalized data as two different ways to sell a sandwich to a consumer. Normalized data is like getting a sandwich from a supermarket. First, you must visit the bakery to get the bread, then the meat department for some sliced meat, then the condiment aisle for the mayonnaise, then the produce department for some lettuce, then the dairy section for some cheese. You then check out and take all the pieces to the parking lot where you can assemble your "normalized" sandwich. This type of organization is optimized for operations. It is very easy to restock the store with additional product. Pallet loads of additional product can simply be dropped in the specific department, such as mayonnaise in the condiment aisle, and the shelves quickly and easily restocked. The consumer has to work much harder, but the operations people who maintain the stock are very efficient and happy.

Denormalized data is like buying a sandwich at a convenience store, such as 7-11. You walk in and they've got all the ingredients already combined into sandwiches wrapped up in cellophane for you. Pick your sandwich, pay at the counter, walk out, and you're ready to eat. This type of organization is optimized for consumers. The operations people must work much harder to preconstruct the sandwiches, but the consumers are very happy.

Just as our "normalized" sandwich required extensive knowledge of the store and its contents, normalized data design requires extensive detailed knowledge of the data on the part of the user to be effective. In addition, standard business users' questions heavily tax RDBMS (Relational Data Base Management System) engines using normalized schemas (designs). Data warehouse and data mart design instead places all the data together in prepackaged sets that are optimized for business user access and utilization. In addition to being easily understandable, these denormalized data sets also minimize the number of joins, or connections of multiple tables, that the database must perform in order to generate the answer to the business users questions.

For instance, if a business user asks "what are the sales for large yellow and red nylon jackets on weekend days to major customers in Seattle" in a normalized design, the user must know in detail about the structure of the database in order to access the proper tables to select the fields of interest and the database would be forced to perform 10 joins and to access 11 tables in order to generate the answer. (See Figure 3.12.)

In contrast, a denormalized design can answer this question with three joins and four tables. (See Figure 3.13.) The database performs much less work, and the answer comes back much quicker. Quick answers equals happy users. Happy users are happy to provide funding. This is a pretty linear relationship.

In data warehouse and data mart design, the goal is for users to get their answers from one, or at most two, database tables 80% of the time. This goal is primarily accomplished by building focused aggregation sets provided as summary tables. Even in the case of a detail query, where the system must access detailed transaction records in conjunction with descriptive business view information, denormalization allows the designer to provide a highly responsive, easy-to-understand system.

Denormalization can also lessen the burden of extensive MQE (Managed Query Environment) semantic layer management and maintenance. These layers are built and

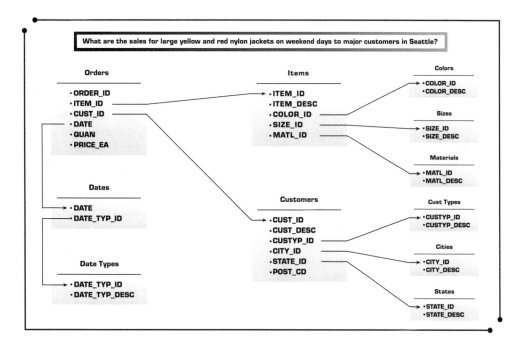

Figure 3.12 Normalized design

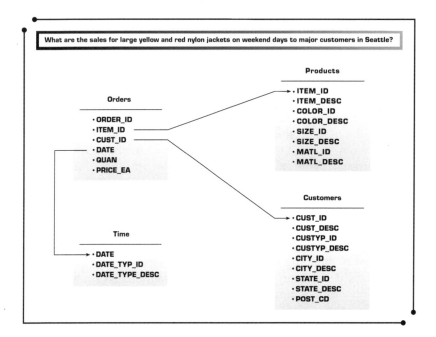

Figure 3.13   Denormalized design

maintained to shield the business users from the complexities and structure of the underlying database. Denormalization, coupled with field duplication and star schema design, allows the direct importation of the database schema into the MQE environment, thereby lessening or eliminating the extensive MQE semantic layer maintenance that can be a large hidden cost of some MQE implementations.

There are often two schools of thought in enterprise data warehouse design. Members of the ER (Entity Relationship) normalized school, which believes in building a data warehouse that is fundamentally normalized and then spawning off subset data marts that are denormalized, are called "Inmonites," for their reflection of Bill Inmon's enterprise data warehouse principles. Those who believe in a consistent, denormalized star schema environment across the entire enterprise data warehouse system are called "Kimballites," for their adherence to the design principles of Ralph Kimball. It is common for raging debates, panel discussions, and countless conversations to be held at industry conferences, on Internet forums, at user group meetings, and around water coolers in a vain effort to determine which approach is "better." Many teams fear that the denormalized design will be unwieldy for their particular industry, in banking or health care, for instance, with their requirements for a very large number of business dimensions. Other teams are reluctant to take on the additional maintenance requirements of a denormalized design in the ever-shifting world of business requirements.

In the end, it must be recognized that enterprise data warehouse systems are built to serve the needs of business users. Denormalized designs are easier for business users to use, although they are more challenging for technical implementation teams to design and maintain. When debating the merits of one design against the other, the ease of maintenance of the normalized design versus the business orientation of the denormalized design, the mandate of "ease of use" must carry the day. Enterprise data warehouse systems and associated data mart systems are not built for the convenience of the design or implementation teams; they are built for the convenience and ease of use of the business community. You must never lose sight of this fact.

> **REALITY CHECK** Much is made of the two warring camps in data warehouse design, the Inmonites and the Kimballites. It might trouble those stoking the flames to learn that I have actually seen Bill Inmon and Ralph Kimball in the same room—and they were talking pleasantly to one another. The fact is, I don't think we're ever going to see a segment of trash TV with Bill and Ralph at each other's throats. As is usually the case, the acolytes display more zealotry than the prophets.
>
> From the reality of the implementation side, you would be hard pressed to find a data warehouse or data mart system anywhere that is a pure reflection of Bill's or Ralph's designs. Reality demands compromise. Your first clue as to someone's practical, reality-based experience is how rigidly they cling to a design mantra or methodology. Experienced practitioners have one common theme: whatever works. The "rule of thumb" for data warehouse and data mart design is: if users are going to access the data, use a star schema. If you are building a warehouse strictly to supply data marts, then an ER design is fine.

Star Schema

To facilitate the access to information from the business user's point of view, the "star schema" has evolved. Largely defined and popularized by Ralph Kimball, the star schema provides an open, scaleable, optimized decision support environment that is perfect for data warehouse and data mart systems. A fully detailed description of the star schema design can be found in Ralph's book *The Data Warehouse Toolkit* (1996, John Wiley & Sons).

The star schema consists of a central fact table that contains transaction level information, surrounded by dimension tables that contain business perspectives of the transactions. (See Figure 3.14.)

The fact table contains the metrics of the transaction (such as quantity and price), the primary key of the transaction (such as order number), and any necessary external, or foreign, keys necessary to join to the dimension tables. Examples of foreign keys are date, customer ID (unique identifier), sales rep ID, and product ID. In systems that store

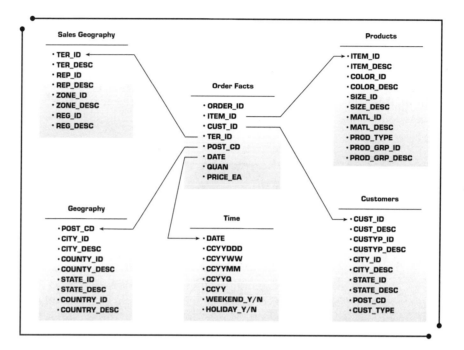

Figure 3.14   Star schema

very large amounts of transaction detail such as in retail businesses that track every UPC (Universal Product Code) scan from every purchase, these fact tables are highly normalized and hold many millions of rows. In a lower transaction volume business such as heavy manufacturing, the fact tables can be denormalized to various degrees.

The dimension tables consist of data necessary to support the summarization and analysis of the transactions by the various perspectives the business commonly uses such as product, customer, time, geography, and sales geography. The dimension tables also contain the associated hierarchies of the dimensions such as customer, sales rep, territory, zone, and region in the sales geography dimension. In addition, the dimension tables commonly contain metrics such as Total Sales Year to Date and Total Sales Prior Year to Date. The dimension tables are highly denormalized and contain all description and name fields associated with all IDs and keys, such as product description. Dimension tables are shared across multiple subject areas.

The star schema allows business users to access the information in an intuitive way, using business terms and perspectives they are familiar with. The star schema is also conducive to the multidimensional analyses fundamental to OLAP (On-Line Analytical Processing). It provides a data structure and organization that is fully extensible, manageable, aggregated, subsetted, and replicated.

Summaries

For the majority of data warehouse users, the summaries or aggregations created from the base detail facts and dimensions are the primary point of entry and use of the system. Derived from analysis of business needs, user interviews, and usage monitoring, summary tables are generated from combinations of facts and dimensions. (See Figure 3.15.)

Summary data sets contain many duplicated fields from the dimension tables along with the aggregated facts from the detail fact table. Instead of forcing users and the database to join together multiple tables to generate the desired answer, the descriptions, names, and other "value add" data points are included in the summary tables. For instance, a customer and product summary table would contain complete customer name and type information, as well as product description, product group, and so on. This allows the system designer to achieve the goal of having the summary tables provide 80% of the answers from the data warehouse or data mart.

Summary tables may be simple, single-dimension aggregations such as "orders by week" (using only detail facts and the time dimension), or they may be multidimensional aggregations such as "sales by product by customer by month by territory" (using detail facts and the product, customer, time, and sales geography dimensions). Note that multidimensional tables escalate very rapidly in size on a logarithmic scale with the addition of each new dimension. (See Figure 3.16.)

Summary tables contain only elements contained in or derived from the fact and dimension tables. External feeds are never introduced to support summary tables. It is essential that all elements of the data warehouse and data mart system(s) audit to each other. Any external fact or dimension element introduced solely for a summary data set will preclude this and sabotage the integrity of the data warehouse and data mart environment.

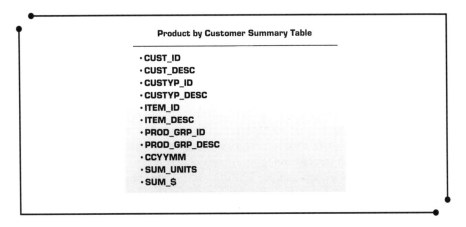

Product by Customer Summary Table

- **CUST_ID**
- **CUST_DESC**
- **CUSTYP_ID**
- **CUSTYP_DESC**
- **ITEM_ID**
- **ITEM_DESC**
- **PROD_GRP_ID**
- **PROD_GRP_DESC**
- **CCYYMM**
- **SUM_UNITS**
- **SUM_$**

Figure 3.15   Replicated data in summary tables

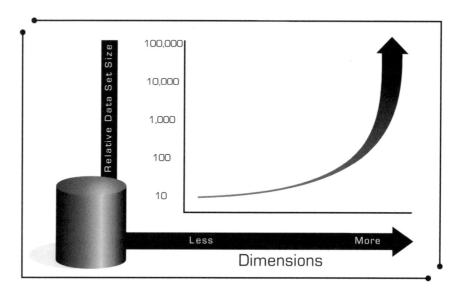

Figure 3.16   Data set size increases related to dimensions

Summary tables form the basis of, and define the reason for the existence of, data marts in classic enterprise data warehouse architecture. (See Figure 3.17.) In this view, data marts are containers of medium to highly summarized data targeted as specific user groups or users of a particular MOLAP application. As we have seen, this limited view of data marts has been rejected by the marketplace, which has often insisted on the presence of fully detailed data in the subset data marts.

History Tables

A common challenge that data warehouse and data mart system designers face is how to deal with the business's propensity to change its underlying relationships between business entities over time. A common example is the relationship between customer and sales representative. Over time, a customer may have relationships with multiple sales representatives, and vice versa. The customer may be assigned to multiple sales territories, as sales force deployment and organization shift with the changing challenges and priorities of the corporation. A sales geography table normally reflects the current relationship between the customer and the sales rep, however, it is limited in its capability to retain historical relationships. Without some mechanism to answer the question of "how has this sales rep performed this year to date versus last year to date?" when the rep's entire customer base has been redeployed last quarter, the data warehouse or data mart is of limited value.

Although it is possible to denormalize this relationship and create columns in the dimension table for current rep, last rep, and original rep, for instance, this makes

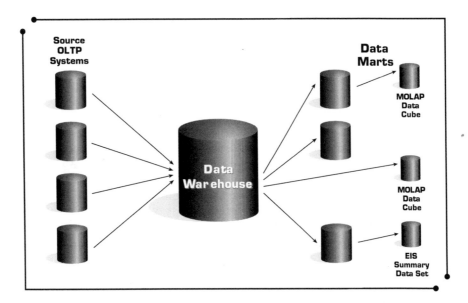

Figure 3.17   Classic data warehouse architecture with summary data marts

querying a complex task, and all other incremental relationships will be lost. Another approach is to create multiple rows in the dimension table, with a new row created each time the customer is reassigned to a sales rep and a new relationship is established. This approach, however, requires duplicate rows for each member of the dimension, incremented and/or multiple part keys, and very complex end-user query requirements that are fraught with caveats and land mines. Users must know, or tools must inherently implement, some mechanism, such as an SQL (Structured Query Language) MAX "where clause," to ensure that only the most recent relationship is the one retrieved in a query. Also, it is fundamentally impossible to answer simple questions such as, "how many customers do we have?" when there are multiple rows per customer in the customer dimension table. The design goal for easy-to-use dimension tables is always one row per subject of the dimension table.

A more elegant and useful solution is the history table, which contains relationships and associated metrics, if any, that the business wants to track over time. The history table contains snapshots of the elements of the relationship and usually also contains date/time stamps to record the time at which the relationship changed or took effect. Common history tables are customer history, to track sales rep relationships; product history, to track cost or price information; and rep history, to track rep and territory deployment.

The advantage of history tables is their full representation of the history of the relationship, while retaining the easy-to-use "one row per member" design of the dimension table. The downside is that you lose the elegance of the transparent change date transitions of the multiple row per member/incremented key approach (this is described in detail in Chapter 12). In my view, it is worth the trade-off to retain the validity and ease of use of the dimension tables.

A full discussion of dealing with history can be found in Chapter 12, under "Slowly Changing Dimensions and History."

ODS (Operational Data Store)

Some organizations find that it is efficient and useful to create an ODS (Operational Data Store) from which to extract the data warehouse. An ODS is basically a read/write data warehouse without any history or summary data sets. Such ODS resources can be used to query detailed operational transactional status information. This allows a clean and stable foundation on which dependent informational resources can be developed. This structure is often the basis of virtual data warehouse construction, using data marts derived from the ODS. A full discussion of the ODS concept can be found in *Building the Operational Data Store* by Bill Inmon, Claudia Imhoff, and Greg Battas (1996 John Wiley & Sons).

Data Warehouse Systems

Fully implemented data warehouse systems consist of multiple subject areas, made up of dozens, scores, or hundreds of fact tables and many shared business dimensions (assuming a star schema design). These subject areas are populated on a regular basis either by scores to hundreds of extract, scrubbing, and transformation programs and resultant flat files or by multiple transformation engine processes. After the loading of the database tables making up the star schema elements, summary data sets are created or updated by aggregating the metrics in the fact tables along various business dimensions and hierarchies contained in the dimension tables. In a classic enterprise data warehouse design, these summary sets, along with the pertinent detail, are then incrementally replicated and distributed to data marts, which are dedicated information assets targeted to specific user groups. Business users use a variety of information access tools and technologies to answer business questions from the data warehouse and the data marts. These business answers are made available in libraries that other business users can access to request copies of analyses, reports, and other assets. (See Figure 3.18.)

The entire process—from EMT (Extract, Mapping, and Transformation), database loading and indexing, aggregation, replication, and access to distribution—is monitored and managed by system tools. These management and monitoring tools assist the data warehouse and data mart team to identify and correct problems, predict and minimize system bottlenecks and slowdowns, identify business user utilization patterns, and identify summary opportunities.

The entire data warehouse system depends on its meta data repository, which is populated, maintained, and accessed by every tool and technology in the process. A logically common, open, and extensible meta data repository is the enabling technology for the data warehouse and is the only route to successful implementation and sustenance.

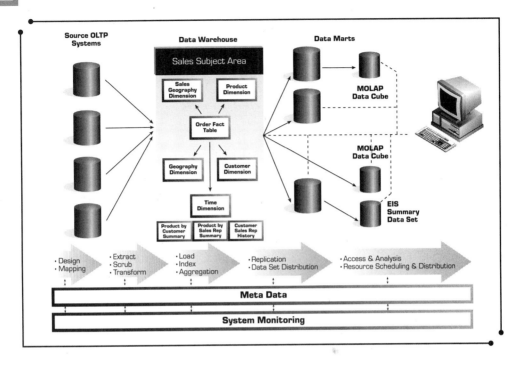

Figure 3.18 Data warehouse systems

Data Warehouse Challenges

As we saw in Chapter 2, data warehouses face many challenges in terms of cost and delivery time. Many organizations, when faced with the prospect of an investment of $2 to 3 million dollars, and more importantly, 12 to 36 months before measurable impact on the business, have turned to incremental data marts as a solution for their information needs.

The scope and resource requirements of an enterprise, or galactic data warehouse, are very daunting, especially for IS (Information Systems) organizations that are overburdened with OLTP system maintenance, new client server OLTP system implementations, and BPR (Business Process Reengineering) initiatives. It is very challenging to marshal and sustain the required political will and resulting budgeting resources over the extended research, planning, design, construction, and implementation phases of a full-scale data warehouse initiative. As a result, most organizations are turning away from a "top down" enterprise approach to data warehousing and are moving toward a "bottom up," or incremental methodology, building on a series of incremental data marts to arrive at the end goal of an enterprise data warehouse.

Incremental Data Mart Challenges

Although the "bottom up" incremental approach is both practical and accomplishable, the trend is often toward the implementation of nonintegrated, nonarchitected stand-alone data marts in as rapid a succession as possible. These nonintegrated data marts are popped out left and right, in an effort to solve as many tactical business problems as possible. The logic is often to provide rationale or to demonstrate the value of the data warehousing concept.

The Curse of LegaMarts

Unfortunately these disparate data marts are being constructed without the prerequisite enterprise data mart architecture that is required in a successful incremental data mart approach. Without an enterprise data mart architecture that defines subject areas, common dimensions, common metrics, common semantics, common business rules, and common source systems of record, these data marts are Trojan horses. As they pop up like mushrooms after a spring rain, each with its very own extract, scrubbing, and transformation jobs requiring batch window time and maintenance, they begin to suck maintenance resources. (See Figure 3.19.) Every time a source system changes, each nonintegrated data mart's EMT (Extract, Mapping, and Transformation) process must be changed. Eventually the business will demand that these nonintegrated, nonarchitected data marts be combined to form either a physical or virtual data warehouse. This is a black day because the effort required is enormous and the levels of pain exceedingly high.

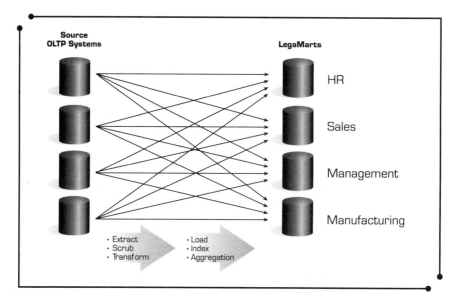

Figure 3.19   Multiple LegaMarts with extract feeds

Because they are nonarchitected and nonintegrated and do not derive from a common enterprise data warehouse source or enterprise data mart architecture, each nonarchitected data mart is likely to contain its own individual version of business semantics and business rules. This inevitably leads to multiple business groups reporting different versions of "truth" for the same business metric, such as sales or profits.

In the example in Table 3.1, the Northern California, Southern California, and Western region nonarchitected data marts are using a different business rule to define sales. The Northern California nonarchitected data mart is calculating sales as net of discounts and returns, whereas the Southern California nonarchitected data mart is reporting sales as equal to gross receipts. The Western region nonarchitected data mart is a third definition, one subtracting only returns from gross receipts to arrive at a "sales" number. This type of confusion is not only likely, it is inevitable when constructing nonintegrated, nonarchitected stand-alone data marts. An enterprise data mart architecture would have ensured that each data mart shared a consistent business rule and a consistent semantic meaning of the label "sales."

Table 3.1 Multiple definitions of sales

	Gross Receipts	Discounts	Returns	Sales
NoCal Data Mart	150,000	–20,000	–10,000	120,000
SoCal Data Mart	120,000	–10,000	–5,000	120,000
Western Region Data Mart	270,000	–30,000	–15,000	255,000

When nonarchitected data marts are frantically created and implemented in an effort to quickly solve the user group's tactical problems, each of them soon takes on a life of its own and becomes mission critical to its user community. It is further modified and tweaked to meet the changing demands of its constituency, all the while pumping out its very own "stove pipe" of isolated and nonintegrated information. (See Figure 3.20.)

Organizations that allow and encourage the construction of nonarchitected, nonintegrated data marts inevitably construct a family of stand-alone legacy systems. They are, in essence, the direct descendants of the problems of information retrieval from legacy OLTP systems to which enterprise data warehouses were supposed to be the solution. They are as separate and disparate as any set of nonintegrated legacy OLTP systems, and they are just as challenging to integrate after the fact. For this reason, we call these nonarchitected data marts LegaMarts.

Sooner or later, the business will accept the argument that these LegaMarts should be integrated into a real enterprise data warehouse. Unfortunately for the IS team in the room at the time, the task at hand is every bit as daunting as the original specter of the galactic enterprise data warehouse. The moral of this story is: Pay me now, or pay me later. You do not avoid the need for integration under an enterprise architecture simply

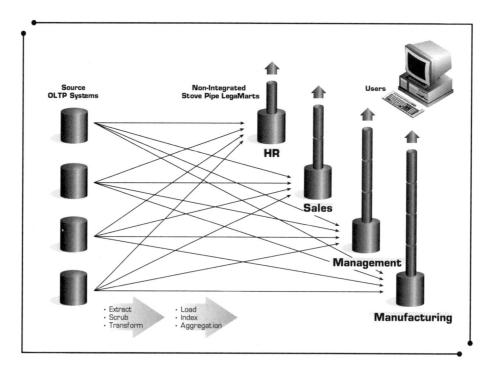

Figure 3.20 "Stove pipe" LegaMarts

by stamping out LegaMarts throughout the enterprise. At some point you will need to "pay the piper," and it will not get any easier by creating LegaMarts that users will defend to the death before allowing changes to their now mission-critical systems.

LegaMarts quickly become a curse upon the unwary who are led onto the rocks by their siren song of quick and easy solutions. They become deeply entrenched, they require massive expense to integrate, and they lead to a false sense of security in nonarchitected and nonintegrated environments.

Successful Incremental Data Marts

Successful incremental data marts are built on a foundation of an enterprise data mart architecture. This enterprise data mart architecture consists of a minimum of:

- *Enterprise Subject Areas*
  You must first establish at a high level what the pertinent subject areas for the enterprise are. Even if an enterprise data warehouse is specifically excluded from short- and long-range plans by your organization, you must still map out the likely subject areas for the entire enterprise. This is the only way to ensure that any incremental data mart will properly account for potential metric duplication and sharing of dimensions. This effort must be kept at a very high level to avoid analysis

paralysis. You are not attempting to model an enterprise data warehouse, only to identify, *at a high level,* what the subject areas would be if an enterprise data warehouse were built.

- *Common Dimensions*
  The next step is to identify common business dimensions—the ways that the business likes to view and analyze itself and its business activity—for all subject areas. Typical business dimensions include date, product, customer, geography, sales geography, promotions, and so on. Common dimensions allow the design of consistent views of business activity across multiple incremental data marts. Common dimensions are usually fairly easy to establish and are simply reflections of the ways the business prefers to analyze its activities.

- *Common Metrics*
  Next you must identify the metrics used in each subject area and each dimension. Metrics are the ways the business measures its activities and operational processes. Common metrics consist of dollars, units, hours, leads, pounds/kilos, and so on.

- *Common Business Rules*
  Having identified the subject areas, business dimensions, and metrics at a high level, you now start to drill into your specific area(s) of interest. You first identify the incremental data mart that you would like to construct, then you examine, in detail, the business rules used to calculate or derive the metrics associated with that area of interest. You must document the business rules for all metrics in your targeted incremental data mart's area, as well as those for duplicate metrics in other areas. For instance, you might have a metric labeled "sales" in your incremental "marketing" data mart, but also a metric labeled "sales" listed under the finance subject area. Upon examination, you will likely find that each of these "sales" fields is calculated differently.

  It is nearly impossible to achieve a successful "bottom up" incremental data mart to enterprise data warehouse implementation without common business rules across the organization. Although it is inevitable that you will be replicating unique definitions of business metrics, for example, Finance "Sales," it is vital that when you populate and present the generic "Sales" data point, all users understand and agree on how that metric is derived. This process is not always easy. After all, you and your predecessors probably have been fighting this battle for years, if not decades, but the rewards are great.

- *Common Source Systems of Record*
  You must now identify the source system from which these data points will be extracted. Without arriving at common sources for facts, metrics, and dimensions, you will sabotage your incremental data mart efforts. Common systems of record are a prerequisite for common business rules. Without a common source, you are laying the groundwork for a confusing matrix of EMT processes and disparate metrics and dimensions.

- *Common Semantics*

  Common semantics allows a business to agree on common definitions of business terms. Obtaining as much consensus as possible on common terms like sales, returns, discounts, and net profit is vitally important. A data mart/data warehouse initiative is a perfect opportunity and forces function to encourage consolidation around common definitions. If you cannot agree on a common semantic term, such as when the Marketing and Finance organizations cannot agree on how to calculate "sales," you must clearly label each field to reflect its unique business rules, for example, "finance sales" and "marketing sales."

Enterprise Data Mart Architecture

What this foundation yields is the ability to construct a data mart environment that can leverage common sources, common dimensions, and common business rule algorithms across the enterprise. To construct this foundation, it is imperative that an investment be made in auditing and assessing the enterprise prior to the design and construction of any data marts, lest they become LegaMarts hanging like millstones around your neck in the near future.

Too often, this effort to assess and define an enterprise architecture takes one of two paths:

1. The team is frozen by analysis paralysis for over a year as they attempt to model every business process, down to the microscopic level. The project is inevitably summarily executed due to lack of tangible benefits in the current or next millennium.

2. The team avoids any attempt to view the enterprise at all, lest they a) get caught in the aforementioned analysis paralysis or b) cause enough noise to get noticed by central management and/or the centralized IS organization and have their "skunk works" data mart squashed under the infinite weight of the bureaucratic morass.

What is required to ensure a successful data mart implementation is *not* a million man-hour enterprise data modeling effort. What is required is a simple one-day to three-week effort to assess and define as many subject areas, semantics, business rules, sources, and common dimensions as possible. If you are spending more than three weeks, you are spending too long. Don't lose the momentum of your project by submersing your team in minutia. Get the basics down, and then move forward, forcibly.

Take the time to interface with other data mart teams in the organization. Work to establish an internal standards organization that can codify the common semantics and business rules as the multiple projects move forward. What is key is to not lose yourself or your team in endless meetings, conferences, and e-mail barrages. Pay close attention to the bandwidth being devoted to marginal issues. The last thing you have time for is the data architecture equivalent of "how many angels can dance on the head of a pin" debate, such as whether the Southern California users can really have their own definition of sales.

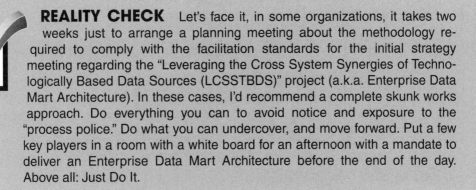

REALITY CHECK Let's face it, in some organizations, it takes two weeks just to arrange a planning meeting about the methodology required to comply with the facilitation standards for the initial strategy meeting regarding the "Leveraging the Cross System Synergies of Technologically Based Data Sources (LCSSTBDS)" project (a.k.a. Enterprise Data Mart Architecture). In these cases, I'd recommend a complete skunk works approach. Do everything you can to avoid notice and exposure to the "process police." Do what you can undercover, and move forward. Put a few key players in a room with a white board for an afternoon with a mandate to deliver an Enterprise Data Mart Architecture before the end of the day. Above all: Just Do It.

By keeping a tight reign on the resources expended on this effort, you can deliver a solid, scaleable, and extensible foundation in one to three weeks. It will not be complete or answer every question, but it will be enough to allow you to begin. As you develop your first incremental data mart, you will supplement the architecture. Each successive incremental data mart will expand the scope and depth of the enterprise data mart architecture. This will allow you to start delivering high-impact integrated and architected data marts, even as you extend and reinforce the enterprise architecture.

Following this approach will allow you to realize the goals of a data mart:

- *Integrated*
  The data mart will integrate the source systems of record identified in the enterprise data mart architecture.

- *Architected*
  The data mart will reflect the enterprise data mart architecture and present a consistent view of "the truth" with every other architected incremental data mart in the enterprise.

- *Leverageable*
  A leverageable data mart serves as a referenceable example of data warehousing principles and data marts as the preferred method for sustainable enterprise-scale decision support systems. In a "bottom up" incremental data warehouse scenario, your initial data marts must be leverageable examples of design, architecture, methodology, process, technology, access, and utilization. If not, your efforts are wasted.

- *High impact*
  A data mart must provide a high-impact solution for real, tangible, and intense business pain. If your data mart does not change people's lives, it will not carry enough impact to be extrapolated across the enterprise. You need enthusiastic

evangelists among the business user and management community in order to survive and prosper.

- *On time and on budget*
  It is incumbent on your data mart team to deliver your solutions on time and on budget. The primary reason most organizations choose the incremental data mart approach is that they fear the "over budget/late and getting later" cloud hanging over the enterprise data warehouse market space. Closely monitor your resources and your project plans. It is imperative that you deliver your first solution in a timely and efficient manner.

Data Mart Architecture

The data mart is not a new creature. In fact, as long as there have been computers, especially personal computers, LANs, and servers, there have been nonintegrated, nonarchitected data marts. In the past we have called them "user reporting systems" when feeling charitable and "data islands" when not. Today we've got a data mart category for all the variations of yesterday's, today's, and tomorrow's user-oriented data set permutations. Consider the variations on the data mart theme presented in Table 3.2.

Table 3.2 Data Mart Variations

Type	Time to Build	Lifetime	Cost	Architected Y/N
Data Mart	2 to 9 months	2+ years	100K–2M	Y
LegaMart	<1 to 9 months	1+ years	100K–2M	N
DisposaMart	<1 to 3 months	<1 year	10–200K	Y or N
InstaMart	<1 day to 1 week	<1 day–3 months	0–10K	Y

Data Marts

As we've seen, data marts go well beyond the classical galactic data warehouse subset definition of "highly summarized" data targeted to a small set of users. They also have evolved well past the pigeonhole of application-specific data sets used to support various MOLAP (Multidimensional On-Line Analytical Processing) applications.

Today data marts serve thousands of users leveraging multiple applications accessing atomic detail as well as multiple levels of summarized data. They range in size from a few gigabytes to hundreds of gigabytes. It is impossible to characterize data marts by these old and inadequate criteria.

Data Marts have the following characteristics:

- *Architected*
  Data marts must be built on an enterprise data mart architecture. At a minimum this architecture identifies enterprise subject areas, common dimensions, common sources, semantics, metrics, and business rules for the organization. Data marts also are based on the design principles and processes of data warehouses as defined earlier in this chapter.

- *Integrated*
  Data marts must be integrated with other data marts in the organization via common sources, metrics, semantics, business rules, and dimensions. If there is only one data mart in the organization, it must be open and ready to integrate with subsequent data marts.

- *Scaleable*
  Data marts must be built on scaleable database and operating platform designs. They must be capable of seamless orders of magnitude growth. The "bottom up" incremental data mart must have no fundamental design barriers preventing it from scaling up to become the core of the enterprise data warehouse.

- *Homogeneous users*
  The data mart must serve a group of users with common interests, challenges, or other homogeneous business needs. These users may be any number, from one to one million, but they must share one or more clearly identifiable homogeneous business needs.

If your existing or planned data marts fall short of these criteria, they are one of the following variations: LegaMarts, DisposaMarts, or InstaMarts.

LegaMarts

As we have seen earlier in this chapter, LegaMarts are classic examples of a Trojan horse. It is generally easy to pop a few out, but sooner or later, someone will have to pay the price to integrate these stovepipe legacy, decision support systems. Their overlapping and duplicative EMT processes quickly become a management nightmare threatening to overwhelm the team, that is, if they don't consume the available batch window first.

LegaMarts have the following characteristics:

- *Nonarchitected*
  The LegaMart does not share common sources, metrics, semantics, business rules, or dimensions with other data marts or the enterprise data warehouse. They often ignore the design principles of data warehousing defined earlier in this chapter. Even if they adhere to the principles, if they are nonarchitected, they are LegaMarts.

- *Nonintegrated*
  The LegaMart is not integrated with other data marts or the enterprise data warehouse. It does not share EMT processes or meta data with other resources.

"LegaMart" assumes the mantle for both the existing nonintegrated, nonarchitected data marts in the enterprise, as well as any new ones being pumped out under the guise of "data mart" legitimacy.

DisposaMarts

DisposaMarts are limited-term data sets created to serve the needs of a specific, limited scope, business need. Although they may be nonarchitected like a LegaMart, they are much more valuable to the enterprise if they are derived from the enterprise data mart architecture. Architecture-derived DisposaMarts also have the advantage of being easier to develop and maintain because they can leverage the existing EMT processes in place for the data marts.

However, one defining characteristic of the DisposaMart is that it is fundamentally a one-time, throwaway data set. The DisposaMart is prime territory for nonintegrated, nonarchitected solutions to be slid out into the business users' space. The challenge is that, as we have all experienced, even the most clear-cut, "it will die in three months, guaranteed" data sets somehow become immortal in that 90-day span. For this reason, deliver nonarchitected DisposaMarts at your own risk. You may be spawning little LegaMart spores that will come back to haunt you in the near future.

DisposaMarts are defined by the following characteristics:

- *Defined, short-to-mid-term life span*

- *Project based; or specific, limited scope, and timeline business need based*
  DisposaMarts are driven by clear-cut, limited life span projects such as a marketing campaign, or by a specific, limited scope business need such as an inventory analysis project.

- *Disposability of all associated processes and data*
  DisposaMarts are fundamentally throwaway processes, code, and data. At the conclusion of the project or business need, everything will be wiped clean, including EMT processes, metrics, and aggregations.

InstaMarts

A close cousin of the DisposaMart is the InstaMart. The InstaMart is an extremely quickly derived, very short life span, point solution to a business information need. InstaMarts are often created by end-user access and analysis tools.

InstaMarts are characterized by:

- *Very short life span*
  An InstaMart may only exist for minutes, hours, or days. Its duration is extremely short; it lives only long enough to provide the answer to a specific question or analysis challenge.

- *Point solution*
  The InstaMart is created to answer a very specific challenge. It is the ultimate tactical weapon in the data mart team's quiver. They are commonly developed to facilitate specific analysis projects, to provide answers for workgroup meetings or management briefings, or simply as an end-user developed answer set that is stored in the database for a brief time.

- *Individual or workgroup audience*
  InstaMarts typically are created to serve the needs of individuals or work groups. They may be created to serve larger audiences for very short-term projects such as budgeting.

- *Subset or aggregation*
  InstaMarts are almost exclusively subsets of parent data marts or the enterprise data warehouse. They may be detailed, summary aggregations or small multidimensional data sets (portable OLAP). It is very common for InstaMart definition to be limited to operations that can be performed using straight SQL against the data mart or data warehouse tables.

Again, although it may be possible to create and distribute multiple InstaMarts outside the umbrella of the enterprise data mart architecture, they too have a tendency to linger on like an unwelcome guest. Before you know it, they've taken up permanent residency and now you're responsible for their upkeep. Better to ensure that all of the InstaMarts created stay warm and dry under the comforting enterprise data mart architecture parasol.

Topologies

Data Warehouse Topologies

Enterprise data warehouses commonly employ a multiple-level physical topology. In a first-generation implementation, the source systems typically reside on a mainframe computer system, with the data warehouse residing on a UNIX or NT server. The business users access the data warehouse from personal computers via a LAN. (See Figure 3.21.)

Second-generation implementations make use of several additional layers of topology. In these implementations, source systems commonly reside on mainframes as well as multiple OLTP application servers. Transformation engine-based DTEAMM environments reside on application servers, whereas separate database servers host the enterprise data warehouse. Additional web and application servers access the enterprise data warehouse and make it available over intranets, extranets, and/or the Internet and LANs for access by thin and thick clients. (See Figure 3.22.)

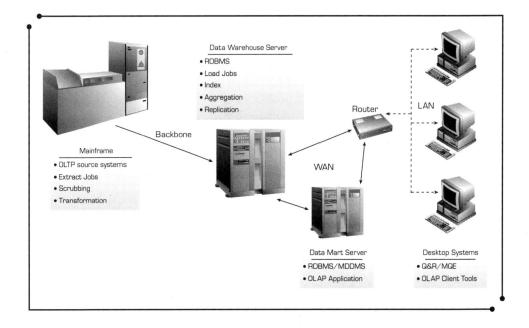

Figure 3.21 First-generation data warehouse physical topology

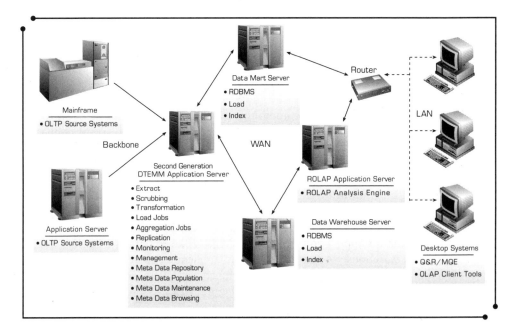

Figure 3.22 Second-generation data warehouse physical topology

Data Mart Topologies

Data marts have shared this same evolution in topology and now are found in myriad physical topology implementations. Table 3.3 lists the applications associated with the single-, two-, and three-tier topologies.

Table 3.3 Applications and Their Topologies

Single Tier	Two Tier	Three Tier
Desktop DB	LowLAP (Low Level Analytical Processing)	ROLAP (Relational On-Line Analytical Processing)
	Query and Reporting	MOLAP (Multidimensional Analytical Processing)
	Report Readers	OCSD (On-Line Content Scheduling and Delivery)
		Intranet
		Internet
		Work Flow
		Collaboration

Single Tier

The smallest data marts are single tier, in which the data mart RDBMS (Relational Data Base Management System) resides alongside the source application itself on a small server. (See Figure 3.23.) These data marts are targeted at individual and workgroup users and would most commonly use a desktop database system and access applications, such as Microsoft Access and Excel. This is a classic "data island" topology. In most enterprises, data islands are used by almost every user group in the organization. They usually form the foundation of a "shadow" DSS infrastructure in the business. They operate outside the auspices of the IT (Information Technology) organization and any accompanying enterprise architecture. Data islands are notorious sources for varying versions of "the truth" used in user reporting and analysis.

Two Tier

In a two-tier topology, the incremental data mart RDBMS lives in a server separate from the source OLTP systems. (See Figure 3.24.) It is commonly found in legacy scenarios where the source systems are centrally located on one or more mainframes. In this

Figure 3.23 Single-tier architecture

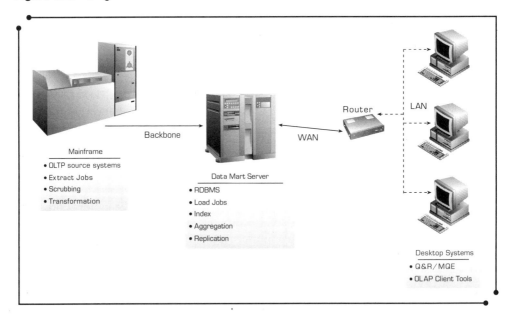

Figure 3.24 Two-tier architecture—MF (Mainframe) to DM (Data Mart)

scenario, it is common to find traditional first-generation EMT tools and thick client access tools.

Three Tier

In three-tier implementations, the incremental data mart RDBMS server is joined by application and DTEAMM servers. (See Figure 3.25.) It is more common to find second-generation transformation engine DTEAMM environments in these configurations, as well as distributed thin client access architectures.

Intranet/Internet

Due to data marts' inherent integrated and scrubbed data, they are natural data sources for intranet and Internet applications. Today's tools allow painless publishing of information to internal audiences in the intranet. These same easy-to-implement tools can open up a carefully subsetted information resource to the external world of the Internet.

The rise of the intranet/Internet topology has allowed the data mart to become one of many information resources sharing the ubiquitous access mechanism provided by the intranet/Internet low-level protocols and resulting cross-platform universal clients.

In this design, the data mart server is joined by web servers, firewalls, application servers, and other data mart servers. (See Figure 3.26.) All the servers work cooperatively

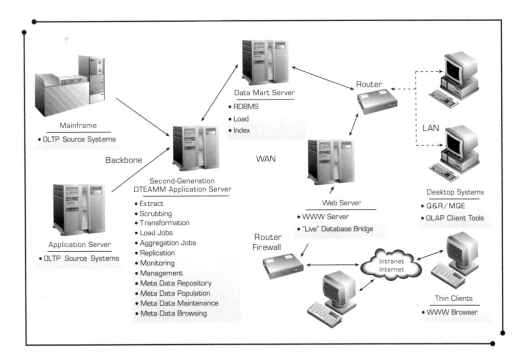

Figure 3.25   Three-tier architecture—ROLAP/MOLAP server

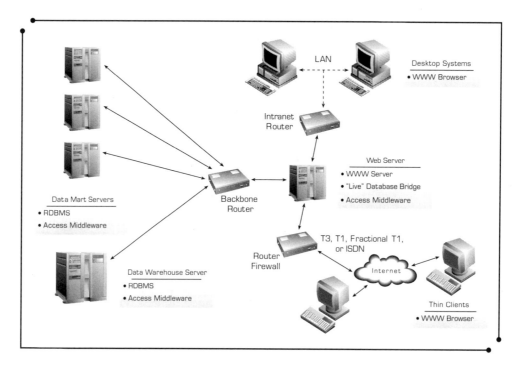

Figure 3.26   Intranet/Internet topology

to provide preformatted and scheduled reports and analyses, as well as ad hoc information to internal and external users worldwide.

In the evolution of the intranet/Internet information access model, we have seen the rapid growth from basic capabilities such as:

- Database access extensions
- Text display of current data
- Simple interactive analysis
- User/consumer self-service

to more sophisticated capabilities such as:

- Content scheduling and delivery
- Controlled release of information
- Open access to customers, partners, and public
- Data delivered with query applets

A fundamental development in the evolution of more sophisticated capabilities in the intranet/Internet model is the move from CGI (Common Gateway Interface)–based data access to more capable "live server" type data access. (See Figure 3.27.)

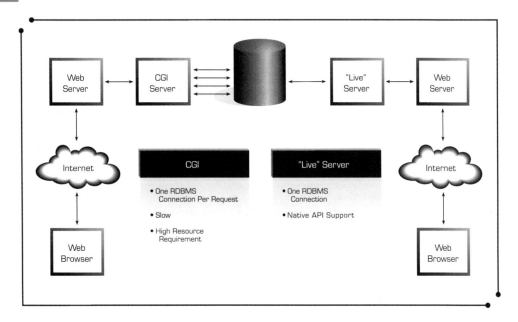

Figure 3.27   CGI vs. live server architecture   *Source: Meta Group*

CGI (Common Gateway Interface) provides a "lowest common denominator" level of access to database information. While being very flexible and relatively easy to develop with, CGI is notoriously slow and resource intensive in actual implementations. It generally requires a dedicated server for hosting, and even then it is generally not regarded as capable of scaleable, enterprise-level intensive data applications.

Characteristics of a CGI implementation include:

- *State-less*
  Native CGI and associated protocols are incapable of maintaining state information about users. It is impossible to retain status of operations or processes, or user history information.

- *Spawns multiple instantiations*
  CGI creates a new instance, or connection to the data base for each access. This is very resource intensive, and quickly chews up available memory.

- *Web-like application*
  CGI applications are not interactive or "on-line." At best they are equal to, and often less capable than, a legacy terminal application of days gone by. They require users to fill in static fields and specifically perform an action, such as pressing a button, in order to gather the inputted information and act on it. There is no interactive GUI.

- *HTML (Hyper Text Markup Language) hot spots with associated URLs (Uniform Resource Locators)*
  CGI applications use HTML hyper links to move users through the application's user interface. Each dialog is created and maintained in an HTML document. There are very few control or UI (User Interface) capabilities or elements available.

A live server environment, however, provides the developer with much the same capability as a client/server development environment. In this model, the developer can employ the full range of GUI (Graphical User Interface) design and leverage the full power of the RDBMS and the display capabilities of the client.

Characteristics of a live server implementation are:

- *Maintains state*
  A live server implementation has full capabilities to maintain state and associated process and user information.

- *Native RDBMS connection*
  Native connections are used to create and maintain RDBMS connectivity. The live server opens only one connection to the database and does not chew up server resources maintaining multiple connections for each database request.

- *Web-live application*
  A live server model uses Java, ActiveX, and other development technologies to provide a full client/server application development environment within the intranet/Internet architecture. This allows developers to provide full client/server applications across any and all platforms to users anywhere in the world, with the short learning curve of the browser as the only barrier to entry.

The Data Mart as Information Resource

Data marts have emerged as a primary entry point to information resources for the enterprise. They are quick, targeted, high ROI implementations that allow businesses to have user-oriented information readily available to overcome both strategic and tactical challenges. Because of their quick ascendancy to the forefront of information access, it is important to understand their roles as the primary information resource for the business and its users.

Roles and Types of Users

Perhaps the most important thing about building a successful data mart is to first understand who will use it, how they will use it, and how those characteristics relate to the available technologies and tools. The first step is to get a fix on who the users of the data mart are going to be, and what roles they play. There are three basic types of users who touch data in any organization: creators, knowledge workers, and consumers.

Creators

Creators are the users of the source OLTP systems that actually generate the majority of data that is used in the data mart. Creators are typically 3–8% of the workforce in the enterprise and are not commonly found among the primary users of the data mart. Creators require access to detailed, transaction-level information that reflects the current status of the OLTP system.

Knowledge Workers

Knowledge workers are the traditional users of the DSS resources of the business. These are the "power users" who work behind the scenes to provide the answers to the management levels of the organization. Knowledge workers are highly skilled, very well versed in the data of the organization, and capable of fully leveraging information access and development environments such as Focus and SAS. They commonly build their own information resources, including extracting and transforming data from source OLTP systems. Historically, knowledge workers typically made up 2–4% of the workforce of an organization and were primary power users of DSS systems.

The primary accomplishment of the Q&R (Query and Reporting) tool vendors of the last few years has been to lower the barrier to entry to becoming a knowledge worker. Now it is possible for anyone who can point and click to query a database to obtain answers for their business questions. Because of this, the percentage of those who can count themselves as knowledge workers will continue to climb, albeit more slowly, from today's levels of 10–15% until it peaks at 20–25% in typical organizations.

Knowledge workers require very robust tools and environments to provide high-end analysis and querying capabilities. They need the ability to collaborate with their fellow knowledge workers through open and shared repositories containing their queries, analysis sets, and reports. Knowledge workers require access to the entire range of data in the data mart, from extensive historical detailed transaction records to multidimensional aggregations.

Consumers

Consumers simply want to consume the answers to the business questions that the knowledge workers have generated. It was a fundamental miscalculation by some who considered that since all you had to do was point and click, everyone would want to become a knowledge worker. This is not, and will not become, the case.

The vast majority of the enterprise will remain primarily consumers, regardless of how easy it becomes to become knowledge workers. Although we will continue to see a rapid graying around the margins, as more and more consumers test the waters with MQE (Managed Query Environment) queries and web-enabled multidimensional analysis, they will remain predominantly consumers of the output of the newly expanded knowledge worker class. It will continue to becomes easier for consumers to access and share the work of the knowledge worker community through the ability to access reports, queries, and analyses in shared repositories. Consumers will also realize significant benefits from collaborative analysis and decision making in this open environment of information resource exchange.

Although more and more will cross over into the realm of active knowledge workers as it becomes easier and easier to surf the corporate data resources, people who are primarily consumers will continue to make up 50–75% of average organizations.

Consumers need the ability to easily browse the available reports, analyses, and queries and to schedule delivery of anything they are interested in. This requires that OCSD (On-Line Content Scheduling and Delivery) capabilities or tools be in place to allow the scheduling and delivery of all types of data mart content to any type of destination via any type of transport. OCSD capabilities or tools allow consumers to browse the available information assets, select one or more that they are interested in, and schedule a one-time copy or a regular subscription in a variety of data formats. For example, a user could request a one-time copy of a multidimensional analysis data cube delivered to their local LAN (Local Area Network) file server, or to subscribe to regular delivery of a report in spreadsheet format attached to an e-mail message every Tuesday afternoon.

Consumers also want the ability to easily access the information resources of the enterprise via very-easy-to-use access tools, such as web browser–based technologies. Consumers can require access to detailed data-derived reports and analyses, but their primary source of information is summary data sets.

It is very important to remember that consumers are your majority audience for the data mart. Those of us on the information side of the business have such a long history of serving the knowledge worker as our primary user group, it is easy to become fixated on their needs and requirements, at the cost of the majority consumer audience.

REALITY CHECK   This point is a big potential trap. As an industry, we have been almost solely focused on the knowledge worker constituency. Regardless of what you think your mission is for your data mart system, in the very near future you will need to effectively serve the majority audience of consumers. Design a system that can fulfill this mission from the start, and insist on tools that can fulfill that mission.

User Requirements Analysis

To ensure that all audiences are adequately served by the data mart resource, a user requirements analysis will be needed. In this analysis, your user's needs and requirements are compared to the capabilities of available tools and technologies.

As we shall see in Chapter 5, it is critical that the business drivers for the data mart be clearly understood and that the resulting tool selection derives from those business drivers. In almost all cases, business needs will demand the implementation of multiple tools to solve the multiple problems the users have. At this time, there is no all-inclusive solution from any vendor that can answer the needs of the average organization. This

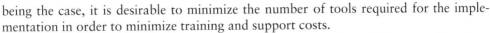

being the case, it is desirable to minimize the number of tools required for the implementation in order to minimize training and support costs.

Regardless of the number of tools chosen, different users have different needs and requirements in the data itself. (See Figure 3.28.) To ensure sustainable utilization levels, you must provide properly designed data sources for each type of business need. This will require both detail and summary data, as well as multidimensional aggregations for specific analysis tools.

Thin and Thick Clients

Regardless of who the users are and what level of detailed data they are looking at, it is becoming increasingly likely that they may be using a thin client tool to do so. Thin client solutions present compelling economic and management arguments and may be an appropriate solution for your implementation.

A "thick client" is a traditional personal computer model in which the personal computer is responsible for presenting and managing the UI (User Interface), storing and executing the application, providing local data storage capabilities, and communicating with remote servers over the network. In this model, the data may be stored on a remote server, but the application processing is accomplished on the "thick" local client. All "state," or user and application status, information is retained on the thick client. All or most of the application data (query results and analysis data sets) is persistent on the thick client as well. Thick clients provide a wealth of local computing power and flexibility for the user. The downside, however, is that they are painfully expensive to

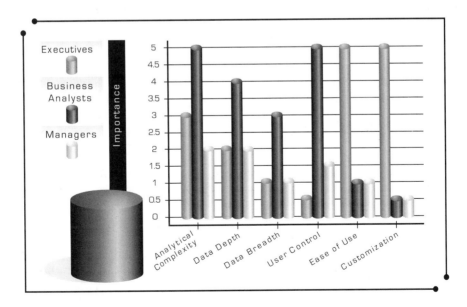

Figure 3.28 User requirements analysis *Source: Meta Group*

support. Personal computers are notorious for having extremely complex configuration files and endless opportunities for software and hardware conflicts.

"Thin clients" are connected to a remote server that maintains the data and the "state" of the user and the user's applications. In some thin client models, the server also performs most or all of the application processing. Thin clients share three common characteristics:

- Their initial purchase price is lower than a traditional PC.

- Their ongoing support costs are lower than a traditional PC (5–40% less according to industry analysts).

- They are "stateless" systems that rely on remote servers to store all volatile user status, application status, data, and software (except for what is cached locally).

The compelling arguments put forth for the thin client model are:

- *Cost*
  The Gartner Group estimates that every PC desktop represents a five-year investment of $44,250 (Windows 3.1) to $38,900 (Windows 95) to purchase and maintain. Although Intel, the primary beneficiary along with Microsoft of the thick client model, weighs in with a lower figure of around $30,000 per thick client desktop, this is still a very significant outlay to equip every worker with computing capability.

  Zona Research places the five-year cost of 15 Windows PCs and a Windows NT server at $217,663. It pegs the five-year cost of an NT Server with 15 thin clients at $94,368. Oracle, a leader of the "thin client" forces, claims an annual cost of only $2,500 for every thin client desktop. It doesn't take too many desktops to add up to some "real money" in savings at those rates.

- *Standards*
  Thin client systems are built to natively support intranet/Internet standards. This allows them to be seamlessly integrated into an existing intranet environment. Thin client design of applications promises to yield ubiquitous availability across all platforms of the enterprise, providing the ultimate open standards system.

- *Scaleability*
  Due to their lower cost of ownership and lower support requirements, thin client platforms are much more supportable across a large number of users. Thin clients are managed from a central source, whereas thick clients require that management tasks be performed on each individual system. Thin client software resides on the server, so an update to the server instantly updates every user. Because the thin client only has to be concerned with connecting to the network and displaying the GUI, the organization can significantly increase the power of the server-based application without upgrading each client system, as is required with a thick client model.

- *Management*
  Thin clients are much easier to manage and support than thick clients. Because all applications are stored on a central server, version control is automatic. Update the server and you've updated everyone in the enterprise. Because the configuration of the thin clients is locked, centrally controlled, or stored on the server (depending on the thin client model), there are no longer any local configuration conflicts.

  Obviously this central management model is heaven for the old guard of centralized IS who have resented the usurpation of absolute power and control that the personal computer has represented since its inception. However, it would be a mistake to blindly pursue a thin client model simply to restore the vision, if not the reality, of the deity of the "glass house."

  Also, the "appliance" nature of thin client platforms makes hardware transparent to the user. If a thin client user system is faulty, it can simply be unplugged and replaced, with no requirement for lengthy setup or configuration because all user, application, and data information is retained on the server.

- *Leverage existing investment*
  Thin client application design allows organizations to extend the lives of existing systems currently installed. Because the only requirement is that the platform must be able to run a "thin client" application layer such as a web browser, JVM (Java Virtual Machine), or a dedicated Net-centric operating system, older systems with relatively low-powered CPUs (Central Processing Units) and low amounts of installed memory can remain viable platforms for much longer than anticipated.

- *Ease of deployment*
  Native thin client platforms have no or very few installation parameters, so setup and installation is quick and easy. There is also the advantage of a small installation footprint when using existing systems.

The downsides to a thin client implementation are:

- *Lack of user autonomy*
  Thin clients are devoid of floppy disk drives and user configurable settings. Users can only execute applications that are provided by central IS management, using only data available on the IS-maintained servers. Because this will be a very challenging cultural hurdle for many organizations, thin clients probably will be most popular in situations where they are replacing "dumb" terminals for vertical applications. In those cases, there is no autonomy to miss.

- *More complex mobile computing model*
  To perform mobile computing on a thin client, the necessary application applets and data must be downloaded to the mobile, thin client, hard disk drive cache prior to disconnecting from the network. Upon reconnection, the user's state must also be synchronized with the server in order to properly restore the user and to handle integrating any new or changed data the user has created on the mobile platform.

• *Higher network/server costs*
Thin client computing can place higher bandwidth requirements on the network and require more robust application and database servers.

Tables 3.4 and 3.5 present the characteristics of thick and thin client users and of the models themselves.

Table 3.4 User Characteristics of Thin and Thick Clients

Thick Client Users	Thin Client Users
Power users	Data creators (OLTP system operators)
Developers	Information consumers
System administrators	Casual users
Support team	Internet/intranet users
Local users	Remote users
Low network capacity	High network capacity

Table 3.5 Characteristics of Popular Thick and Thin Client Models

	Thick Client Model	Thin Client Model
Data	Local persistence	Server persistence
User and application state storage/maintenance	Local	Server
OS (Operating System)	Windows	Various
Processor	Intel (or Intel Compatible)	Various
Local hard disk	Mandatory	Optional
Floppy disk	Mandatory	None
Network	Optional	Mandatory
Portable/Remote operation	Yes	Requires local hard drive cache
Cost	Higher than thin client	Lower than thick client

Table 3.5 Characteristics of Popular Thick and Thin Client Models (continued)

	Thick Client Model	**Thin Client Model**
Management	Local configuration and update	Remote configuration and update
Physical design	Open and accessible	Sealed unit
Replacement/upgrade	Copy all data, update configuration and setup	Unplug old unit, plug in new unit
Maintenance cost	5–40% more than thin clients	5–40% less than thick clients
Program execution	Usually originate and execute on desktop, but can originate and execute on server	Originate on server and execute on desktop or server.
Network capacity/speed requirements	Lower than thin	Higher than thick

Models of Thin Client

There are two popular standards for thin client implementation. (See Figure 3.29.) Both share the goal of an environment sharing all the upside potential mentioned previously,

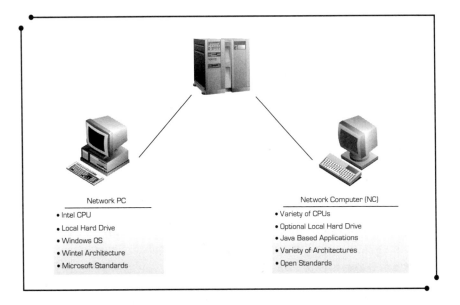

Network PC
- Intel CPU
- Local Hard Drive
- Windows OS
- Wintel Architecture
- Microsoft Standards

Network Computer (NC)
- Variety of CPUs
- Optional Local Hard Drive
- Java Based Applications
- Variety of Architectures
- Open Standards

Figure 3.29 Thin client models

albeit with different approaches. The first, the Network PC, is championed by Intel and Microsoft (popularly known as Wintel), the current majority owners (some would say monopolizers) of the desktop. The second, the Network Computer (NC), is driven by Oracle, Sun, and other non-Wintel players.

Network PC (Wintel)   The Network PC model, to no one's surprise, looks very similar to a personal computer on a LAN. In this model, the applications are stored on the server, but executed on the client. These systems employ a local disk drive that is designated for caching operations. The original specifications called for Intel Pentium or Pentium Pro processors running at speeds at or above 100mhz, and 16 or more megabytes of RAM (Random Access Memory), although they normally require 24–32 megabytes of RAM for adequate performance using Windows as the OS. Management challenges are mitigated by a "zero administration" version of the Windows operating system.

As with any design, there are trade-offs. The upsides of a Network PC model are:

- *Uses existing standard GUI (Windows)*
  Because Windows has become the standard of the desktop world, this model does not require the learning curve of any new GUI.

- *User autonomy*
  Users, once empowered by the advent of networked personal computing, are not enthusiastic about giving up control of their personal computing environment. Huge cultural challenges are inherent in such a transition, as well as practical ones, such as how do you share a file with someone not on your network? Sneaker-net is not an option in a world with no floppy disk drives. As such, pure thin clients, e.g., diskless GUI workstations, are best suited for dedicated OLTP functions, vertical market applications, or other areas with a clearly bounded problem set. The Network PC stands a better chance of providing a familiar, comforting environment to former PC users.

The downsides include:

- *Higher cost*
  Because of their Wintel architecture, the Network PC costs more than the NC (Network Computer) model. Most estimates are in the range of $300–500 for each system.

- *Local configurations issues unresolved*
  Windows and local hard drives inevitably mean nonstandard local applications and thus local configuration issues. Although a network/client management model exists for the Network PC, it is not yet proven to totally eliminate the possibility that a user will download an application and create system conflicts.

- *Local access with disk drives*
  A corollary to the previous challenge is that of local storage and an operating system (Windows) capable of directly utilizing it. Again, with local storage, inevitably comes external access and the possibility of introducing nonstandard applications.

If your goal is total centralized management, configuration control, version control, and application distribution, this would appear to be a fundamental design weakness.

- *Higher maintenance*
Windows GUI + more system parts + local disks + local nonstandard applications = higher maintenance. Windows is a high-maintenance environment. It is not clear how a centrally managed version mitigates the high "hand-holding" characteristics of this environment. Add to this the additional system complexity and the prospect for users to find a way to download nonstandard applications to their local hard drives and it is hard to see how the NC model would not have dramatically lower maintenance costs per system.

- *High windows learning curve*
If your goal is to replace 3270 terminals with new Network PCs operating your new client/server OLTP system, Windows is not necessarily the optimum UI. Although modern versions are more intuitive than their predecessors, there are still plenty of quirks and anomalies to confuse a new user.

- *Non–open standard*
Windows, by definition, is not an open standard OS (Operating System), specification, API, or technology. It is not available in the public domain, and its development and features are controlled by a profit-generating public company. Therefore, it is not necessarily in the best interests of Microsoft's shareholders to popularize or support current or evolving open industry standards. If your goal is to create and maintain an environment that ensures BOB (Best of Breed) solutions, this is not the optimum route.

- *Not universally available on all platforms*
Again, lack of open standards will hinder the integration of a Windows-based Network PC system into a mixed platform environment. If you've got a cross-platform shop, you will not be able to take full advantage of the proprietary features in a Network PC.

NC (Network Computer) The NC (Network Computer) design is very similar to the Network PC with the exception that it does not require or use the Wintel standard CPU or architecture. The NC design relies on applications written in Java and the NC resident JVM (Java Virtual Machine) layer to accomplish all required computing functions. Fortunately for those IS managers leery of betting everything on a development environment such as Java, the NCs are also capable of emulating 3270 and other "dumb" terminals and X terminals, and of executing UNIX and NT applications via various third-party emulators and gateways. Also, because of Java's independence of OS and CPU, NCs are entirely transparent to the network, the server application, and the user. This means that an NC can be replaced with one using a completely different OS and CPU by simply unplugging the old one and plugging in the new one.

The NC thin clients are powered primarily by RISC processors optimized to execute an NC OS, although Intel has announced support for the NC design as well using its CICS processor family. The NC clients are configured with a baseline of 16 megabytes of RAM, but many NCs contain 24–32 megabytes of RAM in real implementations.

The NC clients are responsible for executing the GUI and the applications, and for communicating with the server over the integrated network connection. Because of this "GUI to application communication over the network" design, the network in question needs to be high bandwidth and very highly reliable. In this model, the network is truly the computer. Without it, nothing happens on the client end. Period.

The NC model also has its share of pros and cons. The upsides are:

- *Low cost*
  The systems are simpler and have fewer components. This means they cost less up front and cost less to maintain and support.

- *No local administration*
  There is no local administration whatsoever. No local configuration files to maintain, restore, or rebuild. Ever. Sound like nirvana? That depends on if you're a former personal computer user or a support administrator.

- *Low learning curve*
  This model is targeted toward exploiting intranet/Internet applications with their ubiquitous browser interfaces. They are simple and easy to learn, and ensure quick uptake by the user community.

- *Universal, open model*
  This design is primarily based on exploiting the open standards of the intranet/Internet world. The NC is a much safer bet if you're interested in developing an open environment with the ability to integrate various vendors' solutions, with independent technological road maps. This allows you to develop and deploy a computing environment that is not dependent on only one company for OS development and one company for CPU development.

- *Server centric*
  Because everything is on the server, it is inherently shareable and leverageable across the enterprise. Workgroup applications, collaboration, and shared repositories become a very natural part of application design and implementation. They are inherently able to seamlessly integrate with other intranets and with the Internet.

The downsides include:

- *Higher bandwidth requirements*
  This model is network intensive. Fragile backbones need not apply. Count on high bandwidth requirements and very serious network utilization levels.

- *New architecture/computing model*
  Although basically another cut at a model that has been attempted before (host/terminal), this is still a fundamentally new model for the industry. It is not a panacea and will not find universal appeal or success. The proponents are crossing into

entirely new areas of expertise (Oracle championing a hardware device, for instance), and it is unclear if they can gain widespread market acceptance or succeed in setting new, sustainable standards.

- *Non-Wintel*
This standard is attempting to win against one of the most formidable competitors and market forces ever seen, the Microsoft/Intel juggernaut. Controlling some 95% of the desktop market, these savvy players are in no mood to abdicate it to an upstart coalition of UNIX and database vendors.
    It is a fact of life that the old 1970s saw of "you'll never lose your job for buying IBM" has become "you'll never lose your job for buying Microsoft." The choice has become one not of choosing the best technology or solution, but of choosing the safest one. If this is the primary criteria, the NC has little chance of success.

- *No local capabilities*
The local hard disk drive is optional and only used for caching, and there is no floppy drive. Business users who have grown up with the ability to load applications, configure their local environment, and retain a sense of power and control over their local computing world will not be enthusiastic about this new computing revolution. The same things that make this an extremely compelling vision from the IS and support management standpoint are poisonous from the personal computer's point of view. The NC will be best suited to implementations where an existing dumb terminal application is being replaced with a new GUI OLTP application.

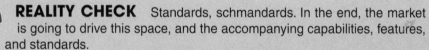

REALITY CHECK   Standards, schmandards. In the end, the market is going to drive this space, and the accompanying capabilities, features, and standards.
   Who's going to win? It's much too early to tell on the Network PC/NC front. Intel is hedging its bets by building for both standards, so they look like a safe bet long term, regardless of the shake out on the standards war side. It looks as though the biggest winner will be the IT departments and the users. Early implementations of NCs have shown low costs and high productivity.

The Future

Thin clients have a bright future. They offer compelling advantages in maintenance cost. About the only questions are variations in platform design, dominant OS/CPU, degree of openness, and degree of dispersion into the general user population.

   Without doubt, thin clients are the heir apparent to the green screen 3270 terminal of character-based systems of yore. The vast general personal computing market, where the huge ROIs lie waiting, is much less a sure bet. It will take a very convincing argument to deliver the general business user over to the thin client world. It appears that yet another religious war awaits, one that will make Windows vs. Apple seem like a minor skirmish before it is over.

DSS (Decision Support System) Tools

Regardless of the platform, thick or thin, the users of the data mart will be using DSS (Decision Support System) tools to access and make use of the data. To understand which among the hundreds of available selections is right for your business, it is necessary to take a few cuts at segmenting the products and their capabilities.

Categorizing Tools

The first cut is to segment the operational needs of the users—reporting, analysis, ad hoc query, and defined applications—and the market segments that are appropriate for each one. (See Figure 3.30.) It is easy to see that many users will have the need to operate in more than one of the quadrants. These users will require multiple tools in order to accomplish their mission. It is equally clear that no one vendor provides a BOB (Best Of Breed) integrated solution across all four quadrants (although the marketing departments at IBI and SAS would probably beg to differ). This, too, implies that multiple vendors will be required in order to provide a complete solution to the business.

Appropriate Business Solutions

In our technology-driven view of the world, we commonly seek out appropriate problems for these technological answers. As we shall see in Chapter 5, this is a fatal flaw when seeking to build and implement sustainable data marts. (See Figure 3.31.)

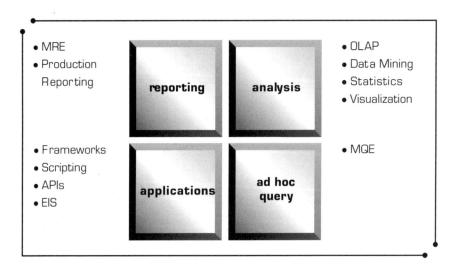

Figure 3.30 Categorizing tools *Source: Meta Group*

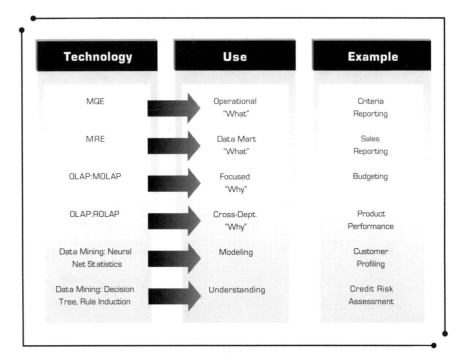

Figure 3.31 Appropriate business applications *Source: Meta Group*

It is much better to turn this around and view the business processes first, and then to seek the appropriate technology to fill the need. In this way, we can identify the needs of the business and fill them with the solutions available, rather than be driven by the pure technology of the tools and applications themselves. (See Figure 3.32.)

Aggregation and Tools

Once the needs of the business have been matched with the appropriate technology, we can proceed to planning how to meet the needs with appropriate data design. Different needs of the business require different levels of detail and aggregation. LOB (Line Of Business) managers using an EIS (Executive Information System) do not require the day-to-day access to historical transactional detail that an analyst leveraging data mining technology to predict behaviors does.

In the past, there was an arbitrary relationship between data marts and levels of aggregation. (See Figure 3.33.) Today, that is no longer the case. Data marts are used to host every level of detail and aggregation imaginable. In the same way, these general relationships between tools and levels of aggregation are not as clear cut as they used to be. Seamless drill through from multidimensional data sets in OLAP (On-Line Analytical Processing) environments into the detail has begun to gray the lines for that segment.

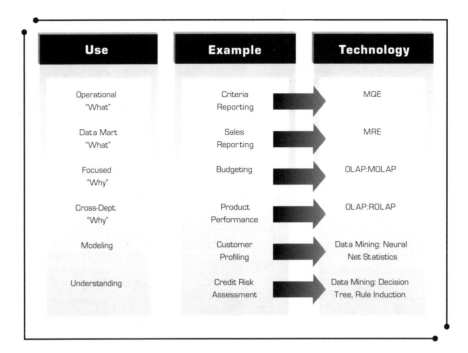

Figure 3.32 Examples driving technology

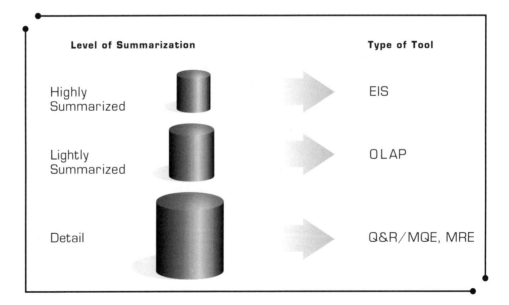

Figure 3.33 Historical relationship of levels of aggregation to categories of tools

EIS systems have traditionally allowed drill down into detail, and Q&R (Query and Reporting) systems are intrinsically capable of using any data set, regardless of level of detail or aggregation.

Table 3.6 presents the various categories of tools, indicating the likely users and purposes for each category.

Table 3.6 Categories of Tools and Their Users

Tool Type	User	Purpose
EIS	Executive management	Business overview, monitor operations
OLAP	Analyst, manager	Understand "Why"
Data Visualization	Analyst	Visually spot and comprehend anomalies and trends
Data Mining	Analyst	Analyze, discover relationships, categorize, predict behavior
Q&R/MQE	Analyst, managers	Understand "What"
ADE (Application Development Environment)	Developers	Build applications

Q&R (Query and Reporting)/MQE (Managed Query Environment)

By far the most ubiquitous type of tool deployed for decision support purposes are Q&R (Query and Reporting) tools. This class of tools is commonly referred to as MQE (Managed Query Environment). An MQE is a system that is built using the Q&R tool's capabilities, tools, and technologies. The goal of the MQE is to shield the user from the underlying data, the database structure, and the complexities of SQL (Structured Query Language), which is the industry-standard programming language used to ask questions of the RDBMS (Relational Data Base Management System) storing the data.

The MQE presents the user with an easy-to-understand semantic layer (SL) that incorporates business terms and uses folders, icons, or other graphic objects to represent

REALITY CHECK Manually maintaining the semantic layer of an MQE can be an unexpected resource drain. Insist on tools that automatically update the semantic layer to reflect changes in database schemas.

the database structures and relationships. This semantic layer is the shield between the user's easy-to-understand and intuitive environment and the cryptic world of SQL and relational database management design.

Q&R tools have been widely distributed in nearly every organization. They have successfully lowered the barrier to entry to becoming a knowledge worker. Those users who have invested the time to go through the necessary learning curve are capable of pointing and clicking their way to their own queries and reports. This has allowed a great deal of self-sufficiency among these users, at least to the level of capability of the tools.

As in all things, however, there is no free lunch. IT organizations have been able to push out a large amount of the day-to-day ad hoc reporting into the user communities via MQE implementations. At the same time, they have discovered that the management and sustenance of the semantic layer is a nontrivial task, especially in first-generation implementations that did not incorporate any systematic maintenance capability.

Q&R/MQE solutions remain popular, especially among organizations that are just stepping off into empowering the user community with direct access to information.

Recently Q&R vendors have begun to integrate low-end OLAP analysis capability into their tools, thus creating a new type of tool, the LowLAP (Low-Level Analytical Processing) tool. These tools combine traditional query and reporting capability with limited abilities to view data along multiple dimensions and perform simple multidimensional operations such as data pivoting. The tools, being thick client oriented, generally bring back data sets to the client and then create proprietary data structures in order to perform these limited OLAP functions. Although they are valuable in terms of providing baseline capability and exposing users to the possibilities of true OLAP functionality, these tools are not sufficient for significant analysis. They are quickly limited by the size of the data set required for meaningful analysis on large data sets, and the resulting time required for the personal computer to process and prepare the proprietary data set. LowLAP tools provide limited functionality and are not scaleable.

We will continue to see the MQE area become a less distinct market segment as the tools continue to move up-market with LowLAP capabilities and the OLAP vendors continue to integrate seamless drill through into the detail data.

The Q&R/MQE tools have their pros and cons. The upsides are:

- *Easy to deploy/maintain*
  Q&R/MQE tools are comparatively easy to install and sustain compared to more complex solutions. They use fairly straightforward technology and do not require a high level of sophistication on the part of support teams.

- *No dedicated data sets to manage/maintain*
  Unlike MOLAP (Multidimensional On-Line Analytical Processing) tools and some ROLAP (Relational On-Line Analytical Processing) tools, Q&R/MQE solutions do not require any specialized data sets or structures in order to provide answers for business users. This allows teams to instantly deploy query and reporting solutions against immature data resources. From the maintenance side, no incremental support resources are required in order to load and maintain specialized data sets.

The downsides include:

- *QFH*
  Q&R/MQE tools are notorious for being prime sources for QFH (Queries From Hell). Because they are thick client tools and are not server centric, the tools work directly from the desktop to the database, with most having no management, monitoring, or screening layer in between. Any user can create a 25-table query in seconds and bring the server to its knees milliseconds later.

- *Semantic layer required*
  The same thing that makes MQEs so wonderful for users requires a significant investment in resources from the IT organization. The semantic layer that shields the users from all that ugly SQL, database schema detail, and underlying data must be maintained every time there's the slightest change in the underlying data, structure, or systems.

- *LowLAP analysis capacities very limited*
  LowLAP tools give great demo, but are much less fun in the real world. They don't scale well into real-world business problems requiring thousands of rows of detail and multiple dimensions.

- *High levels of user support*
  Q&R/MQE tools have the potential to require very high levels of user support. It is critical that a very user friendly database design be used, sufficient training be supplied, and core business meta data questions be no more than a click away. Anything short of this adds up to very high "hand-holding" costs.

- *"Data not found"/high level of data knowledge required*
  One of the biggest detriments to the Q&R/MQE approach is that users find it very easy to build questions to which there is no answer, and to build questions to which they receive, and subsequently publicize, incorrect answers. Even with highly developed and maintained semantic layers, a high level of familiarity with the data is required in order for users to be productive and effective, especially in normalized data model designs.

- *High cost per seat*
  These tools are not cheap; they range from $100 to $800 per seat. Add in support and maintenance costs for the semantic layer and requisite hand-holding for users, and you're looking at a significant investment. Keep in mind that the license fee per seat is by far the smallest part of your overall investment in a Q&R/MQE tool. The investments in user training, in semantic layer construction and maintenance, and in a library of proprietary queries and reports are much greater. Pick a solution with care.

Q&R/MQE tools are an integral part of any data mart solution, short of a dedicated MOLAP or other application-specific data mart. They will continue to move up-market and adopt more OLAP and server-centric capabilities and characteristics. It is important to keep the hidden costs of semantic layer management and maintenance in mind when allocating resources for the deployment and sustenance of these tools.

MRE (Managed Reporting Environments)

Managed reporting environments allow the scheduling and delivery of preexisting report and analysis resources. In much the same way as the MQE tools, the MRE tools shield the users from the source data, its structure, and the SQL required to extract the information used to build the report.

Successful MRE implementations require:

- *Well-defined questions and answers*
  Because MRE environments allow little or no modification of the questions and answers that make up the report, it is essential that the business know what it needs to ask and answer so that the reports are pertinent and valuable.

- *Common, shared repository*
  Users must be able to access a common and shared repository of report and analysis assets.

- *Adequate network bandwidth and stability*
  The enterprise network must be up to the task of transmitting the reports and analyses, and it must be consistently available to the users.

- *Standardized data formats and readers*
  The business must have a reasonable number of standards for reports and analyses. The applications or document readers must be resident on all users' systems.

- *Flexible data and delivery formats*
  The MRE tool must support a variety of data formats, allowing users to order reports in spreadsheet, word processor, or document interchange formats. It also must allow delivery in a variety of ways, such as e-mail or file transfer.

- *Flexible scheduling (time, events)*
  The MRE tool must allow scheduling of reports and analyses based both on time and event triggers. A user must be able to schedule a report every Tuesday afternoon, or every time sales drop below a certain level, for instance.

MRE upsides include:

- *Easy access to information*
  MRE systems provide very easy access to the information with extremely low barriers to entry.

- *Low learning curve*
  MRE tools have very low learning curves. Users can use them with little training or support.

MRE downsides include:

- *Limited ability to explore, change, expand*
  Users have little or no capability to explore the reasons behind a reported event, to change the question that generated the report, or to expand or contract the scope of the report.

- *Possible maintenance nightmare*
  The fundamental questions is: "Who is creating the reports?" If it is the IT organization, you are still in the reporting business, with a lot of resources tied up in minor report tweaks and changes. This is not a fundamental improvement on an old world model of developing green bar reports in COBOL (Common Business Oriented Language).

OLAP (On-Line Analytical Processing)

The fastest growing and highest impact members of the DSS world are the various OLAP (On-Line Analytical Processing) tools and technologies. (See Figure 3.34.) These tools provide the ability to examine information at various levels of summarization along multiple business dimensions in a very flexible and intuitive interface.

In interviewing your user community, you'll find that most of them actually want to do OLAP—they just don't know it exists. They'll consistently relate the desire to look at

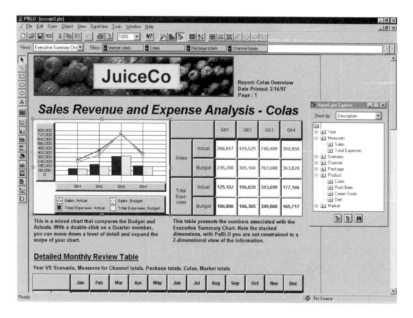

Figure 3.34 Typical OLAP user interface   *Source: Andyne Computing, Ltd.*

data in a variety of "this by that" relationships, as in "sales by product by customer" and then relate the need to quickly be able to look at the data in a different "this by that" way, such as "sales by state by week." They will then hold their right hand in the air, make a mouse-clicking motion with their index finger, and relate the need to "drill down" into this answer to reveal the underlying detail.

All of these desires are grist for the OLAP vendors' marketing mill. The OLAP tools do all of this, and much, much more. They provide the ability to easily reveal and understand relationships and trends that would take weeks using manual methods in Q&R tools.

Obviously these capabilities are highly sought by information users in the organization, and the gold rush is on to provide solutions to the clamoring business users in this fertile market. Consequently a plethora of choices is available, using fundamentally different architectural approaches in an effort to solve common problems. (See Figure 3.35.)

OLAP Elements Fundamentally, every OLAP product variation consists of two common elements: a calculation engine and multidimensional data viewing.

The calculation engine performs operations that are not supported in standard SQL (Structured Query Language) such as:

- Ratios
- Time calculations
- Statistics
- Ranking

The calculation engine usually supports additional calculation capabilities as well:

- Custom formulas/algorithms
- Forecasting and modeling
- Multiple SQL queries

The calculation engine is the core of the OLAP tool and provides the primary technological underpinnings for everything that is layered on top. (The location of this calculation engine is one of the primary segmentation differentiation characteristics, which we shall examine in detail shortly.) When considering an OLAP tool, be careful to look past the sexy GUI and slick demo and closely examine the design and processes of the calculation engine.

Every OLAP tool offers multidimensional data viewing to allow users to examine data in various levels of summarization along common business dimensions such as time, product, or customer. Because this is the normal way business users talk about and relate to the business, the OLAP view is naturally intuitive and is quickly evolving into the default way to present data to end users.

The UI (User Interface) allows users to quickly, easily, and intuitively change the dimensions that they are viewing the data with. This capability is known as "data pivoting" or "slice 'n' dice." Users can move from one view of "unit volume by week" to

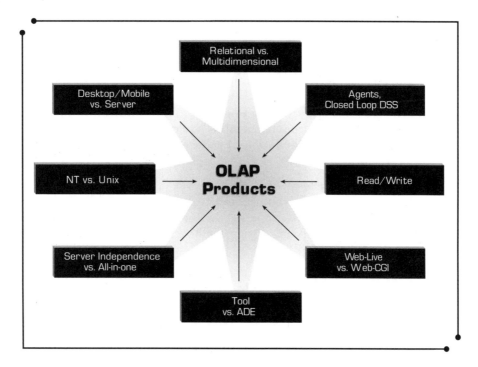

Figure 3.35 Variety of OLAP choices *Source: Meta Group*

"unit volume by product line by customer type" in seconds (response time depends entirely on the type of OLAP tool chosen; your mileage may vary).

Until recently, if users wanted to examine the transaction detail that lay beneath a summary number in their OLAP view, they were forced to move to a different tool to query into the detail. OLAP vendors are now offering the ability to seamlessly "drill" into the data down to the lowest level of detail available. This has negated the requirement for a separate Q&R/MQE tool to accomplish this, thus lowering training and support costs.

OLAP Solution Evaluation Criteria In trying to decide which of the many OLAP solutions is right for you and your implementation, it is important to consider these evaluation criteria:

- *OLAP type*
  Is this a MOLAP, ROLAP, or LowLAP solution? (These will be explained in detail in the next section.)

- *Number of dimensions*
  How many dimensions does your business require? Some OLAP solutions can only practically handle 4 to 5 simultaneous dimensions. LowLAP tools are very limited

in their ability to handle more than 2 to 3 dimensions with any significant number of rows in the answer set.

- *Manageability*
  How manageable is this environment? Does the solution require multiple specialized data sets? How long do they take to update with new information? How does the calculation engine work? Does it generate hundreds of temporary tables or require hundreds of dedicated database tables each requiring care and feeding? How big is the dedicated MOLAP data cube? What if you add another dimension? How big will it be in a year?

- *Number of concurrent users*
  How many people do you plan to have on this system at a time? During a normal day? Month end? Quarter end? Year end? How much server power is required to support that? Can the underlying database support that load in a ROLAP scenario?

- *Maintainability*
  Is it possible to incrementally update the data sets required to support this application? Can the data sets be replicated? How long for initial load? Disaster recovery? Nightly update? How do you recover or rebuild a corrupted proprietary data set?

- *Performance*
  How fast is this solution? How fast with real data, real dimensions, and real user questions? (Ignore demos.) Is a LowLAP solution more than a cruel joke? Is the scaleability of the ROLAP solution worth the slower response time?

- *Spreadsheet support*
  Can your users access the OLAP solutions via a spreadsheet interface? Can they seamlessly, easily, and intuitively transfer results into a spreadsheet? Can results be saved in native spreadsheet format?

- *User-defined abstractions*
  Can user-defined functions be defined and supported? Can they be shared in a common repository?

- *Functions (time, statistics, currency)*
  Does the OLAP tool have the functions your users need to analyze the business? Are complete and powerful selections of time, statistical, and currency functions available? Are the functions easily extensible? Are they shareable?

- *UI/ease of use*
  Is the user experience easy? Is the UI intuitive? How much training and handholding support is this tool going to require? These tools should be understandable and intuitive enough to be productive with virtually no introduction.

- *Language support*
  Is the tool multi-language? Does it support more than 8-bit languages? Are there French, Spanish, German, Japanese, or Chinese versions available?

- *Agents*
  Does the tool support agents that will work off-line to seek out and return answers? Are they time schedule driven? Are they event driven? Can they do different things depending on the answers they find?

- *RDBMS feature exploitation*
  How extensively does the ROLAP solution leverage the underlying database? Does the ROLAP tool take advantage of internal parallelism? Specialized index support?

- *Proprietariness*
  How open is the data set or calculation engine? Is this a closed, proprietary MOLAP solution? Is the calculation engine tightly bound to a single vendor's database? What if you change databases in the future?

- *Aggregate awareness*
  Is the ROLAP tool aggregate aware? (This refers to a tool's ability to know that an existing aggregated or summary data set already exists in the database and it does not need to re-create an identical aggregation set in order to answer a summary question.) Can the tool recommend that aggregations be created to support repeated ad hoc aggregation requests?

- *Application scripting/construction*
  Can users or developers construct preconfigured applications or macros to drive repetitive operations?

- *Complex business questions*
  Can the tool answer complex business questions? At all? Multiple passes? Fully recursive?

- *Shared repository*
  Does the tool have a common, shared repository for analysis and reports that all users can share? Can users easily save and share reports and answer sets? Can users easily browse the available resources?

- *Meta data*
  Does the tool automatically populate meta data? Does it allow simple and easy browsing of meta data? Does the tool support open meta data repositories? Is it tightly bound to a proprietary repository?

- *Drill through*
  Does the tool allow seamless drill through into the detail? Does it require IT team setup? Does it leverage meta data to accomplish this?

- *Read/write and recalculate*
  Do the users need to write to the database? Do they need to quickly recalculate the database, such as in a budgeting or forecasting operation?

Types of OLAP Solutions   The answers to these questions will lead you toward one of the three types of OLAP tools: MOLAP, ROLAP, or LowLAP. Each has its own strengths and weaknesses and is best suited for particular circumstances.

MOLAP *(Multidimensional On-Line Analytical Processing)*

MOLAP (Multidimensional On-Line Analytical Processing) solutions are marked by their use of a dedicated data set to provide answers for the users. This usually takes the form of a proprietary data structure, or "data cube," that can be stored on a variety of platforms. Some MOLAP tools require a dedicated, proprietary multidimensional database; others allow the data cube to be stored on the database server as a set of relational tables, on dedicated data cube servers, on file servers as flat files, or locally on the client.

MOLAP solutions work best when the questions that are being answered are very well defined and of a relatively small scale. This is referred to as a "well-bounded problem set." They are not well suited for discovery type operations, or an "unbounded problem set." In a MOLAP data cube model, every answer to every possible question for the available metrics and dimension members is calculated and stored within the cube.

This gives rise to the primary strength and weakness of a MOLAP solution. Because all the answers are in one place, response times are lightning fast. Conversely, because the data cube is limited to its precalculated answer set, any question dealing with data outside the data cube cannot be answered.

There are three types of MOLAP solutions:

- *Dedicated MDDBMS (Multi-Dimensional Data Base Management System)*
  Some MOLAP solutions employ a full-blown dedicated MDDBMS to host the data and support the calculation operations. These systems are excellent for budgeting and forecasting operations requiring read/write and recalculation operations.

- *Proprietary cube*
  Other MOLAP solutions stop short of a full-blown MDDBMS and simply employ a dedicated proprietary data structure, commonly referred to as a "data cube" or "hypercube." This cube can be subsetted and stored in a variety of places and is an excellent solution for portable or mobile OLAP functionality.

- *Hybrid (sometimes called HOLAP–Hybrid On-Line Analytical Processing)*
  In an effort to solve the difficult scaleability and flexibility challenges facing MOLAP solutions, some vendors have developed a hybrid approach. This allows their tools to rely primarily on a dedicated data cube, but to be able to work outside the cube and leverage the source data mart RDBMS tables when a question exceeds the bounds of the available answers within the cube.

The following common characteristics are the mark of a successful MOLAP implementation:

- *Focused answer/bounded problem set*
  If you have a well-bounded problem set and require focused answers to known questions, a MOLAP solution will work well.

- *Forecasting/budgeting*
  MOLAP solutions are the only practical answer to forecasting and budgeting applications that require database writes and updates across large data sets, and/or quick recalculation.

- *Summarized data*
  Due to the challenges MOLAP solutions face in scaling up to large answer sets, highly summarized data is a more comfortable data set for this design.

- *Highly complex calculations*
  If your well-bounded problem requires very highly complex calculations, a MOLAP may be the only solution that can deliver acceptable performance.

- *Infrequent/small updates*
  Multidimensional data sets become very huge, very quickly. It takes a long time to build and update these structures. If your frequency of update is nightly, and you have large incremental updates, it may not be conducive to a MOLAP solution.

- *Three-tier architecture*
  MOLAP solutions are naturals for a three-tier implementation. They work best on a dedicated, highly optimized server. A three-tier design also facilitates thin client support.

The upsides of a MOLAP solution are:

- *Instant response*
  You will never get faster response than with a MOLAP tool.

- *Impossible to ask question without answer*
  The most frustrating message ever received by users is "no data was found for your query." In a MOLAP world, this is impossible. It is not possible to ask a question for which there is no answer (assuming nonsparse data sets).

- *Value add functions (ranking, % change)*
  MOLAP tools all contain a useful set of functions beyond SQL capabilities.

The downsides of a MOLAP approach are:

- *Long load times*
  It takes a very long time to load a sizable MOLAP data cube. Beware of tools that do not allow incremental updating of the cube. Rebuilding the entire cube on every update is a very painful and extremely resource-intensive task.

- *Very large data sets with multiple dimensions*
  MOLAP data structures become very massive very quickly with the addition of multiple dimensions. Remember that you are calculating and storing every possible answer to every possible question. In other words, every intersection of all possible dimensions with every metric is being calculated and stored. Even with advanced compression techniques, this is a very, very large data set, given a useful number of rows and a normal set of business dimensions.

- *Don't scale well*
  Because of these size limitations, MOLAP solutions do not scale well. They are best suited to tightly focused solutions for a limited number of users using relatively highly summarized data.

ROLAP *(Relational On-Line Analytical Processing)*

To eliminate the boundary set and scale challenges of MOLAP designs, ROLAP vendors have sought a different route. In a ROLAP model, the calculation engine uses the existing data mart database tables of the RDBMS (Relational Database Management System) to provide the data, rather than a proprietary data structure. This allows the ROLAP tool to work well in a discovery mode, where the problem set is totally unbounded. It also allows the ROLAP solution to scale very well. It grows in parallel with the data resources stored within the database.

Because it uses the RDBMS to house its data, the ROLAP engine can leverage the existing investment in the RDBMS as well as any native capabilities, such as specialized index support.

ROLAP solutions are limited by this design as well. Because the RDBMS must seek out and prepare each answer, response times are much, much slower than a MOLAP tool. ROLAP solutions are also not well suited to read/write and recalculate operations such as forecasting and budgeting.

The characteristics of a successful ROLAP implementation include:

- *Unfocused answer/unbounded problems*
  ROLAP solutions are the only answer for discovery operations or where the questions and answers are not well defined.

- *Multi-department data mart*
  ROLAP solutions can scale well, so they can support more users and more problems than a MOLAP design.

- *Transaction detail data*
  ROLAP tools can easily seamlessly drill through into the detail because they are already interacting closely with the host RDBMS.

- *VLDB (Very Large Data Base)*
  ROLAP solutions are the only answer if you have a VLDB. However, with this scaleability comes a price: Be prepared to wait "a while" for your answers.

- *Frequent/large updates*
  ROLAP solutions are transparent to updates. Size and frequency of updates are of no consequence to this design.

- *Aggregate aware*
  ROLAP tools allow you to pre-create aggregation sets that users are commonly requesting and use them as data resources. This prevents needless summarization of detail data with its accompanying penalties of slow response times and resource usage.

- *Monitoring*
  A successful ROLAP implementation requires the monitoring of resource usage. It is critical to know what aggregations are being created on an ad hoc basis and what indexes are being used. The best tools make system optimization recommendations dynamically in response to usage patterns.

- *Three-tier architecture*
  ROLAP solutions are also naturals for a three-tier implementation. They work best when hosted on a dedicated, highly optimized server. This isolates them from the processing demands of RDBMS or client tool execution. A three-tier design facilitates thin client support and allows maximum flexibility and tuning. Avoid thick client ROLAP designs that house the calculation engine on the client because they force a large amount of data through the network and are inherently self-limiting in the amount of data they can process effectively.

The upsides of a ROLAP solution are:

- *Leverage RDBMS capability*
  ROLAP solutions provide the opportunity to leverage the investment in RDBMS. You can take advantage of advanced technology built into the database. There is no requirement to learn a new MDDBMS or to support one with staff and resources.

- *Value add functions (ranking, % change)*
  As in MOLAP, all ROLAP tools provide very valuable business-oriented functions for users.

- *No additional loads*
  Because there is no dedicated data set, there are no additional loads to schedule or monitor. This is significant in multiple data mart implementations.

- *No additional data sets to manage*
  ROLAP tools use the data mart RDBMS as the source of the data. They do not require dedicated, proprietary data sets to provide the answers. This frees you from the requirement to design, implement, and maintain a very large scale proprietary data structure.

- *Very scaleable*
  ROLAP systems are inherently scaleable and open. They function well in rapidly growing environments, or in implementations where the question and answer sets are not well bounded or defined.

The downsides of a ROLAP solution are:

- *Slow response time*
  ROLAP implementations are much slower than MOLAP solutions. They must turn to the RDBMS to seek out the required data, perform any required aggregation or calculation, and then provide the answer. Be prepared to wait for answers to large questions. It is critical that ROLAP tools be very aggregate aware to mitigate this challenge as much as possible.

- *Requires robust monitoring*
  A successful ROLAP implementation requires very complete and capable monitoring of table usage and ad hoc aggregation utilization patterns. It is critical to know

what summaries are being requested on a regular basis, what indexes are being used, and where the opportunities are to provide new ones when required.

- *Watch out for architecture*
  It is very important to pay close attention to the design of ROLAP tools. The demos are so slick and compelling that it is tempting to buy without a full analysis and examination. Of particular importance is the location of the analysis/calculation engine. If it is located in the thick client, look elsewhere. These thick client–oriented solutions do not scale and are inherently self-limiting. Also, pay close attention to the network load implications of the design. Some designs require the movement of huge blocks of data to the calculation engine where they are parsed down to the required answer set. Be sure to compare this to your existing backbone and available bandwidth during peak load periods.

LowLAP *(Low-Level Analytical Processing)*

Q&R/MQE tool vendors have begun to add OLAP type functionality to their product lines. This has led to the evolution of a new class of tool, the LowLAP (Low-Level Analytical Processing) solutions. These tools are marked by being thick client resident and having limited processing capabilities. They offer the advantages of an integrated user environment with a common GUI and a feature-rich work space. It is important to understand, however, that these tools are in no way replacements for a true OLAP solution.

LowLAP tools function much like MOLAP solutions in that they rely on a proprietary data set for their OLAP capabilities. To do this, they pull an answer set from the database down to the client platform and then prepare a proprietary data set, referred to as a "data cube" or "hypercube." This data cube is used as the source for the answers to the questions the user will pose. Because these multidimensional data cubes are bound by the same rules as their much larger MOLAP cousin's data cubes, they get very large, very quickly. Consequently LowLAP tools are inherently self-limiting and are suitable for only very small data sets. They demo very well, but you'll notice that the demo data sets are a few hundred to a few thousand rows at most. Practical, real-world data sets begin in the many thousands of rows.

LowLAP tools are excellent in providing an example of basic OLAP functionality to users and in giving them a place to explore small sets of data on their desktops. However, they do not scale, and it is critically important to inform users in advance of the LowLAP tool's limitations.

Perhaps the greatest strength of LowLAP tools is in providing mobile OLAP. These tools can allow users to slice off a portion of a larger data cube, or create a small scale one, and take it along with them on their laptops to remote locations.

The characteristics of a successful LowLAP implementation include:

- *Small answer sets*
  LowLAP tools cannot handle much in the way of data volume. They are only suited to situations where users are content with small answer sets or extremely long waits for business-scale data cubes to be constructed (think in terms of hours).

- *Users are well informed of limitations*
  It is a cruel joke to take a user from a slick and sexy LowLAP demo to the harsh realities of the limitations in a large-scale business environment. You must clearly communicate the intended use of these tools and their inherent limitations.

- *Mobile OLAP primary mission*
  LowLAP tools are outstanding at providing the ability to take the analysis along, given proper scale. If this is the primary challenge you are trying to solve, you've come to the right place.

- *Robust network infrastructure*
  LowLAP tools pull lots of data across the network to feed their local data cubes. Make sure your network is up to the task.

- *Robust client platforms*
  Because the processing is all performed locally, including the formation of the data cube, your users will require very, very powerful desktop platforms. They will need high-speed processors, lots of RAM, and many gigabytes of free disk space.

The upsides of a LowLAP solution are:

- *Easy to deploy*
  These tools are self-sustaining and require no specialized RDBMS design or server-hosted data cubes. While not quite plug and play, they are close to it.

- *Nice entry point to OLAP for users*
  This is an excellent way to introduce basic OLAP functionality to your organization.

- *Excellent mobile OLAP*
  LowLAP tools are the number one way to provide your mobile users with OLAP functionality. An excellent solution for this challenge and a tremendous additional capability for mobile users long cut off from data and analysis.

- *Integrated environment*
  LowLAP tools present a consistent user experience for both Q&R/MQE and basic OLAP functions. This is much easier for the users and much less support overhead than two distinct tools.

The downsides of a LowLAP solution are:

- *Not scaleable*
  These tools do not scale, period. They are best suited to point solutions for small problem sets. Do not expect these tools to provide the OLAP solution for your enterprise or even your data mart.

- *Limited functionality (small number of rows)*
  These tools cannot handle large answer sets. Do not expect them to handle enterprise-sized questions.

- *Network traffic*
  Some designs can be incredible resource hogs. Be careful of how much data they pull down the wire to the desktop to feed their data cubes.

- *Very slow response to large answers*
  These tools can take hours (days? weeks?) to calculate their data cubes for large answer sets. Do not try to use them for big problems.

- *Disappointed users*
  This is the greatest challenge of all. Don't let your users base their operational expectations on a sexy and slick demo. Make sure they understand the implications of a demo data set containing a few hundred rows. It is critical to properly manage users' expectations with these tools.

- *Uncertain growth path to three tier*
  Closely investigate the vendor's technological road map for growth paths from thick client to three-tier implementations. Is the path leading to MOLAP or ROLAP? Which is suitable for your enterprise-scale challenges? If there is no growth path, you are facing a transition to an entirely new tool as your users grow in sophistication and needs. (Typically this growth will happen very, very quickly.)

- *Thin client capabilities*
  Unless the vendor offers a three-tier version of the calculation engine used in the LowLAP tool, you will have no ability to provide OLAP functionality via a thin client. This can be a crippling shortcoming.

OLAP Topologies   OLAP solutions come in a variety of topologies, each with their own implications in terms of network bandwidth, support, and server requirements.

A typical MOLAP topology is a three-tier design, with the proprietary data structure, or data cube, hosted on the same server as the calculation/analysis engine. (See Figure 3.36.) Due to the high processing requirements required for data cube creation, loading, maintenance, and utilization, these servers are required to be very robust platforms.

Note that the database from which the MOLAP data cube is derived is not typically connected to the MOLAP server in a live or on-line manner. Incremental updates to the data cube arrive nightly, weekly, or monthly and are added to the data cube. Otherwise, the MOLAP engine is dynamically connected only to the users.

ROLAP implementations are also typically three-tier designs. (See Figure 3.37.) In this case the middle tier hosts only the calculation/analysis engine. The ROLAP server is constantly connected with the RDBMS hosting the data mart data at all times.

Because the ROLAP server functions only as a calculation/analysis engine, it is possible that it can be implemented with much lower DASD (Direct Access Storage Device, or disk drive) requirements than a MOLAP solution.

LowLAP implementations are primarily one- or two-tier designs. (See Figure 3.38.) In the simplest implementations the desktop database and LowLAP application reside on the same client platform. This is a good solution for small workgroups with small-scale needs. For wider scale implementations, a two-tier design is used. In this design,

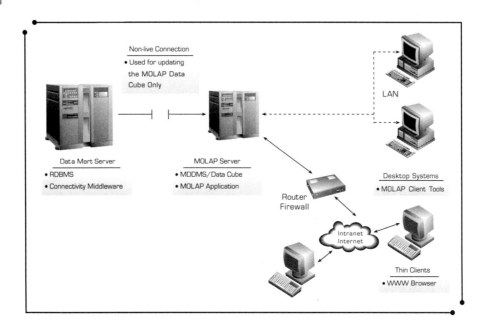

Figure 3.36 MOLAP topology

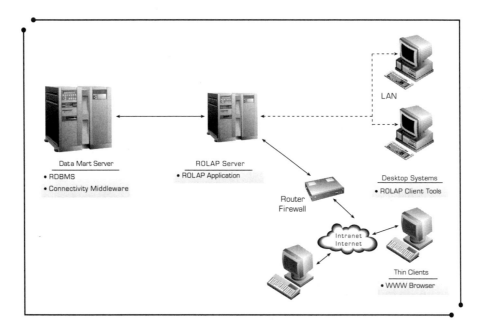

Figure 3.37 ROLAP topology

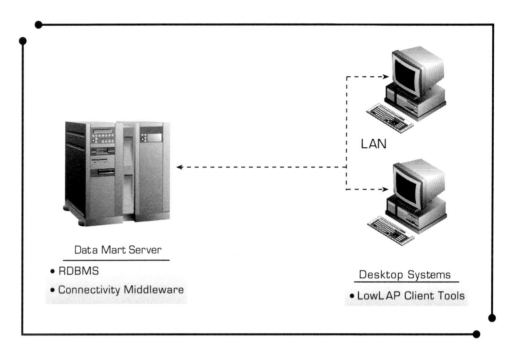

Figure 3.38 LowLAP topology

the client platforms access the RDMS to extract detailed data to construct their data cubes on the client platforms. A robust network and very high powered client platforms are prerequisites for success for this design.

Table 3.7 summarizes the features and functions of the three variations of OLAP solutions.

Each tool and topology design has its own unique ramifications on network and client requirements. You must carefully examine the underlying architecture and technologies to fully understand the implications. Common pitfalls include:

- Inadequate network backbone
- Inadequate network bandwidth
- Inadequate client platforms
- Inadequate servers
- Inadequate user training and support

Research and investigate your candidate tools carefully to avoid these traps and ensure a successful implementation.

Table 3.7 OLAP Variations and Implications

	MOLAP (3 tier)	ROLAP (3 tier)	LowLAP (1 or 2 tier)
Client requirements	Low	Low	Very high
Server to client—network bandwidth requirements	Low	Low	Very high
Server to client—network pipe size	Small	Small	Medium to large
DM to server—network bandwidth requirements	Very high for updates; very low operationally	Very high	N/A
DM to server—network pipe size	Very large for updates; small operationally	Very large	N/A
Cost	$50–250K for data mart scale solution	$50–250K for data mart scale solution	$400–900 per seat
Scaleability	Very limited scaleability	Very scaleable	Not scaleable
Number of users	Department/25	Enterprise/500+	Individual-Workgroup/1–20
Thin client support	Yes	Yes	No
Intranet/Internet capable	Limited audience for intranet/Internet use	Very scaleable to intranet/Internet use	Not usable for intranet/Internet
Scope of problem set	Small/inflexible	Large/flexible	Limited to very small scope
Bounded problem set	Required	Not required	Not required
Maintenance level	High	Medium	Client intensive
Response time	Very, very fast	Can be very slow; aggregation aware dependent	Glacial for large answer sets; fast for small answer sets
Maximum number of dimensions (practical limit)	5–6 (data set size and update time become unmanageable at high numbers of dimensions)	6+ (response time is very long for many dimensions)	2–3 (local cube creation time becomes prohibitive at higher numbers)

REALITY CHECK You need OLAP. Whether you realize it or not, this is the preferred view into the data for almost all of your users. If you are coming out of an environment of little to no user data access, you are probably just looking to provide basic reporting capability. Don't ignore the OLAP segment. To reach the full potential impact of the data mart system on the organization, you will need to deliver OLAP capability to the masses.

EIS (Executive Information System)

The EIS (Executive Information System) has been around for about as long as there have been computers. This is no surprise because the executives making the decisions to fund multi-million dollar computing systems are a natural audience for the output of those systems. EISs form a closed loop between the executives committing significant portions of the corporation's resources into information processing and the potential ROI (Return On Investment) of that system: the information used to manage the business. From the IS standpoint, EISs offer the best possible venue upon which to demonstrate the worth and value of the data and their capabilities.

An EIS's mission is to provide the executives of the business with an intuitive, easy-to-use entry point into critical information about the status of key processes and functions of the business. EISs function as a "dashboard" for the operations of the enterprise, indicating the current status of selected operations and issuing suitable warnings when key metrics get out of safe operating range. An EIS also provides the capability for the user to easily drill down and across the information presented to examine the detailed reasons for warnings and status readings.

Because response time is such a critical issue to this audience, it is very important to prepare dedicated aggregation sets for EIS use. These are sometimes referred to as "CEO tables." These are very high priority data sets, and their care and feeding should be on the top of your priority list.

A successful EIS implementation will demonstrate:

- *Extremely easy to use and understand*
  The tool must be very intuitive and require little to no training or support. Executives have little time for nonintuitive interfaces.

- *All levels of information available*
  From highly summarized to transaction detail, all information must be available through one UI.

- *Flexible drilling capabilities*
  The user must be able to easily drill across or down through the supporting data. Users must be able to instantly zoom into the underlying detail if desired.

- *Flexible data visualization and display*
  The tool must provide a wide variety of charting and display formats. Reports must integrate a wide variety of objects including text, graphics, charts, and multimedia.

- *Near real-time data*
  The data underlying the EIS must be as close to real time as possible. An alarm that signals a problem does little good if the data is a month old.

- *Integrated, scrubbed data*
  The data underlying the system must be integrated and scrubbed. This implies an ODS, enterprise data warehouse, or data mart as the source.

The upsides to EIS include:

- *Excellent exposure for the enterprise data warehouse/data mart system*
  The EIS is an outstanding way to expose executives to the value of the enterprise data warehouse/data mart system. It is much easier to retain sponsorship and sustain political will in the organization when a system is an everyday part of management's lives.

- *Allows easy and flexible executive information access*
  A well-designed EIS is the optimum way to provide information to executives. The easy-to-use interface and unlimited drilling capabilities are an optimum monitoring and investigative resource.

- *Mission-critical system for the business*
  There is no higher profile than to be the primary link between executives and the business they manage. In very short order, EISs are viewed as mission critical and are budgeted and supported as such.

The downsides to EIS include:

- *Maximum political exposure*
  Along with all the exposure comes corresponding risk. If the EIS design, implementation, or maintenance are botched, it can be a very significant CLM (Career Limiting Move).

- *High technology requirements*
  The underlying technology to enable full EIS functionality is nontrivial. It requires a fully functioning ODS, enterprise data warehouse, or data mart, a very powerful EIS development environment, and powerful client platforms.

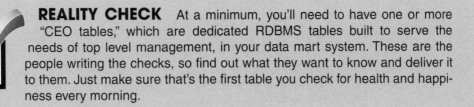

REALITY CHECK   At a minimum, you'll need to have one or more "CEO tables," which are dedicated RDBMS tables built to serve the needs of top level management, in your data mart system. These are the people writing the checks, so find out what they want to know and deliver it to them. Just make sure that's the first table you check for health and happiness every morning.

Data Mining

Data mining tools examine the historical detail transactions of a business in order to identify trends, to establish and reveal hidden relationships, and to predict future behavior. It is this predictive capability that is of particular value. All other tools can easily discover what has happened in the past. Data mining tools are unique in their ability to predict outcomes based on past events.

Data mining tools use statistical analysis and various knowledge discovery techniques such as neural networks to glean meaning from the data and provide anomaly detection, relationship matching, dependencies, and classifications.

Data mining tools require access to extensive collections of detailed data and very powerful computing platforms to host the applications. They also require the care and feeding of the application by analysts with extensive knowledge of the source systems and underlying data.

Characteristics of a successful data mining implementation are:

• *Extensive historical detail data*
  Data mining requires access to extensive amounts of detail data. The more detail you feed in, the more reliable and accurate the output. If your data mart contains only summarized data, you are unable to leverage this technology.

• *Very powerful application servers*
  Data mining technologies examine millions of rows of detailed transactions along with hundreds of associated attributes and dimensions for each bit of detail. These technologies leverage sophisticated algorithms from the far reaches of AI (Artificial Intelligence), image analysis, signal processing, and defense-related research. This all adds up to very serious computing power requirements. For this reason, data mining is an excellent candidate for outsourcing to an organization that has built the heavy-duty infrastructure necessary for reasonable throughput rates.

• *Available resources*
  The organization must dedicate the necessary IS and business analyst resources that these tools require. These resources are not insignificant and are ongoing in nature.

The upsides to data mining include:

• *Discovery of previously unknown relationships, trends, anomalies, etc.*
  Data mining provides the only possible way to reveal deeply hidden and obscure relationships and trends in the data. They are unparalleled in their abilities to sift through mountains of data and return the single gem of information that is relevant and has maximum value. It is not possible to duplicate their capabilities by any manual or otherwise automated process.

• *Powerful competitive weapon*
  Data mining provides a potent competitive weapon for today's technology and marketing savvy company. The ability to discover obscure customer affinities and associated behavior are invaluable in today's hyper-competitive and fast-moving marketplace.

- *Automation of repetitive analysis*
  Organizations are likely to be attempting a minuscule subset of data mining's capabilities by performing repetitive manual analysis of operational activity. Data mining not only automates this task, but delivers heretofore unattainable levels of insight and analysis.

- *Predictive capabilities*
  Data mining tools are unique in their ability to predict behavior based on patterns and relationships established in historical detail. No other technology or tool allows you to make predictions based on this level of examination and predictive modeling.

The downsides to data mining include:

- *Knowledge discovery technology immature*
  Although the statistical analysis technologies used in data mining are stable and mature, the knowledge discovery technologies are still somewhat immature and are rapidly evolving.

- *Long learning and tuning cycles for some technologies*
  Some technologies, such as certain types of neural nets, require significant investments in "training" and tuning the sets of rules and variables they rely on to provide the analysis of the data. In these instances, the quality of the tuning, or "learning," experience will determine the quality of the entire utilization of the tool. It is very, very important to establish a quality "learning" experience for these tools.

- *"Black box" technology minimizes confidence*
  Because of the almost mystical nature attributed to data mining and the more esoteric technologies used, business managers can be slow in anointing the results with the holy water of confidence. It can take a long time for the business as a whole to begin to rely on the results and models of predictive behavior and pattern matching. Pick a good solid "win" from your early results sets and publicize it heavily to overcome this early reticence.

REALITY CHECK Data mining has been carrying the mantle of "the next big thing" for some time. Expect continued rapid development in this area. These tools will get easier to use, less expensive, and more credible as they propagate through the business community. Make sure you understand the basics and can speak intelligently with senior management about what these tools can and cannot do. The execs are being bombarded with data mining headlines in business management publications and with success stories at executive management conferences. They will look to you to be prepared.

- *VLDB (Very Large Data Base) requirements*
  Due to the requirements of enormous amounts of detailed data, you can quickly find yourself in the business of managing and maintaining a rapidly growing VLDB. Do not underestimate the challenges associated with this task when evaluating the implications of adopting data mining technologies.

Data Visualization

Data visualization is simply the graphical display of information to aid in the understanding in interpretation of the underlying data. Although useful in simple presentations and basic analysis, it is a prerequisite for the effective comprehension of very large data sets.

Any data mart implementation using modern tools will have a vast array of data visualization capabilities. At the low end will be spreadsheets and presentation packages; in the mid tier are the OLAP analysis tools; and at the top end are specialized data visualization environments.

These emerging top-end tools require significant processing power, but they are revolutionary in their ability to quickly communicate anomalies and underlying structures in massive data sets.

ADE (Application Development Environments)

Although data marts are designed and constructed primarily for DSS (Decision Support System) purposes, it usually isn't long before the application development organizations discover this treasure trove of integrated, scrubbed, and historical detail data. It is a natural for them to leverage this asset in creating new applications for the various business processes constantly evolving around them.

ADEs range from third-generation procedural languages such as COBOL to fourth-generation, visual, object-oriented environments that tightly integrate with multidimensional data structures and other data sources. You can expect all of these to be used to develop applications that will directly access and leverage your data mart. It is important to keep this in mind when doing capacity, throughput, uptime, and disaster recovery planning for the data mart system.

Summary

The data mart has emerged from under the shadow of the enterprise data warehouse to take a position at the forefront of business decision support and information distribution resources. By building on the proven foundation of data warehouse design principles, data marts can deliver the high-impact value of targeted integrated, scrubbed data sets to users throughout the organization. Data marts offer the opportunity for organizations to select an incremental approach to the goal of an enterprise data warehouse. By constructing a series of integrated data marts under an enterprise data mart architecture, IS organizations can test tools, designs, methodologies, vendors, and

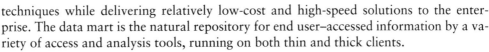

techniques while delivering relatively low-cost and high-speed solutions to the enterprise. The data mart is the natural repository for end user–accessed information by a variety of access and analysis tools, running on both thin and thick clients.

The data mart is:

- *Responsive to business needs*
  The data mart is targeted directly to clear business needs. It has a focused audience and a tightly defined scope.

- *Scaleable*
  Because the data mart is built within an enterprise architecture, it is scaleable to any size, up to and including evolving into the enterprise data warehouse itself.

- *Flexible*
  Because the data mart is built using proven architectures and design techniques, it can be quickly modified to reflect rapidly changing environments and requirements.

- *Quick impact*
  Data marts can be constructed and implemented in two to nine months, providing immediate impact on business challenges.

- *Low cost*
  Data marts can be constructed for as little as $100,000, a fraction of the cost of an enterprise data warehouse.

All of these characteristics add up to a fundamental building block of decision support in the modern business enterprise. The data mart is now the key component in meeting the needs for information access and delivery in the business.

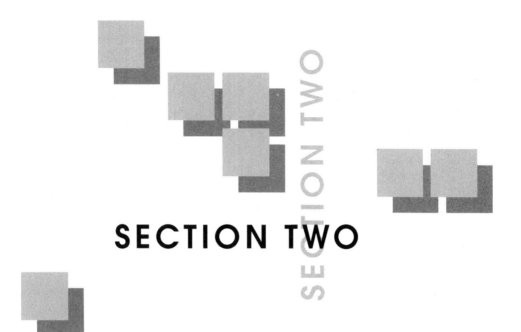

SECTION TWO

▶ *Preparation and Planning*

Site and Team Assessment

Readiness Assessment/Site Check

In the world of traveling show business, such as touring companies with Broadway shows or multiple city corporate events, an advance party is always scouting the territory. Weeks or months in advance of the show's arrival, they visit each future site, or venue, on the tour. Their mission is to evaluate and investigate each aspect of the venue related to the successful execution of the event. Advance parties look for things like the size of the loading dock, available power, height of ceilings, maximum weight of suspended lighting and sound systems, and even obscure things such as directions to the closest 7-11. In the world of show business, this process is known as a "site check."

Data warehousing has its version of a site check, commonly known as a "readiness assessment" or "capability evaluation." Most consulting organizations offer them, most at a preset package price. They are a good investment, allowing you to leverage the experience and knowledge of the consultants to provide you with a quick benchmark of your enterprise prior to the large expenditures of the design, construction, implementation, and sustenance process. In short, you'll be able to find out if the loading dock door is too narrow for "Bronto the Elephant Fact Table" before you light up the marquee for opening night of your data mart show.

You can perform your own preliminary site check, with a scaled-down version of a typical consultant's checklist. You won't have all the knowledge and experience to allow you to understand all of the implications of each site check data point, but you'll find the answers invaluable in your communications with vendors, consultants, your team, and business management. Not only will it save you and your vendors a lot of time otherwise spent in repeated information gathering sessions, it will also prove as an invaluable aid in early detection of potential problem areas, such as network bottlenecks.

Here's a basic framework for a data warehouse/data mart site check, broken down into three main categories: Business, Team, and Technology.

Business

In the Business Section, you will establish the general parameters for the project: business type, budget, pain level (level of urgency and importance), user group size, and so on. These overall parameters guide you as you begin to make your initial choices as to suitable platforms, topologies, and design.

Type of Business

- Manufacturing
- Financial services
- Insurance
- Banking
- Aerospace
- Automotive
- Pharmaceuticals
- Health care
- Publishing
- Transportation
- Lodging
- Broadcasting/cable
- Service
- Retail
- Telecommunications
- Other

Purpose: This data point obviously will not be used internally, but it will be very valuable to your vendors. They may have experience in other businesses of your type and will be able to share "best practices" gleaned from that experience.

Annual Sales

- Over $50 B
- $25–50 B
- $10–25 B
- $5–10 B
- $1–5 B
- $750–1 B
- $500–750M
- $250–500M
- $100–250M

- $50–100M
- $10–50M
- $1–10M

Purpose: Primarily used as a "rule of thumb" sizing device, this data point allows vendors to get a quick handle on how best to fit into a business of your size.

Business Driver (what is driving the need for the project)

- Strategic
- Tactical
- Both

Purpose: This data point establishes the baseline for political will in the organization for the project and is very valuable for all parties. If this is a strategically driven project, it ensures longer lasting political will. Tactical drivers are much more susceptible to loss of political will or abandonment due to changing internal and external business conditions.

Timeline

- 24 months or greater
- 18–24 months
- 12–18 months
- 6–12 months
- 3–6 months
- 1–3 months
- Immediate (You may want to run away with the circus if this is the choice.)

Purpose: Although it may seem self-evident, the timeline of the project functions as the primary gating factor when making most technological and scope decisions. This is also a major factor in making build/buy decisions, especially with human resources. This data point forms a direct linear relationship with budget.

Political Will (level of organization willing to commit sustained resources)

- Board of directors
- CEO (chief executive officer)
- President
- VP (vice president)
- LOB (line of business) manager
- Department manager
- Work group

Purpose: This data point identifies specific roles and levels in the organization willing to commit sustained, dedicated resources to the project. This is very closely related to business driver and timeline. The higher the level of political will, the longer the window of opportunity for funding will remain open.

Political Will Sustainability Window (how long will it last)
- 24 months or greater
- 18–24 months
- 12–18 months
- 6–12 months
- 3–6 months
- 1–3 months

Purpose: This is the primary driver in establishing how long you really have to do this project. It doesn't really matter what the stated timeline is, the political will sustainability window actually determines time to delivery.

Sponsorship Level (highest level willing to tie their career to success/failure)
- CEO (chief executive officer)
- President
- VP (vice president)
- LOB (line of business) manager
- Department manager
- Work group leader

Purpose: This data point establishes the bottom line on how far this project is going to go in the organization. If the project runs into trouble or the usual unexpected delays or challenges arise, the sponsorship level will determine its fate. The higher the better, for making the project happen. This data point is linearly directly related to political exposure.

Budget—Design, Build, and Implement (labor, hardware, software, consulting)
- $3–5M
- $1.5–3M
- $750K–1.5M
- $500–750K
- $250–500K
- $100–250K
- $50–100K
- $25–50K
- $10–25K

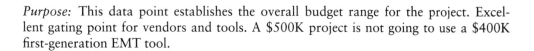

Purpose: This data point establishes the overall budget range for the project. Excellent gating point for vendors and tools. A $500K project is not going to use a $400K first-generation EMT tool.

Budget—Maintenance, Growth, and Sustenance (labor, hardware, software, consulting) (% of Design & Build budget)

- 80% +
- 50–80%
- 30–50%
- 10–30%
- 1–10% (Start thinking seriously about that circus career at these low levels.)

Purpose: This data point establishes a couple of very important points right up front: how realistic has the budgeting process been up to now, and how long term has the thinking been regarding management and sustenance for this project. A good rule of thumb is to budget 40–60%+ of the resource build price to maintain an incremental data mart in its first year of operation. Your site may vary from 20% to 150%, but until you have some real-world experience at your unique site, you will not know the exact amount to expect.

Commonality of Need (diversity of groups in need of this solution)

- Very diverse/very heterogeneous, all units/divisions
- Diverse/heterogeneous
- Fairly common/shared metrics, views
- Homogenous metrics, views
- Single group/division
- Multiple workgroups
- Workgroup

Purpose: Establishing both the constituency base for the project and the user scope, data point is related directly to level of business driver and level of political will and sponsorship. If all are high, an enterprise data warehouse may be the proper end goal, with incremental data marts used to build consensus and prove ROI along the way.

Number of Users

- 1000+
- 500–1000
- 250–500
- 100–250

- 50–100
- 25–50
- 1–25

Purpose: This data point establishes the baseline for calculating network loads, topology requirements, and number of copies, or "seats," of end-user tools. As the project moves forward, you will need to break the users down into more detailed segments, for example, analyst, manager, information resource consumer.

Access Locations

- Worldwide
- North America
- United States (all)
- United States (continental / lower 48)
- Region
- State/territory
- City
- Campus
- Building
- Workgroup

Purpose: Establishes the WAN and remote server location requirements.

Locations of Users (number of discrete user locations)

- 50 +
- 25–50
- 15–25
- 10–15
- 5–10
- 3–5
- 2
- 1

Purpose: Establishes the WAN and remote server location requirements along with the scale of the access locations in the previous point.

Access Requirements (time)

- 24×7
- 24×5

- 18×7
- 18×5
- 12×7
- 12×5
- 8×7
- 8×5

Purpose: Used in conjunction with geographic location and time zone requirements to establish available update and maintenance windows.

Time Zones

- Global, all
- Subglobal, >15
- Subglobal, >10
- Subglobal, >5
- U.S. only
- 4
- <4

Purpose: Used with access requirements and geographic locations to establish available update and maintenance windows start and stop times.

Level of Pain

- Extremely high—business survival at stake
- High—#1 Priority
- Somewhat high—top 5 priority
- Medium—top 10 priority
- Low—top 25 priority

Purpose: The primary driver gauge for the project, this data point can change the actual reality of the project's context, even if other items are reflecting low support and funding. Conversely, if you are looking at low pain levels here, steer clear.

Scale of Pain

- Enterprisewide
- Division
- LOB
- Geographic
- Function

- Department
- Multiple workgroups
- Workgroup

Purpose: Establishes the true scale of the project. Small-scale pain can only be mitigated by very high levels of political will and levels of influence.

Politics of Pain (level of influence of pain owner)

- Top level, maximum influence
- High level, high influence
- High level, low influence
- Medium level, high influence
- Medium level, low influence
- Low level, low influence

Purpose: Used to establish the real level of the political will in the organization. When it comes down to crunch time, the political pull of the pain owner will make or break the allocation of resources to the project. This data point is closely linked to the politics and utilization measures. To be successful, all three measures need to be in the high range.

Politics of Pilot (impact and marketability of pilot group)

- High visibility, high ROI (return on investment of data mart team resources to pilot this group)
- High visibility, low ROI
- Medium visibility, medium ROI
- Low visibility, low ROI

Purpose: Used to get an early read on the proposed pilot group. Avoid pilot groups that are low on this scale.

Use of Pilot (frequency of use and number of users)

- High utilization, wide use (lots of use, many users)
- High utilization, narrow use (lots of use, few users)
- Medium utilization, wide use
- Medium utilization, low use
- Low utilization, low use

Purpose: It does no good to pilot the project with a group of users who are too busy to use the resource, or who have no record of technological utilization. You must demonstrate impact, and you cannot have impact without utilization. Avoid anything but "high" rankings on this scale.

Outsourcing Policy

- No restrictions, outsource at will
- Outsource to existing suppliers only
- Prefer to use internal resources, outsource if required
- Must use internal resources

Purpose: Establishes a baseline for buy/build decisions.

Enterprise Data Model/Architecture

- Exists, well understood
- Exists, not well understood
- Doesn't exist

Purpose: Establishes the existence of an enterprise data model or architecture and the corresponding level of understanding. This is a critical factor in determining overall project timeline.

Level of Understanding of Business Rules

- Very high
- High
- Moderate
- Low
- Very low

Purpose: Used to establish a baseline for organizationwide understanding of the underlying business rules of the enterprise, and to gauge resource requirements for developing enterprise data mart architecture and source integration.

Existing Source System Extracts

- Many, highly reliable
- Many, somewhat reliable
- Many, unreliable
- Few, highly reliable
- Few, somewhat reliable
- Few, unreliable
- None

Purpose: Used to determine the level of organization experience of DSS (Decision Support System) extracts from OLTP (On-Line Transaction Processing) systems and confidence levels of the business users in existing systems.

Confidence in Existing Reports

- Total confidence
- Somewhat confident
- Low confidence
- No confidence

Purpose: Establishes the business users' trust in existing IT (Information Technology) systems and is used to build political will for data mart system. Compare this data point closely to earlier questions regarding IT/user relationships.

Team

The Team Section establishes the general characteristics of the people who will be tasked with building, implementing, and maintaining the data mart system. This section is very important in determining outsourcing requirements and spotting weaknesses early in the process.

Implementation Team Resources

- Unlimited internal/external—whatever is required to solve problem
- Unlimited internal/external as needed
- Core internal/external as needed
- Limited internal/external as needed
- Limited internal only
- LOB technical team
- Alpha geek (workgroup member most conversant with technology and tools)

Purposes: Determines the baseline for human resources on the project; directly determines scope and timeline for development and implementation.

Implementation Team Experience

- OLTP (On-Line Transaction Processing System), DSS (Decision Support System), Data Warehouse/Data Mart—all platforms
- OLTP, non–Data Warehouse/Data Mart DSS—all platforms
- OLTP, non–Data Warehouse/Data Mart DSS—C/S (Client Server) only
- OLTP, non–Data Warehouse/Data Mart DSS—Mainframe only
- Non–Data Warehouse/Data Mart DSS—C/S only
- Workgroup DSS—extracts/flat files
- Desktop DB (Data Base)
- Spreadsheets

Purpose: This is the critical, overall data point for spotting weaknesses in the team. Look here to spot needs for outsourcing and training. Teams with little DSS experience will be hard-pressed to do this project quickly without outside mentoring.

RDBMS (Relational Data Base Management System) Experience/Capability

- Mainframe + Oracle/Informix/Red Brick C/S
- Oracle/Informix/Red Brick C/S
- DB2—multiple platforms
- Sybase
- Mainframe only
- Desktop DB

Purpose: Establishes baseline need for RDBMS (Relational Data Base Management System) consulting, training, or outsourcing. If you have no experienced team members in the RDBMS of choice, make an early decision on outsourcing. If you are going to train, start now. Count on consulting help to get the system tuned for DSS. It will take a minimum of six months to build an acceptable level of capability in a team that has no RDBMS experience.

Server Administration Experience

- Mainframe
- UNIX
- NT
- Novell
- Workgroup server

Purpose: Establishes baseline need for server administration consulting, training, or outsourcing. If you're going to build this expertise in house, get started early.

Tool Experience/Capability—Design and Build

- COBOL/Code generators
- CASE (Computer Aided Software Engineering)
- Repository
- Transformation engines
- C/C++
- Perl
- Basic/VBA (Visual Basic for Applications)

Purpose: Sets the framework for any in house–developed code. Extensive capabilities opens up the possibility of doing some or all of the work manually in house. Low levels of expertise point you toward an EMT (Extract, Mapping, and Transformation)/

DTEAMM (Design, Transformation, Extract, Access, Monitoring, and Management) solution.

Tool Experience/Capability—Access

- Data Mining
- OLAP (On-Line Analytical Processing) /ROLAP (Relational OLAP) /MOLAP (Multidimensional OLAP)
- Q&R (Query & Reporting) / MQE (Managed Query Environment)
- Q&R no MQE
- Mainframe tools (QMF, Focus, etc.)
- LowLAP (Low-Level Analytical Processing) (client-based Q&R tools incorporating low-end OLAP features)
- Desktop DB
- Spreadsheets

Purpose: You will need expertise in these tools for your implementation. If you don't have any now, start your tool selection process early so you can get some people adequately trained.

Tool Experience/Capability—Replication

- Native DB tool
- Replication server
- Flat files
- FTP (File Transfer Protocol)

Purpose: It is very likely that you will require replication tool capability in your implementation. If you have no expertise or low levels of it, you will require consulting or training.

Tool Experience/Capability—Monitoring and Scheduling

- Network
- Database
- Query
- Index/optimizer
- DB load
- JCL (Job Control Language)
- UNIX schedulers

Purpose: Monitoring is a requirement for success. If you don't see much capability here, buy or build some fast.

DSS Experience

- Multiple enterprise data warehouses
- Enterprise data warehouse
- Enterprise data warehouse under construction/deployment
- Architected data marts
- Architected data marts under construction/deployment
- Nonarchitected data marts
- Nonarchitected data marts under construction/deployment
- Extract/replicated OLTP-based DSS

Purpose: Primarily used to root out teams that have little to no DSS experience. There are major cultural issues with teams moving from a pure OLTP background to an entirely user-driven DSS world. Early warning flag with low experience levels.

User Friendliness of Team and Relationship With User Community

- Very high; close working relationship
- High; history of successful projects
- Good; high-quality communications
- Poor; not trusted
- Very poor; bad reputation—outsourcing preferred
- Not applicable—user group implementation

Purpose: Used to establish the human relations baseline for the project. If the team is already alienated from the user community, this project will not be easy. Think about positioning the project as a "new start" if this is the case. Don't be afraid to turn to outside cultural consultants if things are ugly.

Backlog

- Over 24 months
- 18–24 months
- 12–18 months
- 6–12 months
- 3–6 months
- 1–3 months
- 0 (congratulations!)

Purpose: Used to establish the current working environment of the team. If the team is currently backlogged heavily, the chances of adequate resources for the project are slim. Long backlogs also point to a dissatisfied user community, regardless of the response to the previous data point.

Average Turnaround for DSS Requests
- over 6 months
- 4–6 months
- 2–4 months
- 1–2 months
- 15–30 days
- 3–15 days
- 1–3 days
- Less than 24 hours (congratulations!)

Purpose: Used in conjunction with the previous two data points to get to the real status of the relationship with the user community. If the time is long, the users will not be happy with the IS team. This lemon can be turned into lemonade, however, by reinforcing the point that users will no longer have to suffer through this wait with direct access to the data mart.

Technology

The Technology Section establishes the technological framework in which the data mart must be constructed. It is very helpful for spotting problems and bottlenecks early on, and invaluable for vendors seeking to spot incompatibilities or "sweet spots" for their solutions.

Platforms Available for Data Warehouse/Data Mart(s)
- Unlimited (just solve the problem)
- MPP (Massively Parallel Processing)
- SMP (Symmetrical Multi-Processing) cluster(s)
- SMP 64 bit
- SMP 32 bit
- Single CPU (Central Processing Unit) RISC (Reduced Instruction Set Computer)
- Single CPU non-RISC

Purpose: Directly determines the scale and scope of the data mart. Do not try to put a data mart on an inadequate server platform. This will guarantee failure. Do not put any data mart on a nonscaleable platform. Small platforms are best left for small DisposaMarts and InstaMarts.

WAN (Wide Area Network) or Inter-Site Network
- ATM (Asynchronous Transfer Mode)
- OC3/T3
- T1

- Fractional T1
- Frame relay
- ISDN (Integrated Services Digital Network)
- 64/56K
- 28.8 dial up

Purpose: Establishes the baseline for distributed information and user tools. Low bandwidth precludes moving major chunks of data to remote locations. This has major implications on incremental updates and aggregations. Small pipes also rule out many thick client OLAP tools and LowLAP solutions.

Internet Access Speed

- ATM
- OC3/T3
- T1
- Fractional T1
- Frame relay
- ISDN
- 64/56K
- 28.8 dial up

Purpose: Primary gating factor for Internet utilization, both as an information resource and as a portal to the user community. Also has primary implications for distribution and replication in sites using secure tunneling protocols for a distribution medium.

OLTP Systems

- Mainframe only
- Mainframe/client server (nonintegrated applications)
- Mainframe/client server (integrated applications)
- Client server (nonintegrated applications)
- Client server (integrated applications)
- Workgroup application server

Purpose: Determines the sources of the data to be mapped to the data mart. Establishes baseline requirements for EMT and DTEAMM tools. Integration of applications has direct impact on the scope and scale of the extract and especially scrubbing jobs.

Source Data

- Mainframe legacy/client server—very diverse
- Mainframe legacy only—very diverse

- Mainframe legacy only—fairly diverse
- Mainframe legacy only—homogenous
- Mainframe legacy—relational only
- Client/server—relational—diverse
- Client/server—relational—homogenous
- Desktop DB

Purpose: Used to tunnel directly to the requirements for extract tools and programs. Will be of primary interest to EMT and DTEAMM vendors. Diverse environments will be more costly as most solutions are based on "per source" pricing models.

Access Types

- Internet
- Intranet
- WAN (Wide Area Network)
- LAN (Local Area Network)
- Workgroup

Purpose: Determines WAN and LAN requirements; used in conjunction with the user and location counts in the business section.

Strategic Direction—Platforms

- ASAP (As Soon As Possible) transition from mainframe to client/server
- Gradual transition from mainframe to client/server
- Retain mainframe, implement client/server where appropriate
- Client/server only, expand as required
- Test client/server—Pilot
- Mainframe only, no plans to implement client/server
- PC (Personal Computer) only, workgroup application and file servers

Purpose: Determines overall choices for data mart platforms; of primary use to server and RDBMS vendors.

Thin Client Strategy

- Core strategy—in production
- Core strategy—in development/pilot
- Considering—in evaluation
- Interested—researching
- No interest/need

Purpose: Used to determine thin client requirements of the tools selected for the data mart solution; can establish a hard and fast gating point for all proposed solutions. Most sites need a thin client strategy; the data mart can serve as a forcing function to drive this process.

Infrastructure Timeline (status of infrastructure support of DW/DM, time to completion)

- Robust, ready now
- Somewhat robust, ready in 30–90 days
- Needs work, ready in 30–90 days
- Needs work, ready in 6 months
- Overhaul/replace, ready in 12–24 months

Purpose: Used to spot problems with the underlying infrastructure required to support the data mart system implementation; used to drive budgeting and resource allocation for infrastructure improvements and overhauls required to support the implementation.

Existing Solutions (solutions in production)

- IBM
- IBI
- SAS
- Platinum
- Prism
- Carlton
- ETI
- Informatica
- D2K
- Intellidex
- Other

Purpose: This data point is of great value to consultants and vendors. Existing solutions can be leveraged for the data mart project. Existing solutions also provide a gating factor for other vendors and tools, assuming that integration is required.

Existing Standards (RDBMS)

- IBM DB/2
- Oracle
- Informix
- Sybase

- Red Brick
- SQL Server
- Other UNIX
- Other mainframe
- Desktop DB

Purpose: Used by consultants and vendors to spot incompatibilities and opportunities for integration.

Existing Standards (Server)

- IBM
- DEC
- HP
- Sun
- SGI
- NCR
- Other/RISC
- Other/ non-RISC

Purpose: Primarily used as a gating factor for server and tool vendors.

Available Servers (available for dedicated use for DW/DM)

- IBM
- DEC
- HP
- Sun
- SGI
- NCR
- Other/RISC
- Other/ non-RISC
- None

Purpose: Used to determine if existing servers can be dedicated solely to the data mart project. This directly effects the scale and scope of the project, as well as potential tools and technologies. Watch out for antiquated platforms. The data mart requires industrial strength speed, especially in I/O. Do not attempt to save money by implementing on a nonscaleable platform. You will pay more later to make up for that myopic thinking than you could ever save.

Technology Acquisition Restrictions

- None, solve problem
- None, comply with corporate standards
- Prefer to use existing technology if possible
- Must use existing technology

Purpose: Establishes opportunity level for all technology purchases. If you must use existing technology, carefully revisit the proposed scope.

Proprietary Nature of Environment (level of proprietary solutions allowed)

- None allowed, open solutions only
- Some existent, phasing out
- Some existent, long phase out as they are replaced
- Existing, will retain
- Majority proprietary, some open
- Prefer proprietary solutions

Purpose: Determines if open or proprietary solutions are the only paths available. Can establish basic gating factors on all technologies and tools.

Extract Process Window

- 12+ hours
- 10–12 hours
- 8–10 hours
- 6–8 hours
- 4–6 hours
- 2–4 hours
- 1–2 hours
- < 1 hour (Polish that circus-oriented résumé.)

Purpose: Used to flag a potential problem early on. Very short extract windows have a direct effect on scope and capability. Make this one of the first questions you get answered. If you have a very short window, be very careful about establishing the scope of the data mart.

Intra-Site Bandwidth Utilization (peak)

- 10–25%
- 25–50%
- 50–75%
- 75–100%

Purpose: Used to spot infrastructure weaknesses early on in the process. Some client tools can be bandwidth hogs. If you're already overloading your WAN or LAN at peak times, you'll be in trouble with the data mart. Make sure and measure this with DSS in mind, for example, at month and quarter end.

Using the Site Check

Although this site check framework doesn't come bundled with the expertise and experience required to generate recommendations, you will find it invaluable in quickly assessing your situation. It will save you significant time in vendor evaluations and considerable expense in consultant evaluations. A copy of the site check will allow vendors to quickly evaluate if their products are a good fit with your opportunity. A qualified enterprise data warehousing/data mart consultant can use the results to jump start, supplement, or replace their readiness assessment methodology.

You and your team can also use the site check to provide direction for initial project readiness, direction, technology fit, and "red flag" identification. If your enterprise's needs are immediate, your sponsorship level low, your pain focused and local, your user group's needs homogenous, and your budget limited, you're obviously headed for a data mart solution. If you have high-level pain, long-term political will, high-impact sponsorship, and a robust infrastructure, you can point to an enterprise data warehouse as your ultimate goal.

Just as in show business, a site check is a prerequisite for success for any production. It provides the foundation for project direction, vendor selection and evaluation, technology requirements, and resource requirements planning. It even gives early notice to the little things that become critically important in the heat of battle, such as the location of the nearest 7-11 at 2 AM when the star of the show requires M&Ms (red ones only, of course!), or a 56K pipe to a remote location in need of 25-gigabyte nightly updates to its data mart. Used wisely, a site check is one of the most valuable tools in the plethora of data mart techniques, processes, and methodologies.

REALITY CHECK   A lot of teams will turn up their nose at doing yet another readiness assessment. They are the same teams that will usually have the project blow up later over something they would have noticed early on if they had taken the time to stop and examine what lay ahead. Just as in the Broadway play *The Music Man,* "You gotta know the territory."

Team Definition and Development

Once you've prepared a site check and gotten a handle on what the project's fundamental characteristics are, you're ready to move on with assembling a team to deliver your data mart(s) to the organization. The following template is for a standard set of roles and responsibilities that need to be filled in order for your project to be a success. In some cases, you may be wearing all or most of these hats; in others, you will be a cog in a vast machine pumping out data marts at a prodigious rate. In any case, it is vitally important that all of these basic functions and activities be specifically assigned to an individual name. It doesn't matter if the name is the same for every function in the beginning. Someone must take responsibility and ownership for each of these areas.

This outline of the roles and responsibilities is not presented with detailed descriptions of each role and function. It would take an entire book to adequately cover the role of each member of the team and to describe each responsibility in detail. Instead, the goal here is to get each element out on the table and to provide a framework in which you can spot holes in capabilities within your team.

CIO (Chief Information Officer)

- Manage politics
- Cultivate and maintain sponsorship
- Cultivate and maintain resources
- Establish project metrics

No project can make headway without someone to run interference at the top. If you don't have buy-in here, carefully rethink your options regarding this project. If you're on a quick hit/60 day plan, you can probably still make it work. If you're on an "incremental data mart route to enterprise data warehouse" building mission, however, do not proceed without air cover.

In a non-IS scenario, this slot will be covered by a president, executive vice president, or even a high-profile LOB manager in a pinch. The same rules apply; you cannot move forward without presence at these levels.

IS Department Manager

- Identify, specify, and maintain exclusive resources
- Recruit and retain talent
- Procure technology

Someone must take responsibility for assigning and retaining exclusive resources for the data mart project. As the world continues to throw changes and new challenges at the organization, it will remain an ongoing battle to retain the required resources to complete the project. Make sure that the data mart project is number one on this person's list; otherwise, you will die the death of a thousand paper cuts as little by little your team and technology base is whittled away.

Business Driver Leader

- Identify business driver candidates
  - Monitor business
  - Identify pain
  - Rank candidates
- Qualify drivers
  - Investigate politics
  - Rank sustainability
- Manage communications
  - Nature of project
  - Ongoing resource requirements
  - Updates
  - Requests for change
  - Integration requests

At the center of your universe must be a solid business driver for the project. There must be a person who is responsible for identifying, qualifying, and nurturing these drivers. This is probably the most important role on the team. Without them, the project will be a solution in search of a problem, or an abandoned effort that didn't serve a core need of the business. Once the project is up and running, this person facilitates communication and the many change requests that will arise in the user community.

Project Leader

- Manage technology review and selection
  - Vendors
  - Products
- Manage talent requirement definition, recruitment, and implementation
  - Internal staff
  - Contractors
  - Consultants
- Manage project definition and solution set
  - Type of solution
  - Timeline
  - Technology requirements
  - Resource requirements
- Manage project design
  - Match scope to resources
  - Match scope to timeline
  - Match scope to technology
  - Ensure user-oriented design

  - Ensure available network bandwidth/infrastructure
  - Ensure support availability
- Manage project implementation
  - Changing resource requirements
- Manage technology implementation
  - Network/infrastructure:
    - Backbone
    - Internet links
    - WAN links
    - LAN links
  - Server(s):
    - RDBMS servers
    - MDDBMS Servers
    - Application Servers
  - RDBMS:
    - Core DBMS Engine
    - Core DBMS Tuning
    - DBMS Extensions
  - Three-tier tools:
    - Server layer
    - Client layer
    - Specialized databases
  - Middleware:
    - Version testing
    - RDBMS/Server install
    - Client footprint/compatibility testing
    - Client upgrade
    - Client install
    - Client testing
  - Thick client tools:
    - Footprint testing
    - Upgrades
    - Installation
    - Testing
  - Thin client tools:
    - Footprint testing
    - Upgrade

- Installation
- Testing
- EMT (Extract, Mapping, and Transformation) tools
- Repositories
- Design tools
- Management tools
- EMT process:
  - Balance resource requirements
  - Manage source system expert availability
  - Manage Q/A process
- Limit/eliminate scope creep
- Limit/eliminate compromise creep
- Manage project pilot
  - Candidate group criteria definition
  - Candidate group selection
  - Pilot technology implementation
  - Q/A (Quality Assurance)
  - Assessment and evaluation
  - Improvement implementation
- Manage project roll-out
  - Final scope definition
  - Final scope communication
  - Change request process
  - Enhancement request process
  - Definition of team roll-out metrics
  - Design of support plan
  - Development and management of roll-out plan
  - Metric and process monitoring
  - Process improvement

Obviously no one on the team has more on their plate than the project leaders. They are responsible for the overall design, construction, implementation, and maintenance of the data mart. As such, they touch each aspect of the project, from beginning to end. It is critical that this person be widely experienced and well educated in all aspects of the project and have excellent communication, organization, and leadership skills. It is a prerequisite that the project leader have a very strong customer focus and be entirely user driven. Technology driven managers are not good candidates for this slot.

Design/Implementation Team Leader

- Data architect
- Logical design
- Process flow

- Data flow
- Aggregation strategy

- Source OLTP system team leader
  - Source OLTP system owner
  - Source OLTP system data owner

- Source OLTP extract/mapping/transformation (EMT) team leader
  - EMT developer(s)
  - EMT meta data population/maintenance leader

- Data island team leader
  - Data island integration/standards
  - Data island system owner
  - Data island data owner
  - Data island EMT
  - Data island meta data

- Network/infrastructure leader
  - Network designer
  - Network implementation
  - Network management
  - Network maintenance

- DM server administration leader
  - Server design: Vendor evaluation and product selection
  - Server implementation:
    - Coordination with vendor
    - Installation
    - Initial configuration
    - Testing
    - Tuning
  - Server disaster recovery:
    - Design, test, and implement
  - Server maintenance:
    - Upgrades
    - Disk fragmentation
  - Server management:
    - Monitoring
    - Metric evaluation
    - Up-time
    - Recovery
    - Loads
    - Replication

- Aggregation
- Query performance
- Memory utilization
- CPU utilization
- DM DBA Leader
  - DBA Design:
    - Physical model
  - DBA implementation:
    - Create and load tables
  - DBA management:
    - Problem resolution
    - Resource assignment
  - DBA monitoring:
    - Load
    - Index utilization
    - Runaway queries
    - Aggregation opportunities
  - DBA maintenance/modification:
    - Change requests
    - Problem fix
    - Enhancement requests
    - Aggregations
  - DBA disaster recovery:
    - Plan
    - Test
    - Implement

Probably the key technical players are the design/implementation team leaders. They are directly responsible for the structure and content of the data resource relied on by the users. They touch every aspect of the server and database underpinnings of the system, from design to extract to data mart server platforms. Their team must be capable, focused, and oriented to high-speed results rather than long iterations of analysis and discussion.

Team Conclusion

These basic roles will be expanded to even finer levels of detail in large organizations that are implementing simultaneous subset or incremental data mart efforts. In smaller organizations, only a few individuals will be responsible for all of the roles and respon-

> **REALITY CHECK** So what about the users? Although no specific
> user roles are defined, they play a critical part in the success of the data
> mart system. You must have users who are capable and willing to make use
> of the system. It doesn't do much good to deliver a system to an audience
> that is either so overloaded they can't make use of it or so apathetic that
> they are unwilling to try.

sibilities delineated. Again, the most important thing is that every role and responsibility have a name assigned to it. If they all have the same name, and you are alone in the data mart effort, it is a good clue that the enterprise will need to allocate additional resources if it hopes to see a data mart of any kind within the next few years. In this case, this roles and responsibility description can be a wonderful lobbying tool.

Summary

The review, analysis, and assessment of a site's readiness is one of the most time- and resource-saving steps of any data mart project. During the data mart process, you will have seemingly endless opportunities and needs to communicate the state and status of your site and your team. Between business management, consultants, vendors, and your team there will be no shortage of opportunities to communicate this information. Whatever investment you make in time and resources to determine the answers to the questions in this chapter will be repaid many times over as your data mart project progresses.

Development and Communication Methodology

Now that you've assessed your site's readiness for the project, addressed any critical issues, and assembled a team of top line talent to design, implement, and sustain your data mart, you're lacking only two key elements to begin the project: a development methodology and a project planning and reporting methodology. Now I can imagine that if you're like me, you are thinking, "Great, just what we need, yet another methodology." As you can tell, I'm not "big" on methodologies and their associated proponents, whose level of zealotry is unsurpassed by any fringe political or religious group known to man.

Hard-core methodologists tend to be a bit glassy eyed and possessed by an insatiable desire to fit all human activities into their chosen methodology. You've probably seen them at conferences, mumbling alone in the corners or seizing the microphone to complain bitterly that the luncheon service was not planned and executed following the fourth order of compliance to the Splinderphlott development methodology. They possess an unbendable will and are best characterized by the old line:

Question: "What's the difference between a terrorist and a methodologist?"

Answer: "You can negotiate with a terrorist."

As in most human activities, rigid, galactic-scale methodologies don't hold up well in the fast-moving, ever-changing world of data marts. It is likely that you will find that onerous "top down" approaches will hinder your efforts rather than facilitate them.

Having said all this, however, you will also find that approaching the task of successfully designing, implementing, and sustaining a data mart without any methodology is akin to attempting to construct the Brooklyn bridge on the fly. So, there we are. We don't necessarily want one, but we've got to have one, if we're going to have any chance at all of success. In that light, it is important to select and implement a methodology that is oriented toward our challenge of data mart solutions in the enterprise. This chapter reviews, at a high level, the requirements for a successful data mart methodology.

Waterfall Method

The standard approach to IT (Information Technology) challenges is some variation on the "waterfall" methodology. (See Figure 5.1.) In this approach, each step is fully completed prior to commencement of the next activity. The upside of this approach is that every step is fully implemented, with no messy loose ends or unanswered questions. Every anomaly and variation is predicted, researched, and solved. The downside to this approach is its innate glacial speed. Any step along the way, especially the early ones, is a fertile breeding ground for analysis paralysis. Many galactic data warehouses have attempted this approach. I don't know of any that have emerged alive. Due to the "speed to market" requirements of a data mart solution, the waterfall methodology is not a viable alternative.

REALITY CHECK The waterfall methodology doesn't work for data marts. Period. If you are wedded to this one, get out of the data mart world before you hurt yourself or those around you.

Spiral Design

To support the more pressing timeline requirements of data marts and other DSS (Decision Support System) implementations, the "spiral" methodology has evolved. (See Fig-

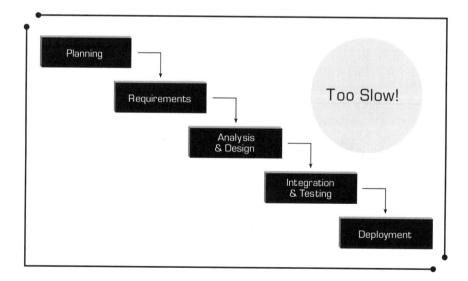

Figure 5.1 Waterfall methodology

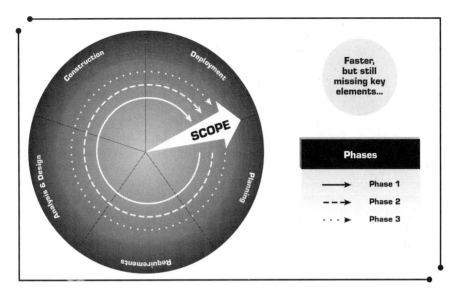

Figure 5.2 Spiral methodology

ure 5.2.) In this approach, each element of the processes is "chunked" off a little at a time. In the first iteration, the scope is limited and very tightly focused, allowing the project to complete the circuit in a relatively short amount of time. In this way, functionality is delivered to the user community in fairly short order. Then the team can make another loop around, while expanding the scope, and deliver additional capability, again in a relatively short amount of time. For instance, the team might start with a very small scope of only one region's sales of a specific product type for the first iteration loop. Once that loop is completed, and the data mart up and running with the small set of data required to support this requirement, the team can start another iteration loop and add another region, or another product type.

The spiral methodology forms the foundation of the functional steps involved in successfully implementing data marts. However, the classic spiral methodology is missing several key elements required for data mart success. Hence, we have the data mart spiral methodology, whose eleven discrete steps are shown in Figure 5.3.

1. Business Driver

The data mart must start with a business driver, so that forms the first step. It is essential that this be the foundation for your efforts, as we shall see in detail later in this chapter. Do not attempt the "build it and they will come" approach to data mart implementation. It leads to solutions looking for problems, along with their concomitant challenges of ongoing sponsorship and budgeting.

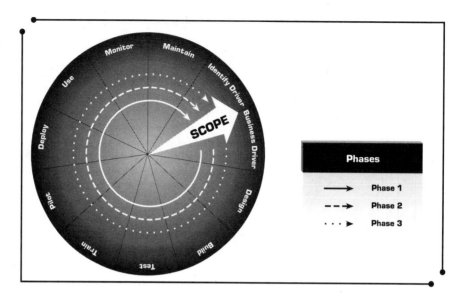

Figure 5.3 Data mart spiral methodology

Data marts must be built solely for the solution of definable business pain. Many teams see the potential ROIs of data mart projects, the quick time lines, the low cost, the low political risk, and the seductive technology as overwhelmingly tempting. These teams quickly construct a data mart solution for a user group that has low levels of pain, low levels of political influence, and low historical levels of technological uptake and utilization. These projects are doomed, but the teams are often incredulous that the users didn't flock to their new solution. Users will only use what solves pain for them. They will not use a system simply because it's got slick and sexy technology. You must only build data marts that solve specific pain for specific business drivers.

2. Design

Once a business driver has been identified, the team can design a solution appropriate to the challenge and the levels of sustainable political will attached to the driver. It is important to tightly couple the scale of the design to the level of sustainable political will in the organization. Do not build a mountain-sized solution to molehill-sized sponsorship.

3. Build

Building the data mart actually can take very little time compared to the entire project, especially if your team and organization is given to endless planning sessions for the most minute tasks. In the building of the data mart, you will probably find that 70–80% of the work is in the mapping, extract, integration, scrubbing, and transformation portions of the build process. If you have chosen to use a DTEAMM (Design, Transformation, Extract, Access, Monitoring, and Management) tool solution, you will realize significant gains in productivity during the build process, although this is not the biggest reason to choose a tool. The systematic population and maintenance of meta data will prove to be the most valuable attribute of these tools.

4. Test

Before you release your new creation out into an unsuspecting world, it is imperative that you dedicate the necessary QA (Quality Assurance) resources to test the system. Your primary goals of the testing process are: data quality, system loaded response time, and network throughput sustainability. You must ensure that the data will roll up to itself, that is, it will withstand audit. You must simulate a month-end/quarter-end scenario and ensure that the system will deliver adequate response time. Finally, you must ensure that the network infrastructure is adequate for data loads, aggregation distribution, and sustained user access.

Although these three goals are important and a prerequisite, don't stop your testing process there. Make your best efforts to weed out and correct any and all possible problems before release. You only have one chance for a first impression, and bad word of mouth can kill you faster than a low-quality, off-Broadway production.

5. Train

The most overlooked aspect of any deployment is always training. Usually you're overdue with the data mart, the business problems are pressing, and the users just don't have the time to commit to learning new tools and data. Your key targets, the power users, are even less inclined to free up time for the "drudgery" of training. They are oriented to "figuring it out" as they have with other tools in the past. It is, however, imperative that you not only train the pilot users, but you train them on live data in the real system. Do not waste anyone's time training on sample data. You must build a real environment in the tool of your choice against real data in your real data mart to make the training viable. Do not, under any circumstances, allow users to have access to the data prior to training. They will be frustrated with incomplete or inadequate knowledge of the data and the tools. The resulting "bad press" is impossible to overcome.

6. Pilot

Once you've got a solid group of trained users in your pilot user group, you are ready to deploy a pilot test of your system. Make sure you've targeted a group of people who are guaranteed to use the system on a regular basis, understand the nature of "beta" systems, and have good personal relationships with your team. From your side, you must have dedicated resources to work closely with this group to ensure their success. Employ mentors to work with the pilot users to solve real business problems with the system. Document the resulting success stories to form a foundation of profitable use of the system. You will later build on this foundation during roll-out and ongoing utilization.

It is very critical that, prior to the pilot, you have a process in place to handle the inevitable flaws in the data, system irregularities, outages, and other problems that will arise. Although the "real world" testing of the design, extracts, transformations, loads, and tools is significant, the stress testing of your "customer service" process is the most important aspect of the pilot.

7. Deploy

After correcting the flaws found in the system during the pilot and ensuring that the processes for handling user requests and problems is fully functional, you will be ready for full-scale deployment. The same rules for training apply here. Do not, under any circumstances, allow user access to the system prior to training on your data. Use your pilot users as mentors and centers of excellence for the general roll-out user community. Distribute information about the effective use of the system during the pilot, including "cook book" examples of how to answer real business questions.

During the deployment, pay particular attention to monitoring system utilization and potential system bottlenecks, especially during your first month end and quarter end. Be ready for the inevitable requests for new data, and ensure quick response to the equally inescapable discovery of flawed data. Word of mouth is critical in the opening stages of deployment, and it is extremely difficult, if not impossible, to overcome a reputation for poor performance and flawed information.

8. Use

The true test of your system will be in its ongoing use by the user community. If it is not used, you have built a solution begging for a problem; or you did not build a system in response to a clear business driver, with sustainable political will; or you built a system that could not support the demand, and resulting poor performance drove the users back to other solutions; or you built a system with flawed, incomplete, or inconsistent data. If you have done none of these things, and your data mart is quickly and heavily used, you will be responsible for the ongoing care and feeding of a mission-critical information resource for your user community.

The most common outcome to a well-managed data mart project is the "curse of success." If you have built the mart as a response to specific pain, it is most likely that the data mart will be wildly popular. Your user base will expand geometrically, and the team will be inundated by requests for changes, additional data points, and new and changed aggregation sets. Meanwhile, other user groups will be clamoring for their own data marts. Be careful to allocate sufficient resources to deal with the "curse of success" scenario.

9. Monitor

To ensure your system's ongoing health and survival in the ever-changing business climate, you will need to closely monitor many aspects of its performance. In the early stages, baseline performance and choke points are essential metrics. The system will die an untimely death if users are being slowed by a network bottleneck or very slow query response time. Past the initial deployment stages, it becomes more important to monitor index and aggregation utilization and repeated ad hoc aggregations. In the nontechnical monitoring realm, you need to stay in close touch with your user community to monitor the overall business drivers, so that if the business climate is changing, you are ready with fresh data sources to meet the needs of the users.

10. Maintain

Your system forms the interface between the business needs for information and the information sources of the business. Because both of these are constantly changing, the system will require ongoing and constant modification and maintenance. Add to this the unavoidable fact that things will break in the process, and you have a requirement for significant maintenance resources, in perpetuity. Do not neglect this fact when doing resource planning for your data mart. Maintenance and sustenance are the true challenges of successfully delivering data marts to your organization.

11. Identify Additional Business Driver

As things change in the business, you must stay in close touch with new and changing business drivers. These will provide the forcing function for changes in existing data marts and for entirely new data marts. It is your job to stay close to the pulse of the business, to understand the dynamics that drive information needs among your users, and to be ready with new, fresh information resources when new requirements arise. Don't forget to attach a metric of sustainable political will to each business driver. There will be many short-term crises in the course of business that will not carry enough sustainable political will to justify the creation of a data mart resource. You can be led down a path of creating a series of abandoned information resources if you don't pay close attention to this factor.

It is also tempting to ignore this part of the process and to deny the need for a business driver. You will believe, you will know, intuitively, that a data mart is the "right thing" to do for the business. You will know, intuitively, that a data mart is the solution that everyone needs, and if we simply build it, the business will discover it, and it will become the nexus of our future information resource efforts. This approach is fraught with danger and is scattered with the remains of many brave information warriors who have set out to fight the data wars without the armor of a solid business driver. They, like you, if you choose this path, were led astray by the siren song of technology and the perceived glory of résumé development.

Technology-Driven Model

When you look under the covers of a non–business-driven solution, you find that at the center of the process is a technology core. Around this core orbits the entire IS (Information Systems) world, and all of its solutions for the business. (See Figure 5.4.)

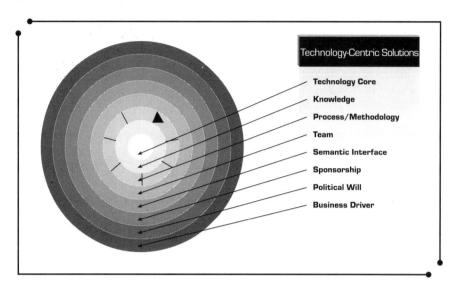

Figure 5.4   Technology-centric solutions

Technology Core

IS team members spend their entire lives looking into the technology core for new and wonderful solutions to emerge that they can bring to their businesses. Magical technologies spring to life here, which are quickly latched onto and implemented, often for no better reason than that they are new and exciting. The assumption is that because they are new and exciting, they must have some intrinsic value that will make them suitable for the business. This "gee whiz" driven phenomenon has been responsible for countless abandoned IS projects that litter the business landscape.

Knowledge

To understand and build solutions from the technology that spin off from the core, the IS (Information Systems) team must have knowledge of the technologies and techniques required to implement them. This need for knowledge drives the burgeoning businesses of professional conferences, seminars, training, and technical books like this one. Often, a knowledge gap is created between new technologies and the mainstream IS population. This gap is filled by consultants, who either simply fill the roles needed to make new technologies "run" or perform a mentoring and knowledge transfer role to educate the IS communities.

Process/Methodology

Once the team has a sufficient level of knowledge to implement the technologies, they will likely turn to some form of implementation methodology to give structure, process, and meaning to the path between knowledge and solution. The methodology forms a foundation on which the team can prepare and package "solutions" to the business based on the technologies it is centered on. An overview of the steps involved in a data mart methodology are covered in detail in Chapter 6.

Team

The layer above the methodology is the lowest sustainable level at which a human organization can exist and function in a business context. They share knowledge of the technology, which separates them from other mere mortals in the business. They also have a methodology that gives reason and logic to their processes of developing and implementing "solutions" for the business. A fully capable data mart team must cover all of the responsibilities outlined in Chapter 4.

Semantic Interface

The team uses a semantic interface to communicate these solutions to the business. The semantic interface consists of language/lexicon (the words used to describe things), syntax (the structure and grouping of terms), and the relations of the lexicon and syntax to the interpreters of them. The semantic interface layer is both the "buzz words" and acronyms used to describe technologies and the understanding of the relationships of the technologies, the solutions, the users, and the business. Traditionally we have found that those who effectively navigate the waters of the semantic interface layer are anointed with special status in the organization. They have the unique ability to "speak the language" of both the business and the technologists.

In smaller organizations, "power users" and "knowledge workers" have filled the role of the semantic interface, acting as an interpretive and buffer layer between the business and the technology organization. Larger organizations often have a formal hierarchical layer, complete with management functions, that is chartered with these semantic interface functions.

Sponsorship

Now that the team has a way to communicate with the business, usually through a few "gatekeepers" who can effectively use the semantic layer to interact with the business, they are ready to seek out a reason for their "solution" to exist. The team's "gatekeepers" then look in the business for sponsorship, for a person or group who will provide funding for the chosen technological "solution." This is usually done under the auspices of solving a problem for the targeted business representative, although it may be a pure "this is neat stuff, let's all play" scenario as well. The key is to find someone with funding who can be seduced into investing it into the technology and the human elements required to deliver it into the business.

Political Will

To justify economic investment on an ongoing basis, a sponsor must generate political will in the organization. This is usually accomplished by generating a business case for the technology. The business case is used to identify a problem that the technology will solve. Most business don't have any shortage of problems, so it is usually not too difficult to find a likely candidate. The problem is examined, and the technological solution is offered up as the ultimate way to permanently eradicate it from the business.

The business case will also include resource (cost) estimates and an ROI (Return On Investment) analysis. Because the cost of the technological "solution" is known, it is often a case of "back filling" to generate a significant enough projected return to justify the cost.

Business Driver

The end result of the process of creating political will is the identification or creation of a business driver. It may be, and usually is, a "force fit" of the technology into a business problem, but it serves the purpose of providing cover for the team's goal of working with the exciting new technology that started this whole thing in the beginning.

Reasons for the Failure of a Technology-Centered Approach

The technology-centered approach to providing data mart solutions to the business is unfortunately predisposed to failure. The primary reasons are: insulation of the team from business drivers, specification-driven processes, the focus on technology, and the inherent out-of-balance condition of this approach.

Insulation of the Team from Business Drivers

When viewed graphically, as in Figure 5.4, you can see that in this model, the team is insulated from the business drivers by three layers. This practically guarantees that the team has little to no contact with what is theoretically the entire reason for their existence.

What soon follows is an insular, xenophobic culture that is both highly suspicious of and entirely dependent on the user community. Because they have little to no direct interaction with the business, the team becomes frustrated by the ever-changing whims of the organization, whose fickle ways drive the team to distraction. In fact, if the team was directly connected with the business drivers, they would see that those "fickle," ever-changing "whims" were direct responses to changing business conditions, not a grand scheme to drive the team to distraction.

Specification-Driven Process

Because the team is living in its own little technological cocoon and must speak to the business through intermediaries versed in the semantic layer, it communicates primarily through specifications. "Specs" become the lingua franca between the IS organization and the business community.

What develops is a large-scale re-creation of the children's game "telephone." The user community identifies a need, and this is communicated to the intermediaries standing guard in the semantic layer. The needs are translated into "specs." The specs are delivered to the IS team. The team interprets and adjusts the specs to fit into the available technologies based on their knowledge, and into the chosen methodology. The team then responds with its own specs that reflect the realities it is working with. These IS specs are passed back out via the semantic layer guardians to the user community for budgeting approval.

The next thing to emerge from the IS cocoon is the "solution." It will be no more and no less than the specs that were approved by the business. The solution will be oblivious to any changes in the needs that started the process in the beginning. The users won't get what is relevant to their current challenges, and the IS team will be further frustrated because they "delivered what the business wanted (what was in the specs)" but it's not "what the business needs (what is required to meet the now changed challenges)". Ergo, the users "never know what they need." Thus begins the death spiral in user/IS relations.

Technology Centered

The technology-centered approach rotates around technology. This creates a deity of technology, beneath which the IS team worships. A mantra quickly evolves: "Everything can be solved by technology." Problems that cannot be "electrified" and solved with a technological solution, are excluded from the problem set. This is a very effective way to avoid the nasty business process challenges that everyone, not just IS, likes to sweep under the rug.

Worshipping at the altar of technology leads directly to solutions looking for problems. The team becomes so enamored with the latest whiz bang hootchicallit that they implement it first, and seek business problems later. Add to this phenomenon the very real pressure to maintain currency with leading-edge technologies to remain viable in a very competitive job market, and you have a very seductive mix.

Personally, I am as enamored with technology as anyone else and have fallen under the spell of the siren song of technology more than once. Unfortunately it inevitably leads to dead-end projects, wasting on the vine. It also is a direct cause of "tin cupping," or going from one department to the next begging for budget to sustain a project with marginal business relevance.

It is important to maintain currency with new technologies and techniques. It is as much a sin to let your organization suffer while new solutions could mitigate the pain as it is to piddle scarce resources away on silver bullet solutions. The "laggard" space on the technology adoption curve is a very safe and comfortable space, but today's dynamic business climate demands quick uptake and adoption of technologies as they become available. The key is to maintain currency, while adopting technologies only when a clear and sustainable business driver demands them.

REALITY CHECK   So how do you know if you're technology driven? Here are some clues:

- If you use acronyms at McDonald's—"Yes, I would LFWT" (Like Fries With That)—you might be technology driven.
- If you prefer to communicate via e-mail rather than voice, even to people in the next cubicle, you might be technology driven.
- If your children want a Peter Norton action figure for their birthday, you might be technology driven.
- If you highly prize your AOL disk collection, you might be technology driven.
- If your collection of *Byte* magazines extends back to 1989, you might be technology driven.
- If you only do business with people who have a web site, you might be technology driven.
- If your social conversation consists entirely of hot web addresses, I/O bandwidth, and processor speeds, you might be technology driven.
- If you prefer to watch the byte counter during long file transfers rather than interact with other humans, you might be technology driven.
- If you view giving up and calling tech support the ultimate sign of personal weakness, you might be technology driven.
- If your children learned to count by saying, "Zero, one, two, three, . . . ," you might be technology driven.
- If you are anxiously awaiting the arrival of your personal T1 line into your home, you might be technology driven.
- If you *know* Dilbert is a documentary, you might be technology driven.
- If you have a pocket protector for your pajamas, you might be technology driven.

Inherently Out of Balance

Technology-driven solutions are like a cancer, they are not self-limiting in any way and inevitably will overrun a boundary that will kill the host. When a technology is introduced simply as a showcase for the technology, it will expand to all available limits, consuming all resources in its path. It will be expanded or used in areas in which it is not well suited, merely to provide additional rationale for its existence. As a consequence, it will ultimately overrun a boundary in resources, suitability, usability, or cost. At this point, the host project will die of mortal wounds of boundary breach. The resulting waste of talents and technology will most likely be mitigated by the next iteration of technology-driven solutions, thus taking the spotlight off the remains of previous failures.

Business-Driven Model

The solution to this unhappy circumstance is to build your organization around a different model. Instead of rotating around a technological axis, make business drivers the core of your organization's efforts. (See Figure 5.5.) In this model, business drivers provide the fundamental forcing function for every activity. As a natural consequence of business need, sponsorship coagulates around opportunity points. Business units and individuals are driven to sponsor solutions to specific, visceral pain in the organization. The semantic interface now becomes a gateway, instead of the gatekeeper function. It functions as a facilitator of communications, ideas, and proposals, instead of a funnel through which only the anointed can pass.

In this model, the team surrounds the opportunities and challenges arising out of the business drivers. The team is driven solely by clear business goals and problems, and once it understands the tactical and strategic context of the business driver, it turns outward to its knowledge of potential technological solutions. Technology can only be applied where appropriate because only appropriate opportunities arise through the business driver, sponsorship, semantic interface, team, and knowledge layers.

Encapsulating the entire process is the methodology, which provides a framework and context for the design and implementation of the technological solution. The

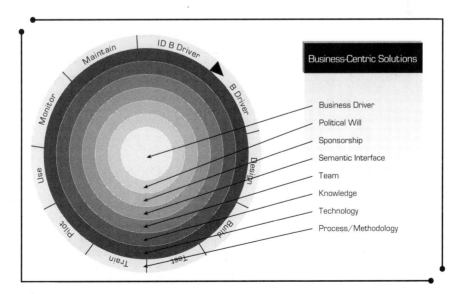

Figure 5.5 Business-centric solutions

methodology is used to implement the appropriate technological solutions that arise through this business-driven model.

Business-Driven Spiral

If we view the business-driven model in three dimensions, we can include the expanding scope of the spiral methodology as the project moves through time. (See Figure 5.6.)

The business-driven model always leads to appropriate solutions to specific problems. This is a formula for success for your data marts. The business-driven model works because it:

- *Is always business driven*
  Business drivers are at the core of the model. Nothing happens until a business driver arises. A "build it and they will come" solution is impossible in this model. Only solutions to specific drivers are designed and implemented.

- *Always provides solutions to specific pain*
  Building solutions to business needs ensures that only specific pain is being addressed with technological solutions. It is a fundamental prerequisite for success that your efforts be directed only toward providing relief to specific, visceral, life-threatening pain. This model ensures that this is the only possible outcome.

- *Integrates political will/budget*
  A business driver gives rise to identifiable pain, which gives rise to integrated political will in the organization, which gives rise to budget and resources in sufficient

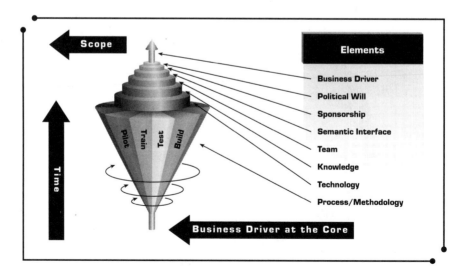

Figure 5.6 Business-centric process spiral

quantity to design and implement an appropriate solution. This model guarantees that by the time a challenge appears on the IS radar screen, it is accompanied by sufficient resources to effect a solution. Challenges without sufficient resources are simply not big enough business drivers to warrant a solution. When they become painful enough, they will come prepackaged with budget and resources. In this way, problems become self-selective, and you can eliminate the clutter of extraneous crises that serve to distract and diffuse your current efforts.

- *Integrates sponsorship*
Problems that have integrated political will, budget, and resources are shrink-wrapped sponsorship magnets. It is very politically advantageous to be identified with a solution to identifiable pain in the organization. By the time a problem has driven itself to the forefront, sponsorship has become another integrated element of the package.

- *Is self-balancing*
This model will never overrun a boundary.
    To surface and become a viable, integrated challenge opportunity, a business driver must overcome:

  - Lethargy (inherent in most organizations)
  - Inertia (commitment of resources to existing problems)
  - Competing resource demands (other projects and problems)
  - Existing solutions (The tendency is to force fit these first.)
  - Culture (corporate and IS)
  - Technology challenges (A technological solution may not be available.)

  These gating factors ensure that only appropriate business drivers will arise to become prepackaged challenge opportunities for the IS team. Because it generates only appropriate solutions to specific pain, technology will never be misapplied or expanded to inappropriate areas.

Beyond these factors, the model is entirely self-balancing and incapable of overreaching its challenge or opportunity axes.

Axes Guarantee Balance

As each iteration of the methodology loop expands the scope of the project, it is balanced by the challenge and opportunity axes inherent in its design. (See Figure 5.7.) The project will continue to expand in scope, and climb the spiral, until the challenge axes outweigh the opportunity axes.

The challenge axes are:

- *Resources*
No project can exceed the resources available for design, construction, implementation, and maintenance.

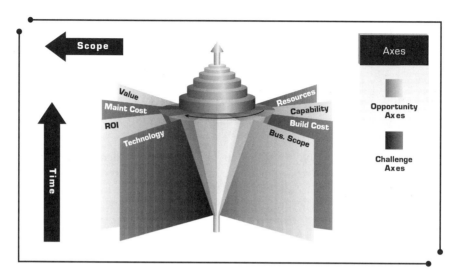

Figure 5.7   Business-centric process spiral with axes

- *Build Cost*
  The project's returns must be balanced against the cost to construct it. If there is no foreseeable ROI, a business case is impossible. The project will proceed until the cost to build it outweighs the potential returns to the business.

- *Technology*
  No project can proceed in a technological vacuum. There must be appropriate and available technology to address the specific pain of this specific opportunity.

- *Maintenance Cost*
  Ongoing maintenance costs of the project must also be weighed against potential returns. If the returns are waning, the project will not proceed in the face of ongoing or expanding maintenance costs.

REALITY CHECK   There's one big challenge axis that is not a formal part of this methodology: politics. It is not all that uncommon to be sailing merrily along with your project and have the rug pulled out from under you and the entire team due to political factors completely out of your control. You can't always anticipate it; all you can do is keep your finger on the pulse of corporate politics. And keep your head down.

The opportunity axes are:

- *ROI*
  Return on investment is the primary financial criterion upon which the project will be evaluated. If the project continues to exhibit a positive ROI, it will continue to climb the spiral.

- *Value*
  A less empirical measure is one of value. What value does this project provide to the business? An increased level of customer service may not be readily apparent in an ROI evaluation, but it could be invaluable in a tightly competitive market. A project that can demonstrate value will continue to live and evolve.

- *Capability*
  The project must demonstrate fundamental capability in a real business process. A project that extends and expands capabilities is of great value.

- *Business Scope*
  How far reaching is this project? Does it affect one key workgroup or an entire department? Is it fundamental to multiple business processes? The greater the business scope, the greater the likelihood of continued growth for the project in question.

Inherently Balanced Projects

The project will always maintain a state of equilibrium between these challenge and opportunity axes. Because it is business driven, it will continue to climb the spiral as long as a specific business need exists, up to the limits of the challenge axes. As long as the business need exists, the project will be prepackaged with political will, budget, and sponsorship. As business needs, resources, technologies, challenges, and opportunities change, the business drivers, challenge axes, and opportunity axes will change to reflect these changing conditions. The project will seek its own level within these forces, as water will seek to level itself in a moving bowl. This means the project is inherently self-limiting, inherently self-balanced, and inherently flexible.

Considering the amount of effort and resources expended attempting to keep all of these balls in the air using other models, it is easy to see why the business-driven spiral model is worth it from the project management standpoint alone. Beyond the time and effort savings of the project manager, the more efficient use of organization resources is reason enough to move your future projects to this model. This model and methodology structure ensures projects with specific purpose, for specific pain, with specific resources that will expand and live only as much and as long as specific business drivers warrant.

Communication Methodology

Of course, no matter how elegant your project methodology, it will all go for naught if you can't successfully communicate with your sponsors, with your users, or among your team. To successfully design, deploy, and sustain a data mart demands a high level of communication on all levels. You must be able to succinctly communicate the mission, scope, and status of the data mart at all times, on all levels, at all scales.

This gives rise to another variation on the "elevator test." In this case, if you get on the elevator in the lobby with a business manager who hits the button for the second floor and at the same time asks you "How's the data mart going?" you must be able to answer the question before the manager exits the elevator. At the same time, you must be able to provide detailed reporting to IS management regarding the status of each element of the data mart project. In addition, you must be able to facilitate effective status meetings with the data mart team, as each group is updating their progress and challenges.

Effective, concise communication is the key enabling element of your entire data mart project. Without it, you are guaranteed failure and disappointment before you begin. Good communication ensures that you are only building solutions to specific business challenges. It facilitates the generation and sustaining of political will. It ensures and smoothes the flow of budget and resource allocation. And it is a prerequisite for effective team management and task execution.

Data warehouse projects, by their very nature, are very large, complex projects. Even a simple, single-business-unit, single-subject-area data mart is a nontrivial responsibility. Effectively communicating, much less understanding, where your data mart project is and where the looming crises are is, in itself, a daunting task. Most teams rely on massive project plans and copious proposals and project-reporting documents to monitor and communicate project scope, process, progress, and requirements.

Unfortunately this is a bit of overkill when all you need to do is answer that LOB (Line of Business) manager's simple question in the elevator of "How's the data mart coming?" Plopping down a 95-page project plan and 150-page project definition document on them is akin to lighting a candle with a blow torch. Certainly effective, but a bit overtaxing on the available resources.

Project plans are certainly valuable, and they are a requirement in most IS cultures. Unfortunately they have been greatly overused, and the situation has digressed to the point that some teams seem to require a project plan to organize a coffee break. As we have seen, they are not appropriate vehicles for cross-functional communication, and they often become incredible resource "black holes," sucking ever greater amounts of project management time, just to maintain the status of innumerable details.

Project Status Report Card

I've found that a much more effective approach is to develop a project status report card (PSRC). These report cards consist of statuses and descriptions for the major elements that make up the data mart system. They are designed in a hierarchical outline form,

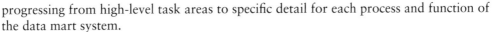

progressing from high-level task areas to specific detail for each process and function of the data mart system.

Due to the hierarchical nature of a PSRC, it is simple to collapse the detail out of a report card and instantly have a simple, high-level status document ready for discussion or distribution to all parties, or to answer that quick "elevator" question. Because they embed the detail of the project, PSRCs are very effective discussion documents for team meetings, with trouble areas easily highlighted. They also function as excellent forcing functions for recalcitrant suppliers and teams, for example, a networking group that hasn't gotten that FDDI (Fiber Distributed Data Interface) backbone in place yet.

Your primary questions at this point are presumably "What does a data mart project report card look like?" and "How do I put one together?" What you're looking for is a document in outline form that you can flesh out as you move forward with the project. You can use any tool you want to create the outline—word processors and spreadsheets work particularly well. Project management packages are also capable of being used in this manner. If you'd like to automate the outline, a spreadsheet is more appropriate.

A spreadsheet allows you to automate the task of arriving at high-level statuses for each project area. You can simply create cells that present a high-level status statement based on the status level of lower levels in the hierarchy. If you choose this approach, I strongly suggest that you use a three-level status method for nonmetric fields: 1 = not known/not started, 2 = in progress/within bounds, 3 = complete/satisfactory. The potential insight afforded by finer levels of detail are wasted in endless hours spent by the team arguing whether the status of researching an index utilization monitoring tool is a 5 or a 6 on a scale of 10. IS teams tend to get dragged down by minutia enough as it is; don't encourage the problem by creating vast new arenas for endless debate.

In the early stages of the project, many topics such as "network infrastructure status" will contain only "we don't know" as an entry. Moving forward, you and the team will fill in each of these with increasing levels of detail and empirical facts. At any time in the life of the project, you'll have a handy guide to measure progress and provide quick status reporting to upper management.

High-Level Subject Areas

The following sections describe suggested high-level subject areas of a data mart project status report card (PSRC). Each high-level area is accompanied by a detailed breakdown of the pertinent elements.

Mission Statement

What is the reason for the existence of this data mart? This should be easy to answer if you're using the business-driven methodology discussed earlier in this chapter. It will be a direct reflection of the business driver responsible for this solution.

Subject Area

What is the subject area of this data mart? Again, this will be a direct reflection of the specific pain this data mart is designed to address.

Source Systems (Internal and External)

What source OLTP (On-Line Transaction Processing) systems will be drawn upon to provide data for this data mart? What external third-party data sets will be used to provide additional data points? This high-level subject area has many levels of detail, down to the source field level.

Content

This section contains high-level table descriptions. As the project progresses, this should be accompanied by an appendix that details fields and descriptions. Make sure to highlight known exceptions and missing data points requested by users. As an alternative approach, you may want to specifically describe the fact, dimension, history, and summary tables if you are using a star schema.

Fact Tables

What detail fact tables will be required for this data mart? This high-level area also contains much detail, down to the target field level. This high-level area assumes a star schema design is being used for your data mart.

Dimension Tables

What business dimensions will be required for this data mart? Are any already in use for other marts? Again, expect very detailed levels in this report card subject area, down to target fields. As in the previous point, a star schema is assumed.

History Tables

What relationships do you need to capture and trend over time? This will most likely be unknown early on, but will be revealed as you closely investigate detailed user needs. Pay close attention to relationships that need to be embedded in the fact table(s). Again, a star schema is assumed, although history tables can be used with any design.

Summary Tables

What aggregation summaries will be required prior to roll-out? Can users identify regularly required multidimensional aggregations? It is important to have several summary tables prepared prior to the general release of the data mart. Expect significant churn and high utilization in the summary sets as you move forward with deployment and general use.

Architecture and Topology

This area concerns the system architecture and physical topology. You will delineate server(s), server(s) locations, network "pipes" and sizes, network topology, connection to desktops, and so on. Pay close attention to this area for red flags early in the project, especially in the areas of network capacity and utilization levels.

Physical Device Information

This is another area that will be filled with "we don't know" early in the game. Here you're looking for server manufacturer, model, configuration, desktop client minimum configurations, and so on.

Process Flow

In this area you are defining the data mart system process flow, that is, where things are going to be done and when. This includes extract, scrub, integration, transformation, transfer, load, summarization, access, batch window, and so on. Don't forget to detail what happens in the user access process in this section. Watch for red flags here, such as requirements for replicated, large, dedicated data sets for MOLAP (Multidimensional On-Line Analytical Processing) tools.

Data Flow

This area is very important to flesh out early in the process. You need to delineate where the data goes, for example, DB2 temp files, output queues, temp load tables, or transformation engines. From the technical side of things, data marts are basically a data movement business, so much of what the eventual design will look like is determined in this section. Early EMT (Extract, Mapping, and Transformation)/DTEAMM (Design, Transformation, Extract, Access, Monitoring, and Management) tool selection can drastically improve your level of detail in this area.

Process and Task Ownership

This is a very, very important project report card subject area that is too often overlooked until late in the project life cycle. It is extremely important to establish ownership as early in the project as possible. Ugly turf wars and orphan processes are too often the result when these questions are left unanswered for too long. Establish who owns JCL (Job Control Language), who owns RDBMS (Relational Data Base Management System) loads, who owns triggers and stored procedures, who owns user change requests, and so on. Don't leave these questions unanswered a day longer than needed.

Roles and Responsibilities

This is an extremely useful and valuable team roster and "score card." It needs to be updated regularly as team members join and leave the group. It should include data mart team roster, steering committee or executive sponsorship committee members, individual sponsors, end-user contacts, consultants, vendors, and so on. Include names, phone numbers, addresses, and e-mail addresses. It is most useful when this portion of the document is embedded from a live version kept on line and easily accessible by all parties.

Meta Data

If there is one area that you will want to focus on early, this is it. Meta data is absolutely required for success, and early population of the meta data is a big part of that success.

Start by listing meta data description, content, extent, population, maintenance, and availability with various tools, and so on. A large portion of the fate of your data mart project hangs on meta data. Don't ignore or defer it.

Known Caveats

Inexorably there will be missing data points, performance issues, tool limitations, and so on associated with your data mart project. Start listing them early, and communicate them openly and often. Make this area your top priority for properly managing expectations.

Schedule and Resource Requirements for Missing Elements

Inevitably the product you deliver will be short of the grand vision that the team had when beginning the project. In this section include the time and resources required to fulfill the vision. If the business driver at the core of the project remains viable, you will eventually make enough iteration loops of the implementation methodology to fulfill the vision and fill in the missing elements and capabilities.

Data Marts

In the case of a multiple data mart environment, or one where your mission is to integrate disparate LegaMarts (you poor soul), you will need a place to provide an overall view of each data mart. This will include description, content, replication strategy, subject areas, and so on. In the case of a multiple data mart or LegaMart scenario, this area will be quite detailed.

Schedule and Resource Requirements for Data Marts

If you are constructing an enterprise, or "galactic" data warehouse, and then extracting subset data marts from it, don't over commit. Make sure to allow some recovery time after the "galactic" roll-out. There will be problems to fix prior to being able to stamp out subset data marts on a regular basis. You will most likely be overly optimistic when predicting the resources required to design, extract, replicate, and sustain the subset data marts. Prudence and restraint is the wise path. "Under-commit and over-deliver" is a good strategy for subset data mart survival and happiness.

Q/A Process and Level

If you have a remote chance to deliver a functioning and successful data mart, you must have a clear Q/A (Quality Assurance) process. In this area describe the overall level of Q/A requirements/commitments at current and future milestones, and the Q/A process for various deliverables. Do not shortchange your project in this area.

RDBMS Response Times

This is an area that will contain "we don't know" for most of the project, until such time that you have some test data and an instance of your RDBMS running on your target server. Once you can do some baseline testing, you will need to establish some benchmark results with real-world data and real-world queries. Establish solid metrics for typical real-world usage, such as: a summary query to a single aggregate table X seconds on average, for a detail query to 2 dimensions and the fact table Y minutes. As soon as you have these times in hand, communicate them to your target pilot users. If there is an overwhelming hue and cry, you still have time to address their concerns. If you wait until pilot, or worse yet, roll-out, for the users to discover the real performance of the system, you can be in an unrecoverable political disaster. Again, you only have one chance to make a first impression, and bad "word of mouth" in the initial stages is almost impossible to recover from.

Service Level Agreements

This area details the agreements you have established with all vendors and suppliers to the data mart project. This includes internal suppliers such as UNIX Administrators and network support and external suppliers such as server up-time agreements. Any service level commitments the data mart team provides to the user community are also detailed in this section.

Security

Every data mart will have security concerns. This area is another place to look for early red flags. If there are unrealistic security expectations among management, address them early. It is of no use to build a solution that will never be released into use due to security fears among the sponsors and drivers of the project. Use this area to delineate your overall strategy, specific tools, security levels, access methods, administration, and so on.

Resource Scheduling and Distribution

Because most of your users are information consumers, a key capability is to allow them to access, share, schedule, and distribute the existing information resources in the enterprise such as reports and analyses. This section describes the tools, strategies, architectures, and so on used for the scheduling and delivery of these resources.

Tools

The data mart system will comprise multiple tools. This section describes each tool used in the system, including RDBMS, monitoring, design, mapping, extract, transformation, management, data access, data visualization, and so on. Include technical specifications as well as capabilities and known limitations, such as the maximum number of rows to return to a desktop "LowLAP" (Low-Level Analytical Processing) tool and still get results in a reasonable time. Known limitations should be communicated to the user community as soon as they are known and confirmed.

Project Plan

This section contains the project plan itself. This allows the team to maintain the plan, if required, and to include the status of the creation and maintenance of the plan in the overall status report of the project.

Site Specific

Your individual project will contain PSRC subject areas that are unique to your circumstances and environment. The PSRC is inherently infinitely scaleable, so you can expand it at will to include additional categories.

Project Status Report Card Utilization

You can use this project status report card (PSRC) in many ways, including management reporting, project management, vendor communication, user group communication, and team meetings and communication.

The PSRC is invaluable for quickly and efficiently communicating to management the status of the data mart project. If desired, the top levels can be sliced off, along with their statuses, and delivered to management with a summary report. The entire PSRC can be made available on line, so that management can drill down into the detail at will to investigate specific areas of the project. If a "red flag" is discovered anywhere in the project's life, the PSRC can be used as the vehicle to communicate the status and importance of the critical factor.

From the project management standpoint, the PSRC is a very efficient tool for maintaining and monitoring project status on all levels. Data mart projects can become fairly large in scope, and it is easy to get lost in the "trees" of the details and sometimes lose site of where the project is in the overall context. The PSRC allows the project manager to drill up and down to any level of detail in the project and have an instant read on the status of any or all elements. It is a very flexible, infinitely scaleable, project management tool.

Vendors also greatly appreciate the PSRC. It allows them to minimize the time and resources required from them and your team in order for them to assess your project and where their tools would fit in. When used in conjunction with the site check described in Chapter 4, the PSRC gives any vendor anything they could require to understand your project and their tool's potential role in it.

For user group communication, the PSRC can be used as a high-level status communication document. This is especially important for fast-track projects answering a specific high-level pain in the organization. If you've got a user group breathing down your neck, it is very handy and efficient to have a standard reporting and communication medium for the duration of the project. If you start with a PSRC and use it throughout your project, the user community not only becomes comfortable with the format, but can literally watch the project progress as elements are defined and populated.

Perhaps the most valuable use of the PSRC is to facilitate team status and development meetings. It allows you to quickly review a project's overall status, as well as quickly drill into problem areas or "red flags" that have appeared.

Be careful not to let teams get bogged down in "analysis paralysis" driving down the atomic levels of detail in each PSRC category, especially during the initial stages of a project. You will find it much more useful if the team spends no more than a couple of minutes on each point in each review session. Drill down until you hit a wall, put in a "we don't know yet" entry into the PSRC, then move on to the next point. The "we don't know yet" points can then be assigned to off-line research or task groups. In this way, you can use the report card to drive status meetings that are an hour in length rather than an afternoon of endless churn.

If possible, keep the PSRC on line so that the team can access it and update the areas dynamically. This provides a common repository for information about the project and provides a natural source feed for your data mart meta data.

REALITY CHECK   You don't need a fancy communications methodology to be effective; all you need is communication. You may hate to do it, your team may hate to do it, but you must enforce regular communications among the team members and especially with the business community. Keep the users in the loop!

Summary

Although methodologies are often taken to extremes, they are required to ensure success for your data mart project. The key is to manage the methodology, not to have the methodology manage you. In choosing a development methodology, it is essential that it reflect a business-driven process. Anything short of that will guarantee failure. A communication methodology is also required for success. One that is hierarchical and scaleable is both required and a key to data mart project success.

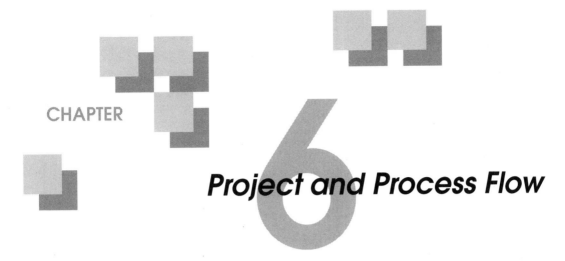

Project and Process Flow

As we saw in Chapter 5, the development and implementation of a data mart information resource involves multiple iteration loops, each of expanding business scope or scale. If properly implemented, the project continues to expand in scope as it progresses through time, until it reaches a point of natural balance between the business driver that is powering the project and the opportunity and challenges axes.

During this life cycle, the data mart project has the following steps on the iterative methodology spiral that make up the project flow:

1. Identify Business Driver(s)
2. Identify and Quantify Political Will
3. Identify Sponsorship
4. Conduct Readiness Assessment / Site Check
5. Survey User Needs
6. Build Enterprise Data Mart Architecture
7. Pick Initial Subject Area
8. Research and Implement DW (Data Warehouse) / DM (Data Mart) Tools
9. Design Target
10. Build Data Mapping, Extract, Transformation, and Scrub
11. Build Aggregation, Replication, and Distribution
12. Research and Implement User Tools
13. Test
14. Train
15. Pilot
16. Deploy
17. Use
18. Monitor

19. Maintain

The first iteration loop of the project demonstrates all nineteen elements of the project flow; however, succeeding iterations of the loop contain, at a minimum:

1. Identify Additional Business Driver(s)
2. Identify and Quantify Additional Political Will
3. Identify Additional Sponsorship
4. Survey User Needs
5. Design Target Additions/Modifications
6. Build Data Mapping, Extract, Transformation, and Scrub
7. Research and Implement Additional User Tools (if required)
8. Test
9. Train
10. Pilot
11. Deploy
12. Use
13. Monitor
14. Maintain

Note that, in both cases, these steps need not be executed serially. Where appropriate and possible, teams should execute as many steps as possible, in parallel.

Project Flow

In lieu of presenting a complete data mart methodology, which would take much more than a chapter, I will give a high-level review of the nineteen core steps of the project flow to a data mart system. Although not a replacement for a full-scale methodology, this foundation will prove adequate for the needs of many teams. Many of these steps are covered in much more detail elsewhere in the book, and appropriate chapter references are provided.

Each element of the iterative steps that make up the project flow is significant and probably deserves an entire chapter, if not volume, of its own. I won't attempt that level of detail for each step, but I will cover each one and provide additional detail for crucial steps.

1. Identify Business Driver(s)

As demonstrated in Chapter 5, business drivers are the fundamental prerequisite for a successful data mart. You must identify the valid business drivers that represent deep and visceral pain in a definable business process, function, or organization. As defined in Chapter 4, the business driver leader is responsible for monitoring the business, identifying candidate opportunities, ranking opportunities in terms of support and importance to the business, and gauging the sustainability of candidates.

It is a challenging and politically sensitive task to separate various business driver candidates into "doable" and "not-doable" camps. It is inevitable that you and your team will get forced into creating data marts for "loser" business drivers via political agendas and other unavoidable facts of corporate life. Do everything you can to defer these until you have at least one viable "winner" business driver data mart in place and functioning. You will need a viable reference to a functioning and sustainable data mart to continue the process. If you begin with a nonsustainable data mart, you will be poisoning the waters.

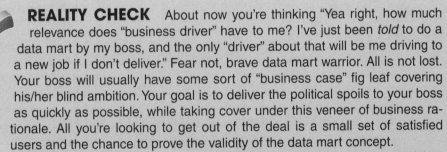

REALITY CHECK About now you're thinking "Yea right, how much relevance does "business driver" have to me? I've just been *told* to do a data mart by my boss, and the only "driver" about that will be me driving to a new job if I don't deliver." Fear not, brave data mart warrior. All is not lost. Your boss will usually have some sort of "business case" fig leaf covering his/her blind ambition. Your goal is to deliver the political spoils to your boss as quickly as possible, while taking cover under this veneer of business rationale. All you're looking to get out of the deal is a small set of satisfied users and the chance to prove the validity of the data mart concept.

Before you fight to the death on the issue, remember the sage advice: "You have to pick the hill you're willing to die on." Are you willing to die on this hill? It might be better to save yourself for when your boss wants to build a whole series of politically driven nonarchitected LegaMarts. Now that's a hill worth dying on.

2. Identify and Quantify Political Will

A valid business driver will always come prepackaged with sufficient political will to drive the creation and initial maintenance of a solution. If you cannot discern viable political will attached to a business driver candidate, avoid it like the plague. If it is truly a critical issue, it will come back around at a later date with additional political will attached. The trick is to avoid these weak business drivers until they can cycle through the organization long enough to attract enough political will to make them viable candidates for a data mart.

3. Identify Sponsorship

Viable business drivers with valid levels of political will always come prepackaged with budget and resources. Any entity floating around an organization with budget attached to it will attract sponsorship like ants to a picnic. An entity that represents a solution to a business problem, with budget attached, is even more attractive. This is the most desirable opportunity for anyone with even a faint heartbeat of political ambition. The chance to solve a critical problem for the business is a singular opportunity to garner political favor and bank valuable points for future trading. Your challenge is to separate the winners from the losers in this contest of political one-upmanship.

Valid sponsorship requires a frank assessment of the political realities surrounding the individuals wearing the sponsor mantle. Factors to consider are:

- *Level of influence in the organization*
  Does this person have the ability to influence the organization? Will his or her testimony as to the effect of the data mart carry any weight? Is this person a heavyweight or a lightweight? An up-and-comer or someone playing out the string? For your first few data marts, you are looking for heavyweights or "fast trackers" who are guaranteed to have the influence to break through any red tape you might encounter and to be heeded when they testify to the effectiveness and impact of the data mart.

- *Stability*
  How stable is this person in his or her position? Is he or she on the hot seat or targeted by anyone higher in the food chain? Once you've got a few data marts under your belt, you can take a chance on a fringe rebel, but starting out, you need people who are secure and stable, with as few powerful enemies as possible. Avoid at all costs a high-risk person for your initial efforts; your team will probably never lose the stain of "guilt by association."

- *IS (Information Systems) Relationship/History*
  What is this person's relationship with IS? Does he or she exhibit open hostility, doubt, or lack of confidence? Do you have a history of success working with this person? Do not use the initial data marts as an opportunity to turn around sour relationships. The last thing you need in the beginning is an assassin taking pot shots at every opportunity. You will experience problems and delays, and you cannot afford to have your sponsor stabbing you in the back with management every time you stub your toe.

- *Track Record*
  Does this person have a history of success? Has he or she been associated with winning projects and initiatives? Does this person exhibit a history of successful communications with project teams? Data marts are great things, but they are not capable of personality transformations. If the potential sponsor has no bona fides to bring to the table, steer clear.

If your potential sponsors pass these hurdles, they represent safe opportunities for your team. Be very wary in the opening stages of data mart implementation in your organization. If you get stuck with a loser early, you must make a tough call. If there is no hope, begin to search for another valid business driver immediately. It will take some time for the "loser" mart to fail, and with any luck, you can get a "winner" up and running in time to take some of the attention away from the demise of the initial effort.

4. Conduct Readiness Assessment / Site Check

Once you have aligned valid sponsorship with a viable business driven need, you are ready to assess the "state of the state" in your organization. Chapter 4 details the process of conducting a readiness assessment, or site check, for your opportunity. This site check will prove invaluable in spotting potential land mines at your site and in quickly and effectively communicating the characteristics of your project and organization to potential vendors.

5. Survey User Needs

It is impossible to deliver a truly business-driven data mart without an intimate understanding of the user community. A "build it and they will come" approach leads to abandoned projects, disillusioned management, frustrated and angry users, and opportunities to explore career options in your local community. A data mart that answers the needs of the users requires you to spend time interviewing the user community to define the functional and operational requirements of the data mart system.

One thing you will discover about data warehousing and data marts, if you haven't figured it out already, is that it is not rocket science. The basic principles are readily understood. As in most things related to technology, a lot of people make a lot of money trying to make it as complicated as possible, offering themselves and their organizations as the path through the maze. Along these lines, you will find that you can drive to the heart of data mart design requirements with a very limited number of well-placed questions to the user community. The six core questions are:

1. Subject area (What do you need to know about?)
2. Atomic level of fact detail (What level of detail do you need?)
3. Length of fact detail history (How far back in time do you need that detail?)
4. Required business dimensions (How do you like to view, or "slice," the business? By product? By customer?)
5. Multidimensional aggregation requirements (What combination of "views," or "slices," is valuable to you in a report or analysis? Sales by customer? By product?)
6. History tables (What relationships do you need to capture, track, and/or trend?)

If you asked nothing else, the answers to these six questions would allow you to design, build, and deploy a valuable corporate information asset. The key to success with a "fast track" approach such as this is to concentrate on what the user's business processes are. In other words, what is their purpose? What are they trying to accomplish? If you focus on these issues and get the answers to these key six questions, you will have a solid foundation to build a design on.

Sensing that the preceding six questions alone may leave your appetite for information about this area unsatisfied, I have elected to give you the "full boat" end-user interview structure. These elements are not ranked in order of importance, and some may be irrelevant to your particular situation.

Goals of Interviews

The first step in the user interview process is to establish clear goals for your interviews with the user community. Fundamentally you are mapping the user's needs into the available technology. We do this through the data warehouse and data mart architecture, topologies, and data access and analysis technologies discussed in Chapter 3. Because the data mart star schema design defines our fundamental elements, one of our primary goals is to define the content and structure of these design elements.

Subject Area   Our first task in the user interview process is to establish the subject area the users are interested in. Because data marts tend to be very focused solutions to point problems, they are predominantly single-subject-area designs, although not exclusively so.

In your discussions with the users, your goals related to subject areas are to determine if the proposed subject area will meet the following requirements. The subject area must:

- *Be definable*

  The subject area must be definable in business terms. A subject area of "customer satisfaction" is not viable unless specific data points are associated with customer satisfaction in the organization.

- *Be measurable*

  Along these same lines, the subject area must be measurable. A subject area of "sales" clearly has measurable components such as orders and returns. A proposed subject area of "quality of life" may not have these elements.

- *Have discrete metrics*

  The subject area must have discrete metrics available for storage, access, and analysis. A subject area of "sales" has discrete metrics of sale amount in dollars, number of units sold, and date of transaction. More ethereal subject areas such as "quality of life" may not have these discrete metrics available. An alternative may be a combination of subject areas that would deliver the same goal, such as "economic index," "air quality," and "number of transportation methods."

- *Have a data source available*

  This may seem obvious, but the subject area must have a source of data available to feed it. Users sometimes have a hard time grasping that the data mart does not create any data, it only stores it. They sometimes think that by decreeing a subject area of "Sales Rep Productivity," all the required measurements of sales, customer marketing, and contact activity are available. Actually, the SFA (Sales Force Automation) system that could provide these could be unavailable, unreachable, or still a gleam in the eye of the VP (Vice President) of sales.

If the proposed subject area does not meet these criteria, you will need to design alternatives that meet the user's needs or to defer the opportunity until there is sufficient political will to overcome the deficiencies.

Source Systems   Your goal related to source systems is to define, to the maximum extent possible, where the required data will come from to populate the subject area. You are seeking to identify:

- *OLTP (On-Line Transaction Processing) systems*
  The primary source for most subject areas will be existing OLTP systems in the business. Be very wary of new OLTP systems as primary sources. If the system is being implemented in parallel with your data mart, it is very likely that the OLTP implementation team will have little to no available bandwidth for you and your team. You must have a high level of resource commitment from OLTP system experts and owners in the initial stages of design and mapping.

- *Third-party data*
  Many subject areas, especially those associated with marketing, rely heavily on third-party data purchased or acquired from outside the organization. Market survey data such as AC Neilson ratings, market segmentation data, and financial rating data are all popular third-party data sources. These can be resource tar pits, so be wary of them. You must commit resources very early in the project to determine how much integration effort will be required to bring third-party data in. Ongoing resources will also be required, as all third-party data suppliers have a nasty habit of "improving" their data formats on a regular basis.

- *Data islands*
  Another hidden resource black hole are data islands. These isolated, nonintegrated operational and analysis systems are very popular among users and are assumed by them to be valid data sources. It can take tremendous amounts of initial and ongoing effort to integrate, scrub, and extract data from the various data islands scattered around your organization. Identify these sources early and commit resources immediately to ascertaining the time and effort necessary to bring their data into the data mart.

Business Rules   Every organization has a huge collection of written and unwritten business rules for deriving intelligence from raw data. Each level of the organization has business rules that are specific to their functions and tasks. To provide a valid information resource for your user community, you must understand the applicable business rules for this group. Your business rule goals during your user interviews are:

- *Definition*
  You must document and define the business rules that your user group uses. You must understand and document these rules to the lowest level of detail, especially where they concern detail facts. For instance, you must fully understand how they calculate "net sales."

- *Alignment with corporate directives*
  It is vitally important to compare your user group's business rules to corporate standards. If the corporation calculates "net sales" differently than your audience, you are headed for integration hell if you label their data mart's column

"NET_SALES." You must always be thinking in an enterprise data mart architecture mode, even when focused on a specific data mart for a unique group of users.

- *Document disparities*
  Any divergence from corporate business rule standards or other data mart business rule standards must be documented fully. Business rule meta data is among the most valuable.

Semantics Semantics form the linguistic representation of business rules and implied knowledge. Probably the greatest challenge in any organization is to get disparate user communities to agree on common terms for business entities, items, functions, and organizations. Your goals in the interview process are:

- *Definition*
  Document and define all semantics that your data mart audience uses. Capture the meaning behind common terms that otherwise would go unnoticed in a casual business conversation such as refund, net, volume, throughput, and so on. In the world of data marts, it is critically important to fully understand exactly what is meant by common terms such as sales, returns, shipped, employed, discharged, and so on.

- *Detail*
  Take whatever time is required to obtain all the intricate detail necessary to fully define each and every semantic term used in the detail facts and business dimensions.

During these initial interviews, don't even consider working for semantic consensus with other groups. Your mission at this time is strictly one of information gathering. Complete alignment of semantics across an organization requires massive amounts of political will and is rarely achieved. It will fall to the later integration and architecture efforts to target that goal.

Detail Facts One of the primary construction elements in the data mart architecture is the detail fact table of the star schema (star schema design is discussed in detail in Chapter 12). Because of its elemental nature, your user interviews must answer four key questions:

- *Metrics/content*
  The most fundamental question is simply, "What do you want to know about?" You need to determine the content of the detail fact table and the metrics required to support meaningful analysis of that content.

- *Level of atomic detail*
  This question comes down to: "What is the lowest level of detail you want to store and have access to?" The answer has huge ramifications on the amount of data you are going to store and the resulting response times for users. Make sure that the users truly require the level of detail that they are requesting. Have them

thoroughly discuss the business processes that require access to the detail. The result of this conversation will yield the primary key for the detail fact table. If the users require order line item detail, the key will be order number and order line number. If the users only require order header level detail, the key will be order number.

Make sure your users understand that if they settle for any level of aggregation in the detail fact table, they will never have future access to the lower levels of detail. It is much easier to later summarize from detail to improve performance than to rebuild five years of line item detail to support an overlooked business process.

- *Width of facts*
This line of questioning is trying to establish how wide the fact table will be, that is, how many fields will it carry. The basic question is, "How much do you need to know about this detailed transaction?" The fundamental elements of the sales transaction, for instance, are date, customer ID, product ID, quantity, and price. Most sales detail fact tables also carry additional fields such as discount applied, sales rep ID, cost, product group, and company. It is these additional fields that you are interested in during these conversations.

Many of these fields are related to the business dimensions and history tables detailed later in this chapter. Others are related to specific business processes that require that characteristics of each individual transaction be captured in detail and be available as part of the detail fact history. It is the latter category that you must identify.

- *Depth of fact history*
Detail fact tables can be thought of as having three dimensions. The width is set by the "how much" question. The height is determined by how many detailed transactions are produced by the OLTP system in a given day or snapshot time period. The depth is set by asking the users, "How long do you need to store this detail?"

The answer to this last question is the primary source of apoplexy in DBAs (Data Base Administrators) associated with data mart projects. They quiver at the thought of storing and managing two, five, or ten years of transaction detail data. Aside from these oftentimes unwarranted fears, there are very real performance and overhead implications of very deep detail fact user requirements. Thus you must investigate in detail the business processes that will be used against the historical detail. If you discover that it is a once-a-year process such as an annual strategic budget, moving the majority of detail history to near-line or off-line storage media may be appropriate.

The requirements for handling the "roll off" of history—that is, what to do with the oldest year's worth of history when you start a new year—must also be established. Do you throw it away, or archive it onto off-line or near-line media? Throwing the detail away is usually not a good strategy. Business users have a nasty habit of coming back later with a valid business need for things that you have just thrown away.

Business Dimensions The second elemental building block of the data warehouse architecture are the business dimensions of the star schema. You must answer three questions regarding the business dimensions during your discussions with the users:

- *Required dimensions*
  You simply need to determine what business dimensions are required for the subject areas contained within the data mart. Common sales and marketing business dimensions include time, customer, products, geography, and sales geography. Because business dimensions are shared across subject areas and data marts, it is important to communicate to your target users that the dimensions are standardized across the organization to the maximum extent possible.

- *Key level of dimensions*
  A prerequisite of successful data mart use is an intuitive understanding of the data resources in the system. A major part of this essential ease-of-use metric is simplicity of design of the business dimension tables. To be easy to use and understand, the dimension tables should consist of one row per fundamental subject or member of the dimension, that is, one row per customer in the customer table. Your goal in discussing this with the users is to confirm that the key or "one row per" level of the dimension tables conforms to their business rules and requirements.

- *Width of dimensions*
  You must determine how much information the users require in the business dimensions. Hierarchical information may be contained in the business dimension that is of no use to your target user group and may be excluded in their data mart. An example would be a product dimension that included product ID, product description, product group, product class, and product type. Your users may have no use for any product information beyond product description.

Dimension specific metrics are also commonly included in dimension tables. Examples include current product inventory and total product sales YTD (year to date). Your audience may require all of these or additional metrics to accommodate their business needs.

Aggregations Over time, your data mart users will concentrate their access and utilization on the aggregations or summary data sets that you provide. It is a great advantage to understand early in the process their requirements for summary data. You can expect that some of the summaries defined in this interview process will not be used as much as anticipated, and it is guaranteed that new summaries will be required and defined in the future. However, it is a huge boon to the initial utilization of the data mart system to have a set of summary tables prepared and deployed based on user input.

Your goals in the user interviews related to aggregations are:

- *Metrics*
  All summaries are simple combinations of metrics and business dimensions. The first step is to determine the metrics required, that is, units, dollars, and so on.

- *Dimensions*
  The second essential element is which business dimension needs to be combined with the metrics. For instance, a "sales by customer" summary combines the detail fact table's sales metrics of order amount and quantity with the customer dimension to produce a table containing total sales by customer.

- *Time slice*
  Most users are not particularly interested in all the metrics associated with a dimension since the beginning of time. They prefer that the summary be sliced up into discrete chunks of time, for example, month, quarter, or year. If the time slice is month, our prior example would yield total sales by customer by month, a much more usable data set.

- *Depth of time*
  The last defining characteristic of the summary table is how "deep" the table is going to be, or how far back in time do the users need to perform analysis or trending on these metrics with these dimensions. Many business metrics are based on current versus prior year measurements, so users commonly require a rolling two years or rolling 13 months in summary tables.

Multidimensional Aggregations   The combination of metrics with multiple business dimensions yields a multidimensional aggregation, sometimes called a data cube. For instance, a table that combined sales by territory by customer by product by month would use four business dimension tables: sales geography, customer, product, and time. This data structure would allow the user to examine and analyze sales by any of these dimensions. These multidimensional data structures form the underlying foundation of OLAP (On-Line Analytical Process) analysis tools. They may also be accessed by any Q&R (Query and Reporting)/MQE (Managed Query Environment) tool as well, assuming they reside in standard RDBMS (Relational Data Base Management System) tables. Multidimensional aggregations are extremely powerful and flexible data sets, and they are very popular with users, once they discover the possibilities inherent in their design.

Because these tables contain the intersections of multiple dimensions, they become very large, very fast. They present specific management challenges in terms of update, replication, and distribution. For these reasons, you must investigate closely the requirements for each dimension in each defined multidimensional aggregation.

Your goals for interviewing users are the same as for standard summary tables. You must define:

- Metrics
- Dimensions
- Time slice
- Depth of time/history

In addition, you must determine:

- *Frequency of update*
  How often will the users need this aggregation to be updated? Recalculating massive multidimensional data cubes can take more hours than you have available in your nightly batch/processing window. Weekly updates may be required due to this limitation.

- *Type of use*
  What will this data structure be used for? Will the users require the ability to perform both read and write operations, as in budgeting and forecasting? Will the users need to rapidly recalculate "what if" values within the data set? Is the problem set the users are addressing well bounded? Do the users require the ability to ask any multidimensional question they choose in an ad hoc manner?

All of these questions will help you to define the type of OLAP solution that is appropriate for their use. A read/write requirement and a well-bounded problem set suggest a dedicated MOLAP (Multidimensional On-Line Analytical Processing) data structure, probably within a proprietary MDDBMS (Multidimensional Data Base Management System), along with its update and scaleability challenges. An unbounded, ad hoc problem set requires a ROLAP (Relational On-Line Analytical Processing) solution and its attendant performance penalties.

All users will want to "slice 'n' dice" the multidimensional aggregation. Invest the time to fully understand the users' requirements in this area. LowLAP (Low-Level Analytical Processing) tools may provide sufficient capability for simple requirements. Moderate to advanced requirements will demand an industrial strength solution, along with their more challenging and resource-intensive implementations.

The multidimensional requirements of your users and the resulting tool choices will drive a large portion of the topology and infrastructure requirements of your data mart system. Invest the resources to understand the requirements early and fully. The last thing you need is a last-minute surprise requirement for a 75-gigabyte data cube that must be recalculated nightly.

History Tables   One of the primary values derived from the data warehouse architecture and its implementation in data marts is the availability of historical information. History is kept not only in transaction detail, but also in dedicated history tables.

History tables are used to capture the status of changing relationships in slowly changing dimensions, such as what sales rep is assigned to a customer. History tables may be composed of regular snapshots of an entire dimension data set, for example, snapshots may be made of a product dimension table at every month end to capture the current cost, selling price, and inventory levels. They also may comprise specific discrete elements, such as customer ID and sales rep ID, that are captured only when the relationship changes. A detailed discussion of history tables and slowly changing dimensions can be found in Chapter 12.

The goals for history tables in the user interview process are to establish what relationships need to be captured, how they need to be captured, and how long they need to be maintained. Common histories include: customer/sales rep, customer/territory, product/inventory, product/cost-price, product/product group-type.

Predefined Queries and Reports   At many sites, the user interview process begins and ends with this topic. It is a fatal error to limit your conversations with users to discussing what existing reports they use and what new ones they would like to see.

In this area, your goals are to fully understand the user's existing business requirements and how they are being met or not met by existing resources. You must also learn about potential future business requirements. Although no one has a crystal ball, you must have a clear picture of known and anticipated business developments that would impact decision support requirements. When the system is released, these predefined requirements must be met by easily accessed queries, reports, and analysis data sets that your team has created and prepared for use by the user community.

DSS (Decision Support System) Requirements   Known and anticipated requirements for end-user access tools must also be researched and documented. The user interview process is the primary means for determining business needs and mapping these needs into available technologies and solutions.

Your goals for this area are to determine what types of tools are required and the necessary features of each type of tool. At the end of this process, you should have a clear understanding if Q&R/MQE, MRE (Managed Reporting Environment), OLAP, EIS (Executive Information System), ADE (Application Development Environment), Data Mining, or Data Visualization tools are required in your data mart implementation. You should also have answers to the major criteria questions for the type of OLAP solution required, i.e., MOLAP, ROLAP, or LowLAP. (DSS tools are discussed in detail in Chapter 3.)

What to Ask

Your user interview process will expose you to a wide variety of people at various levels of the organization. Each person you speak with has valuable information for you to capture and add to the knowledge base of your project. Each role has a different perspective of your project and different expectations as to what it will deliver to them. Your mission as you interview these different people is to focus on capturing pertinent information from that role.

What to Ask Executives   Executives will be in a position to greatly assist or sabotage your data mart project. They have specific agendas, personally and professionally, and tend to view your project in terms of what impact it will have on that agenda. Package and position your data mart so that it will always appear to be a positive impact on the agenda of the person you are speaking with.

When working with this level, it is essential to know the political landscape prior to initiating discussions. Use whatever means necessary to obtain background information on the executives involved and their respective agendas before you interview anyone. It is vital to know who is allied with whom in the executive realm in order to successfully navigate these sometimes treacherous waters. Do not volunteer information lightly, or make casual off-hand comments, especially about other executives, past or current projects of this or other executives, or any other personal or professional relationship with executives. It is painfully easy to inadvertently offend, or worse yet, unintentionally create a permanent enemy.

Your primary goals when interviewing executives are to discover the high-level issues, challenges, initiatives, and business processes present in the organization, as well as to ascertain the present and future political environment. From these executives, you need to discover:

- *Mission of division/group*
  What is their mission and that of their organization?

- *Business processes*
  At the global level, what business processes are utilized by their organization.

- *High-visibility initiatives/programs*
  What initiatives or programs are these executives involved in? Corporatewide steering committees or standards bodies, quality initiatives, and so on are the types of things you are looking for. If possible, fit your data mart into the context of one of these programs, for example, "The data mart will improve speed to market, which is in line with the corporate 'Market Drivers 2000' program you are leading."

REALITY CHECK   As we saw in the previous section, in a pinch, you can design a data mart from the answers to six questions:

- What do you need to know about? (establishes subject area and sources)
- How much detail do you need? (establishes the lowest level of detail in the detail facts)
- How much history do you need? (establishes the depth of the fact table)
- How do you want to slice it? (establishes the dimensions)
- How do you want to analyze it? (establishes multidimensional aggregations)
- What changing relationships do you need to capture, track, and/or trend? (establishes history tables)

Keep this simple framework in mind, especially if you are working with one of the big consulting firms that tend to have multiple binders full of end-user interview requirements and methodologies. It is very easy to lose sight of your fundamental mission and this simple six-step route to the core requirements in the vast quantity of documentation they provide.

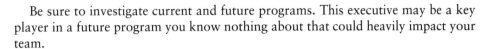

Be sure to investigate current and future programs. This executive may be a key player in a future program you know nothing about that could heavily impact your team.

- *Global issues/challenges*
Ask for the top five global issues and challenges that the organization is facing. Ask for the top three anticipated future challenges. Look for opportunities for current and future business drivers. This is an excellent opportunity to peek down the tracks toward future trains coming at you and your data mart team.

- *Relationships/partnerships*
What key relationships do these executives have with internal and external parties. Are they closely aligned with another division of the company? Do they work closely with other industry partners? Tread carefully here, but there are big opportunities for valuable nuggets. You are searching for current and future partnering opportunities. For instance, you may someday be tasked with integrating disparate incremental data marts into an enterprise data warehouse. At that point, you will need executives who have strong cross-functional and cross-organizational ties to drive political will across the enterprise.

- *Relationship with IS (Information Systems)*
How do these executives view the IS organization? Do they have a history of frustration or of success? The answers to these questions can color everything else you derive from your conversation.

- *Buy in for technology*
Do the executives believe in technological solutions? Do they understand the fundamental value of information? If they are Luddites, you can't expect much support for your efforts. Conversely, if they firmly believe the world will be saved by bits and bytes, you may have a solid source of support, along with an expectation management challenge. You must ensure that if they believe in technology, they clearly understand its limitations.

- *Hidden agendas*
They are very tough to ascertain in direct conversation, but hidden agendas are important to distill. Is one executive out to slay another for a key promotion? If that competitor is your primary sponsor, your data mart may become a convenient way to undermine the sponsor's career path. Is a particular executive fighting a guerrilla war to empower lower levels of decision making in the enterprise? You may have just found a very valuable ally.

- *Politics*
Perhaps the most important and pertinent arena of discussion with executives is one of politics. You need to determine through prior research or careful questions regarding roles where an executive ranks in the organization. It is vital that you determine how much political influence this person has. In short, is this executive a "player"?

You also need to find out who the executive's mentor is, if any, and whom that person is currently mentoring and has mentored in the past. Is this executive on the fast track? What is the growth path out of the executive's current position? Is this person headed up, down, or stuck in a holding pattern?

The answers to these questions provide the threads that make up the complex tapestry of corporate politics. Your project will live and die within that context. It is best to do whatever you can to discover and understand all aspects of that world.

What to Ask Managers The ever-dwindling ranks of middle management have suffered severe attrition as corporate hierarchies have flattened in recent years. Those who remain or have ascended to these roles are sharp players and experts at survival. They have the means and abilities to champion your data mart to the proper audiences to ensure ongoing support. Due to the size of commonly implemented data marts, they are also the primary customers of data mart initiatives.

Your goals in interviewing managers are to develop a very detailed understanding of the processes and functions the group is involved in, as well as an operational understanding of the political context of the manager.

You need to discover:

- *Mission of department/group*
  You must understand what the mission of the manager's group is, and how it fits into the context of the overall business.

- *Group/department business processes*
  What business processes are used by the group? These processes directly define the content and purpose of the data mart. Try to isolate the primary business process, and identify all secondary processes.

- *Group/department issues/challenges*
  Have the managers list the top five issues or challenges they face. Also have them list the top three future or anticipated issues and challenges. Your goal is to identify commonality with other groups for future use. In the short term, your data mart must be a direct solution to one of the top two challenges of each manager. If it is not, you are building the wrong solution for the wrong person.

- *Relationships/partnerships with other groups/departments*
  Do managers maintain close relationships or partnerships with other internal or external groups? You are looking for opportunities to build consensus and a group of allied managers with similar needs and challenges. Do managers have close relationships with external suppliers or vendors? You may be swimming against the current if they are allied closely with outside solution providers and you are building a competitive internal solution.

- *Major functional areas*
  What is the primary functional area that this group is involved with? Understand in detail the primary functional area, and identify all secondary functions. Your data

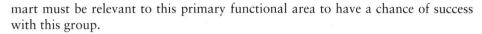

mart must be relevant to this primary functional area to have a chance of success with this group.

- *Current DSS processes*
Determine the current DSS systems used and the group resources committed to all DSS functions. The systems will identify likely sources for the data mart, and the resources used will be a good clue for potential pilot users and the level of available bandwidth you can expect from the users.

- *Required information*
What information is required by this group? What is used with current processes? What will be required to support future processes? Your data mart scope must meet these needs.

- *Available resources*
What group resources are available for the data mart project? How much can be dedicated to the project? How much split time? How much is available for input sessions and pilot? What level of utilization can you expect from this group? These answers define your reality in terms of user resources. You must adjust your time-lines and deliverables accordingly if limited group resources are available for the project.

- *History of IS relationship*
What history do managers have with the IS organization? Have past projects been successful or painful failures? Ask around the IS group prior to the interviews and find out what has happened in the past.

- *IS programs*
With what current IS programs are the managers involved? What is the project status? Research this prior to the interview so you can talk intelligently about the situation. Speak with the IS project manager and get an update on any open or unresolved issues.

- *Hidden agendas*
As with executives, it is very important to plumb the murky waters of hidden agendas among managers. Due to the high levels of internecine warfare common at this level of the organization, tread lightly, but endeavor to discover any pertinent information. Be especially careful of alliances and vendettas among managers. People at this level are especially hungry for anything that will help them stand out from their competition, and conversely help to undercut a potential rival. A high-visibility solution to a major business problem like a data mart attracts much attention in this environment.

- *Politics*
Dipping your toe into the Machiavellian waters of manager-level politics is always a risky proposition. Be careful to remain as neutral as possible, while seeking out the answers you need. You must establish the manager's ranking in the organization and level of influence. Are you dealing with a fast tracker, a "player"? Who is

mentoring this manager? To whom is the manager beholden? Is this person engaged in an active vendetta? Is the manager a potential assassin due to your political ties?

Attempt to keep your data mart project as politically neutral as possible at this level. It will inevitably become identified with a manager at some point, so try to pick and choose who that will be, to the extent that you can. Align yourself with someone who is attached to a stable executive who fits with your strategic plans. Avoid high-flying, risk-taking managers in early implementations, they may get shot down by a jealous rival before you have a chance to gain your own political viability with a successful roll-out.

What to Ask Users   The projected users of the data mart system are the litmus test for the interview process. If you do not extract the information needed to design and deliver a solution to their problems, your entire project will fail. You must invest as much time and resources as required to fully understand their mission, roles, challenges, and specific pain. If you do not solve their problems and relieve their pain, you will have expended your time and resources for nothing.

You must discover:

- *Mission*
  What is the mission of the users and their workgroup? How does it fit into the context of the department or group mission? How does it fit into the mission of the business? You are seeking to discover if the mission of the users is aligned with those higher in the hierarchical structure. Beware of user groups who are off on their own quixotic missions. You need your users' mission(s) to be tightly aligned with those of management.

- *Issues/challenges*
  What are the top five issues and challenges facing the users? What are the top three anticipated future challenges they will face? Your project must deliver a total solution to specific pain contained in the #1 challenge of the majority of your users. A defocused data mart that is solving the #4 and #5 problem for users will quickly become marginalized and wither on the vine as support and resources are diverted to higher priorities.

- *Business processes*
  With what business processes are the users directly involved? What OLTP systems? What DSS systems? These answers point directly to data sources and current capabilities you must match and exceed.

- *Required information*
  What information is required to support the current and future business processes of the users? Your project scope must be aligned with these answers.

- *Available time*
  What time can users personally commit to the data mart project? Pay close attention to these answers. If the entire group has no time to commit, you are in trouble.

Usually someone will be tasked with participating with no relief from existing duties, which leads to resentment of the project.

- *Utilization level*
  What utilization level do the users expect with the data mart system? Look for potential power users to cultivate, mentor, and support.

- *Technology rating*
  How comfortable are users with technology? Are they an information consumer or a knowledge worker? How much experience do they have with tools? Are they chomping at the bit to get at the information? Again, be on the lookout for potential pilot participants and power users.

- *User type (creator, knowledge worker, consumer)*
  If your entire user community is made up of information consumers, you are facing the prospect of being solely responsible for building and maintaining all of the information resources (queries, reports, analysis) for the entire group. Avoid these scenarios unless you are blessed with more resources than you know what to do with.

- *Hidden agendas*
  Like everyone else, users also have their share of hidden agendas. Watch out for users who are harboring ill will toward managers. If your sponsor happens to be the target of the resentment, the data mart could be the unwitting victim. A sustained "bad word of mouth" campaign against the data mart among the user community will dampen utilization and subsequent support and resources.

- *Politics*
  The politics of users is no less harsh and unforgiving than that of any other level. You need to find a way to ascertain the ranking of the users, especially where they fit on the influence scale. If they are upwardly mobile and under the wing of a powerful mentor, you need to be aware of that before involving them in the project.

  What is the growth path of the users? Are they headed anywhere, or marking time? This can be a prime source of frustration and resentment toward management, so seek to understand the context of the users' careers.

Evaluating and Consolidating Interviews

The interview process will give you a complete picture of the target market for your data mart. You will be conversant in the business processes, lexicon, challenges, personalities, and politics of the entire data mart user organization. To arrive at this complete picture, you need to consolidate and evaluate the interviews.

Mission   When consolidating the various mission statements, look for nonalignment up and down the chain. Any nonalignment of missions is a large red flag for the project. Seek to reaffirm the missions of the various roles if you discover nonalignment.

Business Processes   Map the business processes to OLTP systems and other data sources. Watch for discontinuity between the processes identified by the various levels. This signals a dysfunctional organization that is doing something other than what it thinks it is doing.

Challenges/Issues   The primary challenges and issues identified by each role must be congruous. Disparate challenges between the different layers signals an organization with severe communication and perception challenges.

The challenges and issues should be the same from top to the bottom of the group, and they represent the primary channel for political will and resulting sponsorship for the project. You must be able to identify clear, life-threatening pain in the challenges. Your data mart must completely relieve this pain.

You must also pay close attention to the future challenges. If disparity exists between the anticipated future challenges of various levels, you are dealing with an organization with different perceptions and visions of their future direction. This is a huge red flag.

Future challenges are also your key for planning for future growth and ongoing resource allocation. You can plan on growth anyway, but look for clues for major expansions in the future challenges. Think scaleability!

REALITY CHECK   Your data mart must solve the #1 problem for the users and the managers. You'll never get any utilization if it doesn't.

Relationships/Partners   This is a pretty simple job of looking for partners. Try to discover political alliances among the players and internal and external partners. Keep your eyes open for partners for your data mart effort, and for strategic partners for growth paths from your incremental data marts into an enterprise data warehouse.

External relationships can signal third-party data sources or external competition for information solutions. Be cautious around external partnerships, these can be wildcards.

Functional Areas   Functional areas should map closely to business processes and existing OLTP systems. Watch for outliers that do not belong to any clearly defined process or system. View any nonalignment of functional areas between the levels in the interviews with great alarm. Not knowing *why* they are doing something is fairly common, but not knowing *what* they are doing is a sign of an organization severely out of touch with itself and its reason for existence.

Current DSS Processes   Current DSS processes and systems serve as an excellent starting point for source system mapping and as an outstanding guide for existing information requirements.

The data mart must meet and exceed the existing system capabilities. It also must audit to all existing DSS resources. You will find many errors in existing systems, and your efforts to scrub and integrate the data will result in many deltas between what existing systems report and have reported for years, and what the data mart will deliver. It is absolutely essential to document these deltas, and clearly explain why the data mart answer is different and correct, *prior* to roll-out of the data mart system.

OLTP systems that are currently used for DSS purposes are the primary means to identify status table opportunities in the data mart design.

Required Information   Required information becomes your primary source for fundamental requirements. This is the area from which you will derive the subject area, fact tables, and business dimensions used in the data mart design. Pay very close attention to future requirements; they will drive much core system expansion in the future.

Available Time   You must achieve an unequivocal commitment for group resources from the very top of the organization. You must have user resources committed to the project in order to succeed. If definite user group resources are not dedicated to the project, do your best to defer or abandon the project.

Hidden Agendas   Carefully build an understanding of the intertwined hidden agendas across the user group. These represent both your greatest source of political land mines in the project and the source of your greatest political opportunities.

Map Politics   Build a map of the political relationships in the user community. Look for mentor chains from top executives down to the user groups, and exploit them if each member is stable and a data mart proponent. They are your quickest route to the top rungs of the executive ladder.

Steer a wide path around turf wars and vendettas. You will never profit by adding your project as another bargaining chip on the table.

Keep an eye open for potential assassins. Carefully analyze your sponsorship and target users in the political context. Is there anyone gunning for your sponsor or your target manager?

Audit IS Relationship   Check the history and current status of IS relations carefully. Do everything you can to avoid personality conflicts between the user community and team members. You will have enough challenges without playing referee between mortal enemies in both camps.

Business Rules   Align all business rules that you can and document disparities. Seek a second round with the user community to seek consensus if it is politically possible. If it is not possible to arrive at consensus alignment, prepare to carry duplicate data points and to publish and document the disparities in the meta data.

Semantics Semantics should also be aligned if at all possible. This is a hard nut to crack, but the data mart can provide an excellent forcing function to generate the necessary political will to correct long overdue disparities between user groups. Document the disparities and drive hard for consensus. If you cannot reach agreement, design duplicates into the data sets and document them in the meta data.

Facts Assuming that the mission, processes, and functions are reasonably aligned, the facts should be fairly homogenous across your target user audience. The most common differences are in the area of width (quantity of facts) and depth (length of history). If you find major disparities here, resist the urge to create multiple fact tables. Build the deepest one with the lowest level of detail initially and then closely monitor ongoing user requirements. The one exception to this rule is that it is very common to create a detail fact table containing all the historical detail and a separate detail fact table containing only current year and prior year data to facilitate quick response to the predominant prior year delta analysis that most users require.

Dimensions Dimension tables often harbor semantic differences between user groups, especially in the hierarchies found there. For instance, it is common for one user group to have product classes, whereas another uses product types. Your primary goal is to align the key level or "one row per what" of the required dimensions. You will also need to pay close attention to the requested metrics, lest disparate business rules be required to create similar metrics.

Aggregates Summary data sets offer the best opportunity for consolidation among various user groups. It is very common for a variety of user groups to share a multidimensional data set. Consolidation, however, may require that one user group use a summary data set that is aggregated to a lower level of detail than they require. For example, one group may only require sales by customer by quarter, but you may prefer they share a "sales by customer by month" table rather than support two individual tables. Your goal is to align common metrics and dimensions among the various summaries defined by the users and to look for consolidation opportunities.

During this process, you need to pay close attention to read/write requirements, bounded/unbounded problems sets, and required frequency of update.

History History tables also offer the opportunity to consolidate the requirements of multiple user groups into shared tables. Your goal is to align common relationships and metrics. Strive for consolidation in history tables because they tend to proliferate as users discover the ability to trend relationships over time.

Mobility On the personal and team front, you will want to take a step back and look at the overall project's opportunities to leverage visibility for yourself and the team. If you've got a good mentor chain and a solid business driver with high-level pain, it's a

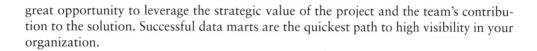

great opportunity to leverage the strategic value of the project and the team's contribution to the solution. Successful data marts are the quickest path to high visibility in your organization.

Survey User Needs Summary

Data marts are end-user driven systems. The survey process is your key to delivering a system that reflects the needs of your user community and will be a valued and essential part of their daily business processes. You cannot drop the ball on this step. You must invest the resources and time in user interviews required to shape a complete understanding of your user community and its needs.

6. Build Enterprise Data Mart Architecture

Your next task is to design an enterprise data mart architecture. This need not be a huge and lengthy task. Unfortunately it is too often an opportunity for the IS team to lose itself in analysis paralysis for months on end while crushing business problems go unanswered. Spend no more than three weeks on the effort for an incremental data mart strategy and no more than four weeks for an enterprise data warehouse/subset data mart strategy. Initially, it is optimum to spend as little as an afternoon on this effort. This forces the team to work at a very high level, and helps prevent "analysis paralysis."

Obviously you will not answer every question you will have or discover in this time frame. What is important is to stick to the primary goal of the enterprise data mart architecture, which is to identify:

* Enterprise subject areas
* Common dimensions
* Common metrics
* Common business rules
* Common source systems of record
* Common semantics

The enterprise data mart architecture will also establish the logically common meta data repository that can be shared by all information resources in the system, that is, data marts and the enterprise data warehouse.

Your goal is to establish the framework within which each data mart will be constructed. This allows multiple data marts to share common resources, such as extraction, scrubbing, and transformation processes. The establishment of common business rules and semantics will save you person-years of effort when the time comes to integrate disparate incremental data marts into a common virtual or physical enterprise data warehouse.

The construction of the enterprise data mart architecture is an ongoing process, which will not be complete after the initial one day to three weeks, nor after the completion of the first data mart. As you construct your initial and additional incremental data marts, you will flesh out the architecture.

Do not, under any circumstances, commence construction of incremental data marts without an enterprise data mart architecture in place. Nonarchitected incremental data marts are instantly transformed into LegaMarts that will be incredibly painful to integrate at a later date, and in the meantime be continuous sources of various versions of "the truth." An enterprise architecture is a prerequisite for success and can no more be deferred or omitted than meta data. You must perform this step.

An overview of the enterprise data mart architecture is presented in Chapter 3, and it is covered in detail in Chapters 11 and 12.

7. Pick Initial Subject Area

Because data marts are primarily single subject area entities, your hands may be tied in this regard. If you are constructing a divisional or functional data mart, however, you will most likely have multiple subject areas.

The selection of an initial subject area is driven by three variables:

- *Pain*
  You must start with an area that is in severe and visible pain that this subject area and data mart will relieve. The target user group must be able to clearly articulate the nature of the pain in business terms. Vague references such as "It'd sure be nice to have production volume numbers" won't cut it. "We'll go out of business without accurate and timely sales information" is what you need.

- *Politics*
  The users of the initial subject area must have the political influence to make a difference. It does no good to invest your initial efforts into delivering information to a marginal business process. In other words, it does no good to save a group's life if no one cares. Look for core functional groups with high visibility and high levels of influence in the organization.

- *Utilization*
  The target users of your initial subject area must use the data mart system. You cannot build momentum and ROI (Return On Investment) if users do not take advantage of the data mart system. Pick users with a solid track record of quick uptake of new technological solutions. Go for initial groups with a high ratio of knowledge workers.

You must balance these three factors to arrive at the best candidate for your initial efforts.

8. Research and Implement DW (Data Warehousing) / DM (Data Mart) Tools

At this point, you're ready to begin the sometimes painful process of researching, evaluating, and implementing tools to aid in the design, construction, operation, monitoring, maintenance, and management of your data mart system. This process can be extremely resource intensive if it is not managed effectively.

The most efficient approach is to assign or hire a dedicated resource to facilitate the vendor and tool evaluation process. An experienced, vendor neutral consultant provides excellent return on investment during this process. This vendor evaluation leader (VEL) is responsible for:

- *Facilitating vendor communication*
  The VEL performs the function of being the single point of contact for vendors into the organization. This allows vendors to hear a consistent, informed message instead of 20 conflicting versions of reality from a variety of team members. It also prevents the team from being endlessly distracted by vendor calls and messages.

- *Facilitating evaluation matrix*
  The VEL is responsible for the preparation and implementation of the vendor/tool evaluation matrix. The VEL must be experienced and knowledgeable in the field and very familiar with the various offerings of the vendors in the market and the requirements of a typical data mart implementation. The VEL surveys the site's requirements and prepares an evaluation matrix that combines the pertinent product performance features and capabilities along with weightings for each.

- *Leading and facilitating discussion at demos*
  The VEL is responsible for leading and facilitating discussion at demos and product evaluation team meetings. The VEL is responsible for ensuring that all pertinent points are covered and discussed, and that all applicable product performance and capability items are brought to light.

- *Monitoring and managing process at meetings/demos*
  The VEL is responsible for managing process at team evaluation meetings and demos. The VEL ensures that the team sticks to the required agenda, meets time lines, and accomplishes the required deliverables.

- *"Wheat from the chaff" research*
  The VEL is responsible for narrowing the potential vendor solutions down to the tools and products that are applicable to your particular site. The VEL uses the results of the site check (detailed in Chapter 4) to ensure that only products that meet the characteristics of the site and opportunity are considered. The VEL also narrows the field based on empirical metrics such as vendor financial reports, market share, and alliances/partnerships. Vendor strategic positioning such as thin client strategy and hybrid database capability is also aligned with the site's priorities. Vendors are also selected based on their technological road map, trade show presence, and trade publication reviews and reports.

Once the field has been narrowed to a manageable size, prepare a copy of the site check and a project status report card (PSRC) for distribution to the vendor short list. These documents inform the vendors of your site's characteristics and requirements in a very efficient manner. The alternative is to spend hours on the phone with each potential vendor, endlessly repeating the same information.

At this point, some vendors drop out due to incompatibilities and "poor fit" between their potential solutions and your opportunity. The remaining vendors coordinate with the VEL to schedule initial demos of the products in question. The VEL also coordinates the formation of a vendor evaluation team.

This vendor evaluation team should consist of a mix of technical and business participants. A team that is strictly technical can tend to be swayed by "gee whiz" bells and whistles, whereas a business-only audience can be blind to massive implementation issues hidden under the covers of a slick demo. User support and network infrastructure should also be represented on the team. Team members may rotate, but if you choose this route, you lose considerable validity in evaluation metrics. Continuity is important, so vendor evaluation team members must fully commit to the process.

This is where the importance of political will becomes particularly apparent. If there is little to no political will, team members will be distracted by other pressing issues. High-level political will and high-level pain ensures participation.

From the productivity standpoint, this is a very critical juncture in the project. Anyone who attends the vendor demos will lose a minimum of a half day with each vendor. When you get past the first round of demos, you will probably have at least one to two additional half day sessions with the finalists. Between all the various categories of tools involved in a data mart system, you can easily be dealing with over a dozen vendors. This quickly adds up to ten to fifteen person-days of "demo time" for each member of the evaluation team. This is a huge drain on resources, and if these evaluation team members are the same people you are relying on to be designing and building your system, you can face significant resource shortages.

The first round of demos are usually heavily front-loaded with marketing information about the vendor. This includes their financial performance, number of employees,

REALITY CHECK The data warehouse / data mart market is getting too crowded with fast-moving vendors to have a realistic chance at knowing enough to pick the winners from the losers. Don't attempt to pick a tool without hiring an analyst to give you an idea of who's a good fit for your site short and long term. If you've got a contract with the big players in this space (Meta Group, Gartner Group, Data Base Associates International, Patricia Seybold Group, Aberdeen Group), leverage it to tap the knowledge of their analysts. It's pretty hard to beat their resources.

Note that the big firms are also contracted by the vendors in this market. Just as you pay them to give you a read on the market, the vendors are paying the same analyst for services. You are relying on the analyst's personal integrity to give you a balanced view of all the vendors, even though the analyst may be profiting from one vendor and not from the other.

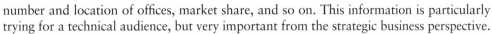

number and location of offices, market share, and so on. This information is particularly trying for a technical audience, but very important from the strategic business perspective.

Most of these tool vendors are relatively small companies; $15–80 million in annual revenues is fairly typical. Many of the companies with the best technology are start-up operations, with little to no track record, and little to go on other than some venture capital and the reputations of the management team. It is very important to weigh these factors when selecting a vendor partner. You certainly don't want to implement a tool from a company that will be gone tomorrow. Another grim possibility is that they may be purchased by another company that puts your product on the shelf and stops development and support. On the other hand, you don't want to buy an inferior solution merely because the vendor has dominant market share and a longer track record than a fast-rising start-up operation. These are difficult choices, and a very clear-cut answer rarely emerges.

The first-round demos are normally conducted by a two-person team consisting of a sales representative and a sales engineer (SE). The sales rep commonly handles the schmoozing and the vendor company hype portion of the meeting, with the SE handling the technical demonstration of the product. Presentation skills and technical expertise vary wildly among vendors, so don't expect a consistent level of presentation. Try to avoid basing a decision solely on the lack of expertise on the part of a bumbling SE, although it is hard to take a company seriously if it can't even train its own SE force.

First-round demos rarely satisfy the curiosity of the technical members of the team. They are generally surface demonstrations of the user interface and the latest flashy features of the products using very small, carefully crafted sample data sets. Be courteous, but don't believe much of what you see. Probe as hard as you can to get real answers to critical differentiating questions during this first-round session. Make sure there is a speaker phone in the room, and encourage the rep and SE to call support if needed to answer tough questions beyond their knowledge.

After the first round, the VEL will be deluged by calls from the sales reps inquiring as to how they did versus their competition. It is very important to rigidly maintain the VEL "single point of contact" during this phase. If not, you can throw productivity out the window because the vendors will shamelessly assault everyone from the CIO (Chief Information Officer) down to the night watchman in a effort to get the inside track on this opportunity.

The first-round demos, along with some follow-up questions by the VEL, will give the vendor evaluation team enough information to make some tool selections outright and get the other categories down to two or three finalists. The VEL handles the task of informing the vendors who were not selected that they will not have the chance to continue with this opportunity. The VEL should be very honest and forthright in informing the vendors who did not make the cut what the issues were in their nonselection. The only way a company can improve is to hear where and how it fell short in relation to its competition. Don't think you're doing anybody any favors by not being honest, brutally honest if required.

Once you're down to the finalists in the categories in which there was not an outright selection, it's time for the "bake off" and proof of concept implementation by the vendors. The prerequisites are that you prepare a sample data set and a suitable source, server, and client test environment for the vendors to share. The environment must be identical for each vendor. Given this environment, the vendor must provide sufficient SE and training resources to construct and implement a "proof of concept" environment with their tool(s). Any vendor who is unwilling to participate in this is obviously not willing to work hard for your business and should be eliminated from contention.

Give each vendor the same amount of time (a few days or a week) to get its implementation up and running under your watchful eye at your site, then have the team evaluate the process and the resulting environment. For end-user tools, such as a meta data browser, the vendor must provide sufficient training (at least half a day) to enable a sample set of pilot users to gain reasonable proficiency. The users should then spend a day or two working with the tools and your sample data. It is extremely important that no vendor be allowed to use its own sample data. You must prepare and provide a representative sample of your own, real data. Don't worry about spending a lot of time on scrubbing, transforming, and so on. Just pull a subset of the raw data out and do the minimum work necessary to make it usable during this testing process. Make sure to communicate to the testers that this is not representative of the production data mart and is being used for testing only.

At the end of this "proof of concept" process, you should have all the metrics you need to fully populate the vendor evaluation matrix. Do not make vendor selections without preparing and populating an evaluation matrix with a reasonable number of criteria. The selection of a vendor and tool may be a "no brainer" to you and the team, but you will need the evaluation matrix and its empirical justification for management reporting and to justify your choice in the face of shifting political winds or unexpected vendor/executive partnerships.

Some additional survival tips for the vendor/tool evaluation process include:

- *Develop a viable short list.*
  The optimum result of the "wheat from the chaff" process is a short list of the top players and one or two leading-edge contenders in each market segment.

- *Don't be swayed by personalities.*
  Probe a little bit and you'll probably find that the rep who's so anxious to find out your daughter's birthday has been with the vendor for less than a year. The SE has typically been with the firm less than 14 months. In short, it's a very small world, and these people are sales professionals who go where the opportunity is the greatest. Chances are, after the sale, you'll never see these people again. Your closest friend will be an 800 number for technical support.

- *It's a long-term relationship.*
  This is more than a short-term "dating" relationship. Think marriage. You'll be living with the database you choose until time eternal. An end-user tool is a three- to five-year relationship, easy. Combined with the previous point, this leads to the conclusion you should insist on a high-level relationship with the people who are really calling the shots at the vendor before you sign anything.

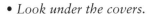

- *Look under the covers.*
  A lot of slick presentations and sexy UIs are layered on top of truly Neanderthal technology. Resist the urge to be seduced by glossy marketing and smooth, high zoot presentations and demos. Take a close look at what the tool is built in. Insist on a real proof of concept implementation in your environment with your data and your server and your network and your users. And remember, benchmarks are essentially meaningless until you conduct your own.

- *Read the map.*
  Don't buy into anything without a high-level presentation of the technological road map from the vendor. Go under NDA (Non-Disclosure Agreement) and see what they are planning for the future. Insist on budget numbers that are committed for research and development and quality assurance. If they can't articulate a concise vision, with demonstrated abilities and resources to deliver it, steer clear.

- *Walk the back aisles.*
  Keep your eyes open for the Next Big Thing. I've found some of today's biggest players in 10 by 10 booths at the fringes of yesterday's industry trade shows. You can pay a ton for market-share dominating, antiquated technology or buy a cheap seat on an E ticket ride by staying awake to the possibilities of new players with better solutions.

Once the tools have been selected, the design and implementation team will require time for training and to become proficient with the new tools and technologies. Don't forget to allocate sufficient training time when you are doing your project and resource planning. Don't expect your team members to go off to a three-day training class and come back rockin' and rollin' with a new tool. It will most likely take a few weeks to climb the learning curve and become reasonably productive, despite the claims you will hear from your vendors.

9. Design Target

You now have the information, knowledge, and tools in hand to begin the design of the target data mart environment. If you have selected an integrated DTEAMM (Design, Transformation, Extract, Access, Monitoring, and Management) environment, this capability will be an integral part of your world. The automatic population of the logically common meta data repository during this process is a very valuable part of what these tools bring to the marketplace. If you have separate tools for the design process, you will need to set up an export/import process for the transfer and population of the meta data from the design tool to the meta data repository.

The design process is basically mapping the user requirements into the data warehouse architecture and star schema elements. Your user interview process will have provided you with the essential user requirements, and you may choose to include additional data points, metrics, or aggregations if your experience suggests that this information will be of value or probably will be quickly requested soon after roll-out.

At the end of the design process, you should have a relational database schema that includes detail fact, business dimension, aggregation, history, and status tables. Samples of this design are included in Chapters 3 and 12.

10. Build Data Mapping, Extract, Transformation, and Scrub

Depending on the tools, suites, and environments you have selected, the mapping process may be an integral part of the design of the target data mart. In this approach, the mapping of source and target are part of the design process, along with all associated extract, transformation, and scrubbing operations.

Mapping consists of identifying a source field for a given target data mart data field. The source field is then assigned to populate one or more fields in the data mart. Most tools integrate the mapping, extract, and transformation aspects of the data mart design and population process into a common tool or integrated suite.

Extraction is simply the process of accessing the source database and extracting the data. In first-generation EMT (Extract, Mapping, and Transformation) tools, the extraction programs are COBOL or C programs that execute on the system that is hosting the database where the source data is stored. These programs generate flat files of the extracted data. These flat files are then transferred to the target data mart system where they are loaded into the target database.

In second-generation DTEAMM environments, the source data is extracted directly from the host database by an "engine" running on a server. The engine extracts the data via a live database connection, transforms it in memory, and inserts the result directly into the target data mart database via a live database connection. These two types of tools are discussed in Chapter 3, and we will examine these two models in more detail later in this chapter.

Transformation is the process of applying business and design rules to the source data prior to adding it to the target data mart. (See Figure 6.1.) This is done by modifying or combining the source data before it is loaded into the target data mart.

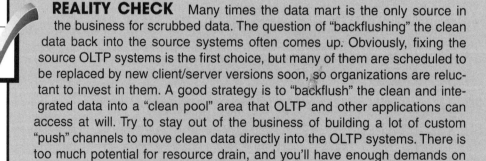

REALITY CHECK Many times the data mart is the only source in the business for scrubbed data. The question of "backflushing" the clean data back into the source systems often comes up. Obviously, fixing the source OLTP systems is the first choice, but many of them are scheduled to be replaced by new client/server versions soon, so organizations are reluctant to invest in them. A good strategy is to "backflush" the clean and integrated data into a "clean pool" area that OLTP and other applications can access at will. Try to stay out of the business of building a lot of custom "push" channels to move clean data directly into the OLTP systems. There is too much potential for resource drain, and you'll have enough demands on your team resources as it is.

"Scrubbing," or correcting flaws in the data, is commonly done as part of the transformation process.

Types of data transformation are:

- *Simple mapping*
Simple mapping is a straight transfer of a source field directly into the target database field. If you are blessed with relatively new source OLTP systems that generate clean data, you will be able to do a lot of straight mapping.

- *Concatenation*
Concatenation is the process of adding two or more fields together to form a single output field. It is common to combine multiple part keys from the source system to single field concatenated keys for the data mart.

- *Separation*
Separation is simply breaking up a single field into multiple target fields. This is commonly applied to source systems where multiple pieces of valuable information are kept in one field, such as a "comments" field. You can expect to generate very complicated parsing logic to break out customer and transaction attributes from "comments" or "description" fields.

- *Lookups*
Lookups are used to add descriptions and user-friendly terms to keys, codes, and other obscure data points. Common examples include adding product descriptions to product IDs, customer description to customer IDs, and transaction type

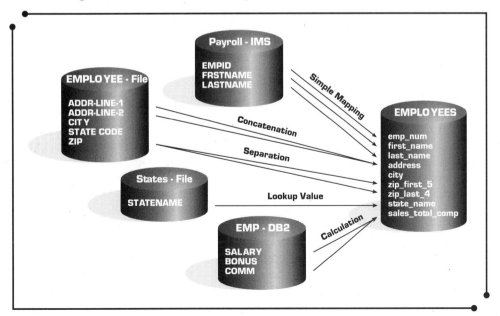

Figure 6.1 Types of transformation   *Source: Meta Group*

descriptions to type codes. Lookups are also extensively used in scrubbing operations to check for valid values, such as looking up zip codes to confirm they are correct for a given address.

* *Calculation*
Calculations are used to perform field-level aggregations, such as "YTD unit sales," and to provide summary information from multiple data points, such as "Order Amount" derived from "Unit Price" and "Quantity."

11. Build Aggregation, Replication, and Distribution

The next step is to build the aggregations, or summaries, you have defined based on your user input and research.

Aggregation

The fundamental law of aggregation in the data warehouse architecture is that aggregations must be derived only from facts and dimensions contained within the data mart system. This means that you create summaries only from detail fact tables and associated business dimension tables that exist in your data mart. You must never build an aggregation or summary that contains data from a source that is not represented in the data mart system (that is, build a summary that pulls in some data from an extraneous source) because the data mart system must audit to itself, lest it forfeit credibility. If you have a summary that is based on data that exist nowhere but in that aggregation table, your users have no way to establish the source or credibility of that data. The entire data mart system *must* "roll up," or audit to itself.

Although the construction and management of aggregations involves many factors, the primary things to consider are type and location. Type concerns the approach taken to incremental updates: drop the existing summary table and completely rebuild it or incrementally update the summary with new information. Location refers to the question of where are the aggregations going to be built.

A "drop/rebuild" strategy is much easier to implement, but it has huge processing overhead implications. You will find that summaries are extremely popular with your users. You will probably soon have dozens or scores of summary tables to monitor and manage. The prospect of rebuilding the majority of them every time you do incremental updates to the data mart is a daunting one. Drop/rebuild strategies work best in data marts with summaries that are primarily long time slices, such as month, quarter, or year. This allows you to only have to rebuild the summaries every month, quarter, or year end. If your summary tables are mostly short time slices, such as daily, you will want to implement an incremental aggregation approach.

Incremental aggregation requires you to examine all incremental updates to the data mart, both detail facts and business dimensions, and create new or updated rows for the summary tables where required. For instance, if a new customer is added to the customer dimension, rows must be created and inserted for this customer's activity in all summary tables that concern customers, even if all the metrics are zero. If incremental transactions are added to the detail fact table, all summaries that are within the current

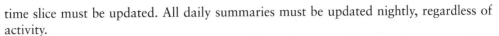

time slice must be updated. All daily summaries must be updated nightly, regardless of activity.

Beware of RDBMS performance in considering incremental aggregation approaches. Although it is fairly straightforward to append a set of transactions to the end of a detail fact table, it can take quite a while to scan a transaction log, compare it to the keys of dimension table, generate new summary rows from the metrics in the detail facts (which may require extensive history), and insert these into the summary table. If you are driven to an incremental, row-by-row update/insert strategy, the RI (Referential Integrity) and index update operations can add significant overhead to each transaction. If you are adding a large number of transactions nightly, it may be physically impossible to accomplish the required processing within the time available.

Aggregation location strategies vary, but there are three primary types: source based, target based, and engine based.

Source Based   Source-based aggregations are built on the source system and transferred as flat files (or native database tables if the source and target RDBMS systems are the same) to the target data mart. This approach is most popular in first-generation EMT sites and manual sites where the team is primarily working in COBOL on mainframe sources. In many cases, these teams have a minimum of UNIX and target RDBMS skills and are only capable of dealing with aggregation in the mainframe environment.

The upside to this approach is that the team is working in a familiar environment with familiar tools. It may also be easier to build and implement a manually constructed incremental aggregation capability.

The downside is that in order to ensure integrity between the two systems, you must build and maintain two identical environments. The source system must contain a perfect duplicate of the target data mart data detail fact and dimension tables used to build the aggregation. This implies that each update of the target data mart must be completed first, then confirmed, and mirrored back into the source system; otherwise, you risk losing synchronization between the two data "worlds." Your worst nightmare would be to have an incremental update of the detail on the data mart fail, and then proceed with a summary creation on the source system, transfer that to the data mart, and have a summary on the data mart that was not reflected in the data mart detail. Significant management overhead is implicit in this approach. Avoid this scenario if at all possible.

Another downside is the additional processing required on the source side. If it is a mainframe environment, you need to perform careful testing and benchmarking to confirm that it is possible to complete aggregation within the processing window available. Be sure to test using peak period load factors, that is, month, quarter, and year end.

Target Based   Target-based aggregations are built on the target data mart server system within the target database. They are popular at sites that have reasonable levels of target server OS (Operating System) and target database skills, but have not implemented a second-generation DTEAMM environment.

The simplest approach to target-based aggregations is to issue a series of SQL (Structured Query Language) statements to the RDBMS and have it perform the grouping and calculations operations necessary to build and populate the aggregation tables. This is viable in small data mart environments with limited summary table sizes. For larger data marts with millions of rows of detail, performance usually becomes an issue because it can easily take hours for the RDBMS to build a single summary table with this brute force approach.

The upside to a target-based location strategy is that the team never has to worry about the aggregation data sets accurately reflecting the detail and dimension tables in the data mart. Because they are directly derived from them, management overhead is very limited.

The downside is that unless the target data mart RDBMS natively supports incremental aggregation, and you want to use basic SQL to build the aggregations, you are forced into a drop/rebuild scenario where you must drop the summary tables and rebuild them every time you add incremental transactions or information to the data mart. If you manually construct an incremental aggregation capability, you may be limited to single row updates of the target summary table. This is a fairly slow process, so you must pay close attention to the processing time required. Again, careful testing is required, using peak load volumes.

Engine Based   At sites that have implemented second-generation DTEAMM environments a third option exists, engine-based aggregation. These tools offer the capability of performing aggregation operations during the extract and transformation process. This allows the "on the fly" creation and update of aggregations on the target data mart.

The upsides to this approach are speed and integration. The "transformation engine" design used in DTEAMM solutions allows the tools to internally leverage the multithreaded, parallel processing capabilities of the servers. This can yield much higher data throughput than first-generation EMT single-threaded approaches in optimum scenarios. The fact that the extraction, transformation, and population operations are integrated within one application allows the tool to optimize all processes and coordinate tasks. It is much simpler to accomplish incremental aggregation in this scenario than by any "brute force" method you can build manually.

The downside to the engine-based aggregation approach is native source support. DTEAMM solutions are optimized for relational sources. If your source data is in a nonrelational source or flat files, you may need to implement an additional gateway in order to directly access the data in its native environment or suffer the performance and management overhead penalty of working with flat file sources for the data.

Replication and Distribution

Replication and distribution are commonly required in full-featured data mart environments and are part and parcel for a subset data mart environment. Like the extract, transformation, and scrubbing processes, replication and distribution can be built by hand, performed by dedicated point solution tools, or be incorporated into a DTEAMM environment.

Fundamentally, replication and distribution is the process of copying and delivering the data to additional information resources in the enterprise. Like most things in the world of data warehousing and data marts, it is conceptually simple and fraught with many real world challenges.

Flat File The simplest form of replication and distribution is the export of the parent RDBMS table to a flat file, the transfer of the flat file to the target subset data mart destination, and the import and load of the flat file into the target subset data mart RDBMS. This "crude but effective" approach is easy to implement and has very low barriers to entry, and a short learning curve, but carries the penalty of significant management overhead.

Native RDBMS Services Next on the evolutionary scale are native RDBMS replication and distribution services. These work great if you have the same RDBMS on both the parent and the target subset data mart. Keep in mind that it's not enough to have the same *brand* of database; it usually requires that they be *exactly* the same, that is, the same version or release. RDBMS vendors are famous for crippling incompatibilities between different releases of their products, so don't make any assumptions in this regard until you actually see it work with your systems, your databases, and your data.

The native RDBMS solutions usually provide at a minimum unidirectional synchronization, meaning that you can set up a "master" database, and all the "copy" databases will automatically be updated to be exact duplicates. Because data marts are read-only DSS systems, we usually don't have to worry about the various flavors of bidirectional synchronization and advanced unidirectional synchronization such as TPC (Two Phase Commit). For this we can be thankful.

Dedicated Tools If you have a heterogeneous environment, or require more advanced scheduling or distribution capabilities than the native solutions can provide, you will require a dedicated database replication and distribution tool. These tools will provide much additional capability, but they require additional management as well. Key things to watch for are meta data population and architecture. Make sure that the tool supports the automatic population of your common meta data repository. It will be vital that both the technical and business users have access to current information about the update of the information resources. Also, pay close attention to the architecture of the tool. If it is based on a single server and that server is down, do all replication and distribution services stop? Does it use distributed services? If so, how do they communicate? Your goal is to acquire a tool that can deal elegantly with system problems, has redundant processes, and communicates and performs efficiently.

DTEAMM Services Enterprise DTEAMM solutions provide the capability to populate multiple targets with the output of an extraction and transformation process. By populating all required targets with data simultaneously, these tools can eliminate the need for external replication and distribution. The resulting reduction in management overhead is a big payoff to this approach.

12. Research and Implement User Tools

The process of researching, selecting, and implementing end-user tools is essentially the same as for data mart tools discussed in Section 8.

It is of the utmost importance when selecting these tools that the end-user community be primary participants in the process. Once the "wheat from the chaff" process is complete, it must be an end user–driven process to select the winner from the finalists. For this reason, you must never allow a vendor to become a finalist who has a significant technical flaw that would make that solution onerous to implement.

The finalists must construct a representative environment using your systems, your database, and your sample data. The end users must undergo sufficient training (usually at least a half day) to operate the tool in this environment. Then, the users must spend enough time with each of the finalist tools to vote on a winner.

During this process it is up to you and your team to explain the technical ramifications of each choice. MOLAP tools, for instance, may place significant overhead on the server during update operations. It is impossible for me to emphasize enough how important it is for you to clearly and repeatedly communicate any known limitations of the candidate tools. For example, you must tell the users about the limitations of LowLAP solutions. It is easy for users to become fixated on nifty features demonstrated with 1000 row sample data sets. Unless you demonstrate to them what happens with a real-world business question of 20,000 rows, they will never know that it is impossible for them to use those nifty features with large data sets. Hell hath no fury like a misled user.

Be sure to budget adequate time for the construction of an end-user environment with the winning tool of choice. It is impossible to attend a one-day administrator class and immediately design and build an effective and efficient end-user environment. Either plan for your end-user tool administrator to invest a few weeks to get up to speed or bring in a tool consultant to quickly build a complete environment while your administrator candidate assists and learns.

13. Test

Before rushing forward with a roll-out and release to your users, fully test the entire system. In the interests of your physical and mental health, do not begin roll-out until you simulate a month, quarter, and year-end process. The morning after your first month end is a very bad time to learn that your source system extract window is too short.

Do not, under any circumstances, implement your system without performing a complete disaster recovery scenario. It is unfortunately not a matter of *if*, but only a matter of *when*, your system will fail. When it does go down, you do not want to have your team on a research and discovery mission as to what is required to restore the data mart.

Ensure that the team takes the system entirely down and rebuilds it from the ground up. This does not mean turn the system power off and pretend to rebuild the components as the system loads. This does not mean sitting around a conference room and discussing the steps that your server and RDBMS consultants sketched out on a legal pad immediately prior to catching a plane. This means turning the server(s) off and:

- Reformatting the disk drives
- Reinstalling the operating system
- Reinstalling the database
- Reinstalling the tools
- Repopulating the data
- Re-creating the aggregations

This process needs to be repeated for each server in the system, and for each type of end-user platform. The resulting recovery process must be fully documented, down to the tiniest detail. The documentation must be easily available to the server administrators, the database administrators, and the end-user support team.

Stress test all of your user tools under every nightmare scenario you can cook up. Do massive result set downloads. Perform 100,000 row "what ifs." Create fifteen dimension cross tabs. Do everything you can to break the user environment in every way possible. Carefully document system performance metrics. You must know how long it takes to get real answers to real business questions using your real data prior to roll-out.

Team up with a target pilot user and spend a day beating on the system in every way possible. If you discover major performance issues, immediately address them prior to roll-out. When it comes time to put this system in the hands of the users, you must perform full disclosure on every known caveat and issue related to the system. The users must be aware of all known shortcomings of tools, data, and performance. Do not let them discover the bad news on their own.

14. Train

Training is the third most often neglected portion of data mart projects, after disaster recovery preparation and meta data population. Your technical and business users must be adequately trained on all tools used in the data mart system. Most importantly, they must be trained on your data, on your database, on your client platforms using your network. Training business users on sample data sets is almost entirely worthless.

It is important to prepare a training process and program prior to roll-out. This process should never allow a user to access the data prior to training. Untrained access leads to frustrated users and high support costs. The process also must address the overriding issue that the data mart is not a collection of individual tools and technologies, but an entire holistic system. The training of the data mart users must clearly communicate this fact and give them sufficient context to allow them to function effectively within it. The training must give them a reasonable amount of background knowledge on the technologies and topologies employed and a detailed understanding of the data in the data mart system, as well as practical "how to" instruction on the specific tools used.

Data mart system training issues are addressed in detail in Chapter 14.

15. Pilot

Before a wide scale roll-out across the entire user group, it is essential to do a small scale "pilot" implementation with a limited number of users. This allows the team to work the kinks out of the user roll-out process, including workstation setup, tool installation, middleware, networks, and user communication. A reasonable pilot will last two to four weeks and involve a dozen or less users.

The goals are to finalize the user implementation process, seek out flawed data, identify weaknesses in design, ensure meta data usability and viability, and isolate end-user tool strengths and weaknesses. You must develop and encourage extensive and open communication with the pilot user group to accomplish these goals.

Less than two weeks does not give you enough time to allow enough things to go wrong. It will usually take at least that long for busy users to find the time to work with the new system. A very short pilot of less than a week is of limited value, because your users are not likely to be able to provide valuable feedback in that time frame. Also, you must ensure that the pilot period extends over at least one major utilization period for the data mart system, for example, month end. You probably won't have the luxury of waiting for a quarter-end reporting period, but it is essential that you get some idea of what happens when real users are doing real work during a month-end process. If this is impossible, you must coordinate a simulation with the pilot user group in which the users perform their normal month-end or quarter-end reporting and analysis.

A very small group of pilot users, such as one or two, is also of limited value. These users are very unlikely to demonstrate the depth and breadth of usage that will give you a clear picture of what is to come from the entire user community. You may elect to start with one or two pilot users and then ramp up to a larger group. This is a good way to manage a situation where your user implementation processes are still evolving, but you are under extreme pressure to implement.

Strive for a representative sampling among your pilot users that will reflect your user community. A pure "power user" sampling in your pilot group will skew your results and mask challenges for neophytes. If you are doing a graduated ramp up of the number of pilot users, it is not a bad idea to start with a couple of power users who are conversant with technology. This helps you quickly develop a user implementation process around these users, while the fact they are on the system producing results helps take some of the "turn it on now" heat off of you and the team.

The pilot user group is your "opening night," and there is practically no way to recover from bad "word of mouth" from this initial audience. Because the stakes are so high, you must ensure that the system is as tested and ready as possible and that your pilot group has been carefully selected.

Often the political situation demands that your pilot include representatives from all user constituency groups. In this case, you will find it more difficult to work with a carefully selected group. The optimum scenario is being able to hand pick the cream of the user crop for your pilot program.

The factors to weigh in selecting pilot users are:

- *Motivation*

  You need very motivated participants in the pilot. Users who are not personally motivated to participate in the pilot, use the system, and provide feedback are of no value. You need people who are willing to put up with the inevitable hiccups of a new system, and this is impossible without personal motivation. Avoid people who are mandated to participate by managers and executives. They are very likely to be a source of deadly "word of mouth" in the face of the unavoidable frustrations of a pilot.

- *Utilization*

  The pilot users must guarantee that they will use the system, period. They must use all aspects of the system that are available and applicable to their business situation. You also need pilot users who will simply explore and push the system. In short, you need some trustworthy users who will try to break the system, but not spread bad reviews in response to successful efforts to push and exceed the envelope. Users who are mandated to participate will most likely not use the system, and if they do, will do so halfheartedly.

- *Proficiency*

  You need users who have or are willing to attain a reasonable level of proficiency with the tools and technologies involved with the system. They must be willing and able to attend the required training classes. "Killer" power users who are too busy to attend class, but assure that they will "figure it out as I go along" are of no value. You do not have the time or resources to babysit untrained users during the pilot.

- *Comfort*

  Pilot users must be comfortable with a system that may not be entirely stable. If your pilot is of value, it will uncover problems with the system. The pilot users must be accepting and understanding of this phenomenon. Avoid brittle personalities who don't deal well with flexible, changing situations.

- *Communication*

  The pilot users must have good communication skills and reasonable relationships with the development and implementation team. You are relying on the pilot users to provide immediate and well-balanced feedback on the processes and data mart system. Establish a process for feedback prior to the pilot program. You must not have a process where user feedback goes to a "black hole" e-mail address and the users never hear back from the team regarding the status of their discovery or request.

- *Bandwidth*

  The pilot users must have the bandwidth available to commit time and resources to the pilot project. High-level sponsorship and political will are particularly important. Pilot users must have their responsibilities adjusted to allow time not only to use the system, but also to participate in feedback sessions, pilot user group meetings, mentoring sessions, and to wait out system down time.

- *Politics*

  Your pilot user group can provide invaluable and irreplaceable public relations for your data mart project. Seek out pilot users who are well connected politically and exert influence over decision makers. At the time of pilot and as roll-out nears, you will be under extreme pressure to demonstrate ROI (Return On Investment) for the data mart. A few well-placed glowing reviews from your pilot users can go a long ways to relieving the anxieties of management and provide enough breathing room for you and the team to implement the data mart system without the suffocating pressure to demonstrate ROI.

A successful pilot program results in a fully developed and tested user implementation and change request process; a complete testing of the data mart system's capabilities and resources; the identification and correction of a number of data, process, and system problems; and a solid core of enthusiastic, experienced data mart users ready to lead the charge of full user community roll-out.

16. Deploy

After taking whatever time is required to correct the problems identified in the pilot process, you will be ready for full-scale deployment.

Do not attempt to do a full-scale user deployment prior to:

- Performing a full-scale disaster recovery test
- Correcting known problems in the data mart data, processes, and systems
- Documenting and communicating all known caveats or flaws in data or tools
- Documenting and communicating all deltas between the data mart and prior reporting and DSS systems
- Developing and testing user change request processes
- Ensuring adequate training, installation, infrastructure, and user support resources
- Preparing site-specific "user guides," documentation, and "cook books"
- Testing, testing, and retesting the technological infrastructure, especially replication, distribution, and wide and local area networks. Make sure you test month-end, quarter-end, and year-end scenarios.

Under no circumstances allow users to have access to the system prior to receiving training. The resulting frustration and "bad press" will kill you if the endless support requirements don't first. It is essential that users attend a training class that teaches them the entire system, including the data and techniques, not just how to use a tool on a sample data set. Only upon completion of this training should users receive passwords and access to the system. A successful deployment requires a process as described in detail in the training section in Chapter 14.

It is wise to conduct a staged deployment, in which groups of users are trained and enabled. The system is then monitored to ensure that the technological and user support resources and systems are adequate to support the new group. Only after support requirements have dropped to levels that will allow additional users should new user groups be brought on line.

Keep a close eye on system response times as the user community grows. Remember the watchword of successful data marts "scaleability, scaleability, scaleability." This is when the time and effort spent on architecture and system design based on scaleability will pay off. You may discover that you need to quickly add RAM (Random Access Memory) to your server to increase cache space. You may require additional I/O (Input/Output) channels as the system chokes on the additional DASD (Direct Access Storage Device) read/write requests. You may require additional WAN (Wide Area Network) bandwidth to remote user groups. These are all common occurrences as the system requirements change to reflect an actual deployment to real users. Remain flexible and focused on growth and scaleability. Accept no vendor solutions that back you into a corner and do not allow continued growth.

17. Use

The ongoing utilization of the system by the entire user community will bring you into the realm of full production, and the evolution of the data mart into a mission critical system. This phase of the project requires:

- *Ongoing communication*
  The team must maintain a very high rate and state of communication among management, the user community, and the development and support organizations. Success stories must be sought out, documented, and publicized. Mentors must make regular rounds among the user community to share techniques and encourage utilization, skill, and confidence growth. User groups must be formed, meetings coordinated, topics developed, and information delivered. User change requests and problem reports must be documented, responded to, implemented, and delivered. E-mail and voice mail distribution lists must be created and maintained. Tips, tricks, and suggestions must be collected and disseminated. Management must be kept up to date on the progress, performance, and impact of the data mart system. Vendors must be informed of bugs and problems. Tool version, problem, update, and feature information must be disseminated. New users and team members must be brought up to speed on the data mart system and its business context as well as the user community and its purpose and utilization. Nothing happens without communication, and the project will soon fail if these elements and examples of communication are not present in your implementation.

- *User-focused support and development team*
  The user support and data mart development team must be entirely user focused. They must have an end-user orientation and outlook. They must be sympathetic to and understanding of the challenges of the end-user experience. The data mart is an entirely end user–driven system, existing only to serve the current and ongoing needs of the end-user community. The support and development teams must understand this, be comfortable with this, and be happy to live and work in this context.

- *Ongoing change and growth*
  The data mart forms the interface between the ever-changing needs of the business and the ever-changing information resources. This creates a very dynamic, fast-moving environment. You must retain, cultivate, and build a team that is comfortable in this environment. You must also develop and manage expectations with management that reflect this state of ever-changing needs, requirements, and growth.

- *Mission critical mindset*
  The data mart is usually the first exposure the user community has ever had to integrated, scrubbed, and historical data in an easily accessible, user-oriented system. They will first audit the data mart against existing reporting and DSS systems. If you have properly documented the deltas between your system and these prior resources, the users will quickly adopt the data mart as the "system of record" for decision support.

  Answers provided by the data mart percolate to the top of the organization in very short order. Don't be surprised if major tactical and strategic business decisions are being made on data mart information within weeks after the audit process is complete. Due to this immediate and very high level use, the data mart almost instantly becomes "mission critical" to the enterprise. Day-to-day tactical and long-term strategic decisions are based on the data mart's information and resources. If the data mart is not available, decisions are not available. In today's fast-paced business environment, this is an untenable position, with the severest of consequences.

  The data mart development, support, and implementation teams must have a very clear "mission critical" mindset. The data mart must be viewed as being as important as any OLTP system in the business. Anything short of this leads to a variety of small and large crippling compromises that will eventually cause the system to fail and consequently spell the doom of those caught in the cross-hairs of enraged management and users.

- *"Service business" mindset*
  Data marts are not a data business, nor a technology business, nor a decision support business. Data marts are a service business. They exist solely to serve the current and future needs of the user community. Your data mart cannot survive unless and until the entire data mart team understands this fact. It is a difficult but necessary cultural shift for your team to make if you hope to be successful not only in creating data marts, but also in sustaining them over time.

- *Customer satisfaction metrics*
  The mere statement of a "service business" mandate is meaningless unless the team is measured and rewarded for specific customer satisfaction metrics. Metrics such as change request turnaround time, hold time, frequency of communication, meta data population and maintenance, query response time, system up time, tool and system update, and so on must become the basis of performance evaluation.

Ongoing, effective use of the data mart system is the true measure of success. It is painfully easy to pop out a data set and call it a data mart. It is challenging and rewarding to build and implement architected data mart systems that are valuable, flexible, supported, user oriented, and relied on as a critical and irreplaceable part of the business decision-making process.

18. Monitor

To meet the needs of your users, anticipate needs, optimize performance, and avoid potential bottlenecks and performance disasters, you must have robust monitoring capabilities for your data mart system. All of your monitoring tools must provide automatic population of the meta data repository, and the ability to alert the data mart team to an out-of-range parameter or other anomaly.

Monitoring includes:

- *EMT processes*
  All extract, mapping, and transformation processes must be monitored. Both the technical and business users must know immediately if an extract process failed to deliver incremental data to the data mart system.

- *Loads*
  The load of the target data mart database must be monitored and recorded. It is vital that business users be able to quickly ascertain via the meta data when the last update was made of the information they are accessing.

- *Indexes*
  Index construction and updates must be monitored. The technical team must be alerted if an index fails to update or be built/rebuilt after a load or update. Users can experience ruinous performance degradation if indexes are not available for use. The resulting load on the server can essentially bring down the entire data mart system.

- *Aggregations*
  The creation and/or update of aggregations must be monitored and recorded in the meta data. In one of the nightmare scenarios that data mart managers fear most, the detail facts and dimensions are updated, but the aggregations do not successfully incorporate the new information. Users can then base far-reaching business decisions on incomplete or out-of-date information, with disastrous results for all concerned.

- *Dedicated data sets*
  Some end-user analysis tools require dedicated proprietary data sets, most commonly MOLAP tools using multidimensional data cubes. These data sets can incorporate many business dimensions and multiple metrics, resulting in very long processing jobs to create or update the data cube. If this process does not successfully complete, users can be left with a partially populated or corrupt data structure. The construction and/or update of these proprietary data sets must be closely

monitored, with appropriate alarms and notification mechanisms in place to alert the data mart team and users.

- *Index utilization*
  In addition to monitoring the ongoing extraction, transformation, and loading of the data mart, you must monitor the usage of the system. First and foremost you are going to need to monitor the use of your existing database indexes. If they are not being used, you will want to remove them to free up some space. You will also need to closely monitor the query activity to spot opportunities for additional indexes that would positively impact query response time and server load.

- *Ad hoc aggregation*
  One of the best places to look for opportunities to drastically reduce server load and improve user response time is in the elimination of the repeated creation of ad hoc aggregations. By watching for users who are rolling up the same summary information every day or week, you can find perfect candidates for precreated aggregations to add to the nightly, weekly, or monthly update jobs. If you monitor nothing else, monitor this.

- *Resource utilization*
  You need to monitor the utilization level of all information resources in the data mart system. You will inevitably identify summaries, reports, analyses, histories, status tables, and even business dimensions and fact tables that the user community is not using. Summaries especially suffer from the ever-changing needs of the business. The area of greatest change will be in the aggregation or summary tables, with some falling into disuse. Reports and analyses are also common victims of changing requirements. Once identified, these resources become candidates for elimination, with resulting savings in management and monitoring resources.

  Conversely you will find resources that are used very heavily. Careful analysis may reveal opportunities for system optimization, server load reduction, and improved response time. For instance, a detail table may be used very heavily for current and prior year information, while the preceding three years of detail are used very little. In this case, everyone profits handsomely by the creation of a CYPY (Current Year and Prior Year) detail table and a separate, five-year detail table. Or, you may choose to simply partition the detail by year or year/month to reflect this type of activity and improve performance. The server will work much less and the users will experience much faster response times.

19. Maintain

Every data mart system requires a high level of ongoing maintenance. This is a common trap for unwary organizations and project managers. They assume that a data mart will be similar to a typical OLTP application and that once delivered, it will require low levels of resources to handle the occasional maintenance task. In reality, the data mart, due to its highly volatile nature, requires a very high level of resources for ongoing maintenance and modification.

There will be constant changes in the data sources, in the business environment driving requirements, and in the underlying tools and technologies. These three drivers combine to form a very demanding ongoing maintenance challenge. In your project and resource planning, you need to assume that the maintenance of the data mart will require 40–60% of the resources required to design and build it. If you start with this percentage, you will have adequate resources to respond to maintenance requirements in the first year of the data mart's implementation. Only through actual use and maintenance will you be able to determine the actual resources required for your unique site and data mart system(s).

The maintenance process requires a dedicated process and set of resources to handle changes coming from all three directions: source, business, and technology. Business driven changes, especially, must have a clear and direct path to implementation. Changes in the business take you back to step one of the project flow, to begin another iteration loop through the project flow.

Project Flow Implementation

The 19 steps of the project flow outlined here will provide a basis for a fundamental methodology if you do not develop or obtain a more detailed one for your data mart project. By ensuring that each of these steps are adequately addressed, you will take a large step toward delivering a successful and sustainable data mart system.

Process Flow

Steps nine through twelve of the project flow require a detailed understanding of the process and data flow of a data mart environment.

The subset data mart process shows the relationship of each process involved in the design and implementation of a subset data mart. (See Figure 6.2.) In this case, the extraction, transformation, and initial load processes are performed against the parent enterprise data warehouse. Subset data mart data sets are subsequently replicated from the parent data warehouse and distributed to the appropriate target subset data mart servers.

In the case of an incremental data mart, the extraction, transformation, and load processes are performed against the target data mart directly. (See Figure 6.3.) It is common for subset data marts to be subsequently extracted from this "parent" data mart.

The importance of an enterprise data mart architecture becomes clear in this scenario, as the implications of duplicating identical extraction, integration, transformation, and scrubbing process for each target data mart are clear. Not only does a non-architected approach waste processing resources, the ongoing maintenance of duplicate processes for each data mart is a tremendous drain on resources.

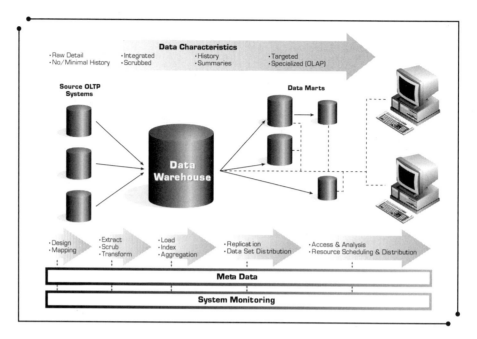

Figure 6.2   Subset data mart process flow

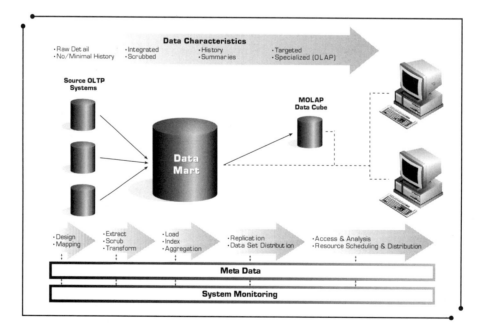

Figure 6.3   Incremental data mart process flow

Integration of Tools

Each step along the process flow requires specific tools and technologies to implement. A wide variety of existing and new tools and technologies have been modified or developed to answer the needs of the data warehouse and data mart marketplace. (See Figure 6.4.)

The primary choice in establishing a strategy for tools and technologies related to the data mart process is one of point solutions or integrated suites and environments. An enterprise-scale DTEAMM environment can provide an inclusive solution from the beginning to the end of your project. A BOB (Best Of Breed) approach that uses a variety of point solutions from various vendors can be more robust in specific areas, such as source support, but present very significant challenges for tool integration and meta data sharing and support.

Data Flow

Depending on the choices made in implementing tools, you will have two primary types of data flow in the data mart system: flat file model and transformation engine model.

Flat File Model

If you choose to build the system manually, or implement a first-generation EMT (Extract, Mapping, and Transformation) tool, you will be dealing with a flat file model for

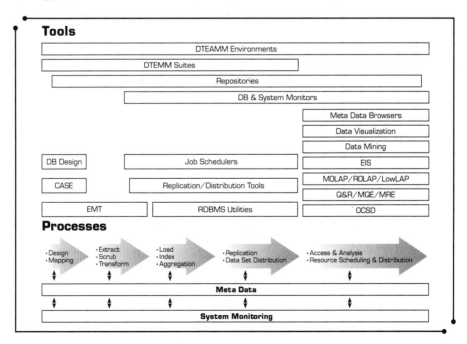

Figure 6.4 Data mart process and related tools

data flow. (See Figure 6.5.) This model uses a series of discrete programs running on a variety of platforms to perform the required processes necessary to extract, transform, and deliver the data to the data mart system.

The upsides for this model are:

- *Familiar skill set*
  These tools and methods use skill sets and tools that are familiar to development staffs, particularly in mainframe-oriented implementations that require extensive COBOL skills and have low levels of client/server expertise.

- *Familiar management methods*
  Because this model is very similar to other extractions done by the organization to support prior DSS systems, the processes, time lines, resource requirements, and so on are familiar and comfortable for IS management and team members.

- *Supports complex rules*
  Because a manual or first-generation EMT code generator approach requires manual coding for complex transformations and mappings, these complex problems present no special challenges or limitations.

- *Native support for MF (mainframe) file formats*
  First-generation EMT tools have extensive support for mainframe file formats. Shops that choose to develop their systems manually usually already have gateways or mechanisms in place to access and/or extract the mainframe-based data.

- *Clear process ownership boundaries*
  The flat file model is very conducive to drawing distinct lines in the sand between organizations and departments. There are clear breakpoints where flat files can be handed off between groups, for instance, from mainframe developers to data mart server database administrators.

The downsides for the flat file model are:

- *High learning curves*
  Historically some of the first-generation EMT tools have had a high and long learning curve. These robust but complex tools generally do not yield quick results.

- *Product capabilities/performance*
  Early implementations of the tools in this category had significant gaps in capabilities and performance limitations. Recent versions have mitigated these issues somewhat, but lingering challenges remain.

- *Cultural shift*
  Like CASE (Computer Aided Software Engineering) tools, these EMT tools require a cultural shift in the organization. Due to the nature of these code generator tools, all work, no matter how trivial, must be done via the tool and its UI or else the meta data chain is broken. This is very frustrating for native COBOL and C programmers, who usually consider their code to be superior to that of the output of the tools. If the use of the tool is mandated from above, resentment and misuse can result.

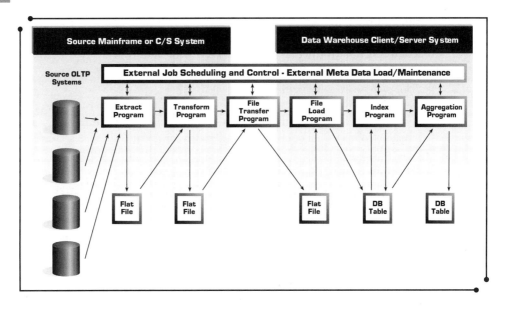

Figure 6.5 First-generation EMT data flow

- *Long implementation and maintenance cycles*
  Because of the requirement to regenerate the source code, recompile, and redistribute the program segments for any and all changes to the system, maintenance cycles can be long and cumbersome. The required process mandates the coordination of many roles and several functions, which represent significant investment in resources and time.

- *High price*
  Early implementations in the EMT tool segment were extremely expensive, with typical implementations ranging from $250–400,000. This is well out of range for many, if not most, data mart implementations. Recently, the majority of first-generation vendors have delivered data mart–specific packages and bundles in the $50–150,000 range. You can expect continued price pressure in this segment to drive prices for a viable solution below $25,000. It is not known if the first-generation EMT tool vendors can survive at these price points.

- *Point solution*
  EMT tools are point solutions to only a part of the data mart system challenge. A sizable array of products from different vendors must be married to these tools to create and maintain a viable system.

- *Spotty meta data support and integration*
  Support for meta data with this model is very spotty as you move across the data mart process. If you are constructing your system manually, it will be up to you to automate the population and maintenance of the common meta data repository.

Some of the point solution tools in this model use their own proprietary meta data repository, which doesn't synchronize with other vendors or your common meta data repository. Often these proprietary meta data repositories are not of a universally open, logically common, or fully extensible design.

- *Tool and process integration*
  The flat file model requires the integration of a wide array of products from a variety of vendors. Although a variety of two-player and three-player marketing alliances promise interoperability, the reality of getting these disparate tools to play well together remains a very challenging and frustrating experience.

- *High management overhead*
  The inherent nature of the flat file model guarantees a very large number of code segments, programs, scheduling jobs, tools, vendors, roles, functions, and processes to coordinate and manage, now and forever. This factor is often minimized in the initial stages of design and construction, but it can come back to haunt unsuspecting organizations.

- *Single-threaded execution*
  Manually produced code and that generated by flat file model tools are almost exclusively single threaded. The resulting programs cannot perform internally multi-threaded parallel or coordinated operations. Although it is possible to manually manage and execute multiple single-threaded programs simultaneously, this still leaves the majority of the power of parallel server technology untapped, thus limiting scaleability.

Transformation Engine Model

If you have chosen to implement a DTEAMM environment, you will have the opportunity to leverage a transformation engine data flow model. (See Figure 6.6.) This approach minimizes I/O activity to storage media and interacts directly with source and target databases.

The upsides to this model are:

- *Suite/integrated solution*
  Because the products combine the entire data mart process within one suite of tools or environment, you gain tremendous savings in effort and overhead associated with integrating multiple tools from different vendors. The elements of the products all naturally work together and integrate smoothly. Management overhead is reduced by several orders of magnitude.

- *Lower cost*
  These tools start at a price point that is a fraction of the cost of traditional EMT tools. Price points of $25–100,000 are common, and continuing price pressure will drop these in the future.

- *Consistent UI*
  Because each function in the tool is part of the same environment from the same vendor, users experience a consistent look and feel across the entire data mart

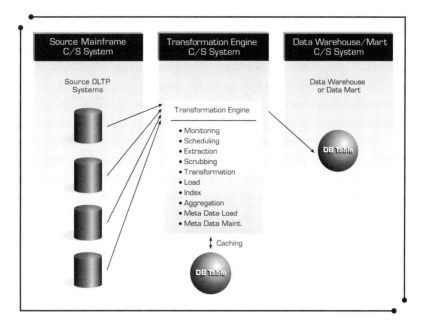

Figure 6.6   Second-generation DTEAMM tool data flow

process. This means a short and quick learning curve, and none of the confusion and challenges inherent with multiple tools from multiple vendors.

• *Quick implementation*
The consistent UI and short learning curves add up to very quick implementations of these tools. It is not uncommon for teams to be effective within two to three weeks.

• *Distributed processes*
Transformation engine–based products are built to function in a client server environment. This architecture allows these tools to break apart their functionality and locate various portions of their processing on multiple physical devices. For instance, you can have one server that performs the transformations while another concentrates on extraction.

• *Integrated meta data repositories*
Perhaps the greatest advantage of the transformation engine model approach is the inherent integrated meta data repository of this design. All elements of the data mart process, from beginning to end, share and leverage the same meta data repository. This ensures that all elements of the process, from design to monitoring, can leverage information from previous or subsequent elements.

• *Multithreaded execution*
Because these DTEAMM systems are built to leverage parallel technology, they make full use of multithreaded, coordinated execution. They can perform internally

managed simultaneous extraction, transformation, and loading operations. They offer tremendous potential performance advantages compared to serial execution of a flat file model and tremendous management advantages compared to attempting to coordinate parallel execution of single-threaded dependent applications of a flat file model.

- *High throughput*
Because of the distributed and parallel design of these systems, they can provide much higher data throughput rates than flat file models. Although no industry benchmarks currently exist to allow true "apples to apples" comparison, DTEAMM tools can reach sustained throughput rates many times greater than flat file models in optimum scenarios.

- *Dynamic granular changes*
Because there is no code to regenerate, recompile, and distribute, incremental changes are much faster and easier to implement than in a flat file model. Designers and implementers can make quick changes to the DTEAMM system that are instantly reflected in the system's output.

The downsides to the transformation engine model are:

- *Lower on maturity scale*
Because DTEAMM tools are newer to the market, they are lower on the technological maturity scale than first-generation tools. This means younger companies, shorter track records, and in some cases, incomplete feature sets.

- *Fewer natively supported sources*
DTEAMM tools tend to be very RDBMS oriented. Their support for nonrelational data is spotty and usually requires either a third-party gateway to directly access the nonrelational data sources or the export of the data to flat files, negating a portion of their speed, throughput, and object management advantages.

- *Fewer supported targets*
Because of their youth in the marketplace, there are fewer natively supported targets for the DTEAMM tools at this time. This is primarily a concern for those sites with non–market leading RDBMS products. All leading products are supported natively.

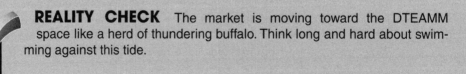

REALITY CHECK The market is moving toward the DTEAMM space like a herd of thundering buffalo. Think long and hard about swimming against this tide.

Summary

The project flow described in this chapter forms the foundation of your data mart project. Its elements will be executed each time an iteration loop is performed for data mart construction, modification, and growth. Knowledge of and successful execution of the nineteen steps of the project flow will help to ensure your data mart project's success, regardless of type.

A variety of tools and technologies can be employed in the core functionalities of the EMT process. The two most popular models are the flat file model and the transformation engine model. Although each has its unique strengths, the transformation engine model is a very powerful and cost-effective approach for data mart system design, creation, and maintenance.

Understanding and Implementing Meta Data

The most ballyhooed yet consistently neglected element in the brief history of data warehouses and data marts is most certainly meta data. Everyone talks about it and respected sources from all sides assure us that it is absolutely required for success, yet actual implementations are less than common. Those sites that actually do implement meta data usually end up with a more scaled back application of the meta data concept than they expected during the planning stages of their projects. What are the reasons for these dichotomies? What exactly is meta data? How much do you need? How do you use it?

Meta Data Description

Card Catalog

Meta data is information about the data that is contained in the data mart, and the environment that makes up the data mart environment and system. Oftentimes, a comparison to a library's card catalog is made when explaining meta data. Although this is accurate for a small subset of meta data's potential functions, it falls well short of the full implications and capabilities of a valuable and leverageable meta data implementation.

To continue the library analogy, a meta data source for a library would contain not only the card catalog listing the available content information (titles, authors, subjects), but also a variety of information about the library itself and its operations. This information would include organizational/social information (address, phone, e-mail address), structural information (architect, construction materials, infrastructure capacities such as size of electrical entrance and water feeds and drains), management information (manager, librarians, board of directors, maintenance personnel), scheduling information (hours of operation, delivery schedules of books and periodicals, availability notification such as children's reading room sessions), contact information for all processes and personnel (phone extensions, pager numbers, cell phone numbers), and technical information for all equipment and assets (model and serial numbers, installation dates, configurations, options). As you can see, the description of meta data as simply the card catalog falls well short of the potential and realities of what meta data encompasses.

If we transfer these meta data examples to a data mart implementation, we would see meta data examples along the following lines:

- Organizational
  - Data mart owner (department, division, function)
  - Owner location (physical address, location)
- Structural
  - System designer
  - Physical topology (device locations, capacities)
- Management Information
  - System owner
  - Process owners
  - Data owners
- Scheduling Information
  - Extract/transform/load schedules
  - Table/field frequency of update
  - Backup schedules
- Contact Information
  - Phone extensions
  - Help line numbers
  - Beeper numbers
  - E-mail addresses
- Technical Information
  - Server model number
  - Server configuration

Fully designed and implemented meta data for a data mart resource includes many more elements from each of these categories, as we shall see in detail later in this chapter.

Why Do You Need Meta Data?

Every successful and sustainable data mart implementation requires meta data that is easily accessible (one click away), understandable (uses appropriate terminology for the target audience), and leverageable (can be populated and utilized by the full range of tools used). What may work in Hollywood's version of Iowa cornfields—"Build it and they will come"—does not work in real-world data marts. If you implement a mart without meta data, you will quickly find that they may come, but they will also leave.

The reason they will flee is that a collection of data, no matter how accessible, is just that: a collection of data. Until the user can understand the context and meaning of the data, its value is severely diminished. It is critical that the supporting descriptions and explanations underlying the data be available to the user. Only then will the data become information that can be used.

If business users are confronted with thousands of available fields, with no supporting context or explanation, they will be unable to leverage this business asset. If they find a field labeled "sales," that field will remain useless unless users can ascertain that "sales" is defined to mean "gross sales, less discount and returns." A field labeled "CUSTID" is questionable unless users can discover that the source system that provided the CUSTID is indeed the service contract system that they rely on for all operational customer activity.

Sites that prefer to forgo the physical implementations of meta data and instead concentrate on extensive training and support to provide the "meta data" for their data warehouses and data mart systems have found that the turnover rates for typical business users have required a huge commitment in ongoing training and support. Their users move on, are promoted, or switch to new assignments so frequently that very few reach the level of self-sufficiency that this model requires. Consequently their ongoing support and training costs have far outstripped the cost for implementing and maintaining a viable meta data source.

Meta data provides the understanding, rationale, audit trail, and confidence that users require in order to make use of and believe in your data mart. Without understanding, they cannot place the available data in context to their needs. Without the underlying rationale of the transformations and scrubs, they are incapable of understanding how these facts were derived. Without the audit trail of sources, scrubs, and transformations, they have no foundation to build confidence. Without confidence, they are unwilling to take the political risk in utilizing this data resource. Without utilization, your data mart will die away, unfunded and unsupported.

Meta data is a prerequisite for success. You will not achieve full utilization without it. You will not achieve sustenance without it. You will not succeed without it.

REALITY CHECK Are you tired of hearing this message yet? Vendors, analysts, writers, pundits, and gurus have been pounding this message into your heads for the last couple of years. Yet, you protest, some data warehouses and data marts are running without much, if any, meta data. How can this be? They are examples of information resources that are underutilized by their organizations and will never reach their potential of positive impact on the enterprise. Many organizations are so starved for information that the tepid waters of a system lacking meta data will be initially satisfying. Unfortunately these users will never experience the fulfillment and enjoyment of a full meal that a system enabled with meta data provides.

Types of Meta Data

The "build and maintain" team's meta data is referred to as "technical meta data," whereas the business user's meta data is referred to as "business meta data." Both groups have a common goal: to research, discover, build, and share corporate resources resident in the data mart system(s) of the enterprise.

Amount of Meta Data

How much meta data do you need? The short answer is: "As much as you can possibly support!" Regardless of the type of data mart you are constructing, you will require a minimum set of meta data in order to succeed. For the extent of meta data you will provide, there are two primary gating points:

• Data mart type
• Available resources

A full-scale data mart implementation requires as much meta data as you can possibly build and maintain. A DisposaMart, due to its limited life span and tightly focused scope, can exist with a smaller set of meta data. An InstaMart, by definition, is limited to subsetted meta data from a parent source that can be quickly and easily segmented and acquired.

The Meta Data Conundrum

The most powerful gating factor in any data mart meta data implementation is the "meta data conundrum." Although it is clear that meta data is absolutely required for utilization, impact, and resulting success, it is also clear that data mart teams are finding it excruciatingly difficult to field and maintain a robust meta data resource for themselves and their users. The overriding reason for this is a brutal truth that the tool vendors and pundits are not talking about very often right now: meta data is primarily a manual process.

Although many data mart tools make much of their capability to populate meta data as part of their functionality, what they fail to mention is that very little of that populated meta data is done in an automated or required fashion. For instance, take a look under the covers of a leading first-generation code generator EMT (Extract, Mapping, and Transformation) tool and you'll find that very, very few meta data fields are required or are automatically populated. A little investigation reveals that beyond source field, target field, and transformation, just about every other meta data field is optional, and manually populated. Obviously, if you're creating your own EMT programs, or other elements of the data mart system, you'll be doing all the pertinent meta data population by hand as well.

Some quick math reveals the scope of this challenge. Let's say that you've got 5,000 data fields in your data mart environment. A modest goal of 10 meta data fields per data field yields 50,000 total meta data fields. Even if you have a tool that is going to populate the source, target, and transformation fields, you've still got 35,000 (5,000 × 7) meta data fields to manually populate. And if that isn't daunting enough, just wait until it's time to manually *maintain* those 35,000 fields, *forever.*

This, then, is the core of the meta data conundrum. You absolutely must have it to succeed, survive, and prosper, but it is a resource black hole that can consume your team faster than you can say, "Show me everything you've got on sales."

The keys to overcoming this challenge are to:

- Budget dedicated resources at the beginning of the process for meta data creation.
- Budget dedicated resources for meta data maintenance.
- Carefully manage meta data scope.
- Push for tools, suites, and environments that systematically populate and maintain as much meta data as possible.

REALITY CHECK This is another issue that the industry doesn't want to talk too much about these days. Manual meta data is the biggest resource black hole in the entire data warehousing/data mart universe. Only commit to the amount of meta data that you can maintain, in perpetuity.

Meta Data Content

In the meantime, you still need to decide how much meta data you need to be viable. We can break meta data down into three capability levels:

- Core
- Basic
- Deluxe

If we take the two basic kinds of meta data, technical and business, and subset them into these capability levels, we can derive a foundation for a flexible and scaleable meta data implementation.

Technical Meta Data

Core

A core level of technical meta data is primarily limited to mapping:

- Source field
- Target field
- Transformation (algorithms, many to one, one to many, etc.)

This gives you the minimum technical functionality to track source systems and target fields in the data warehouse. It also gives you the ability to answer the most common technical meta data question: What's the impact if this source field gets changed?

Basic

Basic-level technical data gives you the ability to actually track the data across the system and provide basic troubleshooting support.

- History of transformation changes
- Business rules
- Source program/system name
- Source program author/owner
- Extract program name and version
- Extract program author/owner
- Extract JCL (Job Control Language)/Script name
- Extract JCL/Script author/owner
- Load JCL/Script name
- Load JCL/Script author/owner
- Load frequency
- Extract dependencies
- Transformation dependencies
- Load dependencies
- Load completion date/time stamp
- Load completion record count
- Load status

Deluxe

Deluxe-level technical meta data provides additional and valuable utilization, support, and resource information. Systematic utilization meta data maintenance is usually accomplished with a database monitoring tool.

- Source system platform
- Source system network address
- Source system support contact
- Source system support phone/beeper
- Target system platform
- Target system network address
- Target system support contact
- Target system support phone/beeper

- Network support contact
- Network support phone/beeper
- Target utilization total selects
- Target utilization PYTD (Prior Year To Date) selects
- Target utilization YTD (Year To Date) selects
- Target utilization PYMTD (Prior Year Month To Date) selects
- Target utilization MTD (Month To Date) selects
- Target utilization total aggregations
- Target utilization PYTD aggregations
- Target utilization YTD aggregations
- Target utilization PYMTD aggregations
- Target utilization MTD aggregations

Business Meta Data

Core

Core user meta data provides basic field description information.

- Field/object description
- Confidence level
- Frequency of update

Basic

Basic user meta data provides the foundation for understanding the content and source of the information.

- Source system name
- Valid entries (that is, "there are three valid codes: A, B, C")
- Formats (that is, Contract Date: 4/30/82)
- Business rules used to calculate or derive the data
- Changes in business rules over time

Deluxe

Deluxe user meta data allows the user to understand the entire context of the information.

- Data owner
- Data owner contact information
- Typical uses
- Level of summarization

- Related fields/objects
- Existing queries/reports using this field/object
- Estimated size (tables/objects)

How much meta data do you need? Perhaps now you see the need to answer first the question: "How much meta data can we support?" You will absolutely need the core level to function, and a subset of the basic level is required for any real usability of the data mart environment. On the business side, field description, confidence level, frequency of update, and business rule are the practical minimums. For technical meta data, source, target, business rule history, and transformation are the bare minimum.

Meta Data Functions

For a successful data mart implementation you must not only collect meta data of sufficient quantity, but also be able to use it. Both your technical and business users have clearly defined needs and requirements for meta data functionality.

Technical

In the technical realm, meta data is primarily used for the "big M's": maintenance and metrics. Technical meta data also facilitates troubleshooting and documentation.

Maintenance

In the world of maintenance, the most common use of meta data is the production of "impact reports." These detail the impact of a change to a source field or system on the data mart. Because of the ever-changing nature of source OLTP (On-Line Transaction Processing) systems, this is a very common occurrence, and one that you must be in a position to handle efficiently.

Without core meta data to answer the "what happens to the data mart(s) if we change this source field?" question, you are reduced to doing word searches on source code and to manually reviewing extract, mapping, and transformation program listings. The minimum amount of meta data required to answer this question is:

- Source field
- Target field

You will probably find the inclusion of the transformation meta data to be a necessity as well because just knowing where the field goes isn't of much value without knowing what happens to it along the way.

Metrics

Metrics, or the logging of what is happening with the data mart, is also a primary function of technical meta data. Common metrics include:

- Extract process status
- Extract process start and completion date/time stamp
- Scrub process status
- Scrub process start and completion date/time stamp
- Transformation process status
- Transformation process start and completion date/time stamp
- Load process status
- Load process start and completion date/time stamp
- Index process status
- Index process start and completion date/time stamp
- Index utilization
- Table utilization
- Field utilization
- Resource utilization (queries, reports, analysis sets)
- Ad hoc aggregations

Meta data metrics allow monitoring and trending of maintenance operations and utilization by business users. Start and completion date/time stamps are particularly useful for trending and predicting extract window problems as the volume of data transferred into the data mart grows as utilization increases.

Business user utilization, especially of ad hoc aggregations, is extremely valuable as you work to optimize the ongoing operational design of the data mart. If you see a user in marketing spinning up a massive aggregation every Tuesday afternoon that bogs the server down for hours, it is a good opportunity to carefully examine the business need and create a dedicated aggregation set during off-hours. Pay careful attention to the capabilities of RDBMS (Relational Data Base Management System) monitoring tools and of ROLAP (Relational On-Line Analytical Processing) tools in the areas of logging ad hoc aggregation sets.

Utilization metrics are also invaluable for trending and reporting time variant utilization patterns. End-of-month, end-of-quarter, and year-end time periods place large demands on the data mart resource(s). These are easily predictable, but without a method for logging the usage and response times, you will have no evidence to support requests for increased processing capability to efficiently handle the periodical increased loads.

You will also experience seemingly random peak loads, not linked to any apparent time event. Utilization meta data metrics allow you to identify the source of the work, and to research the business drivers for the unexpected demands. Marketing campaigns, previously unknown production cycles, major industry events such as trade shows, and corporate planning initiatives are all commonly identified as hidden utilization drivers. Quickly identifying and planning for these utilization peaks can prevent the unexpected melt down of performance and response time when two of these non–time variant business drivers overlap.

Troubleshooting

Troubleshooting is nearly impossible without a basic set of technical meta data. One of the first things to happen when you roll out the data mart into production is that users will discover "dirty data." Regardless of how much time and resources you apply to this challenge, some flawed data always slips through. When this happens, the ability to quickly map back to the transformation algorithms and the source fields is required in order to address these problems with a reasonable amount of resources.

Dirty data requires you to have technical meta data including:

• Source

• Target

• Transformation algorithm

• Source data owner

One of the most common occurrences upon production roll-out is for users to find sparse data sets in columns they want to use as hierarchical groupings, or members of a dimension. If "customer type" is not fully populated, no analysis of the business metrics is possible using this attribute. You will find that missing and dirty data, although a challenge in the short term, serves as a remarkably effective forcing function for producing budget to correct these flaws.

Many times, repeated budget proposals have been made to correct problems in the source OLTP (On-Line Transaction Processing) system that is producing sparse or dirty data. These requests are often pruned in the budgeting process year after year. However, once the data mart opens the door to accessing the data easily and users find that these long-tolerated problems that have been swept under the budget rug are now major lumps under their carpet of business analysis, budget dollars somehow magically appear to quickly address these problems.

This is a prime example of the data mart as forcing function for process improvement in the business. Until the users are given easy access to the full range of information assets in their domain, they will have no need to fund or drive process or technology improvements. The data mart opens this cornucopia of information assets to them, along with any long-resident flies in the ointment. It is a wonderful way to bring long-dormant data challenges to the fore.

Documentation

The last major function of technical meta data is to document the systems and processes that make up the data mart system. A common repository of documentation for the infrastructure, elements, processes, and owners of the data mart system is extremely useful.

If we revisit the example we used in the opening of the chapter, we can see that most of these examples fall into the realm of documentation:

• Organizational:
  - Data mart owner (department, division, function)
  - Owner location (physical address, location)

- Structural:
  - System designer
  - Physical topology (device locations, connections)
- Management Information
  - System owner
  - Process owners
  - Data owners
- Contact Information
  - Phone extensions
  - Help line numbers
  - Beeper numbers
  - E-mail addresses
- Technical Information
  - Server model number
  - Server configuration

Most of the discussion and attention paid to technical meta data concerns the earlier examples maintenance and troubleshooting. Documentation, over time, proves to be among the most important and valuable data points you can populate and maintain.

Note that because the majority of these data points are not related to field level granularity, it is a much smaller task to populate and maintain this information over time. This is offset by the high degree of volatility in this set of meta data. Contact information, for instance, changes frequently. It is very important to have a solid process in place to facilitate timely update of this type of information.

Business

Business users have two primary meta data questions:

- Where do I?
- How do I?

If you do not easily and effectively answer each of these questions, with no more than a click of a mouse, your data mart is doomed to failure. Through neglect, underutilization, abandonment, or political abdication, your data mart will meet an untimely death. It is essential that the business users have quick and easy access to meta data required to answer these two fundamental questions.

Where Do I?

Where Do I Find: Information   The first type of "where do I?" questions you need to answer for business users concerns information:

- "Where do I find all the information about sales?"
- "Where is the output ratio information?"

- "Where is the customer description?"
- "Where are the net profits for international divisions?"

These are all examples of users requests to locate information in the data mart.

To support information "where do I?" questions from business users, you will need the following meta data fields:

- Field type (summary, descriptive, metric)
- Field description (to support text searches)
- Field key word (to support category searches, i.e., SALES)

Information "where do I?" meta data is primarily field atomic level, so resource implications for population and maintenance are extremely high. Due to the nature of the meta data, it is almost certainly manually populated and maintained. Be extremely careful when committing to a large amount of this type of information. You must be certain that you have the required resources not only to populate these fields, but most importantly, to maintain them over time.

Of course, if you don't deliver the ability to answer the information "where do I?" questions with a simple click, your data mart is doomed before it starts. This quandary is one of many in balancing business value and available resources in the process of designing, implementing, and maintaining data marts.

Where Do I Find: Resources

The next wave of "where do I?" questions relates to finding information resources that others have created and the business user wants to utilize, share, or modify:

- "Where are all the queries about model type inventory?"
- "Where is the weekly management report?"
- "Where is Bob's hypercube?"

These types of resource "where do I?" meta data questions follow quickly on the heels of information "where do I?" requests.

One of the fastest growing segments of capabilities in the tools, suites, and environments offered in the data mart space is that of resource cataloging and sharing. Pay particular attention to the vendor's products that you review for your implementation for this capability. The ability to share and distribute existing information resources is a key differentiater in the market, and one you should require from your solution providers.

To support resource "where do I?" requests, you will need these meta data fields:

- Resource type (query, report, analysis data set)
- Resource description
- Resource owner
- Resource creation date

- Resource modification date
- Resource key word (to support category searches)

Because the number of available resources is several orders of magnitude lower than the number of data fields, we have the luxury of much more easily providing this set of meta data. Don't scrimp in this area; it's relatively easy to populate and maintain this information and extremely valuable for business users.

An important issue is the challenge of implementing a process whereby the business users consistently populate the resource meta data as they create and store the resources. The audience for the data mart is not limited to knowledge workers; it includes users of every type and capability. It is extremely important to effectively communicate the importance to all users to populate and maintain the meta data associated with the resources they build and share.

In general, "where do I?" questions can be answered systematically. User tools provide a variety of ways to group and segment information resources including:

- Color
- Icons
- Folders
- Windows

It is critical to leverage the business users tools' UIs (User Interfaces) to present a very intuitive answer to the "where do I?" question. The business user should be able to answer 80% of the "where do I?" questions simply by looking at the UI you present.

Humans are primarily visual creatures. Leverage this asset by making your UI work hard for you. Humans' second-tier communication methods are primarily oral. This means that if they can't discern the answer by looking at the UI, they are going to call you for support. This implies increased support costs and lower productivity for both the business users and the support team.

How Do I?

Much more challenging answers to provide a business user are in response to "how do I?" questions:

- "How do I calculate western region net sales of new items?"
- "How do I rank the slowest moving items manufactured in the last quarter?"
- "How do I pull out the elements not resident in either sample set?"

All these questions concern processes and techniques in accessing and analyzing the data. It is very challenging to answer a "how do I?" question systematically. They are primarily knowledge transfer issues best addressed through training and ongoing communication. Of course, knowledge transfer processes are inherently resource demanding of all parties involved, and are required on an infinitely ongoing timeframe due to attrition and turnover. It is best if we can leverage any systematic way possible to answer these questions.

Some ways to address these questions systematically are:

- Sample queries
- Sample reports
- Sample "cook book" exercises working through common business problems

From the knowledge transfer standpoint, you need to ensure that the primary "how do I?" questions are answered in your user training classes, user guides, and other system documentation.

"How do I?" questions never go away, and as soon as you teach one person, he or she gets transferred and you'll have to train the replacement. This is why it is much more efficient to rely on a knowledge storage and publishing system such as a web site to communicate these answers than it is to use a resource-intensive personal trainer or mentor method.

Ongoing "how do I?" questions can be answered through:

- Intranet web site (very good option)
- Newsletters (avoid these; they are very resource intensive)
- User group meetings (there is no replacement for personal contact)
- Brown bag lunches (great informal setting)
- Mentoring teams (best for power techniques)

Other Business User Questions

Business users also require the answers to such questions as: "What does this mean?", "Can I trust this?", "What are valid codes?", and "How is this formatted?" These questions are answered by:

- Field description
- Confidence level
- Valid entry codes
- Formatting samples

Aside from field description, which is absolutely required, confidence level is perhaps the most valuable. It is important when populating this field to have only a few possible values. I suggest using 1, 2, and 3, with 1 being CEO (Chief Executive Officer) worthy and 3 being "use at your own risk." A larger number of variables inevitably leads to a vast amount of lost time as the team debates whether a particular field should be, for example, a 7 or an 8 on a scale of 10.

Valid entry codes contain all the possible valid codes for this field. For instance, a customer type code field might have A (active) and I (Inactive) as valid codes.

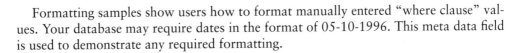

Formatting samples show users how to format manually entered "where clause" values. Your database may require dates in the format of 05-10-1996. This meta data field is used to demonstrate any required formatting.

Business Meta Data Conclusion

The business user is the central driver and the entire reason that we create and maintain data marts. It is impossible for these users to effectively utilize and leverage the data mart without easily accessible meta data. Consequently it is equally impossible for your data mart project(s) to succeed without quickly and easily answering the "where do I?" and "how do I?" questions.

Utilization History

The types and usage of meta data are by definition practically limitless, given sufficient resources. You will undoubtedly find many additional fields to add to the suggestions contained in this chapter. One additional and very useful category is history. You will find it extremely useful to capture and maintain specific utilization histories of departments, workgroups, and individuals.

If you are in an incremental data mart scenario, one of the important decisions you may be required to make is when to scale up one of the incremental data marts, or the multiple incremental data mart systems to an enterprise data warehouse, and who is going to drive it politically. A solid history of utilization of the incremental data mart systems is a great way to build a foundation of requirements and recruit sponsors.

Meta Data Location

Obviously this collection of meta data soon becomes quite large and requires its own set of management and access tools, but first and most importantly, it requires a place to reside. Although it is possible to keep meta data in hard copy form, in word processor files, or in spreadsheets, these formats are typically only adequate for small workgroup data marts. For a realistic and usable meta data resource, you will need a formal repository for the meta data.

Meta Data Repositories

Meta data repositories range from dedicated mainframe-resident environments to ad hoc desktop databases. Since meta data's ascension into the forefront of the data warehousing and data mart market space, it has become central to the functionality of the variety of tool suites and DTEAMM (Design, Transformation, Extract, Access, Monitor, and Management) environments offered by vendors. All of these offerings are centered around a meta data repository that is shared by the various elements. This allows the extraction, scrubbing, transformation, replication, access, and monitoring elements to leverage common meta data and resources.

For dedicated, stand-alone meta data repositories, normalized RDBMS implementations are the most popular. This approach allows teams to use familiar tools and processes to build and maintain a meta data store that is open, flexible, and easily extensible. OODBs (Object Oriented Data Bases) are more popular in the proprietary solutions sector.

Requirements for Meta Data Success

From the "build and maintain team" side, we are very interested in management capabilities that provide for automatic population and propagation of the constant ongoing changes affecting the data sources, the data mart design, and the data mart system and environment. We also require the same easy access to the meta data, once it has been populated, that users do in their quest to discover information assets and use them effectively and efficiently.

Some information appeals only to the technical audience, such as the owner of a particular data extraction and transformation process. Other information appeals commonly to both audiences, such as field definitions and load schedules. Users also have information that is primarily targeted to their needs, for example, the distribution list for a departmental report.

Browser Interface

Both groups share the need for an easy-to-use meta data browser that will allow them to peruse the available meta data information and easily drill down into the underlying or related information. (See Figure 7.1.)

They all require the ability to leverage existing resources such as queries, reports, analysis, or utilization logs, modify them if necessary, and store their version back into the meta data repository. Both technical and business users need to be able to schedule processes and events, such as reports, and manage the distribution of the results.

Logically Common Repository

Both technical and business users have a strong need for a logically common meta data repository. A logically common meta data repository presents one point of entry into the meta data resources of the data mart system. The physical meta data may be stored in multiple locations, but to the user it appears as one coherent meta data resource. A logically common repository allows the technical team to track the utilization of source data across multiple data marts, leverage common business rules, and share meta data that is pertinent to all audiences, such as the source system for the data field. This minimizes the maintenance and data replication challenges associated with multiple repository scenarios.

Logically common repositories are required for a coordinated, architected approach to an incremental strategy to data mart to data warehouse construction. Noninte-grated multiple repositories become legacy, stovepipe meta data OLTP applications,

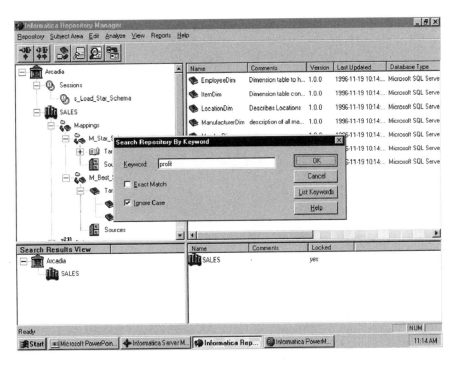

Figure 7.1 Screen shot of meta data browser *Source: Informatica*

each spinning off its own little stovepipe of information. A logically common meta data repository enables common semantics, common business rules, and most importantly, the ability to run an extract, scrub, and transformation once and populate all pertinent data marts with the result.

The alternative is to run the extract, scrub, transformation, and population operation once for each target data mart. It is easy to see how inefficient this is, and how it can quickly consume extract window and network resources, especially in the case of aggregations. (Compare Figures 7.2 and 7.3.)

REALITY CHECK Don't get hung up on one physical location for the meta data. In distributed data mart systems, the meta data is most likely going to be distributed as well. The key point is a single point of entry. Regardless of what's going on behind the scenes, it must look like one common source.

Business users profit from a logically common repository's ability to present them with data resident in other data marts, along with timely and accurate meta data regarding their primary information resource. Nonintegrated multiple repositories require

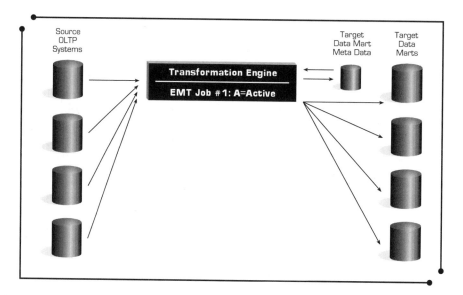

Figure 7.2 Multiple targets per EMT iteration (Extract Once, Populate Many)

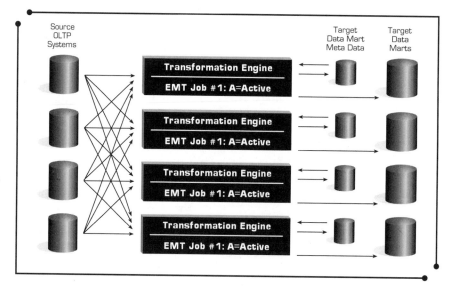

Figure 7.3 Single target per EMT iteration

users to access multiple entry points into the information resources. (See Figure 7.4.) A logically common repository allows users to access one single, consistent entry point to the information resources. (See Figure 7.5.)

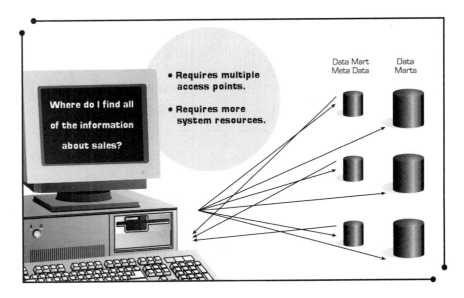

Figure 7.4   Disparate meta data repositories

Figure 7.5   Common meta data repository

Table 7.1 presents the advantages and disadvantages of a logically common repository and those of multiple repositories.

Some meta data repositories and data mart tools keep the business and technical sets of meta data in separate repositories, requiring duplicate updates of common changes and separate entry points, which is not an optimum scenario. It is important to pay close attention to potential solution providers' meta data architectures and their ability to share and leverage common resources, especially algorithms, business rules, and information resources.

Table 7.1   Pros/Cons of Common vs. Multiple Repositories

	Pros	Cons
Logically Common Repository	• Avoids replication challenges • Allows central management/ access • Allows sharing of algorithms/ business rules • Facilitates "transform once, populate many"	• Requires remote access for remote DMs • More network infrastructure • May require gateways
Multiple Repositories	• Local instance, quick response • Local view; users don't have to wade through other's material	• No ability to share algorithms/ business rules • Advanced replication • Distributed maintenance resources • Susceptible to local schema modifications

Openness

A logically common meta data repository that is open to external access also serves as a common resource for point solution tools to share information and processes. A closed repository is very quickly self-limiting, given the heterogeneous nature of data mart systems. Open, common meta data repositories enable:

• *Scheduling*

  Logically common meta data repositories allow disparate tools to work from a common process schedule. This allows tools such as extraction tools, scrubbing tools, transformation tools, loaders, replicaters, monitors, and job scheduling and management applications to share a common resource for scheduling and status. OCSD (Online Content Scheduling and Distribution) applications can also leverage this common event schedule repository to coordinate their activities with fresh data loads.

- *Sharing of Algorithms and Business Rules*
  Multiple scrubbing and transformation programs, applications, or instances may share common algorithms and business rules. For instance, there may be a standard way to resolve postal codes containing illegal characters or incomplete population. This common algorithm can be used both on supplier and customer addresses, although two completely different programs, processes, or applications may be performing the transformation and scrubbing for these two data sources.

- *Logging*
  A logically common meta data repository allows multiple applications to share status information regarding previous and dependent processes. An MRE (Managed Reporting Environment) application can check the status of a table load before executing, thereby ensuring the integrity of the contents of the distributed report.

- *Sharing of Resources*
  A logically common repository allows the various tools that the business uses to answer its informational challenges to store and share the queries, reports, and analysis developed by the various knowledge workers and other users of the tools. Without a common repository, users are doomed to a fate of re-creating the wheel that a counterpart built, but couldn't share. With a common, open repository, any authorized user can view, select, load, modify, and execute any resource created by any user in the enterprise. This sharing of information resources is one of the key ROI (Return On Investment) generators of a data mart implementation.

Extensibility

Another key requirement for meta data repositories is extensibility. Unless you can easily extend the design, capabilities, and accessibility of the meta data repository, you will be locked into the vendor's limited vision of a meta data solution. It is almost guaranteed that their vision will fall well short of the hard requirements of your reality.

This is the primary challenge for the OODB meta data repositories offered by various vendors. Although they are the perfect vehicle for combining the disparate types of data that you may want to collect in your meta data repository (queries, descriptions, algorithms, unstructured text, and so on), they are very challenging to modify or extend in their primarily proprietary implementations. Although vendors offer APIs or SQL (Structured Query Language) views that can be queried with SQL, you are limited to the views that the vendor provides into the repository.

Open RDBMS repositories, although greatly challenged to smoothly integrate disparate data types, are easily extensible by modifying schemas, adding tables, and creating joins. By their very nature, they can be easily queried by the very MQE (Managed Query Environment) tools used to query the data, in addition to the meta data–specific browsers provided by repository vendors. As hybrid object/relational DBMSs continue to evolve and gain capability, this choice may disappear entirely.

Table 7.2 Pros/Cons of Object Oriented vs. Relational Repositories

	Pros	Cons
OODB	• Easily integrates disparate data types	• Closed, proprietary environments • SQL access limited to set views • Challenging to extend • Minimal third-party support
RDBMS	• Easily extensible • Open, easy access to queries and other tools • Robust third-party support	• Challenging to smoothly integrate multiple data types

Table 7.2 presents the advantages and disadvantages of an OODB meta data repository and those of an RDBMS meta data repository.

Vision vs. Reality

Although several vendors have delivered portions of an optimum common, open, and extensible meta data repository vision, an inclusive and comprehensive solution has remained elusive. The industry has struggled with sharing meta data for many years, with no clear standard emerging. Up to now, there have been a variety of "partnering" solutions, consisting of two to four vendors sharing a proprietary meta data repository. Being tightly bound to these closed solutions, many of them OODB resident, no common, open, extensible standard has yet emerged.

A batch-oriented standard was recently agreed upon by the Meta Data Coalition, an industry standards group attempting to provide a common way to exchange the meta data produced by their various tools. It remains unclear whether this standard will be widely adopted and supported to the extent necessary to provide a clear and indisputable solution. Even if a set of two or three widely adopted standards evolves, it would be a huge improvement over the plethora of repository standards currently in the marketplace.

Meta Data Process

Meta data is a key fundamental element of the entire process of data mart design, construction, implementation, and sustenance. As such, meta data population and maintenance start at the beginning of the project and continue for the entire project life. It is a critical, and usually fatal, error to consider meta data something you populate in the end stages of the construction portion of the project. (See Figure 7.6.)

To the contrary, meta data begins with the general and progressively moves toward the specific. In the beginning stages of the project, you are populating data mart owners,

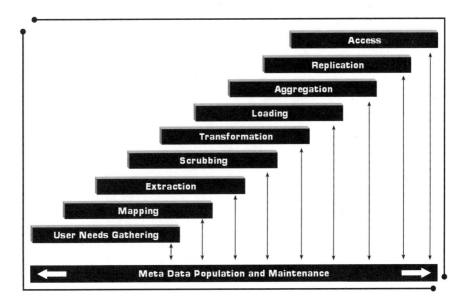

Figure 7.6 Data mart processes and meta data population

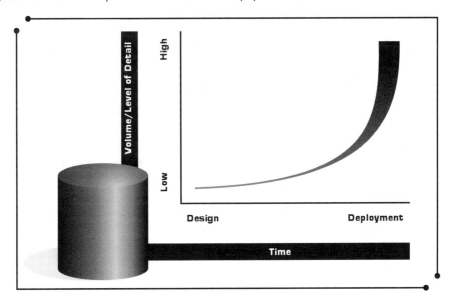

Figure 7.7 Meta data population rates

source systems (in the general sense, that is, order entry), and other high-level general topics. As the project moves forward, the meta data becomes progressively more detailed.
(See Figure 7.7.) The key is to populate the meta data consistently and compulsively as

the project moves forward. The population of meta data needs to be a key metric for team members. It is as important or more important than any other deliverable on the project. To achieve meta data population and maintenance as a core part of the team's activities, you will find it necessary to base performance reviews on the meta data metrics such as population and maintenance rates. Otherwise, the team will claim "responsibility overload" and the meta data will be abandoned.

Too often, meta data is the first thing to fall off the crowded plate of the data mart team. It is extremely tempting to adopt a "we can always go back and populate the meta data" attitude. This is a direct corollary to "we can always go back and document the code," in other words, it is never going to happen retroactively. You will be up to your ears dealing with sparse data, change requests, and new aggregations, and will have no resources, time, or desire to take on the Herculean task of populating thousands of meta data fields after the fact. This is an unfortunate and nearly always fatal choice.

You will find that you will need specific and dedicated resources for meta data throughout the project. Specific rates of population and accompanying performance metrics are required to maintain consistent and accurate population and to resist the pervasive temptation to defer this sometimes onerous task.

It is at this point that you will come to appreciate tools, suites, and environments that aid in the population, management, and monitoring of meta data. EMT (Extract, Mapping, and Transformation) tools and DTEAMM environments that contain integrated meta data repositories begin to lay the foundation for considerable ROI during these stages of the project's life. The ability to systematically populate and maintain any portion of the meta data, regardless of how small, is extremely valuable when the resource pool continues to diminish in the face of scope creep, changing requirements, or aggregation requests.

The maintenance of meta data is critical for ongoing validity and utilization of the data mart. You must budget sufficient ongoing resources for meta data maintenance. Again, specific meta data maintenance metrics must be attached to team member's activities. Specific results require specific metrics, and you will find that the meta data's synchronization with reality quickly fades without ongoing team metrics and resulting evaluations directly tied to maintenance activities.

Meta Data Challenges

Meta data remains the greatest challenge of the entire data mart design, construction, implementation, and maintenance process. It is central to the successful design, implementation, and especially utilization of the data mart. In fact, it is practically impossible to have a sustainable, successful implementation without it. At the same time, it is usually the first major element of the project to be abandoned or deferred, especially once the "meta data conundrum" becomes apparent. If that's not enough of a challenge to bury meta data at the back of the project plan, the realities of maintenance soon finish the task.

Summary

Data mart success is predicated on meta data success. Meta data success requires careful resource planning, ongoing team- and management-expectation management, specific team metrics, detailed project management, sound architectural design, and as much enabling technology as you can acquire.

SECTION THREE

▶ *Development and Implementation*

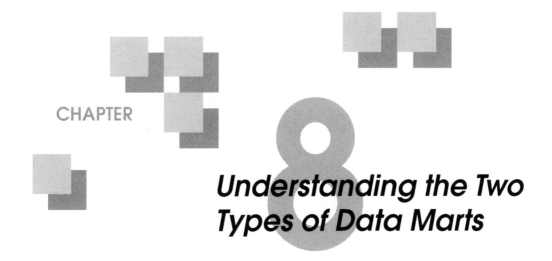

CHAPTER

8

Understanding the Two Types of Data Marts

Data marts fall into two broad categories:

1. Subset data marts created from a parent data warehouse or parent data mart
2. Incremental data marts used as independent information resources or as data warehouse building blocks.

These categories reflect the two approaches to data warehousing that have evolved: top-down (subset) and bottom-up (incremental).

In the classic top-down approach, an enterprise or galactic data warehouse is constructed and populated. Subset data marts are then created by taking portions of the enterprise data warehouse and creating information resources to serve specific user groups with homogenous characteristics or needs. The downside to the top-down method is that it is very lengthy and very costly. Enterprise data warehouses typically take two to three years to construct and cost over $2–3 million dollars on average. Due to its sequential nature, no data mart can serve a user group until the enterprise data warehouse is completed. The upside to the top-down approach is that all subset data marts are inherently architected, sharing the same meta data, business dimensions, business rules, metrics, and semantics. Top-down subset data marts are also very quick and easy to design, create, and populate. Often they require nothing more than standard SQL (Structured Query Language) commands to create. The enterprise data warehouse also provides a centralized repository for meta data and information resources, including replication and distribution.

Subset data marts are also created from parent data marts. In this way, two, three, four, or more "generations" of subset data marts may be derived from one parent. Subset data marts can be derived from either a parent enterprise data warehouse or a parent data mart. In either case, they inherit the meta data, architecture, semantics, business rules, and metrics of the parent.

The incremental bottom-up approach to data warehousing uses incremental data marts as the building blocks of the enterprise data warehouse. Individual incremental data marts are created and deployed. They are used to test and perfect the methodologies, processes, and tools used in the creation of the corporate information resources. As the data marts prove themselves to be valuable corporate resources, the organization can justify the time and expense associated with the enterprise data warehouse.

243

The downside to this approach is that all too often, unarchitected incremental data marts are rapidly inserted into the user community where they take root as LegaMarts. Later, when it comes time to bring these data marts together into the enterprise fold, the team is faced with a gargantuan integration task that is very resource intensive. The upside to this approach is that with a proper enterprise data mart architecture in place, incremental data marts can be quickly and inexpensively delivered to users to solve immediate business problems. Using an enterprise data mart architecture as a foundation for the incremental data marts, it becomes very easy to demonstrate high ROIs and significant impact to the organization. Architected data marts are fairly straightforward to join together into a physical or virtual enterprise data warehouse.

Incremental data marts are also used as independent information resources in sites where an enterprise data warehouse is not the end goal. Again, it is critical to create these incremental data marts under an enterprise data mart architecture. Otherwise, each independent nonarchitected incremental data mart will be a source of a unique version of "the truth."

Hybrid environments consist of independent, architected incremental data marts with multiple "child" subset data marts. Each "parent" incremental data mart may have multiple generations of subset data marts. Whichever type of data mart you choose, incremental or subset, it is important to understand the characteristics of these data marts, their common risk factors, and their common prerequisites for success.

Subset Data Marts

Subset data marts are derived from a parent enterprise data warehouse or a parent data mart. (See Figure 8.1.) They have the advantage of inheriting the parent's architecture, along with common semantics, business rules, business dimensions, and meta data. Because subset data marts are comprised of portions of the parent data warehouse or parent data mart data, they are quickly and easily generated, especially if the requirements for subset data marts is taken into account during the design of the parent data warehouse or parent data mart.

Subset data marts are created based on a variety of criteria. They may be based on the level of aggregation of the data; they may be line of business–specific, organizationally focused, functionally focused, or based on geographical segmentation. The creation, population, and maintenance of these subset data marts is greatly eased if attributes providing these segmentation keys are included in the parent data warehouse or parent data mart tables.

For instance, you may foresee the need for a geographical segmentation of the parent data warehouse or parent data mart into targeted subset data marts for West, East, Central, and South sales regions. It then becomes very important to include sales geography information on the individual row level of the atomic transaction data in the parent. Otherwise, re-creating the territory assignments that were current at the time of the transaction in order to re-create accurate sales history for each subset data mart becomes a very challenging task. (See Figure 8.2.)

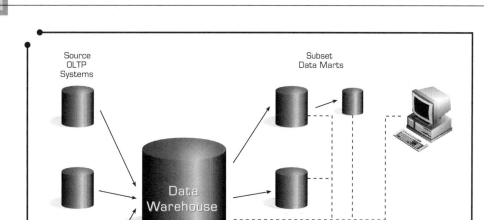

Figure 8.1   Subset architecture

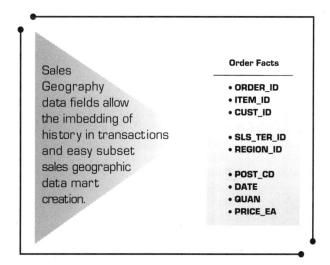

Figure 8.2   Detail facts with sales geography fields

In an enterprise data warehouse scenario, subset data marts quickly become the primary utilization point of the enterprise data warehouse system. Users like the smaller, targeted data sets that don't require the database server to wade through other people's information in order to answer their questions. Properly designed and targeted subset data marts demonstrate very high levels of utilization, accompanied by very high levels of growth and evolution. You must be careful to allocate sufficient dedicated maintenance and support resources to each subset data mart. Don't let the ease of creation lead you into an insupportable position.

Subset data marts are the fast track to mission-critical status in the enterprise. They are easy and quick to create, which makes them excellent vehicles to meet the fast-changing needs of the business. They deliver highly integrated, accurate, scrubbed, easy to access, targeted information into the hands of the user community. There is no more valuable asset in today's information driven, fast-paced business environment.

Incremental Data Marts

Incremental data marts may exist as separate entities, forever isolated, or they may be joined together to form a virtual or physical enterprise data warehouse. (See Figure 8.3.)

Incremental data marts have become the preferred path to an enterprise data warehouse. They offer a low-risk, low-cost way to test out the theories and realities of data warehouse architecture, design, and construction. They offer a much quicker impact on the business, as quick as two to three months in some cases. Due to their low cost, no one has to risk their career on the success or failure of a specific incremental data mart. These factors of speed, cost, and lower political exposure make incremental data marts the ideal approach to the goal of an enterprise data warehouse.

If one incremental data mart works for a set of users, it is easy to expand the program to design and deliver an incremental data mart for a second group. You can

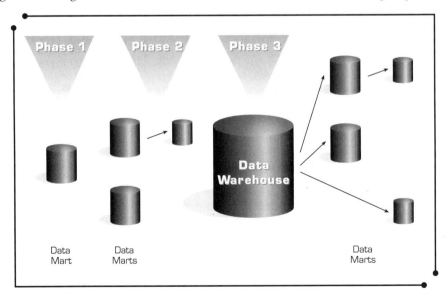

Figure 8.3   Incremental path to data warehousing

incrementally expand the scope, along with the positive ROI (Return On Investment) that the incremental data marts generate. As user groups spread the word about the positive impacts of incremental data marts on their lives, more and more organizations clamor for their own data marts. This quickly generates political will and makes it easy to pick and choose solid business drivers from among the various candidates. The short "time to market" of incremental data marts eliminates the risks found in the very long terms of unrewarded political will in the 18–36 month timeframe typical of enterprise data warehouse projects. All this adds up to an optimum scenario for information delivery to the enterprise.

Unfortunately many teams become seduced by the ease of incremental data mart delivery and the adoration of appreciative users. They avoid or defer the required investment in an initial enterprise data mart architecture providing a road map of enterprise subject areas, common dimensions, common metrics, common business rules, common source systems of record, common semantics, and resulting common meta data. What these unfortunate teams wake up to is a hangover of nonintegrated, nonarchitected LegaMarts scattered throughout the organization. To those unlucky souls who are still around to clean up the mess falls the unenviable task of supporting the many multiple variations of the "truth" spewing out from these collections of different business rules and semantics. To those even unluckier to be in the room when the directive to "integrate the LegaMarts" is delivered falls the almost impossible task of making all these foreign worlds seamlessly integrate and interoperate. (See Figure 8.4.)

The requirement for an enterprise data mart architecture seems to generate a bipolar reaction in data mart teams. They either bury their heads in the sand and pay the inevitable price, or they latch on to the concept of an "enterprise" data mart architecture as the opportunity to process map the entire enterprise down to the application of every

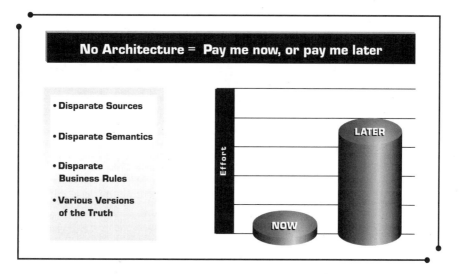

Figure 8.4   LegaMart integration effort before/after

REALITY CHECK Avoid the tragic fate of LegaMarts. Be sure to only construct incremental data marts under the umbrella of an enterprise data mart architecture.

paper clip. The creation of an enterprise data mart architecture is a two-week job, not a two-year project. Spend no more than one to two weeks identifying:

- Enterprise subject areas
- Common business dimensions
- Common metrics
- Common business rules
- Common source systems of record
- Common semantics

Clearly you will not have all the answers to all the questions in only two weeks, but you will have enough to start on the data mart project. The architecture continues to be filled in as you move forward with your initial incremental data mart and as you add new sources and requirements for further data marts.

It is essential that you avoid being caught in the project tar pit of spending weeks, months, and years defining a massive, grandiose, galactic architecture. Even if you are beginning an enterprise data warehouse by building the first incremental data mart, spend no more than two to four weeks on the architecture, and that long only if you are working on a truly massive scale, such as an $80 billion multinational organization. You must not lose the momentum of your project nor the opportunity to make a timely impact on the business by spending months arguing about intricate, minute details.

The bottom-up incremental data mart is the optimum enterprise data warehouse development and deployment strategy for most organizations. It offers a small scale, fast turnaround, and small pilot and user bases. The small scale of the projects allow you to "test and toss without big loss." You can try various methodologies, designs, tools, and strategies quickly, without permanent failure implications. This allows teams to work out the kinks in their site-specific process and methodology before taking on the large-scale enterprise warehouse.

The incremental data mart is a very profitable approach to information resource construction and deployment for your organization. Just keep in mind that you must meet the prerequisites for success, and the biggest one is an enterprise data mart architecture.

Common Risk Factors

Regardless of if you are on a top-down/subset or bottom-up/incremental track, you must understand the common risk factors for each approach. To ensure success, both

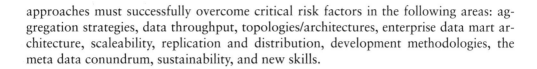

approaches must successfully overcome critical risk factors in the following areas: aggregation strategies, data throughput, topologies/architectures, enterprise data mart architecture, scaleability, replication and distribution, development methodologies, the meta data conundrum, sustainability, and new skills.

Aggregation Strategies

Aggregation strategy involves determining where the summary data sets are going to be created. This is a very important decision, with major implications for network bandwidth requirements, source system capacity, and batch window and server capacities.

The two primary options are to create the aggregations on the source system or to create them on the data mart server.

If you are building a subset data mart derived from an enterprise data warehouse, building the aggregations on the data warehouse platform can be a convenient and practical choice. Often, the enterprise data warehouse server has sufficient horsepower to make these tasks quick and easy. You do need to be careful about the resulting size of the aggregation table and how long it will take to transfer to the target subset data mart over the available network bandwidth.

If you are building an incremental data mart that is directly sourced from OLTP (On-Line Transaction Processing) systems, the choice of building the aggregations on the source system becomes much more complicated. Although it may seem attractive for a team steeped in COBOL experience to do the logic and process operations for the aggregations on the source mainframe system, there are valid reasons to be wary of this approach.

To ensure data mart integrity, the aggregations must be based on only the metrics and keys available in the fact and dimension tables on the incremental data mart server. If you are going to build the aggregations on the mainframe or other source system, you must maintain *exact* duplicates of the incremental data mart fact and dimension tables on the source system. This adds significant DASD (Direct Access Storage Device) and data replication overhead to your incremental data mart system. If you attempt to build your aggregations without deriving them from the fact and dimension tables on the incremental data mart server, you inevitably get out of sync with the incremental data mart. Your users will discover the discrepancy, and your most precious asset, credibility, will be destroyed.

The simplest approach to aggregation creation is to use simple SQL to derive them from the fact and dimension tables on the data mart server in a "drop and re-create" scenario. In this method, the old tables are deleted and new aggregations are created from scratch. This ensures perfect synchronization with all data mart elements and guarantees "auditability" and credibility. The only downside is that you must have a strong enough server to accomplish all the aggregation roll-ups within your available processing window. You must test the aggregation time requirements while simulating a month end, quarter end, and year end in order to get an accurate idea of the processing requirements. This approach often requires more investment in memory and I/O capacity than initially envisioned during data mart server configuration, especially for multidimensional data sets.

Many sites do not have the time or brute horsepower to re-create large aggregation sets on the data mart servers, so they choose incremental aggregation. In this method, only the new information since the last time slice capture of the transactional information is added to the aggregations. On the surface, this is the most elegant approach, however, it can also be very resource intensive, depending on the capabilities of the RDBMS (Relational Data Base Management System) and the tools involved in the aggregation process.

Data Throughput

Data marts are very demanding of networks. They require the movement of large amounts of data throughout the infrastructure. From the backbone, to the Internet gateway, to the desktop, data marts perform daily stress tests of the entire network infrastructure, management, and support systems. To deliver and sustain a successful data mart implementation, you must work closely with the network design and administration teams.

The key factors that drive network utilization and capacity are:

- *System architecture*
  An *n*-tier system (a multi-tier system using more than three tiers) that is based on thin clients accessing the data mart via browsers using your intranet or the Internet has different network requirements than a two-tier model using thick clients and non-open standards. Every one of the myriad architecture and topology variations affects network utilization at various points in the design. You must pay particular attention to backbone requirements and remote data mart server update requirements.

- *End-user access tools*
  The type of tool selected to serve end users' needs has major implications for the required network capacity. MOLAP (Multidimensional On-Line Analytical Processing) tools require massive multidimensional data cubes that must be created, managed, and moved around the infrastructure. LowLAP (Low-Level Analytical Processing) tools pull large answer sets to the desktop to build their local data cubes. ROLAP (Relational On-Line Analytical Processing) tools transfer large data sets between the RDBMS server and the ROLAP analysis engine server. Each type of tool has varying network needs and requirements. Network capacity planning cannot be finalized until these tool decisions are made.

- *Client platform*
  Users may be accessing the system from a variety of client platforms. Personal computers and Network PC platforms perform the bulk of processing and storage locally. Network Computers (NC) perform application and data storage at the server and rely on downloaded applets for client platform processing. Because of the different approaches to application storage, the NC platforms may require more network bandwidth between the server and the client.

- *Frequency of update*
  Your data mart may require updating every night. If so, the network must be able to handle all data transfers of detailed transactions, dimension keys, and aggregations every night, from every source to every target.

- *Source extraction window*
  A close corollary to frequency of update is the length of the extraction window from the source systems to the target data mart. If you are extracting data from a 24×7 OLTP system serving a worldwide user community, your source extraction window may be very limited. You cannot afford to be slowed by thin network pipes if you've only got an hour or two to perform all the source-resident processing and get the transactions off the source and distributed to the data marts.

- *Number of users*
  If your data mart is going to serve thousands of users in an entire business unit, you need extensive network infrastructure resources. Again, the tools chosen for end-user access have major implications for resource requirements.

- *Locations of users*
  If your data mart is functionally or organizationally segmented you may have users scattered all over the globe. The WAN (Wide Area Network) requirements of your data mart are driven by the number of locations, the number of users at each location, and the types of tools users employ at each location. You may also choose to mirror your primary data mart server with duplicates at key remote locations. These mirror sites require very reliable, high-capacity links to the primary data mart server.

Topologies/Architectures

The fundamental topology and architecture of your data mart system drives overall system requirements for servers, network, and client platforms. The topologies are driven primarily by the choice of the data mart and end-user tools. Some first-generation EMT (Extract, Mapping, and Transformation) tools do not require a client server environment. However, if you plan to implement a DTEAMM (Design, Transformation, Extract, Access, Monitoring, and Management) environment and server-centric, thin client–based access tools, you need a multiple-tier client server environment linked by a robust and reliable network.

Enterprise Data Mart Architecture

As previously mentioned, you must have an enterprise data mart architecture in place to design, build, and implement successful data mart systems. There is no getting around this requirement, even if you think you are only building a single, one-off data mart for one user group. If you do not invest the time and resources now, you will pay a heavy, heavy price sometime in the not too distant future.

Scaleability

Data marts are very dynamic. They tend to grow rapidly, extensively, and relentlessly. You will, on average, underestimate the eventual size of your data mart by 25–50%. Due to its overwhelming success, your data mart may eventually scale up to become the core of the enterprise data warehouse.

Due to all of these characteristics and possibilities, you must be intently focused on the scaleability of all elements of every aspect of the data mart system. Scaleability must become your watchword. In fact, when you get up in the morning, one word should be emblazoned on your forehead: scaleability. (See Figure 8.5.)

Your primary gating factor for every decision—be it server model, RDBMS, DTEAMM environment, end-user tool, or data mart utility—must be primarily weighted by scaleability. You cannot afford to be cut off from adequate performance, required growth, or expansion opportunity by a technologically limiting solution. Accept no vendor's solution that cannot demonstrate several orders of magnitude of scaleability.

Replication and Distribution

Your data mart implementation most likely requires replication, now or in the future. You must have a solid replication and distribution strategy in place to ensure success.

Figure 8.5   Scaleability focus

You may choose dedicated replication and distribution utilities, native RDBMS capabilities, or home-grown replication solutions. Whatever your choice, it must support your current environment, as well as one significantly larger as your system grows and additional targets are added.

Development Methodologies

To have any hope of sustainability in your data mart system, you must have a business-driven methodology in place, as described in Chapter 5. The methodology you implement must reflect the required elements of data mart design and implementation, as described in Chapter 6.

Avoid getting side-tracked by dogmas that force you to twist and shape the project to fit within their narrow pigeonholes. If the methodology is not flexible, it is not suitable for data marts.

Meta Data Conundrum

To achieve success with either a subset or incremental data mart approach, you must overcome the meta data conundrum: meta data is both required for success and overwhelmingly manual in nature. You simply must have meta data to have a viable data mart system. You also must have sufficient resources to populate and maintain the amount of meta data you commit to implement.

Meta data is a resource black hole, so be very careful to commit only to what you can maintain today and more importantly, tomorrow. The absolute minimum requirements for meta data are:

- Technical
  - Source
  - Target
  - Transformation/scrub algorithm
- Business
  - Description
  - Confidence level
  - Frequency of update

Any additional meta data you can provide in addition to this is extremely worthwhile and will make your system much more usable and valuable to the enterprise. Be very careful to implement only what you will be able to support over time. Meta Data is discussed in detail in Chapter 7.

Sustainability

To implement a sustainable data mart, you must meet the following criteria:

- *Methodology*
  You must use a business-driven methodology, such as the one described in Chapter 5.

- *Design*
  You must have a user-oriented design. The system must be built to accommodate the needs of users, not the convenience of the data mart team.

- *Politics*
  You must identify and understand the relationships, partnerships, mentors, vendettas, and conflicts in the organization. You must avoid having the data mart caught in the middle of a political conflict between individuals or organizations. Pay close attention to past and current relationships between all players and the IS organization. Avoid personality conflicts between team members and the user community.

- *Resources*
  You must ensure ongoing resources to maintain the data mart. Data mart systems require much higher levels of ongoing maintenance resources than traditional OLTP systems. Be wary of the decreasing level of talent of team members because the "best and the brightest" usually move on to other exciting new projects after roll-out.

- *Technology*
  You must implement technology that is scaleable, capable, and seamlessly integrated into a common meta data repository.

- *Customer satisfaction metrics*
  You must establish and implement clear customer satisfaction–oriented metrics for the entire data mart team. Performance evaluations must be based on such factors as request turnaround time, system up time, and meta data population and maintenance.

Critical data mart sustainability issues are covered in detail in Chapter 15.

REALITY CHECK   Sustainability is a huge issue that you are not going to think about much, if at all, in the first 75% of your project. You will be focused on "buying and building." Someone has to keep this data mart humming along in the future. Back away from the details of your project plan for a few days and consider what it is going to take to keep this data mart happy and healthy a year from now, and two years from now.

New Skills

Data marts require new skills from all members of the team. Management must build an evaluation environment based on customer service metrics and instill in the organization a clear vision of a service business. The data mart architects and designers must adopt an entirely new perspective and build an entirely user-driven system. They must overcome "DASD fear" and become comfortable with denormalization and extensive replication. The builders and maintainers of the system must become comfortable with a very dynamic, growing system that is entirely driven by the needs of the user community. Everyone on the team must be flexible, be adaptable, and be excellent communicators.

Common Prerequisites for Success

Whether you are building an incremental data mart or a subset data mart, your system must possess certain prerequisites in order to be successful. These elements are requirements; they cannot be minimized or ignored if you hope to build and implement a data mart system that will positively impact the organization and be possible to sustain over time.

- *Business driver*
  Your data mart must be an answer to a clear and sustainable business driver.

- *Political will*
  The data mart must be in response to high-level and sustainable political will in the organization. It must not be driven by a single individual's needs or wishes, but answer the needs of a homogenous user group.

- *Sponsorship*
  The data mart must have high-level and sustainable sponsorship. The sponsor must be politically viable and carry sufficient influence in the organization to garner and retain adequate resources for the construction and maintenance of the data mart.

- *Pain*
  The data mart must provide immediate and total relief to definable, clear, and life-threatening pain for a discernible user community or organization. The pain the data mart relieves must be the highest rated problem for the executives, managers, and users associated with this user community or organization.

- *Scope management*
  The data mart must be built to meet the requirements of a very narrowly defined and rigid scope. The data mart must have a finite mission statement that can be expressed in no more than one sentence.

- *Politics*
  The data mart must not be allowed to become caught in the political cross-fire between warring factions or individuals. The data mart must not be allowed to be the victim of a political assassin targeting sponsors or user group individuals.

- *Enterprise data mart architecture*
  The data mart must be built under the auspices of an enterprise data mart architecture. This architecture must not take more than two to three weeks to define and must be the foundation for all data marts in the enterprise.

- *Meta data*
  The data mart must have easily accessible, adequately populated, and well-maintained meta data. The meta data should be in a logically common repository and contain the full range of enterprise information resources (reports, analyses, and so on). The meta data repository must be common to all system elements, open, and extensible.

- *Accessibility*
  The data mart must be easily accessed from all client platforms from all locations. All client platforms must exhibit equal performance and capability. All access tools must exhibit an intuitive, productive, and common user interface.

- *Picking initial subject areas or data marts*
  Initial user groups, data marts, and/or subject areas must be based on the highest possible combination of pain, political influence, and utilization.

- *Supportable topology*
  The organization must have adequate network and support resources to maintain and support the data mart topology.

- *Tools*
  All data mart system tools must be seamlessly integrated and tightly bound to a common meta data repository. All tool vendors must be financially sound, offer products that reflect current technologies and standards, and demonstrate a solid technological road map.

  All tools must be server centric in design and seamlessly support thin clients. All tools must have a common, productive, and intuitive UI (User Interface). All tools and solutions should be based on open standards. Accept no closed proprietary solutions.

- *Auditable*
  The data mart must be fully auditable. All of the data in the data mart must be based solely on the contents of the fact tables and the business dimensions. No external feeds can be used in aggregations other than facts and dimensions. The entire data mart system must audit to itself. The data mart must audit to other information resources in the business. All deltas between the data mart and other information resources must be fully documented and communicated prior to roll-out.

- *Resources*
  The data mart must have dedicated resources. These resources include source system experts, network administrators, data architects, project managers, quality assurance engineers, server administrators, database administrators, developers, tool experts, user support engineers, consultants, vendor SEs (Sales Engineers), vendor technical support, vendor consultants, pilot users, and user representatives.

- *Design*
  The data mart design must be entirely user oriented. It must reflect the needs and requirements of the user community. It must be easy for users to use, easy for users

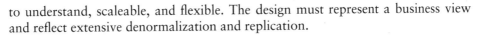

to understand, scaleable, and flexible. The design must represent a business view and reflect extensive denormalization and replication.

- *Perspective*
  The data mart team must be entirely user oriented. The users' needs and requirements must drive all decisions and actions of the team.

- *Philosophy*
  The data mart team must overcome preconceptions and fears, such as "DASD fear," and must operate under a philosophy that reflects the systemic nature of data marts. The team must be solely focused on creating and sustaining "a happy place to be."

- *Culture*
  The data mart team must adopt a service business culture. Customer satisfaction metrics must drive all performance evaluations. The team must be very flexible and respond positively to changes in business requirements and needs.

- *Scaleable technology*
  The data mart system must be constructed entirely of scaleable technology. The system must be capable of quick expansion by several orders of magnitude with linear performance response.

Summary

Regardless of the path you are on, top-down (subsets) or bottom-up (incremental), data marts provide the best return on investment possible for information delivery to the enterprise. Understanding the differences and commonalties between subset and incremental data marts gives you the fundamentals you need to begin data mart system construction using the techniques described in the following chapters.

Successful Subset Data Marts

Subset data marts offer compelling advantages compared to building from the ground up. They are fast and easy, and they are inherently architected, integrated, and prescrubbed. (See Figure 9.1.) In short, it's pretty hard to screw up a subset data mart, however, it has been known to happen. The fundamental key is to identify a clear business driver for the subset data mart. Do not embark on frivolous subset data mart projects for marginal business processes or personal agendas. What you create, you must support.

In this chapter, we'll look at the prerequisites for successful subset data mart implementation and the keys to building and implementing a sustainable subset data mart.

The upsides to subset data marts are:

- *Easy*
  Subset data marts are easy. They usually require no more than some simple SQL (Structured Query Language) to extract the pertinent data from the parent enterprise data warehouse or parent data mart. If they are not easy for you in your data warehouse or parent data mart

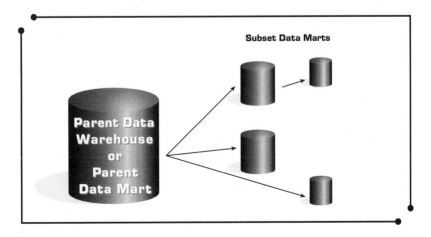

Figure 9.1 Subset data mart

system, it is time to revisit your basic design for the enterprise data warehouse or parent data mart. Data mart segregation fields should be an integral part of the parent enterprise data warehouse or parent data mart design from the beginning.

- *Quick*
  Subset data marts are extremely quick to construct and deploy. Because it is so easy to subset the data, subset data marts can be quickly created in response to changing business needs. This is an excellent attribute to leverage when demonstrating the power and flexibility of the data warehouse architecture to the organization.

- *Architected*
  Because they are derived from an enterprise data warehouse or a parent data mart constructed under an enterprise data mart architecture, subset data marts are inherently architected. This is a tremendously valuable feature, allowing the easy and seamless integration of any business dimension, metric, or summary data set. The subset data marts are naturally based on common dimensions, semantics, metrics, and business rules. This greatly facilitates communications and information sharing in the enterprise. And most importantly, this guarantees that there will only be one version of the "truth" in the enterprise.

The downsides to subset data marts are:

- *Dependent on existence of data warehouse (long time line)*
  The greatest strength of the subset data mart is that it is derived from the enterprise data warehouse. This is also the greatest weakness of the subset data mart in a classic enterprise data warehouse scenario. Because it is dependent on the existence of the enterprise data warehouse, a subset data mart cannot be constructed before the enterprise data warehouse is designed, created, and implemented. This is usually a two- to three-year process. This long timeframe is the direct reason why the incremental data mart has emerged as the preferred way to build and implement an enterprise data warehouse environment. Obviously, subset data marts derived from parent data marts do not share this negative prerequisite attribute of extended time to create the parent.

- *Too easy*
  As noted above, subset data marts are painfully easy. Too easy in fact. They are so easy that you may find that they are multiplying like rabbits in the spring. Soon you will be reminded of the fundamental rule of subset data mart creation: what you create, you must support. It can be a painful experience to wake up to a tsunami of subset data mart support requirements and a handful of support resources.

Prerequisites for Success

There is a clear set of prerequisites for the development and deployment of a successful subset data mart system. Do not attempt to move forward until the following are in place: parent elements, bidirectional data flow, and topology.

Parent Elements Only

Subset data marts are always derived solely from a parent data warehouse or another parent data mart. The subset data mart inherits some or all of the characteristics of the parent and contains nothing that is not contained in the parent. The subset data mart never contains metrics, business dimensions, or any other element that cannot be found in the parent data warehouse or parent data mart. In this way, you ensure that the subset data mart will always audit perfectly to the parent. Introducing any element solely into the subset data mart leads to inevitable disaster when someone wants to combine that new data mart unique element with an element from the parent on the parent platform.

Bidirectional Data Flow

Sometimes a subset data mart can be used in applications where data is generated uniquely in the subset data mart, such as a budgeting or forecasting application using a MOLAP (Multidimensional On-Line Analytical Processing) tool and a dedicated MDDBMS (Multi-Dimensional Data Base Management System). In this case, the second prerequisite of success, bidirectional data flow between the data mart and the parent, is required.

In this scenario, the unique new data created on the data mart must be replicated upstream into the parent data mart and/or parent data warehouse. If you do not provide for this reverse replication of the parent systems, there will be trouble ahead for your data mart team. Users have a nasty habit of sharing information they derive from the information assets of the business. Well-designed data marts are huge hits among users, and the information and analysis from them is quickly disseminated throughout the organization. If you allow a unique data point to exist in a subset data mart, and it is not available to executives or other users accessing other information resources, you can suffer severe political ramifications. Don't give potential political enemies such an easy target.

Topology

The third prerequisite for success for subset data marts involves the topology and physical design of the subset data mart system. The topology and supporting infrastructure must be adequate to support the data flow required by the tools and technologies selected for the system. You must pay particular attention to:

- *Backbone bandwidth*
  It is essential that adequate bandwidth be present between the parent data warehouse or data mart and the subset data mart server. You must make the investment in capacity planning well prior to pilot and roll-out to ensure that the network team can design, implement, and support an adequate backbone for your required topology. Test your system under simulated week-end, month-end, quarter-end, and year-end scenarios prior to pilot and roll-out. Monitor the network between subset data mart ROLAP (Relational On-Line Analytical Processing) or MOLAP

servers and the parent data warehouse or parent data mart closely. They can quickly clog with large data sets required for dynamic processing or data cube updates.

- *Aggregation processing*
Another challenge is to ensure that the subset data mart system has adequate I/O (Input/Output) bandwidth and processing power to build and distribute all required aggregations within the available processing window. Typically, data mart aggregation processing is I/O bound, so you will want to implement servers that are very easily scaleable in terms of I/O channels and controllers. Again, simulations of high-volume processing periods are essential. It is practically impossible to estimate accurate performance times without actually processing your data on your server. Cast a wary eye at estimates provided by server and RDBMS (Relational Data Base Management System) vendors, unless it's an SE (Sales Engineer) you feel you can trust.

- *MDDBMS loads*
MOLAP tools and their dedicated multidimensional data cubes deliver fantastic response times to users. To deliver these nearly instant results, however, they require that all possible answers to all possible combinations of their metrics and dimensions be precalculated and stored in the data cube. This precalculation is extremely computationally and I/O intensive. You must be very, very careful about managing expectations in the user community when designing and implementing a MOLAP system. Users tend to remember only the flashy demonstrations based on a very small data cube. They will expect you to deliver the same twelve dimensions they saw in the demo unless you change that expectation early on. In reality, it is very challenging to deliver more than a handful of dimensions in a data set that can be processed in a reasonable amount of time and hosted on a reasonably sized and priced server. Again, it is nearly impossible to accurately estimate the eventual size of your data cube or the time required to calculate it until you actually implement the system with your data and your server. Start very small, and build slowly from there. Do not promise your users more than a few dimensions initially, until you can get a clear picture of real data cube sizes and processing time requirements.

  Once you are the proud owner of a 35-, 65-, 95-, or 165-gigabyte data cube, you'll quickly understand why the incremental update of these data cubes is such a highly prized feature among the available MOLAP solutions. If the tool supports the incremental update of your nightly or weekly transactions, your processing time may only be a few minutes or hours. However, if you are required to recalculate the entire data cube every time you want to add a few hundred rows of transaction detail, you will be paying a heavy, heavy price every night or every weekend. It is for this reason that MOLAP environments typically deal only with fairly highly summarized data and infrequent time slices.

- *Mid-tier application server MIPS (Millions of Instructions Per Second)*
Your enterprise data mart environment typically consists of a variety of mid-tier applications accessing the data stored on your subset data marts and their parent

information resources, often simultaneously. These mid-tier applications include ROLAP servers, OCSD (On-line Content Scheduling and Delivery) servers, MRE (Managed Reporting Environment) servers, and web access servers. Some of these applications, especially ROLAP analysis engines, can be very demanding of their application server system. It is important to select a server for these applications that is powerful, has significant RAM (Random Access Memory), and is very easily scaleable.

There is no way to predict the load your users will put on a ROLAP server. Usually the greatest challenge of a ROLAP environment is that of response time, so the onus will quickly be on your team to do everything it can to optimize performance of the ROLAP system. Creating, populating, and maintaining aggregations on the data mart (assuming your ROLAP solution is aggregate aware), ensuring adequate backbone pipe size, optimizing RDBMS performance, and maximizing ROLAP application server performance are your primary available avenues.

Keys to Success

The creation and implementation of a successful and sustainable subset data mart is somewhat less daunting than that of a "bottom-up/building block" data mart, but challenging nonetheless. There are six keys to a sustainable subset data mart effort: scope management, single feed, infrastructure, meta data, subset data mart keys in parent, and well-managed pilot/roll-out.

Scope Management

Your greatest enemy in your efforts to deliver a valuable information asset to the organization is scope creep. Scope creep is the ever-expanding mission of the subset data mart project. Scope creep is usually externally driven by users, managers, sponsors, and executives seeking to expand the range of data provided by the subset data mart system.

There is a simple way to help control this challenge: a finite mission statement of no more than one sentence that defines the sum total of the subset data mart's mission and scope. This is commonly referred to as "the elevator test." The example is that you get on the elevator in the lobby with a manager who pushes 2 and then asks you what the subset data mart is for. To pass the elevator test, you must be able to answer the question before the manager exits the elevator one floor later. This is a practical and useful tool for eliminating scope creep from your data mart project.

Establish the "elevator test" mission and scope statement in response to the business driver that is prompting the project. The solution to a clearly defined business driver that has discrete, visceral pain will be a finite mission and scope statement. Ensure that this one-sentence mission and scope statement is written into every initial project document, especially those related to resource allocation and time lines. Any effort to expand the scope of the project can be met with the mission statement. Any request that falls within the scope of the mission statement is reasonable and should be included or scheduled for immediate inclusion at the earliest possible time. Anything outside the mission statement must be referred back to the business driver identification process.

Single Feed

A subset data mart must be exclusively fed by the parent data mart or data warehouse. There are no exceptions to this rule (bidirectional data flow discussed earlier in this chapter does not negate this downstream data flow rule).

One of the fundamental precepts of data warehouse and data mart design is that the entire system *must* audit to itself. Without this fundamental feature, the system has no internal integrity and will suffer inevitable deterioration in user confidence. Introducing an external data feed into a subset data mart is a certain recipe for short- and long-term disaster.

Infrastructure

The enterprise must supply and support an infrastructure that will adequately support the subset data mart today and in the future as it rapidly grows and expands. The infrastructure elements include the network, servers, system support, and user support.

Network

The most commonly neglected element of a subset data mart system is the network. This is not surprising because it is almost impossible to demonstrate a discrete ROI (Return On Investment) for a network investment. Businesses are notoriously reticent to invest in "brick and mortar" that doesn't demonstrate an immediate return within one or two quarters. Because of this attitude, networks generally only get fixed when the business comes to a screeching halt when the network melts down. They generally are only rebuilt, rearchitected, or constructed adequately when the business operations physically relocate into a new facility.

Be this as it may, subset data marts are server-centric systems. They require a robust and healthy network to connect the clients and the server-centric applications and data resources. Subset data mart systems often require the movement of very large data sets between parent data warehouses or parent data marts and the target subset data mart system. MOLAP applications are very popular subset data mart implementations. These applications require very large dedicated data sets that are often moved from larger systems more capable of calculating them in reasonable times. The MOLAP data cubes are often sliced into subsets for mobile OLAP (On-Line Analytical Processing) applications. ROLAP application servers require very healthy network connections to the parent data warehouse or data mart, with large data sets frequently passing between them. Finally, client resident tools, especially the LowLAP (Low-Level Analytical Processing) tools, pull large data sets from the data mart to the client platforms for each question and answer.

The network is both the nervous system and the circulatory system of the data mart system. It must be very stable, high capacity, and well supported. The key elements of

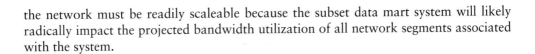

the network must be readily scaleable because the subset data mart system will likely radically impact the projected bandwidth utilization of all network segments associated with the system.

Servers

Subset data marts require healthy, powerful servers. It is not a viable plan to use recycled, outdated, cast-off servers for your subset data mart implementation. The enterprise must provide servers that are not only powerful, but extremely scaleable. It is almost certain that you will require immediate upgrades to your server platform soon after pilot and/or roll-out of the subset data mart system, especially in the area of I/O bandwidth.

Your servers must be industrial strength, properly scaled to your implementation, capable of mirrored or suitable RAID (Redundant Array of Inexpensive Disks) data protection, and have very clear and open growth paths.

It is generally much easier to obtain the required server resources than network resources. Servers are discrete items. Managers and executives can "kick the tires" of a server and come and see it physically installed. In short, a server with an attached disk array is a lot sexier than a rack of routers and patch bays. Servers are also easily dedicated to specific applications and processes in the subset data mart system. It is much simpler to dedicate a server to a ROLAP application than to amortize a 100 mbs (megabit per second) network across every process in the business.

System Support

After networks, the next most neglected element of subset data mart systems is system support. Subset data mart systems have very high maintenance requirements after initial roll-out. Subset data mart systems are constantly changing and evolving as the needs of the business change. Because subset data mart systems exist at the interface of the business needs and the information resources, their destiny is that of constant and neverending change and evolution.

If this wasn't challenging enough, subset data mart systems also very quickly become mission critical to the business. The pace of business today demands that every business make decisions at lightning speed in response to rapidly changing competitive or market conditions. Subset data mart systems are required in order to meet these decision-making demands. If the subset data mart system is "down," decisions are "down." To most organizations that is just as fatal as the order entry system being "down."

Most organizations struggle with these two key concepts and often don't budget adequate resources to maintain the subset data mart system on an ongoing basis. A subset data mart that lacks adequate resources is a time bomb waiting to go off. It is only a matter of time before it takes a large number of casualties with it. If you do not want to be among the body count, you must ensure that you budget adequate support resources for the subset data mart system from the beginning of your project planning. There is little chance you'll be able to slip it in near the end; you must include the maintenance resources required from the initial stages all the way through the project.

User Support

Well-trained, experienced user support is required to achieve a sustainable subset data mart system. For many users, the subset data mart will be their first exposure to directly accessing and utilizing a data resource in the business. These "newbie" users' first and lasting impression of the system will be largely formed by their experiences when dealing with support personnel.

Your user support team must have high levels of understanding of:

- *User mission*

  The support team must clearly understand the users' mission and its context in the business. Many support/user community conflicts are a direct result of the support organization being out of touch with the mandates and missions of the user community. It is much easier to understand and deal with a panicked, frantic user if the support team understands that the annual budgeting exercise the user is working on is always due to the CEO (Chief Executive Officer) tomorrow.

- *Politics*

  The support team needs to be in touch with the fundamental politics of the user community—who reports to whom, who has a direct line to the top, and so on. It is critical to your long-term success to avoid brush fires in the user community incited by out-of-touch and brusque support personnel.

- *User tools*

  The user support team must be completely versed in the intricacies of the user access and analysis tools. The support team must clearly understand how the tools work, how to accomplish real business tasks with the tools in your subset data mart environment, and how to use the tools for basic and advanced tasks. It does no one any good to have your user support team be at the same experience, skill, and training level of your user community. You need more than people who will read users the documentation over the phone. The support team must be able to solve real problems in short timeframes.

- *Troubleshooting*

  Ensure that the support team experiments with troubleshooting. Have them personally reinstall the software, discover how to troubleshoot and solve middleware problems, identify data problems, and identify and correct client platform problems.

- *Data*

  The support organization must be well versed in the data contained in the subset data mart system. It must understand what business processes are represented there, where the data comes from, what happens to it along the way, and how it is stored in the subset data mart. The support team must maintain working knowledge of the ongoing changes in the subset data mart, especially new and modified summary tables.

Most users' process for resolving problems goes something like this:

1. Try to correct problem/answer the question for 30 seconds or so.
2. Call support.

Consequently the support team will be fielding a lot of "how do I" and "where do I" questions from the user community. The support team must be able to answer these questions quickly, competently, and intelligently and to do so, they must have knowledge of the data.

- *Technical infrastructure*
The support team must have a functional understanding of the technical infrastructure that supports the subset data mart system. The team must be aware of the physical locations and connections of the subset data mart system elements. It must have a working understanding of the servers, databases, and networks that connect the elements. This does not mean that the support team must be expert in any of these areas, but it does mean that the support team should invest the time in being educated by the experts to achieve a level of conversant knowledge about the system. Every support team member should understand where the parent system is, what the parent system's scope is, how the parent is connected to the subset data mart server and how big the connection is, where the subset data mart server is located, and what the fundamental physical characteristics of the subset data mart server and associated technology are.

   This technical infrastructure knowledge allows the support team to speak intelligently to users when hiccups develop in the subset data mart system processes. A working knowledge of what physical technologies are involved in the subset data mart system is required for the support team to establish and maintain credibility with the users.

- *Subset data mart process and technologies*
Like the physical technical infrastructure, the support team must develop a working understanding of the subset data mart system processes and associated technologies. The support team must understand completely the relationship of each step of the subset data mart system process, from extract and transformation to load, index, and replication. Again, the goal is not to create a duplicate set of system experts, but to build a foundation of fundamental knowledge that will allow the team to speak intelligently to the users about where things come from and what they represent.

- *Meta data population and maintenance*
The meta data population and maintenance process is especially important for the support team to understand in some detail. The user will have a wealth of questions about the meta data and what it represents. The support team needs to stay in close touch with the meta data repository as it grows and changes over time to ensure that its knowledge of this resource stays current.

The overall level of user support required will be driven by several factors. Chief among them is your level of success in delivering pertinent, easy-to-understand meta data in an environment that is extremely easy to access and utilize. The easier it is for users to answer their questions through the meta data, the fewer "where do I" and "how do I" calls the support team will have to answer.

Another key driver for support is the level and quality of end-user training. Low-quality, tool-centric training leads to very high support requirements. If you hope to maintain reasonable support levels, you must deliver training that is specific to your site, specific to your data, and specific to real business questions.

Finally, the level of expertise of your support team will play a critical role in determining the overall level of support. If your support team is very thin in overall knowledge, the users' questions will go unanswered. This leads to a very high call-back rate, as users and additional support personnel struggle to solve problems. A competent user support team can solve or refer user questions in one call lasting 10 minutes or less.

Overall, your user support team will have a tremendous impact on the success and sustainability of your subset data mart system. The user support function is often neglected and pushed into the shadows as the stars of the subset data mart project receive the lion's share of attention. To ensure success, however, you must dedicate specific and sustained resources to user support.

REALITY CHECK More than you'd probably like to admit, the success of all your efforts will hinge on the support team. All the back room technology is nice, but for the users it comes down to the user access tool and the support experience. Get the support team involved in your project early and ensure they participate in all tool and technology decisions.

Meta Data

Meta data is a requirement for success and sustainability. If you release a subset data mart without meta data, your support costs will be extremely high, your utilization will be low, your user base will be limited to a small audience of knowledge workers, and your project will probably have a very short life span before it falls before the ax of resource allocation or is the victim of a political shift.

To achieve optimum success, you should implement a logically common, extensible, and open meta data repository for the enterprise. Your meta data repository needs to contain both technical and business meta data in sufficient depth to answer the needs of the subset data mart support team and the business users. The meta data must be easily accessible and provide for a seamless drill through into the available enterprise resources, such as reports, analysis, and data sets.

Most importantly, and by far the greatest challenge, your meta data system must be sustainable. Due to its overwhelmingly manual nature, meta data is very challenging to maintain over time, as resources dedicated to the subset data mart drop off. Only implement what you can maintain over time. Out-of-date meta data is worse than no meta data at all.

Subset Data Mart Keys in Parent

If there is one thing you can do to make your life easier in the world of subset data marts, it is to include subset data mart segmentation keys in the parent data warehouse or parent data mart. This a true "no brainer" with 20/20 hindsight, but many teams don't think to include them in the initial data warehouse design.

Subset data mart keys are used to allow the easy segmentation of subset data marts and InstaMarts. If the keys are not included, important historical information may be lost, for instance, in the case of transaction detail that is not tagged with sales region data and is later pulled into a sales region subset data mart. Due to the constant shift of customers and territories among regions, it may be impossible to later establish what region the transaction belonged to when it actually happened. (See Figure 9.2.)

Including subset data mart keys in the parent enterprise data warehouse or parent data mart also allows painless mirroring of subset data mart information in the parent. It is almost always the case that the subset data mart users will evolve their own specific set of summary tables and other representations of the data. These unique data sets will quickly establish an identity of value and ease of use for specific purposes. A quick follow-on will be requests from parent enterprise data warehouse or parent data mart users to have "one of those things the subset data mart users have." The inclusion of subset data mart keys in the parent data warehouse or parent data mart allows the quick and easy creation of duplicate data sets to mirror the information and functionality of the subset data mart.

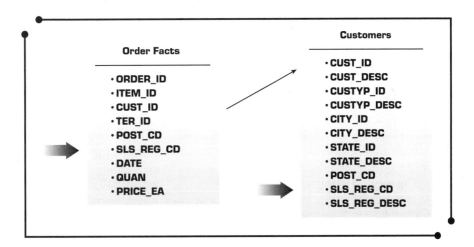

Figure 9.2   Data warehouse schema with data mart keys embedded

Well-managed Pilot/Roll-out

For your subset data mart to be a success you must have a well-managed pilot program and general roll-out. Your goals are to establish viability, establish credibility, gain trial, and build and retain utilization.

Establish Viability

You must first establish a viable subset data mart system and user community. This process is outlined in this book, and even a medium level of adoption of the principles and techniques described in this work will take you to this goal. Critical factors in this area are population and maintenance of a viable meta data repository and adequate levels of user training. If either of these two areas are shorted, you will never establish a viable, sustainable subset data mart system.

Establish Credibility

Your next step is to establish the credibility of the subset data mart system. This process varies depending on the success of the parent enterprise data warehouse or parent data mart. Due to its derivative nature, the subset data mart will be entirely dependent on the credibility of its parent system. Just as you cannot make a silk purse from a sow's ear, you cannot easily build a credible subset data mart from a disparaged and ridiculed parent enterprise data warehouse or parent data mart. In this scenario, it is your unenviable task to change the perception and reputation of a corporate information resource and its team from marginal to mandatory.

This type of project requires a relaunch of the enterprise data warehouse/data mart concept based on a very well-targeted subset data mart relieving specific and life-threatening, high-level pain. A "silk purse" subset data mart requires a high level of investment in business driver and needs analysis, design, QA (Quality Assurance), and user support and development.

In this scenario, you must ensure that the subset data mart you are providing is a specific and complete solution to life-threatening pain to very highly valued individuals, groups, or functions in the business. You don't have room for a marginal payoff subset data mart; you must deliver a high-impact solution to the business. You must invest the time and resources required to identify a pure and solid business driver that your subset data mart can address.

You must also ensure that the "silk purse" subset data mart is entirely free of corrupt, incomplete, or misleading data. The subset data mart must be entirely and completely reliable for the user community. You cannot afford for even one marginal data point to make it into this subset data mart—too much is riding on its success and acceptance by the user community.

In a scenario where the parent enterprise data warehouse or parent data mart has been well accepted by the user community, your task will require much less worry. You will have the opportunity to leverage success stories from the parent enterprise data warehouse or parent data mart user community and establish the subset data mart's credibility from them. Ensure that you have documented and communicated examples of parent enterprise data warehouse or parent data mart success to your pilot and user community of the subset data mart prior to launch.

Gain Trial

Before you can build utilization, you must first convince users that the subset data mart is worthy of trial. Once users try the subset data mart system and experience some success, they will become members of the ongoing user base of the system.

Because you will not be introducing the first example of integrated, scrubbed, and historical data in the organization, you can't count on as much "wow" factor to carry the day for your efforts as a virgin introduction. Again, you will have the advantage of leveraging the success of the parent enterprise data warehouse or parent data mart, and this is your primary weapon.

Data marts, if they have a hope of being sustainable, are built and implemented in response to specific pain of an organization. Many times, the process of gaining trial of the subset data mart merely comes down to demonstrating the process of using the available tools to answer pertinent business questions. Simply preparing "cook book" examples of how to achieve success using the subset data mart system often carries the day to generate sufficient trial to build a viable user base.

The importance of a strong user support organization during this phase cannot be overly stressed. If users have negative experiences during the trial, they will not be predisposed to employ the system in an ongoing manner.

Trial is also the most critical time to put your mentors out into the field. A strong mentor can guide users through their initial experiences with the subset data mart system and lead them to success. An experienced voice is many times the only thing a new user needs to feel comfortable with a new resource. This is the opportunity for mentors to establish ongoing relationships with users and to spot potential power users who can assume the mentoring role within their workgroups and organizations.

Build and Retain Utilization

If you have built a solid subset data mart system, including strong technical and human components, your trial period will yield a solid user base. To remain viable and sustainable in the organization, you must build on this base and drive utilization throughout the homogenous subset data mart system user community.

System monitors take on added importance in this phase, as you seek to identify your users and to spot and track utilization trends. This is the time to demonstrate proactive system management by spotting emerging requirements for summary data sets.

You must build and maintain a very high level of communication with your user base during this phase. Use your mentors to cultivate and nurture power users. Monitor the usage of your target power users and selected "mentorees" very closely. Do everything you can to ensure their success, especially in quick ROI opportunities. As soon as you have a success story publicize it mercilessly. As soon as you have a second, flog it as well. Users are very attracted to positive ROI success stories and will be drawn like moths to the flame toward your subset data mart system. It only takes a few wins to build a solid user base in most organizations.

Customer service orientation becomes critical because continued and expanded use often hinges on turnaround times for requests for support, modifications, and additions. You must ensure that the support team is ready and waiting for the users. The support team must maintain a positive, noncynical outlook at all times in their relations with the user community during this phase of the project. One bad apple in the support team truly will spoil the whole barrel, so do whatever you must to isolate negative personalities on the support team.

Establish and implement clear customer support metrics for the development, maintenance, and support teams well before pilot and roll-out. Don't drop it on their heads in mid stream; that will inevitably lead to resentment and sabotage. You must guarantee that the team members understand that their performance reviews will be based primarily on customer satisfaction metrics. This is the primary cultural challenge you will face during this stage of the project.

Summary

As noted in the opening of this chapter, subset data marts are pretty easy compared with their more challenging cousin, the incremental data mart. Still, as we've seen, they present a clear set of definable challenges that must be overcome in order to deliver and sustain a successful subset data mart that adds value to the organization.

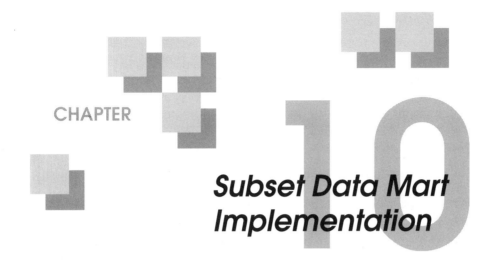

CHAPTER

Subset Data Mart Implementation

Once an organization has invested the time, money, and resources into the long process of creating an enterprise data warehouse, it can begin to reap the rewards of its efforts. Industry studies have shown the average ROI (Return On Investment) of an enterprise data warehouse to be over 400%. The primary vehicle for generating these fantastic returns is subset data marts. Subset data marts allow users to work with data sets that are specifically targeted at their unique challenges, processes, functions, and opportunities. Subset data mart users and their servers don't have to wade through mountains of other people's data in order to glean the pertinent records. The net result is better system response time, a more manageable system, and quicker ROI for the business.

Design

The design of a subset data mart is solely dependent on the needs of the users. It may be large, small, permanent, or temporary. It may support a dedicated application, such as a MOLAP (Multidimensional On-Line Analytical Processing) analysis tool, or be a general-purpose information store for the user group. It may be a temporary data set used to support an afternoon's analysis, or it may be constructed to support a one-year program.

The subset data mart may be a very large system, with multiple subject areas and thousands of users. In prior years, these system were commonly referred to as "departmental data warehouses."

REALITY CHECK   If you've implemented a classic ER design enterprise data warehouse, your only effective vehicle for getting information into the hands of users will be subset data marts. Do not attempt to unleash users on the normalized data warehouse. Build the users some nice, denormalized data marts with star schemas and then turn them loose on the data.

This was primarily due to the "currency" of the data warehouse name at the time. Nobody was handing out money for the construction of anything called a "data mart." Data warehouses were the hot topic, and that was the easiest route to funding and implementation. As the world of data warehousing has evolved, we can now generate political will and subsequent funding support for subset data marts in their own right, without disguising them as downsized data warehouses. Although some organizations continue to prefer to view their systems as a series of distributed data warehouses with a "corporate" data warehouse at the core, a more practical view is that there is only one true data warehouse, that being an enterprise data warehouse that provides depth and breadth of coverage across the enterprise. Any subset of that scope is a subset data mart, of one size or another.

Subset data marts can be derived from other parent data marts, and this is very common in the case of specialized multidimensional data sets, such as those used to support MOLAP tools. Many subset data marts are spawned from a typical departmental or functional parent data mart. Optimally the number of "child" subset data marts is balanced nicely between workgroup data set optimization and the available support resources. Subset data marts are so easy to pop out that many teams rapidly create many subset data marts before they consider the support requirement implications of each one. This can be a fatal mistake for the entire subset data mart effort because the low levels of support and customer satisfaction that are part and parcel of this scenario quickly lead to diminished sponsorship and resource support. Don't let your subset data mart creation efforts get out of hand. Work hard to maintain a good balance between the number of subset data marts and your available support resources.

Regardless of the eventual size of your subset data mart, or its intended life span, it is essential that you construct it following these basic design principles.

Derived Solely from Parents

The subset data mart must be constructed using feeds from the parent enterprise data warehouse or parent data mart only. By now, you are probably getting pretty tired of reading this point, but I cannot over emphasize the importance of never allowing any external data feed into the subset data mart system. All data must come through the sources to the parent data warehouse or parent data mart. External data feeds corrupt the auditability and credibility of your subset data mart system.

No Proprietary Columns

Try to avoid the creation of proprietary columns of data that exist only on the subset data mart. They are especially popular in the area of aggregations and metrics. If the subset data mart is the only place that the "average order process days" column exists, you are setting yourself up for problems down the road. It is inevitable that users of the parent data warehouse or parent data mart will be exposed to this field through shared reports or analysis. They will require it to be integrated upstream into the parent in order to provide a corporate or enterprise view. Although this is not the end of the world, it makes things much smoother and easier to implement and support if all columns are created and distributed from the parent. This ensures consistency of business rules and semantics across all child subset data marts.

Indexable Column-Based Extract

Your subset data mart will be based on some measurable characteristic of the transactions of the parent detail fact table(s) or the parent business dimensions, for example, geographic characteristics such as region or zone, functional characteristics such as manufacturing-oriented information, or organizational characteristics such as sales related only to a specific division. Include these subset data mart keys as a separate indexable column in the parent data mart fact and/or dimension tables. These discrete columns allow simple and easy extraction of subset data mart information. A column containing "division" data allows almost anyone to easily carve out a subset data mart of information specific to a single division's interests. These extractions require nothing more than simple SQL (Structured Query Language) to create, allowing anyone with access to a point and click query tool to subset out data sets for specific needs.

If you do not provide these indexable columns, any and all extractions will require extensive "black box" processing by custom logic to produce viable data sets for the subset data mart. In addition to the creation and maintenance overhead of this approach, you also will be losing the only way to maintain operational history.

It is a Herculean effort to retroactively tag transaction level information with relationship information. Common examples are trying to understand current customer / sales representative / sales territory deployment performance versus historical performance. Unless each transaction is tagged with all pertinent keys, that is, cust ID, rep ID, and territory ID, it will never be possible to perform this analysis. These same relationship tags also form the foundation for later subsets of the information into subset data mart–specific data sets.

Multiple Views

Your subset data marts must be able to support multiple views of the same information. Common examples include the need to see an organization's performance from both a sales and marketing perspective and a finance perspective. These are usually referred to as an S&M (Sales and Marketing) view and a P&L (Profit and Loss) view. In this case, management uses the same subset data mart to view activity from both a sales perspective (How much did I sell?) and a finance perspective (How much did I earn?). An example of this requirement is when a division sells products that they "own," or natively produce, as well as products from other divisions or external partners. In this case, management needs to see not only total sales of every product, but also specific margin performance on only products that the division owns.

This example requires the creation and maintenance of two separate summary data sets, each with their own sets of business rules. One summary data set calculates and summarizes sales of all products, regardless of origin; the other is used for analysis only of sales, costs, and margins of products "owned" by the division.

You will find many examples of multiple views, including commission and noncommission sales; domestic and international sales; internally produced parts versus outsourced parts; all versus hourly versus salaried employees, and so on. Although they will vary by subject area, your summary sets must accommodate these varying views of the same base set of transactions and business dimensions.

Common Semantics

Simple things are often the most challenging in the design of successful data resources. Chief among these simple but daunting challenges is words we use to describe metrics, events, and entities in the business. How many times have you sat through hour-long debates about the meaning of the word "sales"? If your experience mirrors mine, it will be far too many times. Businesses seem to have more ways to express and describe the same concept than is healthy, and that is certainly the case when it is time to codify those descriptions into the architectural framework of the subset data mart system.

Beyond the alignment of common business rules and the resulting semantics such as "sales," "net profit," and "division" lie even murkier waters. For instance, in an organization that has operations and divisions around the globe, what do "international" and "domestic" sales mean?

As you start down the semantic trail, you quickly find that your parent data warehouse or parent data mart will be required to carry multiple columns with a variety of flavors of the same basic metrics. It is not unusual to find parent data warehouses carrying many sales columns, one for each international and domestic view of the global operations or divisional view. This realization often leads to widespread apoplexy among DBAs (Data Base Administrators), but their protestations must be ignored in the face of the greater good of the power of these multiple columns. A common repository of these various sales perspectives allows quick and easy segmentation of the information into subset data marts, while retaining a corporate or overall view of all available metrics from the parent data warehouse or parent data mart. This ensures that when the Asian operation reports a sales figure from their subset data mart, it will match exactly the Asian sales numbers contained in the ASIAN_SALES column in the parent. The countless person-hours saved by this design that would otherwise be spent tracking down

> **REALITY CHECK** Common semantics is about the toughest battle you will fight in your data mart efforts. It is never easy to get people to let go of terms they have used for years. Just imagine trying to get a group of Americans to start saying "boot" instead of "trunk" or "football" instead of "soccer." Semantics is a tough battle, and one worth fighting for the rewards it brings, but usually not a good choice for a hill to die on. Fight the good fight, but keep in mind that it is the rare organization indeed that ever resolves all of its semantic differences.

how the Asian staff calculated their reported sales more than offsets the costs associated with the additional DASD (Direct Access Storage Device) and calming the nerves of the DBAs.

Direct Mapping

Use only direct mapping from the parent when creating your subset data mart. Do not perform any additional transformations, lookups, or scrubbing, with the exception of aggregation. It is essential that no new algorithms be applied to the data during the mapping and population of the subset data mart. The subset data mart must directly reflect the detail facts and business dimensions of the parent data warehouse or parent data mart. Custom transformations, other than aggregation, that are performed for subset data marts are direct pathways to disparities between parent and child, which lead directly to maintenance and support problems. If the requirement for a new transformation is documented as part of the business needs for a subset data mart user group, you will save yourself considerable grief later by creating that column on the parent and doing a direct map to the child subset data mart.

You must ensure that the audience for each data set, parent and child, are always speaking the same language and trading in the same currency. Common semantics ensures the same language, and direct mapping ensures common currency.

Construction Options

Subset data marts are very easy to construct, and as such, are constructed using a wide variety of methods ranging from hand-generated code to DTEAMM (Design, Transformation, Extract, Access, Monitoring, and Management) environments. Each approach has its strengths and weaknesses.

Manual

A subset data mart can be created and populated with a simple "insert into" SQL statement. If the subset data mart is to be hosted in the same instance of the RDBMS (Relational Data Base Management System) as the parent, this may be the most efficient way to pop out a subset data mart.

The upsides to this approach are:

- *No learning curve*
  The team doesn't have to climb any learning curve for this approach. Most team members and most simple query generator tools can perform these operations simply and easily.

- *In-house capabilities*
  No external training or consultants are required for this approach. All the required skills are contained within the team and user groups.

- *Usually simple*
  If the design principles for subset data marts are followed, the required SQL code is usually fairly simple. High-powered development talent is not required, thus lowering the resource requirements of the subset data mart.

- *No culture change/mandate*
  Automated tools, be they first-generation EMT (Extract, Mapping, and Transformation) code generators, or second-generation DTEAMM environments, all require a major culture change in the development and maintenance teams. The required mandate is: "Thou shalt always use the tool." To maintain synchronized meta data, manual editing, or maintenance of any code or process is absolutely forbidden. This is a very challenging cultural transition for many organizations and should not be underestimated when adopting a tool-based approach.

The downsides to a manual code approach are:

- *Manual meta data*
  Manual approaches require the manual population and maintenance of all meta data in the system. This is a very onerous task, and extremely resource intensive. Do not underestimate the resource "black hole" characteristics of manual meta data. Manual meta data too often is like borrowing money from a loan shark. It becomes an endlessly escalating debt that is impossible to erase and eventually overwhelms the debtor, in this case, your subset data mart team.

- *Varying talent levels*
  Data mart teams usually attract high-flying, top talent in their initial stages; however, in the later stages, when maintenance is the primary task, the remaining team members are of a lower skill level. This is a major factor when calculating ongoing resource requirements. It is easy to get spoiled by the productivity and output of highly skilled team members in the formative stages of the project. You will often find that lesser skilled "maintenance" talent is less than 10% as productive. They will also be less informed about the parent systems than the original team members. This is not as much a fatal problem with subset data marts as it is in incremental data marts, but still a major consideration.

- *No automation*
  Manual approaches are just that, manual. Given the extremely productive options available at modest price points in today's market, it is challenging to make a case for a manual solution with its attendant manual meta data challenges. A modern DTEAMM solution will allow even moderately talented team members to create and maintain a subset data mart in hours, not days. All the while, they will be automatically populating the meta data as well as monitoring and managing the entire process. Considering the management challenges associated with manual solutions, it's hard to turn your back on the productivity gains of the automated solutions. Think long and hard before choosing a manual approach.

Tools

The rapid growth of the data warehouse and data mart market segment has fueled the development of a wide variety of tools dedicated to various aspects of data mart design, creation, monitoring, and management. Many of these tools are point solutions aimed at a specific and narrow problem, such as database monitoring. Others are grand in scale and extend from one end of the process to the other, from design to delivery. These tools vary in price and performance, and the segment is rapidly evolving, with companies and tools springing up (and disappearing) like mushrooms after a spring rain. (See Figure 10.1.)

Early on, the market was focused on point solutions, especially in the EMT and Q&R (Query and Reporting)/MQE (Managed Query Environment) and OLAP (On-Line Analytical Processing) segments. Recently the market has been rapidly moving toward the DTEAMM environments due to the seamless integration that they offer. (See Figure 10.2.)

As detailed in Chapter 3, the DTEAMM environments offer compelling features, including seamless integration of tools, consistent UI (User Interface), enterprise scaleability, common meta data repositories, system monitoring and management, and automatic population of the meta data repository by all system processes. Although the market will continue to support a few niche players for specific problems that the

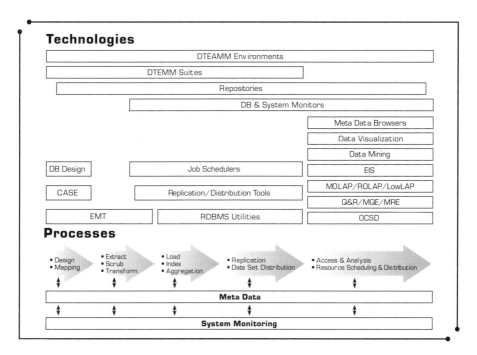

Figure 10.1   Data mart process and tools

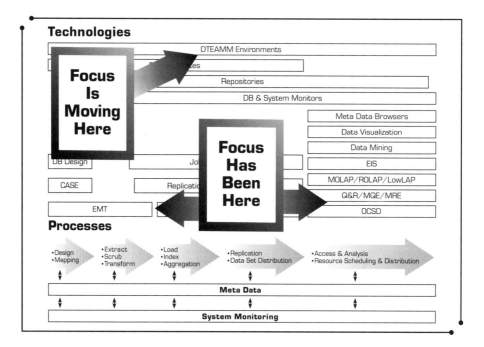

Figure 10.2 Market movement

DTEAMM environments do not fully handle, the clear winners in this segment will be the integrated enterprise DTEAMM solutions.

Whatever type or scale of tool you choose for your subset data mart system, there will be positives and negatives associated with that choice.

The upsides of a tool-based solution are:

• *Lessens talent dependencies*
A tool-based solution makes the talent level of the design, construction, and maintenance team members less of a critical issue. The tool allows users of vastly different skill levels to be productive and effective in all stages of the subset data mart creation and maintenance process.

• *Automatic meta data*
Although many early tools actually systemically populated only a handful of fields, they still had a major positive impact when extrapolated over the thousands of fields typically found in large-scale subset data marts. Second-generation tools and DTEAMM environments can provide much more extensive population and maintenance of the meta data repository. Although tool vendors prefer to concentrate on productivity gains and the nifty GUI (Graphical User Interface) aspects of their products, by far the greatest value these offerings provide is the automated population and maintenance of your meta data repository. A tool that offers no or limited capabilities in this area is nearly worthless in the long term.

- *Efficiencies/productivity*
  Tools also offer modest gains in productivity and developer efficiency compared to manual creation and maintenance. View with much skepticism tool vendors' lavish claims of 10× gains in productivity. As with new cars, your mileage may vary, and in this case, actual mileage will be much less. Expect productivity gains in the range of 2–4× in real-world implementations, over the entire process of the subset data mart system.

- *Meta data repository integration and support*
  Any tool that is viable in today's market will offer integration with your meta data repository. Tools that require a closed proprietary meta data repository or that only interface with one or two proprietary standards are of very limited value. Insist on open standards and logically common, extensible repositories from your tool vendors. Again, a tool that does not support easy and seamless integration with your meta data repository of choice is essentially worthless. Also, don't settle for manual file export/file import schemes. The world has moved beyond these techniques to real-time update and monitoring.

- *Integration*
  DTEAMM environments provide for a consistent GUI and seamlessly integrated components across the subset data mart life cycle process. This full integration of design, mapping, transformation, scrubbing, populating, access, monitoring, and management is a godsend to anyone who has spent countless person-months trying to string together separate products from multiple vendors (or even the same vendor). Nonintegrated approaches guarantee a future of dealing with wildly disparate GUIs, onerous management overhead of file export/import schemes, finger pointing between supposedly closely aligned "partners," and version incompatibilities between multiple products. Integration provides a modern, productive, and effective work environment in which to rapidly design, construct, implement, and sustain subset data marts. Nonintegrated environments place a significant overhead burden on your resources.

- *Schedulers*
  Point solutions tools and integrated environments offer automatic scheduling of all events in the subset data mart process. This eliminates the need to manage the hundreds and thousands of discrete events associated with manual approaches to subset data mart construction, operation, and maintenance. Integrated schedulers also provide automated population of the meta data repository with event information. This "start/stop/duration" type of information is extremely valuable, especially among the technical audience, and is otherwise very challenging to populate with manual approaches.

- *Monitors*
  Integrated environments and specific point solutions also provide system monitoring capabilities and the automated population of the meta data repository with the results of the monitoring process. Point solutions are usually confined to specific

areas, such as network or database system monitoring. Integrated environments offer full-spectrum monitoring and also guarantee seamless integration with the meta data repository.

Monitoring is a prerequisite for sustainability in the subset data mart environment. You must be able to monitor the entire subset data mart process from extract to access, and quickly and easily derive the implications of each monitoring metric. Without monitoring, it is impossible to know if an extract or load was accomplished. Without monitoring, it is impossible to know if a user is creating a massive aggregation every Tuesday afternoon and bringing the server to its knees. Without monitoring, it is impossible to know if a system resource is being under- or overutilized. Monitoring is your window into the subset data mart system. It is impossible to achieve sustainability without it.

The downsides of a tool based approach are:

- *Cost*
  Early first-generation tools in the EMT segment carried a very high price. It was common to see $350–450,000 ADP (Average Deal Price) in this segment. This high price kept many sites from implementing these early tools and resulted in many manually created systems.

  Second-generation tools and DTEAMM environments offer orders of magnitude more capability for a fraction of the cost. Modern tools range in price from well under $35,000 to $100,000 and up. These lower priced solutions are easily justified and provide nearly instant payback.

- *Learning curve*
  Some early first-generation tools had extensive and steep learning curves. Deep, disparate, complex, and nonintuitive UIs contributed to the lengthy times it took teams to become productive with these tools. Modern DTEAMM tools offer intuitive, consistent UIs, so these problems have been greatly mitigated.

- *Enforced culture change*
  By far the greatest challenge for any tool solution is the mandatory usage required by all team members, at all times, for all problems and challenges. Any manual alteration of the environment leads to unsychronized meta data and system failures. Many teams struggle mightily with this mandate, and often this is the sole reason for the failure of a tool at a site and its resulting "shelfware" status. All team members must "buy in to" the requirement of 100% utilization; otherwise, you will be facing inevitable, if inadvertent, sabotage of the subset data mart system.

- *Speed*
  Ironically, some tool implementations are much more time consuming than a straightforward manual approach. This is especially true in the easy and quick world of subset data marts. Some teams, when faced with the prospect of weeks of training and "learning curve climbing" for complex tools, simply choose to do a "down and dirty" manual extract. Although more timely, these manual approaches are orders of magnitude more resource intensive to sustain over time.

Subset Data Mart Examples

DisposaMart Examples and Uses

A subset DisposaMart is a data set created with a known short- to mid-term life for a known scope or bounded problem set. DisposaMarts may be any size, but you know going in how long they are going to be used and what the specific problem is that they are created to solve. A subset environment is a perfect framework for the creation of DisposaMarts. Because subset data marts are inherently architected and share common business rules and semantics, you don't have the wide range of challenges that an incremental DisposaMart scenario poses.

An example of a subset DisposaMart is a data set created to support a targeted marketing program. The program has a known program life, and the data is derived from a parent enterprise data warehouse. At the conclusion of the program, the DisposaMart data set is deleted.

In this case, the subset DisposaMart is derived from a snapshot of customers who have purchased a specific model of equipment from the manufacturer. This model is outdated, and the manufacturer wants to offer a special financing program to this set of customers to allow them to upgrade to a newer model, for less money than they are currently paying for service contracts on the old model. (See Figure 10.3.)

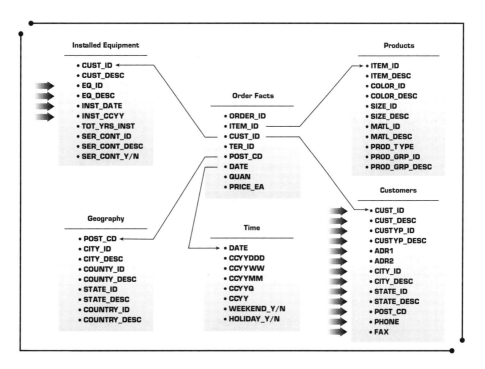

Figure 10.3 Data warehouse star schema with selected DisposaMart fields highlighted

The DisposaMart consists of specific customer and installed equipment detail that will support a targeted direct mail and telemarketing program aimed at generating upgrades and clearing the installed base of equipment of outdated models. The extracted data is derived from the Customers dimension and the Installed Equipment dimension. This information is placed into a large denormalized table, which forms the foundation of the DisposaMart. (See Figure 10.4.)

In this case study, the manufacturer also wanted to track order and upgrade activity in this customer set to measure and monitor program success. In this case, the DisposaMart was hosted in the same instance of the RDBMS as the parent enterprise data warehouse, so the users were able to simply join with the Order Facts, Products, and Installed Equipment dimensions. This allowed the users to monitor daily order and installation activity. At the end of the six-month program, the users were able to present a detailed ROI analysis of the program.

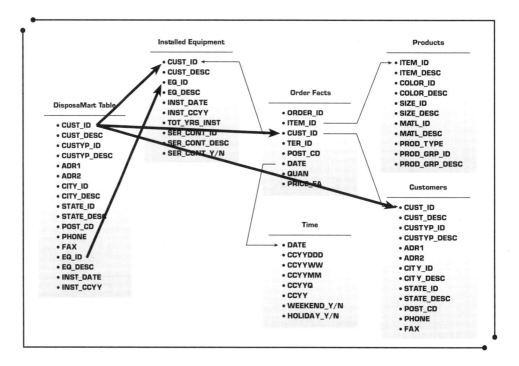

Figure 10.4 DisposaMart table and joins to data warehouse

InstaMart Examples and Uses

An InstaMart is a very short life span data set that is subsetted from a parent data warehouse or parent data mart. They are most commonly used to support iterative analysis and mobile OLAP. InstaMarts have life spans of minutes to days, and they come and go rapidly in user temporary spaces in the subset data mart system. InstaMarts are normally created and deleted by end-user access and analysis tools, with no intervention required from the subset data mart system team.

A common example of an InstaMart is a mobile OLAP data set sliced from a parent data mart and used locally by users. This example is from a client site where sales representatives use mobile OLAP via LowLAP (Low-Level Analytical Processing) tools to provide flexible and portable "slice 'n' dice" information for short-term analysis and decision support. The use is primarily for understanding individual customer buying trends and patterns.

The InstaMart is created from the parent data mart by extracting information from the Order Facts, Customers, Products, and Time dimensions. The goal is to create a multidimensional data set that is targeted at a specific customer's purchases over the last two years to allow trending and analysis. (See Figure 10.5.)

REALITY CHECK Portable OLAP is one of the fastest growing uses of information today. Make sure you are well prepared to enable mobile sales reps and other users to quickly and easily slice off multidimensional data to peruse at their leisure.

The LowLAP tool extracts the information from the parent data mart and uses the answer set to construct a proprietary data cube on the sales representative's laptop computer. The sales rep can then use the cross tab features of the LowLAP tool to "slice 'n' dice" the customer data to better understand the buying patterns and trends of this specific customer prior to making a customer visit. (See Figure 10.6.)

In this example, the LowLAP InstaMart is of a very fine level of detail, down to the individual order and day level. A data cube of this level of detail would be very, very large, and not practical for a LowLAP tool unless there were only a few thousand rows of source transactions. (A few thousand rows of source detail would become 50,000 to 300,000+ elements with several dimensions involved depending on the granularity involved.) Most LowLAP tools are only practical when handling relatively small data sets. It is often required to summarize data to a higher level of detail, such as sales by customer by product by week or month, rather than individual order by day.

Many sites prepare multidimensional aggregations on the parent data mart to speed up the process of InstaMart creation in cases like this where the problem set is well bounded and the operation will be repeated often by an entire mobile sales force. Having all the required dimensions and metrics pre-aggregated in a single table greatly speeds the process of extracting the data from the parent data mart, and it can reduce the long processing times LowLAP tools require to prepare even modestly sized multidimensional aggregation data sets for local use.

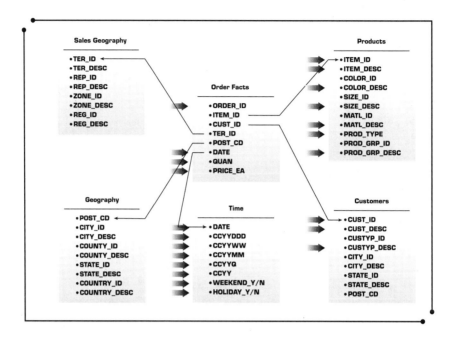

Figure 10.5 Star schema with selected InstaMart fields highlighted

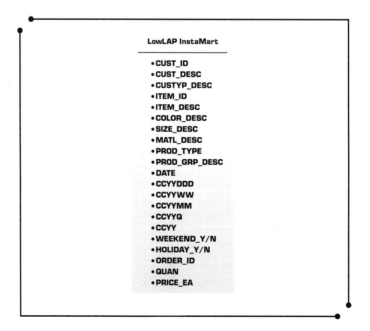

Figure 10.6 LowLAP InstaMart data cube elements

Data Mart Examples and Uses

Subset data marts are used for countless purposes and take innumerable forms. Common examples include functional, organizational, and geographically segmented data sets derived from parent enterprise data warehouses or parent data marts.

An example of a geographic subset data mart is a regional sales subset data mart. This subset data mart is created by replicating the majority of fields from the parent enterprise data warehouse or parent data mart and extracting only the rows that are pertinent to that particular region's performance and activities. (See Figure 10.7.)

In this case, the organization wanted to create subset data marts for each sales division to allow the divisions to have access to data resources that contained only their data. This alleviated security concerns regarding users seeing other regions' sales data, and it speeded up performance because the subset data mart servers could work with much smaller data sets.

The subset data mart was easily created because the parent enterprise data warehouse carried regional columns in the Sales Geography dimension, and each detail transaction in the Order Facts table carried a sales territory tag. This allowed the subset regional sales data marts to carry both a current deployment view, based on the relationship of customers and territory in the Sales Geography dimension, but also the

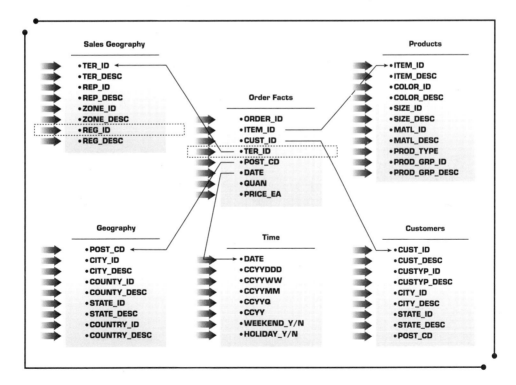

Figure 10.7   Star schema with selected subset data mart fields

historical performance of customers, territories, and sales reps via the columns carried in the detailed transaction history.

Summary

Subset data marts are a wonderful luxury for organizations that have paid the price in time and resources to construct and sustain an enterprise data warehouse or an architected parent data mart. They offer a direct route to the lofty ROIs delivered by well-designed enterprise data warehouses. Subset data marts derived from parent enterprise data warehouses or parent data marts are quick, easy, inherently integrated with other subset data marts, and embedded with the enterprise architecture.

For organizations developing subset data marts from parent data marts, there is less of an enterprisewide payoff, but still a very positive story. As long as the parent data mart is constructed under the auspices of an enterprise data mart architecture, these organizations realize all the benefits of an enterprise data warehouse–spawned subset data mart. These parent data mart–derived subsets are also quick and easy to develop and deploy. They offer users easily accessible targeted data sets that are a direct reflection of the enterprise data mart architecture. They share common dimensions, metrics, semantics, and business rules with other subset data marts in the organization, creating an environment of confidence and auditability.

Successful Incremental Data Marts

The preferred route to enterprise information delivery has moved from a "top-down" enterprise scale data warehouse to a "bottom-up" incremental building block data mart approach. This bottom-up approach using incremental data marts to construct the enterprise information system allows organizations to start small, grow a step at a time, learn valuable lessons along the way, gradually expand their scope, control costs, and maintain low levels of political exposure.

Incremental data marts can be found in a wide variety of flavors, styles, and designs. They range from dedicated MOLAP (Multidimensional On-Line Analytical Processing) data sets used by a handful of users to organizationwide data sets with thousands of users. Many organizations eschew the end goal of an enterprise data warehouse altogether and concentrate on building a dispersed set of incremental data marts closely targeted at various user groups' needs. Others use each incremental data mart as a testing and development laboratory, carefully building the necessary political will and resources required for an enterprise data warehouse. (See Figure 11.1.)

REALITY CHECK   With all the attention paid to data warehouses, be they enterprise or virtual, it is easy to forget how many people just want a simple, point solution data mart to solve a simple point problem. As an industry, we tend to get locked in on the "grand vision" and the "big problem," while forgetting about how many little points of pain are around the business. It may be that we just need the glory that goes along with solving the big problems, or it may be easier to ignore the pesky little problems if we're "100% committed to solving the galactic challenge."

If your mission is a point solution to point pain, a data mart is a great solution. Just don't forget about the "curse of the LegaMart." You still need an architecture.

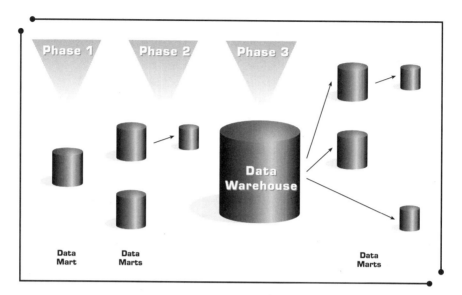

Figure 11.1 Incremental data mart process

Most organizations that embark on an incremental data mart process experience, at a minimum, the requirement to link the independent incremental data marts into a "virtual" enterprise data warehouse to enable enterprisewide views of the information assets. (See Figure 11.2.) This outcome is almost a dead certainty, regardless of what the business management team is saying now. The haunting prospect of incremental data

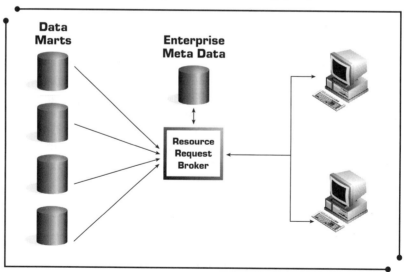

Figure 11.2 Virtual data warehouse architecture

mart integration is the compelling reason why an architected environment is required for all incremental data marts, regardless of currently defined needs.

Prerequisites for Success

Regardless of size, scope, or end goal, every incremental data mart must meet these prerequisites in order to be successful and sustainable.

Architected Environment

The incremental data mart must be constructed under an enterprise data mart architecture. Even if your organization has ruled out ever constructing an enterprise data warehouse, you must invest the one to three weeks to develop an enterprise data mart architecture to achieve sustainability for your incremental data marts. If you do not establish enterprise subject areas, common dimensions, sources, semantics, business rules, and metrics, you will be quickly overwhelmed by the support requirements of managing scores of redundant extract processes and multiple versions of the "truth" generated by the nonarchitected incremental data marts.

The architecture continues to evolve over time as additional business needs are served by the incremental data mart system. The initial enterprise architecture must identify and address:

- *Enterprise subject areas*
  To develop a context for the incremental data mart system, you must begin by defining, at a high level, the enterprise's subject areas. You must take this step, even if the organization has specifically ruled out an enterprise data warehouse as an end goal. Without this context, it is impossible to identify common business dimensions and metrics.

- *Business dimensions*
  You must identify common business dimensions across the business, so that each incremental data mart has one common representation of these dimensions. Common business dimensions used in multiple incremental data marts often include: time, product, customer, employee, and geography. As part of identifying the business dimensions, you must establish each dimension's fundamental key level. In other words, you must answer the question, "This dimension consists of one row per what?"

- *Metrics*
  Metrics are the measure of the enterprise. Sales, orders, returns, discounts, units, and so on are the ways the business measures the operations and subsequent success or failure of the enterprise. To achieve sustenance, you must build a common repository of business metrics that any and all incremental data marts can use. All incremental data marts must share common metrics that are extracted and derived once and shared among the assortment of incremental data marts in the organization. The alternative is measurement anarchy, with a different version of the metric

"truth" resident in each incremental data mart. This is a sure path to decision support havoc and management wrath.

- *Business rules*

  Each incremental data mart must use the same business rule to calculate common metrics and identities. One common business rule must be established for sales and net profit, for instance. If a business group wants to have a different business rule for their incremental data mart's metrics or identities, the column must be labeled uniquely, WEST_REG_SALES, for instance. Do not, under any circumstances, use the same column names for metrics or identities calculated using different business rules on different incremental data marts. The support nightmares will begin immediately, and the integration challenges, daunting enough as they are, will become several times larger.

  Incremental data marts must leverage common business rules or algorithms for transformation and scrubbing on common data points. The extraneous resources required to maintain redundant processes are indefensible, and the additional management overhead required is often fatal. If duplicate business rules are in place, they will inevitably begin to diverge over time as maintenance and modifications are made to one and not the other(s). The optimum goal is a common shared repository of all information assets, including business rule algorithms that can be checked out and shared by all incremental data mart teams.

- *Sources*

  The incremental data mart system must share common source systems of record. It is fatal to have multiple incremental data marts with different source systems of record for the same key or metric. Multiple customer identities or multiple sources of order or production information will play havoc with the enterprise. It is impossible to achieve success with multiple sources for the same dimension key or fact metric. Multiple sources inevitably lead to multiple versions of the "truth," each fervently defended by the constituents of the nonarchitected incremental data mart.

  In many cases, it will be impossible to arrive at a consensus decision in the business as to the proper source "system of record" for a given data point. In this case, specialized point solution integration software is usually required to join together and de-dupe the multiple sources and provide an integrated, scrubbed source for the metric or business dimension. Customer information is very commonly found in multiple source systems and must be integrated and de-duplicated before being brought into the various incremental data marts requiring the customer dimension.

- *Semantics*

  One of the greatest challenges in data warehousing is the effort to gain consensus across the business on semantics related to business processes, functions, organizations, dimensions, and metrics. The ascension of incremental data marts has allowed many teams to avoid this challenging step and simply give each user group a data source that reflects only that user group's view of the organization's elements. Although the team avoids the immediate pain of this challenging task, it is merely deferring it, and making it more difficult in the process. Eventually management is going to want to integrate the incremental data marts. When they do, someone is going to have the unenviable task of integrating a collection of incremental data marts that all use the same words to describe different things. No user group is going to want to change their usage to match some rival organization's, and you quickly have a huge corporate battle that could have been avoided by paying the price up front. Do the hard work in the beginning, and establish common semantics for the organization. You will be saving someone indescribable grief in the future, and it may just be you.

REALITY CHECK There are two simple rules to a successful enterprise data mart architecture:

- Keep it simple to start
- Just Do It

DW (Data Warehouse) Strategy

Your organization must establish an enterprise data warehouse strategy prior to mass proliferation of incremental data marts. Even if the strategy is that there will never be an enterprise data warehouse, you need to establish this fact and mission. If the organization's goals are to eventually create a virtual or physical enterprise data warehouse, each incremental data mart must move the organization forward toward that goal.

If you are moving toward an enterprise data warehouse, your focus must be on:

- *ROI (Return On Investment)*
  Demonstrating and documenting the ROI of your initial incremental data marts is critical in achieving the goal of an enterprise data warehouse. The organization will never commit to the time and resources required for the enterprise data warehouse if the incremental data marts cannot demonstrate quick and positive ROI for the enterprise. Cultivate and nurture power users who can quickly leverage the incremental data mart assets to move their programs and initiatives forward. Capture and publicize each and every success of your users.

- *Process*
  With each iteration of the development methodology of each incremental data mart, and with the creation and sustenance of each incremental data mart, you must establish and hone your development and maintenance process. The enterprise data warehouse will be an undertaking several orders of magnitude larger than your incremental data marts. To succeed with that large-scale project, you must have a well-developed and time-proven process for your team to implement.

  Pay special attention to the sustenance portions of the process: monitoring, management, and change request implementation. Most organizations are overfocused on the "buy/build" portions of the process and neglect the maintenance and sustenance segments, to their eventual ruin.

- *Technology*
  Incremental data marts are excellent test beds for technologies and tools. Each incremental data mart provides the opportunity to "test and toss" tools, technologies, and methodologies. Use the incremental data marts as a prototyping area for vendors' solutions. Don't be afraid to abandon tools that fall short of the vendor's claims and your expectations. In the long run, you'll be much further ahead by adopting a "just do it" approach to data mart tools. Rather than spend months locked in analysis paralysis debating and evaluating, just do it. Implement some tools and see if they work. If they don't work, document what you learned and try something else. In a few months you'll have found something that fits your needs, and you'll be actively producing solutions. The "debate/dicker/dither" approach would still have you creating and filling out massive evaluation matrixes; a "just do it" approach will have you producing high value, high ROI information resources for the business.

  When evaluating technologies, stick to the principles established in this book: logically common, shared, and extensible meta data repository; common UI; seamless integration; and scaleability. To be successful with the eventual enterprise data warehouse, you must have a logically common meta data repository for the entire system, so this will be a requirement for any technology, tool, or environment you evaluate.

- *Scaleability*
  As you construct and implement incremental data marts, you will begin to experience first hand the rapid growth often experienced when users are put in touch with integrated, scrubbed, and historical data. If you've done a good job selecting technologies, you will have an easy time scaling up the network, servers, databases, utilities, and technologies that make up the incremental data mart system. Inevitably you will make mistakes and have bitter lessons to learn. Document these lessons and the solutions to your challenges. It is much better to learn them with an incremental data mart that is below the radar horizon of executive management than it is to be hung out to dry on an enterprise data warehouse that is based on dead-end technology.

  Do not be afraid to refit and redesign older incremental data marts as you learn valuable lessons with later implementations. Almost all data marts will demonstrate growth over time. You might as well bite the bullet now and retrofit early implementations with the lessons learned before it becomes painfully apparent that they have hit the scaleability wall. Keep in mind the planned and eventual size of your incremental data marts as you develop plans for the enterprise data warehouse. Your technologies implemented in the incremental data mart systems will need to support orders of magnitude higher capacities to be viable in that environment.

Wide-Scale/Long-Term View

You must take a wide-scale and long-term view when building incremental data marts to avoid backing yourself into a nonscaleable, nonsustainable corner. Other incremental data marts undoubtedly will follow the ones you are constructing now. It is also almost a certainty that someone in the future will have the brilliant idea of integrating these disparate incremental data marts. Management personalities change regularly, and with them the goals and priorities of the business. Don't lull yourself into a false sense of "we'll never integrate" security. All it takes is a management shakeup, and you will be faced with an integration nightmare of massive proportions.

Avoid LegaMarts at all costs. They will come back to haunt you or your successors. Someone will pay the price, and that price will be many, many times the cost of laying the groundwork for integration now, prior to construction and implementation.

Integration Strategy

Incremental data mart systems require an integration strategy. The team must work within a framework that establishes the design parameters that will facilitate integration when it inevitably happens. An effective integration strategy contains: shared elements, data mart labeled columns, and a data mart to data warehouse road map.

Shared Elements

You must identify all elements and objects that can be shared among the incremental data marts in the business. These elements must be shared across all incremental data marts in the business. You are creating a recipe for certain disaster in having incremental data marts with different business rules, various metrics, and redundant extracts and transformations. You should share, at a minimum:

- Dimensions
- Metrics
- Business rules
- Sources
- Semantics

Data Mart Labeled Columns

When designing the incremental data marts, label data mart view–specific columns with unique identifiers. If the sales column in the West region incremental data mart contains only West region sales, label it WEST_SLS, not SALES. When it comes time for integration, you will have saved yourself countless hours in design and especially maintenance headaches.

REALITY CHECK   This is so simple it is painful, but I couldn't begin to count the sites I've visited where this had not been done. Remember that by labeling data points you are building a semantic environment. The users will become very wedded to what they work with and will vigorously resist change.

Data Mart to Data Warehouse Road Map

Just as you expect your vendors to show you a clear road map to future technology, you must prepare and maintain a road map for the evolution of the incremental data mart system to the enterprise data warehouse. This road map is a living document and will change and evolve as you learn lessons from your incremental data mart experiences and as the business's needs change.

The road map must delineate the path taken for all the technologies, infrastructure, human resources, and vendor relationships required to transition from an incremental data mart system to an enterprise data warehouse centric design. Key elements include:

- Business drivers
- Enterprise architecture
- Infrastructure capacities
- Human resource requirements
- Server, database, and tool scaling
- Topologies
- Meta data repository

Accomplishable Scope

In order for your incremental data mart to have even a remote chance at success, you must tame the wild scope horse. If left unbridled, the scope requirements of your incremental data mart will run wild and leave you with an impossible mission and a short time frame to accomplish it in. To be a success, the scope must be completely defined and rigidly enforced. You must align your scope with a specific business driver in relief of specific pain. Do not allow any scope growth beyond this definition. The scope parameters are:

- Solid, rigid definition of need
- Adequate resources
- Adequate time
- Adequate technology

Keys to Success and Sustainability

Incremental data marts offer a wide variety of implementation scenarios. Once the enterprise data mart architecture is established, incremental data marts can be created to serve a wide variety of needs across the enterprise. To achieve not only the easily attained initial success, but also the much more challenging long-term success of sustainability, you need to ensure that the following keys to success and sustainability are incorporated into your project: elevator test, no creep, deliverables, document process, leverage of best practice, limit to new feeds, good performance, and good tools.

Elevator Test

Above all else, you must be able to pass the "elevator test." This test involves the hypothetical circumstance of getting on the elevator in the lobby with managers from the user community. You push the button for the sixth floor, while they push the button for the first floor. At the same time, they ask you, "what's your data mart for?" You have one floor to answer that question succinctly, completely, and resolutely. In that time, you must define both the mission and the scope of your incremental data mart project.

As you can see, there is no time to lose, and the prerequisite is to use no more than one sentence for the mission of the incremental data mart and one sentence for the scope, and if possible, say it all in one sentence. These one or two sentences form the foundation for all of your efforts in your incremental data mart project. The mission statement should reflect the specific, focused pain that your incremental data mart is solving for a clearly defined set of users who share specific attributes in common. The scope statement must establish a finite and immovable scope that will solve the pain, and nothing more.

A sample mission and scope statement would be: "The data mart system will provide decision support resources for users of the new ACCUS accounting system among headquarters and western region management. The data mart will provide accounting information from the ACCUS system for North American operations only with a rolling three years of historical detail." These two statements clearly define the pain, the users, and the scope. You must prepare similar statements for your effort. Until you can pass the elevator test, your project will be like a ship upon the sea with no destination, constantly battered by the ever-shifting currents of business needs and the driving winds of corporate politics.

No Creep

Your greatest enemy during your incremental data mart project is creep. You will fight this enemy on two fronts: compromise creep and scope creep, both of which are equally dangerous and equally fatal to your project.

Compromise Creep

Compromise creep is an enemy from within. It begins to appear as soon as the team approaches the meat of the work of the project, that space where 80% of the work involved in the entire incremental data mart project resides: extraction, integration, transformation, and scrubbing. Up to this point, the team is usually cooperative in your efforts to bring a source of integrated, scrubbed, historical data to the user masses. However, once the true scale of the work required is revealed during the initial stages of the extraction, transformation, scrubbing, and especially integration efforts, the team begins to backpedal at high speed from the vision and defined deliverables. You begin to hear team members question the need for metrics and dimension information. Suggestions of "deferring" key data points begin to arise. Soon, the development team proposes wholesale abandonment of entire tables.

If left unchecked in the early stages, compromise creep leaves you with a gutted data mart, stripped of its vitality and viability to the user organization. You must nip compromise creep in the bud and not allow it to gain any momentum in the development team. Any initiative to pull back on the deliverables to the user community must be examined very closely and justified extensively. "Because it's hard to get this data" is not sufficient justification.

The simple solution is to require that any deletion of any incremental data mart design element be approved by the project team leader and countersigned by the unit manager or CIO (Chief Information Officer). This should stifle the flood of deletions and deferrals that will otherwise spew forth from the EMT (Extract, Mapping, and Transformation) team once the real work of extracting, scrubbing, and transforming the data on the project begins.

Scope Creep

While compromise creep is the enemy within, scope creep is the ever-lurking danger outside the team. You must draw upon your well-defined, one-sentence, "elevator test" scope statement to defend your project whenever the specter of scope creep rears its ugly head. If a request for additional scope falls outside that rigid definition, you can easily turn it aside, to be considered for future enhancements or additional incremental data marts. If it is within the bounds of your scope statement, you must carefully consider the request, within the political context of your organization.

Runaway scope is one of the leading causes of enterprise data warehouse and incremental data mart failure. Scope control is one of the primary reasons for building incremental data marts only in response to specific, clearly defined business drivers that result from specific pain. If you have amorphous pain, you have undefined scope, and you will not be able to resist requests for additions prior to release. A corollary arises when you are building a solution looking for a problem. To secure budgeting, you will "tin cup" around the business looking for budget dollars. Once someone gives you funding, you will be unable to resist their entreaties for additional scope.

Scope creep will overwhelm your data mart team and leave you with a broad audience of unsatisfied and unhappy customers. You must maintain tight control over scope in order to deliver a deep and sustainable solution to a tightly defined audience that shares specific pain.

Deliverables

You must nail your deliverables in order to achieve success and sustainability for your incremental data mart project. You must be:

- *On pain*
  You must solve specific pain with your incremental data mart. The pain must be definable and be crippling to the target user community. The incremental data mart must completely remove the pain. Do not deliver a partial solution unless you can clearly demonstrate that further iteration loops of the development methodology will deliver the full solution in short order.

- *On scope*
  You must not be consumed by scope creep or compromise creep. The scope of the delivered incremental data mart must be wide enough to solve the pain of the user group and be deep enough to be of long-term value to the organization. Runaway scope saps your resources and prevents you from solving specific pain. Compromise creep waters down your deliverable and leaves your users unsatisfied and unhappy.

- *On time*
  The incremental data mart must be on time. You must provide a timely solution to an overwhelming pain in the organization. You must prevent runaway scope, inappropriate technology, or slow development methodologies from fatally delaying your incremental data mart project.

- *On budget*
  The incremental data mart must not overrun its budget. You must demonstrate a high return from a modest investment. Runaway scope consumes your resources and forces you to be wildly overbudget. It is extremely challenging to make a case for a doubling of budget, even if you provide triple the information resources in the delivered project. Those who request additional scope are almost never around to defend you when you are being crucified for being over the line on budget. Pay very close attention to allocated resources, and beware the resource tar pits of integrating data islands, meta data, and new OLTP (On-Line Transaction Processing) source systems.

Document Process

In the world of incremental data marts, little is more important than to document your processes and experiences in developing and delivering your incremental data marts. This documentation is the corporate memory that will be the foundation for further incremental data mart efforts, and possibly the enterprise data warehouse. You must record each lesson in an open repository so that others can draw upon your experiences. In most organizations, the closest thing to an open document repository is Lotus Notes, which works fine for this purpose. If you don't have Notes and no other type of formal text/document repository is available, simply dedicate a shared, public folder on your file server to word processing documents, spreadsheets, and other types of documentation of your incremental data mart efforts.

If other groups are undergoing parallel incremental data mart development, establish open channels of communication between all groups. Set regular meetings or teleconferences between the groups to facilitate the open exchange of information and best practices that each team can leverage. The biggest challenges you'll face in this effort are jealousy and politics, usually at the management level. To eliminate these stumbling blocks, create your channels of communication among the technical members of the teams directly. Implementers are interested in what works and how to deliver effective solutions. Let the political battles rage above you, while you conduct lunch meetings and swap messages in incremental data mart forums on your intranet.

Leverage Best Practices

During your communication efforts with other teams, you will identify "best practices": ideas, processes, vendors, and technologies that have proven to work in situations similar to your own. You will also be able to identify best practices at industry conferences and seminars, in case studies, and from real-life experiences of consultants and vendors. To make your deliverables, you need to leverage these best practices whenever possible.

If you learn of an interview process that greatly facilitates the design process, use it. If you read of a technology that works in a real-world situation that mirrors your own, try it out. You won't have time to try everything, so attempt to leverage as much existing experience as possible.

REALITY CHECK   One of the best forums for leveraging best practices is the mail list server at www.datawarhousing.com. It is a good spot to seek out answers for problems you are having from fellow practitioners, as well as to spot successful techniques from other sites.

Limit New Feeds

Try to limit the number of new source feeds to your incremental data mart to one or two, if possible, especially in initial incremental data marts and initial iterations. Over 80% of the work involved in incremental data mart projects is in the extraction, integration, and transformation of source system feeds. If you are just starting out in your incremental data mart efforts, you will have to build each source feed from scratch. By limiting the number of feeds in your initial iterations, you will be able to deliver a solution to the enterprise much quicker.

For each source system, you will require the services of a source system expert. In the initial stages of design and mapping, you will need approximately 80% of their time for several weeks. If you are building an incremental data mart to support the reporting requirements of a new OLTP system, be aware that you will have very little, if any, dedicated time from the source system experts. They will be consumed by the daunting task of implementing a new client/server OLTP system in your enterprise. You must gain high-level commitment for their time; otherwise, you will be in deep trouble when it comes time to design and map your incremental data mart. Because the business is unlikely to delay your deliverables, the only effective remedy is to dedicate a "clone" source system expert. This person essentially attaches himself or herself to the primary source system expert and attends all the OLTP system team meetings, monitors the OLTP system project, and strives to bring back as much of the required source system information as possible.

REALITY CHECK If you've got a choice, avoid building data mart systems in parallel with new OLTP systems. It is a very challenging process and not recommended for your first one or two data mart experiences.

Good Performance

Your incremental data mart system must exhibit good performance from all aspects of the entire system. This not only means that queries must be answered by the database server in short order, but that end-user questions of support staff are answered quickly as well. Most organizations focus on RDBMS (Relational Data Base Management System) response time as the primary performance metric of the data mart system. It is indeed very important because sluggish response to user questions leads to low utilization, high user frustration, and a quick end to funding.

Technical system performance problems can usually be solved by "throwing money" at them, so they are relatively easy to fix compared to business issue and human process challenges. To deliver a sustainable solution with long-term value to the business, you must also provide good performance from your support team, your monitoring team, and your development team. Poor user experiences with support will poison the waters. No amount of data or analysis can overcome this. Nonexistent or poor monitoring leaves opportunities for precalculated aggregation sets to go unnoticed. The resulting poor performance of the system lowers utilization levels and leads to dwindling budgets. Slow turnaround of user requests for additions and changes creates a gulf between the team and the user community that is very challenging to bridge once it begins to grow.

You must maintain a "holistic" systemic view of the incremental data mart system and ensure good performance from alpha to omega, in both the technological and human elements of the system.

Good Tools

Quite simply, you must nail this one. You must deliver competent and scaleable technological solutions as part of your incremental data mart effort. Excellent tools are available today to greatly facilitate and enable your incremental data mart efforts. It is almost impossible to make a case for not implementing one of the available solutions, given the low price points and high capability levels that are becoming prevalent in this market segment.

User Tools

From the user side, you must provide server-centric solutions that allow users to easily share information resources in the business. These tools must allow for intuitive access to all available information resources in the business, the easy construction of ad hoc questions, powerful and scaleable OLAP (On-Line Analytical Processing) functionality, robust WYSIWYG (What You See Is What You Get) reporting capability, thin client access, and flexible and powerful scheduling and delivery options. You must not miss on the user tool side of the equation. Your entire incremental data mart system will be judged by what they see on their CRT (Cathode Ray Tube).

It won't matter if you've got 30 terabytes of data on the largest MPP (Massively Parallel Processing) server array in the city running over the fastest network known to man if you give the users an ugly, unproductive, nonintuitive access and/or analysis tool. Bad user tools lead directly to astronomically high support costs and astonishingly low levels of utilization. A variety of proven and powerful user tool solutions are available in the market from a number of market leading vendors. It is possible to deliver what you need; just don't fall short in this area.

From the technical side, demand a solution that is server centric, scaleable, and thin client enabled. A fundamental prerequisite is that the end-user tool seamlessly support a logically common meta data repository.

Data Mart Tools

The emergence of the DTEAMM environments has made the option of building an incremental data mart by hand an almost untenable position. Quite simply, these tools are so powerful and at such low price points that it is pretty senseless to turn your back on the productivity gains, the ease of use, and especially the common meta data repositories that they automatically populate and maintain.

The tool that you choose must enable you to deliver your incremental data mart in a reasonable time. The tool must support your required sources, provide the needed integration, support the required transformations, and directly populate the target RDBMS. The tool must have an open, logically common and extensible repository that is automatically populated and maintained by every element of the tool. It must have a common UI (User Interface) that is intuitive, productive, and more than a slick UI over a "yester-tech" engine. The DTEAMM environment must be fully integrated, with each element sharing and leveraging common resources. This market segment has offerings that fulfill these mandates, so you should demand more than stitched-together Frankenstein solutions.

A modern incremental data mart tool leverages the capabilities of parallel servers to provide multithreaded transformation engines. This allows the tool to accomplish many internally managed operations simultaneously, which vastly increases throughput compared to manually managed single-threaded solutions.

When examining possible solutions, pay close attention to the underlying architecture of the tools and how they go about accomplishing their mission. Your greatest enemy is I/O (Input/Output), so avoid solutions that rely on a plethora of temporary database tables. Your goal is to accomplish as much as possible within memory, with disk I/O confined to caching and very large table integration operations.

As always, demand scaleability. Look for a clear road map to enterprise-scale multiple data mart management and monitoring. Insist on a logically common meta data repository for the enterprise and the ability to share and leverage transformation algorithms among incremental data mart projects. The meta data repository must be open to all internal and external tools, common across the entire incremental data mart process from extract to access, and extensible to allow for easy customization at your site.

Do not attempt to build your incremental data marts by hand. Those days, thankfully, are past, and a variety of very capable and affordable solutions are now available to facilitate the creation and maintenance of data marts in the enterprise.

Summary

Incremental building block data marts are much more challenging than subset data marts. Incremental data marts involve the extraction, integration, transformation, and scrubbing of data from multiple source systems and the population of specifically designed decision support databases provided to answer specific pain for homogenous user groups. All of the land mines that cripple their larger cousin, the enterprise data warehouse, are waiting for the incremental data mart as well. Scope management, compromise creep, appropriate technology, and resource allocation are all waiting in the wings, ready to cripple the unwary incremental data mart project that wanders into their path.

With awareness of these issues, you can steer clear of these obstacles and deliver a high-impact decision support resource to your organization that will be on pain, on scope, on time, and on budget.

Incremental Data Mart Design

Overview

An incremental data mart is designed following the same principles as a full-scale enterprise data warehouse as explained in Chapter 3. Each is fed directly by source systems or a holding/staging area for transactional data such as an ODS (Operational Data Store) or formal data staging area. Each is comprised of integrated, scrubbed, historical, read-only data that exists at a variety of levels of detail and summarization. Each is designed for ease of use and to reflect business users' perspectives, semantics, structures, and organization. Each may be the parent of "child" subset data marts.

The incremental data mart usually has many fewer feeds than an enterprise data warehouse and is correspondingly easier, faster, and less costly to build. Incremental data marts usually have only one or a few subject areas, whereas the enterprise data warehouse contains all subject areas pertinent to the entire enterprise. The incremental data mart is built to answer specific, visceral pain in a tightly defined user group, whereas enterprise data warehouses are often built to answer longer term, more amorphous, and undefined needs in the enterprise. (Compare the data warehouse design in Figure 12.1 with the data mart design in Figure 12.2.)

The primary role of incremental data marts in today's organization is as a "proof of concept" for data warehousing. Incremental data marts are constructed to address the needs of specific user groups and are used to demonstrate ROI (Return On Investment), architecture, methodology, technology, and processes. Once the business case for the incremental data marts can be proven, it is much easier to establish the needs and probable returns to the enterprise for a full-scale enterprise data warehouse. In this bottom-up approach, it is common to find an incremental data mart that is scaled up to become the core of the enterprise data warehouse. This scenario, coupled with the very fast expansion rates of data marts in general, are the primary drivers for the overriding requirement of scaleability in all aspects of the incremental data mart system design and construction.

Incremental data marts normally experience very high initial success with user groups, especially if they are properly designed and supported with a well-populated and maintained meta data repository. In these cases, the greatest challenge for the incremental data mart team is that

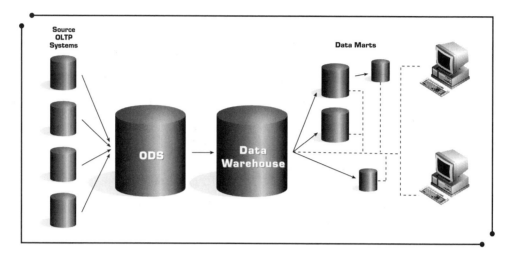

Figure 12.1 DW design with multiple feeds

of overwhelming success, otherwise known as "the curse of success." The target user group for the incremental data mart will bombard the team with change and addition requests, while other user groups in the organization will demand their own incremental data mart targeted at their specific pain.

It is critical that the incremental data mart team not succumb to the temptation to

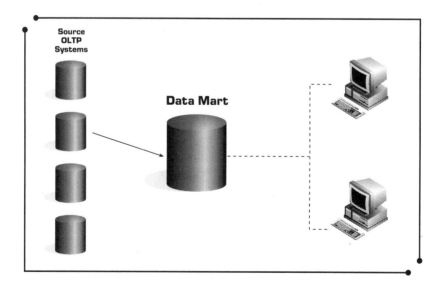

Figure 12.2 DM design with limited feeds

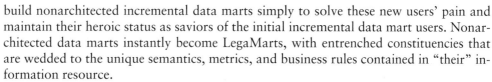

build nonarchitected incremental data marts simply to solve these new users' pain and maintain their heroic status as saviors of the initial incremental data mart users. Nonarchitected data marts instantly become LegaMarts, with entrenched constituencies that are wedded to the unique semantics, metrics, and business rules contained in "their" information resource.

LegaMarts present two primary challenges to the business. First, their redundant extraction and transformation jobs inevitably evolve down divergent paths. This leads directly to multiple representations of the "truth," with each LegaMart's proponents vigorously defending their source and version of information. The resulting crossfire is a very unhealthy place to be caught. Second, these nonarchitected LegaMarts inevitably need to be integrated at a later date. This integration is a massive undertaking, easily several orders of magnitude greater than the effort required to develop a basic enterprise architecture prior to incremental data mart development.

Enterprise Data Mart Architecture

To avoid these organizational nightmares and provide a sustainable information asset for the business, incremental data marts *must* be constructed under an enterprise data mart architecture. An enterprise data mart architecture is designed by the data mart team prior to beginning the design and construction of the incremental data mart(s). The data mart architecture effort should take no more than one to three weeks of the team's time. The danger in taking longer is that the team will usually get caught in analysis paralysis and spend months lost in the minutia of the organization's processes and systems. The definition of each tiny detail is not the goal of the enterprise data mart architecture. It is a high-level effort to define the critical factors at whatever level of detail that can be ascertained in the available timeframe. Not all answers will be known at the end of this period, but you will know enough to get started. The rest of the details will be filled in as you progress in your incremental data mart project and as other incremental data marts follow.

The enterprise data mart architecture must identify:

- *Enterprise subject areas*
  You begin the enterprise data mart architecture process by identifying, at a high level, all the probable subject areas of the entire enterprise. This allows you to identify common dimensions and metrics and to flag semantic trouble areas.

- *Common dimensions*
  Every business looks at its activities in several ways common to most user groups in the organization. Popular examples include Customer, Product, Time, Geography, Sales Geography, and Employee. A primary goal of the enterprise data mart architecture is to identify common business dimensions that are shared across the enterprise subject areas and the multiple targeted user groups for multiple incremental data marts in the organization.

- *Common metrics*

  Organizations have a variety of ways to measure the operations of the business that are referred to as metrics. Common metrics include units, dollars, hours, and other measures of output, throughput, or productivity. Metrics are fundamentally what the business is about and how it measures itself.

- *Common business rules*

  Business rules are the algorithms and logic that the business uses to calculate metrics and derive classification and structure. Various business units commonly use a variety of ways to calculate standard business metrics such as "sales" or "net profit." It is your job during the formation of the enterprise data mart architecture to identify as many common business rules as possible. You must also identify all the different ways the business uses to calculate the same metrics, classifications, and structure. If you are unable to gain consensus on these business rules, you need to carry individual columns identifying each method of calculation. For example, if the international division calculates "net sales" differently from the headquarters staff, you must carry two columns specifically labeled to reflect the user group, e.g., ITL_NET_SLS and HQ_ITL_NET_SLS. You must also populate and maintain the meta data to reflect these two disparate methods of "net sales" calculation.

- *Common sources*

  The enterprise data mart architecture must identify the best system to obtain each required dimension key and metric used in the anticipated enterprise incremental data mart environment. This involves determining the best source system in the business to obtain "Customer ID" information, for example. Once the source system is identified, the first incremental data mart team builds an extract and transformation process to populate their incremental data mart. This extraction process needs to be stored in a central repository where other teams can use it when they need the same information.

  Ideally you don't want to have redundant extraction and transformation programs running against the same source to populate the same data point in multiple targets. This not only is a waste of system resources, but greatly adds to management overhead. To eliminate this duplication, you may choose to use an enterprise DTEAMM (Design, Transformation, Extract, Access, Monitoring, and Management) tool that can support "extract once, populate many" operations. These tools only hit the source system once to extract the needed data. They also only perform the transformation and scrubbing operations once, and then populate each required target directly with the results. This is the preferred solution.

  If you are manually developing your incremental data marts, or using a first-generation code generator tool, you may not have this luxury. To prevent needless duplication of extraction effort, you may choose to create a staging area or mini-ODS that acts as a temporary storage point for each extraction process. In this way, each extraction job is only run once, and each target can then be populated by a separate data replication and distribution program.

The different elements of the organization targeted to be served by incremental data marts often cannot agree on a common source system. For instance, one user group may be wedded to an Accounts Receivable system for customer information, whereas a second group may only find a Sales Force Automation system viable for accurate and complete customer information. In this case, you must integrate these two sources into a common source for the various incremental data marts in the organization. This usually requires a point solution tool dedicated to the scrubbing, integration, and de-duplication mandatory in these circumstances.

- *Common semantics*
Semantic terms are what the business uses to label itself, its elements, its structure, its metrics, and its activities. As elsewhere in life, semantic differences between different elements of the organization lead to many challenges. When two different groups use the same term for two different entities, or use two different terms for the same entity, confusion and frustration reign supreme. It is always a tough battle in trying to gain enterprisewide consensus for semantic terms, but one well worth fighting.

   The construction of an incremental data mart is an excellent opportunity to drive semantic consensus in the business. It is easy to demonstrate the need to agree on what to call the business and its components in order to eliminate not only the resulting confusion, but also the required needless duplication of multiple columns carrying different semantic terms if multiple groups cannot reach consensus.

The creation of the enterprise data mart architecture prior to the design and construction of any incremental data marts is the single most important activity you will execute in the entire incremental data mart project. It is an absolute prerequisite for success, and its absence guarantees the long-term failure of your team's efforts. It is most tempting when faced with the need for only a single incremental data mart solution to avoid or defer this step. You must not fall prey to this temptation. Your initial single solution will soon lead to a proliferation of "single solutions" that will pop up across the landscape of your business like mushrooms after a spring rain. Without a common enterprise data mart architecture to lay the groundwork for common sources, dimensions, metrics, semantics, and business rules, you will be faced with multiple versions of the truth, mass confusion, and frustration about semantic differences and a looming nightmare of LegaMart integration.

REALITY CHECK Don't get intimidated by the sound of "enterprise" data mart architecture. The only thing "enterprise" about it is the potential to extend it across the enterprise. In the beginning, it only addresses the specifics of your first incremental data mart. The point of the exercise is to give you the ability to look up from the details of your individual project and see the enterprise perspective and the context of your incremental data mart system.

Design Fundamentals

Successful incremental data mart design is not terribly difficult, as long as you follow some basic design fundamental guidelines. Overall, the designers must be committed to designing a system that is entirely end-user oriented. If this overriding principle is uppermost in the design team's thinking and execution, you will be well on the way to a successful and sustainable incremental data mart.

To be a success, the incremental data mart must be designed with the following goals as paramount: business focus and ease of use.

Business Focus

The incremental data mart must be designed and built entirely with a business perspective. It must exist solely and only to answer the needs of the business. It must be built to answer specific, visceral pain in the organization, and it must solve this pain as completely as possible. The incremental data mart must be built in response to a solid, sustainable business driver.

Ease of Use

The incremental data mart must be designed, built, and maintained solely for ease of use by the user community. Although seemingly obvious, this principle is often given lip service by data mart design teams while they design and deliver systems whose primary goal is ease of implementation and maintenance by the incremental data mart team. A fundamental law of successful data mart design is: Somebody has to do the work. If you force the onus on the users, your support costs will be very high and your utilization rates will be low.

Easy-to-use incremental data marts are marked by the following characteristics: subject-based design, denormalization, replication, no caveats, and business semantics/lexicon.

Subject-Based Design

The incremental data mart reflects standard data warehouse subject-based design principles. In this design, the information of the business is organized and labeled along perspectives used by the business user community. The transactional information of the business is organized into logical units that reflect the normal business orientation of the users called subject areas. Common subject areas include Orders and Sales, Human Resources, Manufacturing and Inventory, and Financial (G/L).

Denormalization

To build an intuitive productive environment for users, the data is commonly heavily denormalized. Although the normalized design found in OLTP (On-Line Transaction Processing) systems is very good for transaction systems and ease of maintenance by the technical teams, it is the worst possible environment for a user to navigate and attempt to be productive in. A denormalized design is not only optimized for the consumers of the information, it places much less work on the server hosting the incremental data mart. (See Figure 12.3.)

A grocery store is optimized for operations. It is designed and built to make re-stocking the shelves as easy as possible. The onus is placed on the customer to know the locations of every item. A convenience store such as 7-11 is optimized for consumers. The onus is placed on the operational team to pre-build products that are desired by customers. To be successful and sustainable in the data mart business, you must build 7-11s.

Denormalized vs. Normalized Designs Denormalization is the greatest cultural hurdle for most incremental data mart design teams, and you can expect the largest number of cultural challenges in this area. It is common to find massive resistance among the DAs (Data Architects) and DBAs (Data Base Administrators) weaned on OLTP system design and maintenance to the idea of widespread denormalization in the incremental data mart system. In some cases, you may need to find personnel who do not have such deeply held views and are more open to new approaches to system design

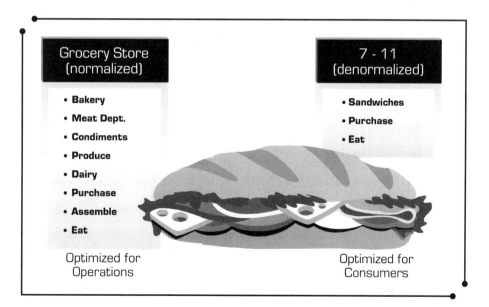

Figure 12.3 The data sandwich

and implementation. Although it is simple for a data architect or a DBA to construct a query in a normalized design, it is a very daunting task for a normal user.

Normalized designs lead to very high support costs because users must constantly be trained and retrained in which of the scores of normalized tables actually hold their data. Although an initial group of power users could be trained to use a normalized system, turnover and attrition will guarantee a very high level of ongoing training and support. Even the trained users will require extensive hand-holding in order to navigate the hundreds of joins and jungle of tables in a normalized system. The high levels of knowledge required by users in a normalized design guarantee a very low utilization rate and a user group limited to an elite segment of power users. Widespread usage among a general user community is impossible with a normalized design without correspondingly high training and support costs.

Normalized designs are very, very slow in responding to users' queries, assuming they can successfully build them. RDBMSs (Relational Data Base Management System) are not quick in processing queries involving a dozen tables and 14 joins, which is a very common scenario with a normalized design and a typical marketing user question. Slow response times by the system also leads directly to low utilization rates. It only takes a few real-world queries to bury an incremental data mart server laboring under the weight of a normalized design, and the resulting 20-minute to hours-long response time will drive away all but the most desperate users.

Many design teams use the rationale that they "don't know what the users want" so it is impossible for them to effectively denormalize the design. They suggest starting with a normalized design until they can ascertain what the users want, then denormalize. This is a fatally flawed approach for two basic reasons:

1. It is almost certain that no one will ever return to change anything in this scenario. Once the system is in place, it will take on a life of its own, and the resulting inertia will tend to dampen any change initiative. Also, once the design is in place and the core of power users is trained in its use, no one will want to duplicate the time and resources required to retrain all the users in a new design.

2. This approach of "we don't know what they want" is the largest red flag imaginable indicating that this team is completely isolated from any business driver that could justify this incremental data mart. Any incremental data mart that is being designed and built in response to a pure and sustainable business driver and its associated clear and visceral pain will be a direct reflection of "what they want." The "we don't know what they want" phrase is the standard design rationale slogan of the "build it and they will come" approach to incremental data marts. This is a nonsustainable approach, doomed to failure. You must only build incremental data marts in response to clear business drivers with identifiable and definable pain. If you do so, you will *always* know "what they want" in intimate detail.

If you are a data mart project manager, you can expect a tremendous amount of "push back" in the area of denormalization. You must resist the urge to please the data architects and DBAs by listening to their pleas of "if they want the data, they can learn the normalized schema just like we did," and "if we denormalize, it will mean a tremendous amount of work for us." Incremental data marts systems are built to serve the needs of the users, not the desires and conveniences of the design and development teams.

Normalized designs are appropriate only in circumstances where:

- *"User" users will never, ever touch the data*
"User" users, or information consumers, are the overwhelming majority of the organization. It is unlikely, if not impossible, for this audience to effectively use a normalized design. If you are building an ODS or other data staging area that will never be touched by this audience and will only be used as a parent for subset or incremental data marts, you can successfully use a normalized design.

- *The data mart is being built solely for a small, elite core of power users*
If you have no intention of ever expanding the user base of the incremental data mart beyond your traditional customers consisting of the "SAS heads" and "FOC Masters" elite power users in the organization, you may have limited success with a normalized design. These users are already steeped in the arcane world of the many tables and joins required to build a question and get an answer in a normalized design, so they can adapt to this type of incremental data mart. You will, however, still be faced with training and supporting this audience at a high level as turnover and attrition take their toll. Performance (or lack thereof) will continue to be a big issue because you simply can't escape the extraordinary load this design will place on the server. And, of course, a limited audience provides a very small and narrow foundation on which to support your incremental data mart system. This is a challenging environment to sustain politically over time, and it is a world easily toppled by unexpected changes in the environment. (See Figure 12.4.)

- *You have unlimited support and training resources*
In the unlikely event that you are blessed with unlimited support and training resources, you may achieve some limited success with a normalized design. Otherwise, the turnover and attrition among the users will bleed your support resources dry because they will require massive amounts of daily hand-holding to navigate the myriad tables and joins of the normalized design.

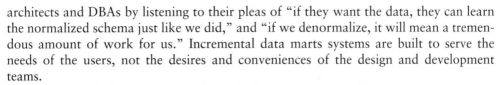

REALITY CHECK In practice, most normalized ER enterprise data warehouses function as nothing more than staging areas for data that is subsetted into data marts for consumption by the users. This is why they are successful with a normalized design; they are not designed for, nor used for, end-user access.

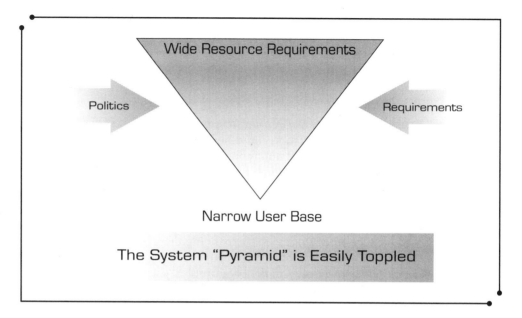

Figure 12.4   Inverted political pyramid

Denormalization Is Required for Success   Although you will probably experience high levels of resistance to this concept among the OLTP veterans of the team, you will find that denormalization is a prerequisite for success for your incremental data mart efforts. The ease of use gained through its intuitive presentation of information, coupled with the much faster response times of a denormalized system, deliver a high performance information resource that is both supportable and sustainable.

Replication

The "rule of thumb" for ease of use–oriented design is for users to get their answer from one to two tables 80% of the time. This leads to very fast response times and a very easy to use and intuitive system for users. To accomplish this goal, you must replicate data profusely throughout the incremental data mart design. This is another area where you can expect near apoplectic responses from data architects and DBAs. Some people have a very difficult time with the concept of carrying a data point in more than one place; they are consumed by "DASD (Direct Access Storage Device) fear." It is a simple fact of

REALITY CHECK   To help break DASD fear early in projects, I usually open my first meeting with the IT technical team with the announcement, "Let's all take a 15-minute break to call our brokers and buy plenty of disk drive stock."

CST_ID	CUST_DESC	TR_ID	TER_DESC	ZN_ID	ZONE_DESC	RG_ID	REG_DESC	CCYYWW	CCYYMM	CCYYQ	CCYY	QUAN	SALES
1001	Al's Quick Mart	185	Chicago North	14	Chicagoland	3	North Central	199708	199702	19971	1997	244	495.38
1002	Dominics Store 283	185	Chicago North	14	Chicagoland	3	North Central	199708	199702	19971	1997	842	1709.47
1003	Jewel Store 288	185	Chicago North	14	Chicagoland	3	North Central	199708	199702	19971	1997	1038	2107.40
1004	Dominics Store 104	187	Chicago West	14	Chicagoland	3	North Central	199708	199702	19971	1997	750	1522.68
1006	Mobil 19951	187	Chicago West	14	Chicagoland	3	North Central	199708	199702	19971	1997	132	267.99
1009	Amoco 2103B	187	Chicago West	14	Chicagoland	3	North Central	199708	199702	19971	1997	68	138.06

Figure 12.5 Replicated data in summaries

life in the world of data marts that you will use a lot of DASD, much more than you plan initially. Thus the team must be able to overcome "DASD fear" and be comfortable in a world where things are replicated freely and provided wherever and whenever it will make the users' lives easier and the environment more intuitive. (See Figure 12.5.)

Replication levels vary in incremental data mart designs, depending on the volume of detail, but they are very commonly found in aggregations. This allows users to build answers from single tables. The resulting quick response times encourage utilization and dramatically lower processing requirements on the server. Again, the fundamental trade-off is who is going to do the work and when. It is much better to do the work on the server in the middle of the night during the update process by replicating data than forcing the user and the server to do the work in the middle of the afternoon at peak load times. The natural inclination of the team, especially those new to the world of data marts and data warehousing, is to push the work out toward the users and the server at query time. You must overcome this inclination and instead deliver to your users a system that is optimized for ease of use through the extensive replication of data.

No Caveats

Historically, IT teams have delivered decision support systems with data structures that were riddled with caveats and land mines waiting to blow up in user's faces. As an industry, we have been famous for requiring qualification on fields such as ACTIVE_CUST_YN (active customer Yes/No). Unsuspecting users the world over have slipped up on these caveats and delivered incorrect information up the chain to executive management, often with disastrous results. To ensure the success, utilization, and sustainability of your incremental data mart, you must eliminate all caveats. A well-designed data mart has zero caveats or land mines for your users.

Philosophically this requires you to adopt a "service business" mindset. No service business would ever be successful if its customers had to endure what users of decision support systems are regularly burdened with. Could you imagine staying in a hotel and being denied maid service simply because you neglected to check the "Guest alive Y/N" box on your registration form? Yet, as an industry, we regularly deliver decision support systems that require an extremely high degree of knowledge and diligence on the part of the users to ensure they do essentially the same thing. A data mart is not a data business nor a technology business. A data mart is a service business, and to be successful, your entire team must adopt this attitude.

The "service business" mindset must be reflected in your incremental data mart design. To achieve a high degree of customer satisfaction, your design must be devoid of all caveats.

Business Semantics/Lexicon

The users of your system are business users, not technical mavens. To provide them with a system they will find accessible, usable, and valuable, your design must speak their language. Table names must be fully descriptive of the contents and subject. All field names must be descriptive and intuitively understandable. If your RDBMS places a short limit on the length of field and table names, you must invest the effort in your MQE (Managed Query Environment) and OLAP (On-Line Analytical Processing) semantic layers to provide fully descriptive and understandable table, field, dimension, and object names. For example, you may be limited to eight, twelve, or sixteen characters for field names. This leads to field names such as TTLNTSLSNA, the meaning of which is not intuitively obvious. In this case, you must ensure that the field description meta data is populated and easily available, and that the user access tool's semantic layer is used to present to the users a field name such as "Total Net Sales for North America."

Design Summary

A successful incremental data mart design can be almost guaranteed if these design fundamentals are followed. Using these fundamentals as a foundation, the design team is ready to address the simple flow of the incremental data mart, from source to target.

Sources

Data marts are merely specially designed repositories of transactional and third-party data that provide easy access and analysis by business users. To construct this collection of information assets for the users, you must first obtain the data from source systems and/or third-party data providers. There are five primary ways of obtaining source information:

- *Direct from source OLTP systems*
  The most common way to obtain data from OLTP systems is to directly extract the data from the OLTP data tables or files stored on the transactional system. Historically most sites have created these extraction programs manually, primarily using COBOL. Some teams implemented first-generation EMT (Extract, Mapping, and Transformation) tools to help generate the code and provide some automatic meta data population and maintenance. Recently, DTEAMM tools have become available to greatly ease the process of extracting data from source OLTP systems and data files.

The greatest danger to the direct extraction of the data is the duplication of effort and disparate business rules among multiple incremental data mart systems. Environments with multiple LegaMarts and new incremental data marts will breed redundant extraction, integration, scrubbing, and transformation processes and the opportunity for many different business rules to introduce various versions of the "truth" into the business.

- *ODS (Operational Data Store)*
  To eliminate the duplication of effort and divergent business rules inherent in multiple simultaneous extractions, an ODS (Operational Data Store) is often implemented. An ODS is essentially a data warehouse without historical or summary information. An ODS is subject oriented, integrated, volatile, current valued (reflects the current state of the data), and fully detailed. The ODS is used to integrate the OLTP systems into subject areas and to transform and scrub the data to provide the business with a reliable operational analysis environment. An ODS makes a superb source for incremental data marts. When you have an ODS available, you can extract out the incremental transactions at your desired frequency with full confidence in the data and with little or no additional transformation or scrubbing. The ODS is described in more detail in Chapter 13.

- *Staging area*
  An ODS requires a full data warehouse–scale effort at data integration and scrubbing, and consequently it is beyond the scope of many organizations who are merely attempting to construct and implement an incremental data mart in short order to answer specific pain in the organization. At the same time, these sites don't want to open up the Pandora's box of redundancy and metric variation of multiple extraction processes. The answer often implemented is a data staging area. This area serves the same purpose of a common source of information as the ODS, without the subject area integration. A data staging area usually contains a fully normalized replication of the transactional systems' data sets, which are scrubbed and transformed to provide a reliable source of data for the incremental data marts of the business. This allows the team to quickly replicate, transform, and scrub only the source systems that are required for the incremental data mart at hand, without taking on the sometimes onerous requirements of a full-scale ODS. As additional incremental data marts are added, more source systems can be tapped and replicated into the staging area. Although a staging area does not provide for the operational analysis capabilities of an ODS, it is often an optimum partner for a fast timeline incremental data mart strategy. Staging areas are explained in detail in Chapter 13.

- *Third party*
  Third-party data sets, sometimes called syndicated data, are any data set that is obtained from outside the organization. Common examples are A.C. Nielson rating data, market segmentation data, industry association sales, and market size data and demographic data. These data sets are available in a variety of magnetic

formats, from nine-track tape to floppy disk, and they are also commonly available via EDI (Electronic Data Interchange) transfer.

Third-party data set integration is not a task to be taken lightly, and it can quickly become a resource tar pit for the unwary. Not only is the initial effort of establishing a file format and performing key integration nontrivial, each of the third-party data vendors seems intent on altering their schema on a semi-annual basis. Usually couched in terms like "improved," "enhanced," and "enriched," these ongoing revisions in the incoming data require constant ongoing maintenance. When you are budgeting resources for your project, make sure to dedicate resources to each incoming third-party data set. If possible, always place the incoming data into an ODS or staging area to prevent needless duplication of effort among incremental data marts sharing this source.

• *Data islands*
Data islands are small, self-contained, nonintegrated OLTP and associated DSSs (Decision Support System) that users have independently created outside the sphere of influence of the IT organization. These are the File Maker Pro, Access, Lotus 123, and Excel systems that are out there humming along being used to create and provide mission-critical information to workgroups and divisions across the organization. It is a very rare occurrence to create an incremental data mart and not have a defined user requirement for the integration of at least one data island. This is another prime resource tar pit in your incremental data mart project. Data island integration is very resource intensive and should not be taken lightly in your resource planning. Data island integration is covered in detail in Chapter 13.

Once you have established the source of the required information for the incremental data mart, your next mission is to design the target data mart.

Targets

Incremental data mart targets may range from general-purpose information assets to be used by thousands of worldwide users to small, specialized MOLAP data sets to be used by a handful of users in one department. Regardless of the amount of data stored in the incremental data mart or the number of users, the target incremental data mart must be in response to a specific business need in order to be a long-term success. The design of the target incremental data mart will be shaped by this well-defined business need and its accompanying specific pain.

Relational Schema Design

Star Schema

By far the most popular denormalized design for data marts is the star schema. Popularized by Ralph Kimball and examined in detail in his book *The Data Warehouse Toolkit* (1996, John Wiley & Sons), the star schema is an ideal way to represent the multiple dimensions and transactional metrics of a business organization in a relational database.

A basic star schema is composed of fact and dimension tables. (See Figure 12.6.) The fact table contains detail information, and the dimension tables contain information regarding the common dimensions of the business, or the ways the business views its activities. A full-production implementation of a star schema normally also includes aggregation tables. History and status tables are also used to track and trend relationships and allow views of snapshot OLTP status.

The star schema consists of the following elements: detail facts table, dimensions, slowly changing dimension elements and history, aggregations, history tables, and status tables.

> **REALITY CHECK** So what about classic ER data models? Why are only star schemas discussed here? Although there are industry-sponsored debates and much discussion about the advantages and disadvantages for both ER and star schema design, I follow one simple rule of thumb: If the users are going to touch (access, query, analyze) the data, put it into a star schema. If the database is exclusively (or almost exclusively with the exception of a few power users) used as a source to populate data marts, ER is fine. Because data marts are built solely to support the access and analysis needs of users, I use star schemas almost exclusively, with the exception of data marts created only for the purpose of supporting a specific application such as a MOLAP data cube.
>
> I find that some of the loudest proponents of ER models for data mart systems are often people more concerned with making systems easy for IS to maintain, rather than making systems easy to use. This is unfortunate because it clouds the issue and obscures the valid advantages ER systems can have as data sources.

Detail Facts Table

The detail facts (or fact) table lies at the center of the star schema and contains the transactional detail from the source OLTP system(s) related to the subject area being modeled. As such, the detail facts table is by far the largest table in a star schema design. In a retail or telecommunications scenario, fact tables often exceed 100 million and, in some cases, one billion rows of transactional detail data.

Due to their potentially enormous size, the fact table is highly normalized in large volume implementations. In these scenarios, the fact table consists solely of keys and metrics. The fact table commonly contains a primary key related to its subject area, for instance, "ORDR_ID" and "ORDR_LN_ID" for a sales order fact table containing order line item detail information. The fact table also contains all the foreign keys that are needed to join to the dimension tables of the star schema. Note that in high-volume applications, the fact table is designed to be as "narrow" as possible, with as few

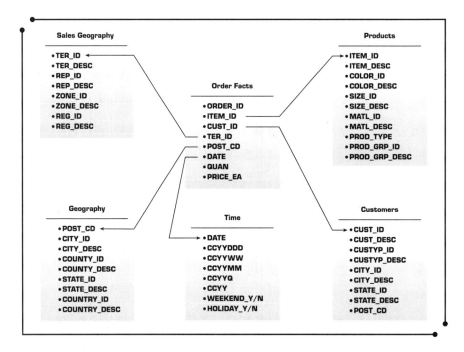

Figure 12.6 Sales and marketing star schema

attributes as can be used and still maintain the necessary abilities to examine the operational activity from all business dimensions and capture required relationships over time.

The metrics carried in the fact table are most commonly numeric values related to the operational activity of the source OLTP system. For instance, in a sales and marketing subject area, the order fact table would normally carry QUANTITY, COST_EACH, and PRICE_EACH as the minimum set of metrics. These metrics allow the easy calculation of gross sales, unit sales, and gross margin along any business dimensions.

REALITY CHECK   So what about specialized DSS databases such as Red Brick? Aren't they supposed to be purpose-built for star schemas? Yes, they are, and if you can afford the additional resources associated with them, they make a fantastic solution. If your organization is locked to a standard RDBMS, all is not lost. All the major merchant RDBMS vendors are supporting extensions or intrinsic capabilities to support star schemas, bit indexes, and other DSS specific technologies.

In day to day queries by users, the metrics carried in a fact table are almost always summarized in some manner. Normal use involves the sum, average, or other mathematical overall operation on the fact table metrics. Actual business users look at total sales along one or more business dimensions, such as Sales by Month by Customer. This involves summing total sales in the detail fact table and grouping by month and by customer from the Time and Customer dimension tables. Normally a qualification is made on the Time dimension to limit the answer to a specific date range, such as prior-year month and current-year month.

Because most actual user analysis is done prior year vs. current year, a rolling thirteen months is the shortest practical historical depth for most detail fact tables. When you are conducting user interviews, historical depth requirements are commonly three to five years. You will greatly improve the response time of the system in this scenario if you create two detail fact tables, one containing the full rolling five years of detail and one containing a rolling thirteen months. You will probably discover through utilization monitoring that at least 85% of the use of the fact tables involves the rolling thirteen-month table. Alternatively, you can partition your data on year/month lines, if your database and user access and analysis tools support partitioned data.

Some businesses are not as high volume as retail or telecommunications, and their fact tables only contain thousands of rows, even with many years of historical detail. This is common in manufacturing scenarios where the units produced have very high prices and very low sales volumes. In these cases, it is very common to denormalize the fact table and carry descriptive information, such as product description and customer name, along with the keys. Do not be tempted to do this in high-volume scenarios; you have enough performance challenges as it is without carrying any additional text over millions of rows.

Another exception to the "keys and metrics only" rule for fact tables is the requirement to record relationship status at the time of the transaction. In many businesses, it is critical to record the status of certain relationships at the time of the transaction so that history can always be easily and accurately re-created. When this is the case, an additional key is stamped into each row of the fact table.

A common example is the customer/sales geography relationship. Sales territories are constantly being redrawn in attempts to gain efficiencies and competitive advantage.

> **REALITY CHECK** Pay close attention to how wide your fact table becomes. No matter what you do with indexing, the database will spend a lot of time scanning the fact tables. You need to measure the maximum sustained I/O throughput of your server, DASD, and RDBMS. The table size divided by the maximum sustained throughput equals the response time for any query that has to scan the fact table. If you keep the fact table width down as much as possible, you can greatly improve the sustained throughput rate.

Territory 101 might have 50 customers this week and 65 customers next week. The Sales Geography dimension of the star schema only reflects the current status of the sales territory/customer relationship. However, when the sales department wants to compare performance of territories, it wants to see prior year versus current year sales for both the old configuration and the new configuration. The new territory 101 configuration comparison is no problem because the current status is contained in the Sales Geography dimension. The users can simply compare total sales for prior year to date to current year to date. However, if the users wanted to see how the average sales per customer of the old territory 101 compared to the average sales per customer of the new territory 101, they would be out of luck because the Sales Geography dimension would not contain any historical customer/territory relationship information. As soon as the Sales Geography dimension is updated with the new territory 101 status, all ability to examine the old territory 101 performance is lost.

The solution to this challenge is to stamp the sales territory key pertinent to the transaction on each row of the detail facts table. In this way, the relationship between the customer (CUSTID) and sales territory (TERID) at the time of the transaction is permanently recorded in history. Sales management has total flexibility in historical comparisons with this relationship. These relationship key historical stamps on the detail facts are used to capture any required relationship history at the detail transaction level. We will examine another approach to capturing relationship history later in this section when we discuss slowly changing dimension elements and history.

Dimensions

Star schema dimensions contain descriptive information about the dimensions of the business, or the ways in which the business examines its activity. Common business dimensions are time, product, customer, geography, sales geography, employee, store, and so on. Dimensions are denormalized flat data structures that contain many attributes regarding their subject. Product and customer dimensions usually contain at least 50 attributes, with over 100 attributes being very common.

Dimension tables are the primary viewpoint of the users and are used extensively to analyze current and historical business activity along single and multiple dimensions. Users "browse" the dimensions at great length to learn about the content of the dimension and characteristics of the dimension members. Dimensions are commonly based on the primary "master" files in the business, such as "customer master" and "product master." It is extremely rare to be able to directly import a "master" file into the incremental data mart. Most "master" files need scrubbing and some transformation to make them useful. At a minimum, descriptive attributes such as the full-text description of codes like CUST_TYP are needed to make them useful for users.

Dimension tables contain three types of attributes:

- *Descriptive*
  Descriptive attributes contain full-text descriptions of the keys and codes that make up most OLTP systems. Descriptive attributes provide the product descriptions, customer names, and status descriptions that users rely on to understand and make

use of the system. No incremental data mart is complete without a full set of dimension descriptive attributes. Do not design a data mart relying on arcane codes and keys. Users may have had to rely on secret decoder rings in the past to understand and leverage the data, but those days are past!

• *Hierarchical*
Hierarchical attributes provide the classifications and hierarchies that businesses use to categorize and segment business activity. Common examples are product, product type, product class, product line, and customer, territory, zone, and region. Most dimension tables contain more than one hierarchy. For instance, different user groups may use a dimension in different ways. A sales-oriented group is interested in customer, customer type, and customer class, whereas a marketing-oriented group is interested in customer, customer title, customer role, and customer profession.

Hierarchies form the basis for most OLAP tools' "slice 'n' dice" multidimensional capabilities. They provide the framework to allow "drill up," "drill down," and "drill across" in OLAP analysis tools. Hierarchies provide most of the replicated data in the denormalized dimensional tables, so hard-core OLTP veterans have a lot of trouble accepting their existence. In this way, they are a good way to weed out those design team members that just can't get over the replication hump.

• *Metrics*
Metric attributes are used to store the activity status of the dimension key. For instance, a product dimension commonly has metric attributes such as current inventory level, total sales prior year, total sales prior year to date, total sales current year to date, volume ranking, and top ten volume product Y/N. Metric attributes are of extremely high value to business users because they allow a quick segmentation of dimension members and a useful and convenient presentation of common performance metrics. A good design will have a standard set of metrics that are shared across all applicable dimensions (product, customer, sales geography, geography, store, employee). The repetition of the standard set of metrics is a tremendous productivity boost for users because they know they can find a "Prior Year to Date Sales" attribute in the same general place in each dimension.

Because most businesses live and die by year-to-year deltas, very popular metric fields are "PYTD (prior year to date) vs. CYTD (current year to date) delta" and "PYTD/CYTD delta %." These fields form the basis of extremely efficient ways for users to separate the winners from the losers across all their business dimensions. A

REALITY CHECK   Many sites miss the opportunity to add metrics to the dimension tables. They are extremely valuable to users and probably provide the biggest "win" of anything that you put into the design.

simple qualification of asking for only the customers whose deltas are less than zero allows users to not only quickly generate a list of all customers with poor sales versus last year, but it can also easily be used to generate an in-depth analysis of the transactional activity associated with those customers. A well-designed set of metrics opens the door for very powerful, very easy utilization of the incremental data mart system.

Slowly Changing Dimension Elements and History

One of the greatest design challenges of dimension tables is handling historical change to the dimension keys. The characteristics of the dimension members such as customer and product are constantly changing over time. Designers must decide how they will deal with the "current cost" field changing in the product dimension, for example. There are four common approaches:

1. *To update in place the dimension member attribute with the new values.* In this scenario, all history is lost and there is no way to recover the past history of the value of the attribute or relationship information. If the history of the attribute in question is of no interest to the business, this a practical approach. An example of this approach is a customer telephone number attribute. Aside from the telecommunications industry, most businesses are not vested in the history of a customer's past phone numbers. This attribute can be updated in place with no dire consequences.

   The advantage of this approach is its simplicity. No additional overhead is required to manage history in any form. The disadvantage is that all history is lost. It is impossible to do any form of accurate historical trending along any field that is updated in this manner.

2. *To create artificial composite keys for each member of the dimension.* When an update is made to a dimension member, the composite key is incremented and a duplicate row created with the new value in place. All transactional activity in the detail fact table after that date contains the new incremented foreign key in the dimension table, thus automatically segmenting the data between the two "identities" of the dimension key. (See Figure 12.7.)

   For example, a customer may change from a low-volume to a medium-volume account. Using this approach, a new row would be created in the Customer dimension table, and the key for that customer would be incremented by one. The original row would stay as it was, and the new row would now have "medium volume" in the customer type field.

   The upside of this approach is that it automatically segments history. After the new incremented composite key is created in the Customer dimension table, all subsequent detail transactions in the detail facts table relating to this customer use the new incremented composite key. This allows the seamless segmentation of transaction activity between the two "identities" of the dimension member. Any previous change activity will use the old composite key, and transactional activity after this change will automatically refer to the newly incremented composite key.

KEY	CST_ID	CUST_DESC	CST YP_ID	CST YP_DESC	CST_ADR1	CST_ADR2	CST_CITY	CSTST_ID	CST ST_DESC	CST_PSTCD
10010	1001	Al's Quick Mart	L	Low Volume	1253 Wilmette Ave		Wilmette	IL	Illinois	50123
10011	1001	Al's Quick Mart	M	Medium Volume	1253 Wilmette Ave		Wilmette	IL	Illinois	50123
10012	1001	Al's Quick Mart	L	Low Volume	1253 Wilmette Ave		Wilmette	IL	Illinois	50123
10020	1002	Dominics Store 283	M	Medium Volume	253 Ridge Ave.		Evanston	IL	Illinois	50110
10021	1002	Dominics Store 283	H	High Volume	253 Ridge Ave.		Evanston	IL	Illinois	50110
10030	1003	Jewel Store 288	H	High Volume	2821 Central		Evanston	IL	Illinois	50111

Figure 12.7   Duplicate dimension rows with incremented keys

The downside is that by selecting this approach, you have just designed a huge caveat into your incremental data mart system. When browsing the dimensions, users will be presented with multiple rows for every member that has experienced a type two change. Users will be unable to ask simple questions such as "how many customers do we have?" without having to remember caveats such as "MAX" clauses on the composite key. Users will be unable to query by well-known keys, such as CUSTID, without carrying multiple key columns, one for the composite key and one for the user known key. Simple questions like "what are my total sales for this customer?" now take on needless complexity. This approach violates the fundamental dimension design rule of "one row per member" and the fundamental data mart design rule of "no caveats."

3. *To create a new attribute for the changed column.* This usually takes the form of a "current status" attribute and an "original status" attribute. An "effective date" attribute is normally required in this scenario in order to track when things changed. This can be an effective "down and dirty" approach to providing limited history in circumstances where the beginning and end states are all that matter. For example, an "original list price" and "current list price" approach might be valid for an organization that doesn't care what the price was at any intermediate time.

   The upside of this approach is its simplicity. The downsides are that it can become a management nightmare to create and administer all the additional attributes required if the approach is widespread. Also, because all intermediate history is lost, no trending can take place on these attributes over time.

4. *To use a separate history table to capture all changes for any relationship in the dimension table that the business wants to capture or trend over time.* For instance, the business may want to track all changes in product cost over time. There are three strategies for capturing history in this approach:

   a. *To snapshot the entire dimension table and append it to a dimension history table on a regular frequency, such as every night.* This allows any attribute to be trended over time. This is simple and easy, but it requires quite a bit of DASD over time (although a pittance compared with the gargantuan detail fact table and the multidimensional aggregations).

b. *To snapshot and append to a dimension history table only the fields in the dimension table that the business wishes to trend or track on a regular time frequency, such as daily.* This allows any of the attributes that are known to change to be trended and tracked over time. Common examples are a nightly snapshot of current product cost for highly volatile industries such as petroleum distribution. This is also straightforward and uses a little less space than the previous strategy. Those wrapped in DASD fear will sleep easier.

c. *To write out a new row into a dedicated attribute history table only at the time a relationship changes and put into that new row only a copy of the attribute that has changed, the dimension key, and the date.* The upside of these dedicated attribute history tables is they are very compact and allow the capture and trending of any specific relationship the business wants to track. The downside to this strategy is that rows are only written when the attribute changes in the dimension table, thus precluding any time series–based trending, for example, product cost trend by week. Also, with this strategy, you must manage a greater number of tables because you will have a dedicated history table for each attribute you want to trend.

A typical dedicated attribute history table would contain Product ID, Product Description, Cost, and Change Date. It is very common to add additional metrics to these dedicated history tables. For instance, you might design a Product History table that contained Product ID, Product Description, Cost, Price, Product Type, Product Class, and Change Date. In this design, any time any one of the attributes changes (with the exception of Change Date, of course), a copy of the new version of the dimension row is stamped into the dedicated attribute history table. Product history (cost, price, and inventory level), sales rep history (territory, customer, quota, and ranking), and customer history (territory, rep, ranking, and sales volume) are all very popular dedicated attribute history tables.

Type four approaches have the advantage of maintaining a complete historical record of all changes in the relationship between two or more attributes while retaining the fundamental "one row per member" design rule of dimensions. Their biggest drawback is that they do not allow for the seamless partitioning of detail history that a type 2 approach allows. To overcome this, some sites use a hybrid approach, in which a composite key is used and incremented with each change, (as in a type 2 approach) but a copy of the new relationship rows are stamped out to a dedicated attribute history table. Only the newest incremented composite key version row for each dimension member is retained in the dimension table. This allows seamless partitioning of history via the dedicated attribute history table, while retaining the ultimate ease of use and "no caveats" integrity of a "one row per member" dimension table.

In summary, the type of approach selected to deal with slowly changing dimensions is determined entirely by the needs of the business. If there is no need or concern for history, Approach 1 will suffice. If the team does not have the resources to manage multiple dedicated attribute history tables but requires seamless partitioning of detail history, Approach 2 might be taken, along with its inherent disadvantages for users. If no intermediate history is required, Approach 3 is adequate. If the retention of the optimum "one row per member" dimension design is desired, along with a full trending history of dimension table attribute relationships, Approach 4 is suitable.

Aggregations

With all the attention paid to detail fact and dimension tables, it is often easy to overlook the aggregation tables that are present in nearly all incremental data mart designs. In fact, the precalculated aggregation tables that you design and create usually receive at least 80% of the utilization of the incremental data mart system. If this isn't enough to attract your attention, the fact that the vast majority of user-requested changes to the incremental data mart system come in the aggregation tables should. Aggregations in many ways form the "front lines" of the data mart system to the users. Users prefer the quick response of a single table answer from the aggregation sets over the much slower response of a detail fact and multiple dimension table query. Remember that the overall design goal of the incremental data mart system is that users should be able to get their answers from one to two tables over 80% of the time. The aggregate tables are the key to accomplishing this goal.

Aggregation tables are simply the combination of the detail facts table and one or more dimension tables. It is critical that you must *never* introduce any attribute into an aggregation table that is not contained in the fact or dimension table. Never introduce a data element into an attribute table downstream of the fact and dimension tables. Doing so immediately corrupts the auditability of the incremental data mart and inevitably leads to multiple versions of the "truth" among various incremental data marts. To retain credibility in the business, the entire incremental data mart system—from detail facts through to the last subset "child" data mart—must "roll up," or audit to each other. A downstream data feed into an aggregation table eliminates this possibility.

The initial set of aggregate tables are your "best guess" as to the anticipated user requirements based on your user interviews. The critical question to ask during the interviews related to aggregations is, "How do you like to view the business activity?" You will receive answers along the lines of, "I like to look at the business by sales by month by customer by product." These answers not only allow you to establish the business dimensions required in the incremental data mart, they also are prime indicators of the aggregation tables that will be most useful to the user community. At the conclusion of the user interviews, you need to consolidate the definitions of the required aggregation tables into as few multidimension aggregation tables as possible. You can usually take the 15 to 20 variations on aggregation expressed in the interviews and consolidate them into four to five multidimensional aggregation tables with multiple levels of hierarchy.

For instance, many of your users may express the need for an aggregation table that presents sales by product by customer by month. You also may have a group of users that requires sales by product by customer by quarter. These two requests are easily consolidated into one aggregation table that contains both the month and quarter members of the time dimension hierarchy. (See Figure 12.8.)

CST_ID	CUST_DESC	PRD_ID	PRD_DESC	CCYYMM	CCYYQ	CCYY	QUAN	SALES
1001	Al's Quick Mart	A28	White Cake	199702	19971	1997	244	495.38
1001	Al's Quick Mart	A36	Long John	199702	19971	1997	132	267.99
1002	Dominics Store 283	A28	White Cake	199702	19971	1997	223	452.74
1002	Dominics Store 283	A36	Long John	199702	19971	1997	105	213.18
1002	Dominics Store 283	B43	Choc Cupcakes	199702	19971	1997	38	77.15
1002	Dominics Store 283	B63	Banana Flip	199702	19971	1997	185	375.60
1002	Dominics Store 283	B75	Fruit Torte	199702	19971	1997	221	448.68
1003	Jewel Store 288	A36	Long John	199702	19971	1997	485	984.67
1003	Jewel Store 288	B43	Choc Cupcakes	199702	19971	1997	295	598.92
1003	Jewel Store 288	B63	Banana Flip	199702	19971	1997	318	645.62
1004	Dominics Store 104	A28	White Cake	199702	19971	1997	501	1017.15
1004	Dominics Store 104	A36	Long John	199702	19971	1997	225	456.81
1006	Mobil 19951	B63	Banana Flip	199702	19971	1997	85	172.57
1006	Mobil 19951	B75	Fruit Torte	199702	19971	1997	35	71.06
1009	Amoco 2103B	A28	White Cake	199702	19971	1997	68	138.06

Figure 12.8   Multidimensional aggregation table with month and quarter

Your primary limitation in preparing aggregation tables is the massive size of aggregations with more than a few dimensions. For instance, in businesses with a large number of customers such as telecommunications, a table that contains sales by customer by product by geography by month quickly becomes very, very large. Multidimensional aggregation tables are flat file versions of the proprietary data cube structures used by the MOLAP tools. Unfortunately simple, single table RDBMS versions do not have the space-saving advantages of the highly compressed proprietary MOLAP structures, nor the specialized indexing and access techniques used to deliver MOLAP's extremely fast response, nor the value add calculations and capabilities such as ranking that native SQL does not support. Even given these limitations, multidimensional aggregations are still orders of magnitude faster for users to browse and access than creating ad hoc aggregations from the fact and dimension tables. Multidimensional aggregations are also the key to acceptable response by aggregate-aware ROLAP tools. By precalculating the aggregations commonly requested by the users, you provide a rich library that the ROLAP tool can call upon to provide very quick answers, as opposed to generating a fresh aggregation from the facts and dimensions. The ROLAP tool also provides the "value add" functions such as ranking that SQL doesn't support. The combination of multidimensional aggregations and a highly aggregate-aware ROLAP tool is a very powerful combination for the average user community.

A second major challenge when dealing with aggregations is the updating of the aggregation data sets with each update of the incremental data mart system. The simplest method is to simply drop the aggregation tables and "brute force" rebuild them based on the updated detail facts and dimension tables. For small, highly summarized aggregation tables, this method works fine. However, for very large aggregations, this method is not preferred and may not even be possible, given the amount of processing time available during the update process. In this case, incremental aggregation must be used to limit the additional aggregation to only the incrementally new transactions and the incrementally new dimension members. If you choose to implement a DTEAMM environment, this capability is normally integrated into the tool. If you are building manually, you need to create an incremental delta table for each dimension and the detail transactions prior to appending them to the dimension and detail facts tables. You must then compare the deltas to the existing dimensions and aggregations, calculate new aggregation rows for any new dimension member that has appropriate detail transaction activity, and then insert the new rows into the appropriate aggregation table.

To be effective, aggregation tables are highly denormalized and contain a large percentage of replicated data. You must resist the urge to save some DASD by not including descriptive text or repeating hierarchical descriptions in the aggregation tables. If a user must join the aggregation table back to two or three dimension tables such as customer and product in order to report the descriptive names of the keys, you have not accomplished much in the way of speeding up response time or lowering the processing demands on the server. Worse yet, you have precluded the users from effectively browsing the aggregation table to explore and discover information. To be most effective, aggregation tables must be highly denormalized and contain a large amount of replicated data. You must overcome DASD fear in order to be successful in data mart design. If your data architect or DBA is having fundamental philosophical problems with denormalization or replication, it might be best to reassign the person to an OLTP project and use someone else for the data mart system.

The incremental data mart system's aggregation tables will quickly evolve into a plethora of data sets answering the needs of many different users of all types. There will be highly summarized aggregations for executive management, massive multidimensional aggregations for managers and analysts, and multiple one, two and three dimension tables for general use by all users. These aggregation sets will be the primary utilization area for the incremental data mart system, and as such will require dedicated resources to ensure their health and well being. When you are planning resource allocation for your incremental data mart system, be sure to allow for dedicated assets for aggregation table creation, modification, and maintenance.

Also, it is very common to create a dedicated aggregation table specifically to meet the needs of senior management. This is usually referred to as the "CEO (Chief Executive Officer) table." Although this is more common in an enterprise data warehouse scenario, you can expect to be hosting these tables in your incremental data marts as well. CEO tables require the highest possible levels of monitoring and maintenance. They provide the ultimate opportunity for positive political exposure and a fast track path to mission-critical status. They also offer the ultimate opportunity for maximum political risk. Make sure they are at the top of the "tables to monitor" list. You want to make sure that these tables are fully populated with every refresh cycle and that any changes requested are executed very promptly and competently. Do not make junior, new, or inexperienced people responsible for the monitoring, modification, or maintenance of "CEO tables."

In summary, aggregations form the primary data interface to the user community. As such, it is critical that they be designed with convenience, ease of use, and user orientation as the top priorities. They must be denormalized and contain a very large amount of replicated data to allow for easy browsing and single table answers. Aggregations present both challenges, in the form of large table management and incremental aggregation, and opportunities, in providing the primary gateway to directly answering users' needs in a very easy to use and timely manner.

REALITY CHECK It is very critical to set your team's expectations properly regarding aggregations. They will change early and often. Don't assign the aggregations to anyone who is neither flexible nor user oriented.

History Tables

History tables are used to capture and store the history of a relationship between two or more attributes of a dimension table. As described in detail in the previous section on slowly changing dimensions and history, there are four approaches to dealing with history. Approach 4 involves the creation and population of history tables. Most incremental data marts contain multiple history tables, with the most popular involving product, customer, and employee histories.

Status Tables

Some incremental data marts also make use of status tables. Status tables are used to provide a consistent user interface for all information access needs. Status tables are snapshots of OLTP data sources, usually taken nightly. These status tables allow the user of the incremental data mart to check on the status of an operational system, as of the last refresh cycle. They are commonly used in manufacturing, orders and sales, and financial systems incremental data marts.

For instance, an order status table enables users to check on the status of an order as of the last refresh cycle (usually last night) without ever leaving the incremental data mart environment. This eliminates the need for users to toggle over to a terminal emulation program and log on to the OLTP system in order to check the current status of an order or other operation.

Status tables are normally not scrubbed or integrated and are pure "down and dirty" snapshots of the operation system. They are created and maintained purely as a convenience for the users, to allow them to maintain a consistent user interface when accessing information. They are not real-time views of the operational system, and they are not meant to replace OLTP access systems.

Status tables are dangerous to the extent that they allow access to nonintegrated, nonscrubbed data within the incremental data mart environment. Care must be taken that users do not combine status table data with the scrubbed and integrated data contained in the rest of the data mart environment. This is usually accomplished by carefully controlling the attributes replicated from the OLTP system, that is, only carrying pure "status" fields in the incremental data mart and avoiding metric fields. For example, an

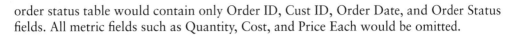

order status table would contain only Order ID, Cust ID, Order Date, and Order Status fields. All metric fields such as Quantity, Cost, and Price Each would be omitted.

Snowflake Schema

A snowflake schema is a variation of the star schema in which the dimensions are partially normalized through the use of snowflake tables. There are three common causes for the use of snowflakes:

- *Many to one relationships*
  In some instances, it is impossible to carry required information in a dimension table due to many to one relationships between the subject of the dimension and the required data. For instance, the cost of a product may vary by manufacturing plant. In this case, a Product Cost snowflake table that contains product, plant, and cost information is joined to the Product dimension table.

- *Many to many relationships*
  In similar instances, it is impossible to carry required information due to many to many relationships. For example, in a publishing scenario it is impossible to include the author in the product dimension, due to products having multiple authors. The same is true for products in the author dimension, due to authors having multiple products. In this case a Product Author snowflake table that contains product and author information is joined to both the Product and Author dimension tables.

- *Data replication*
  In some cases, where there are hundreds of millions of rows of transaction or dimension information, it is undesirable to replicate some data points. For instance, if a credit card company has 40 million customers, they may not wish to replicate a fixed set of customer demographic fields in every row of the customer dimension. In this case, a Customer Demographics snowflake table that contains the demographic information is joined to the Customer dimension. (See Figure 12.9.)

These data replication snowflake tables are often the first manifestation of compromise creep among designers who cannot get over the denormalization "hump." They are often justified as a way to "save some DASD" in the dimensions. In reality, the dimension tables make up so little of the overall system DASD space, any efforts to save DASD space by minimizing or normalizing them is purely wasted time and effort. Compared to the massive fact tables and multidimensional aggregations, the dimension tables consume a very, very small percentage of the data mart system. (See Figure 12.10.)

When used to eliminate the replication of hierarchical, text description, or demographic attributes, snowflake tables will usually save less than 1% of the total system DASD requirements. The tradeoff for saving this small portion of the total DASD requirements is the loss of the user's ability to browse the dimensions. Since browsing the dimensions is the fundamental prerequisite for ad hoc utilization of the star schema, widespread use of these snowflake tables essentially renders the incremental data mart useless for ad hoc use. Consequently, data replication snowflake tables are to be avoided, at nearly any cost.

REALITY CHECK Here's one of those great spots for compromise in the face of reality. Snowflakes are not great, and they pretty much wipe out the chance for users to easily browse the dimension, but there are times when they are unavoidable. As in other areas of design, you do what you have to in order to deliver a viable system to the users. Bottom line: Don't lose sleep over it.

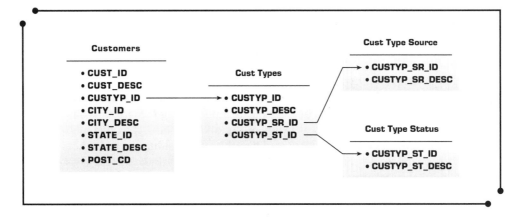

Figure 12.9 Snowflake Schema

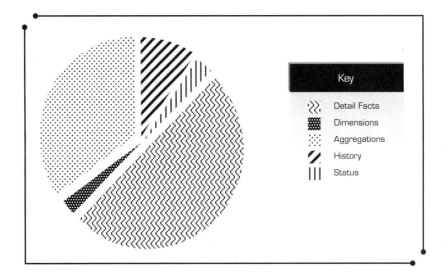

Figure 12.10 Typical system DASD utilization

Examples

Consider the following example of a sales and marketing incremental data mart star schema with accompanying history, aggregation, and status tables. (See Figures 12.11–12.14.)

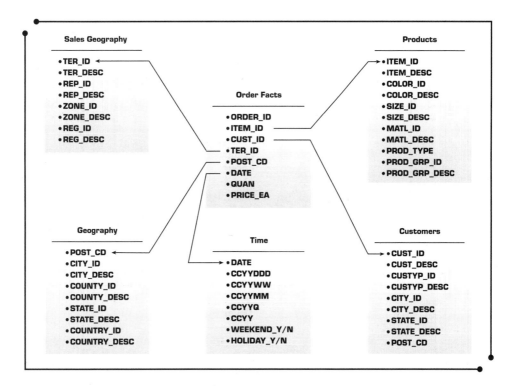

Figure 12.11   Sales and Marketing star schema

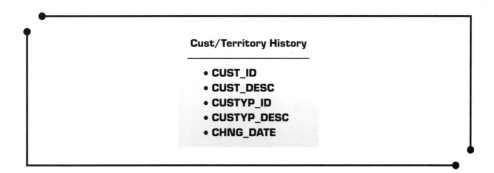

Figure 12.12   Sales and Marketing history

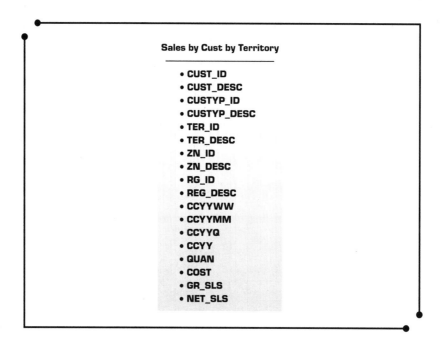

Figure 12.13 Sales and Marketing aggregation

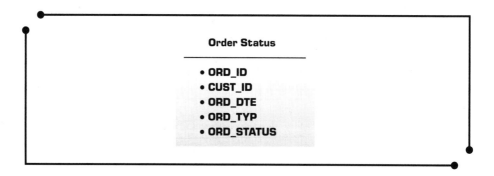

Figure 12.14 Sales and Marketing order status

MOLAP Design

Many incremental data marts exist solely to host specialized data sets required by MOLAP analysis tools. In fact, the term "data mart" was initially popularized by the MOLAP vendors in an effort to codify and legitimatize a mid-tier system to host their required specialized data sets. These data sets are commonly referred to as "data cubes" or "hyper cubes" and are sometimes hosted in a specialized MDDBMS (Multi-Dimensional Data Base Management System).

The MOLAP data sets comprise selected metrics and selected dimensions, along with selected hierarchies from the dimensions. These "data cubes" usually contain all possible answers to every possible question along any of the defined dimensions and hierarchies and the associated metrics. Some MOLAP systems calculate a subset of every possible answer and calculate the rest "on the fly," if required, in a type of hybrid MOLAP/ROLAP approach called HOLAP (Hybrid Online Analytical Processing).

Because the data cubes contain every possible answer to every possible question, they provide two key features for user happiness. First, because all the answers are precalculated, they provide nearly instant response. Users love quick answers, so this is a highly desirable feature. Second, because there is an answer to every possible question, it is impossible for a user to receive the error message "no data was found for your query," which is the bane of the ad hoc query world.

The downsides of the data cubes' containing every possible answer for every possible question are twofold. First, you must be dealing with a very well-defined, bounded, problem set. You must understand in great detail exactly what the users are going to ask. It is impossible for the users to wander outside the range of the data cube for answers, so you must anticipate every possible question. Second, the data cubes are extremely large. It becomes a practical impossibility to build and maintain a MOLAP cube for more than a handful of dimensions at any level of practical detail. MOLAP cubes are primarily effective when used with a limited number of dimensions and highly summarized data, and even then, they are very, very large.

Because of their potential size, the cubes present some specific design challenges. You must first identify all possible questions along each dimension. You must identify the lowest level of detail required. You must then determine the actual load and, more importantly, the actual update time of this size cube. It is not uncommon for initial loads of these large cubes to take days, even weeks, of processing time. An incremental update that takes 20 hours does you no good if your users need a daily refresh cycle. If you cannot update in time, you must limit the cube. The usual approach is to summarize the data to a higher level. This is usually a better approach from the user's standpoint than eliminating dimensions.

Summary

Incremental data mart design follows the same success criteria as designing a data warehouse:

- Pain specific
- Business and user focused
- Ease of use

As long as you focus on these goals, you will deliver a valuable and sustainable information asset to the enterprise.

CHAPTER 13

Incremental Data Mart Construction and Integration Options

Picking a Data Mart Tool

Picking a data mart construction tool is one of the most important elements on the project plan for your data mart project. The downside of data mart tools is that the wrong tool can become a hidden resource tar pit and cost you more in learning curve, bug hunts, vendor consultants, and dead ends than you could ever hope to recoup through increased productivity. The upside of data mart tools is that the market space is rapidly maturing, price points continue to go down as capabilities expand, and you can afford to try a tool and have it fail without fatal project and/or career consequences.

If you were around in the data warehousing market space over the last few years, you experienced the great "new and improved for data warehousing" phenomenon during which every tool and technology lying around the market was repackaged and remarketed as a "data warehousing solution." Between "data warehousing" replicators, monitors, extractors, and tried-and-true access tools, we had everything you could ever imagine for data warehousing, just short of "new and improved for data warehousing" pencils and paper clips. Innumerable examples of ancient technology were covered with a new GUI (Graphical User Interface) or simply new packaging and foisted upon an unsuspecting market. As the market has moved to incremental data marts as the preferred path to providing enterprise information resources, vendors have followed the same methodology that worked so well in the data warehouse segment. Now, all the old technology is being repackaged as "new and improved for data marts." In some cases, the very same products that recently were the absolute salvation of data warehouse teams everywhere are now being marketed as data mart–specific solutions. Although we can certainly salute the flexibility and speed of the vendor marketing teams in responding to a fast-shifting market, the burden of *caveat emptor* remains solely with those of us on the receiving end of their repackaged wares. You must perform the requisite due diligence to ensure that you are not being sold antiquated technology in a fancy new GUI wrapper that is being force fit into the data mart market space.

337

There are several well-known examples of purpose-built technology for the data mart space. Informatica's PowerMart was the first transformation engine–based tool in the data mart space, and it has led the way in establishing the early feature and performance standards for DTEMM (Design, Transformation, Extract, Monitoring, and Management) solutions. PowerMart is an excellent example of a tool built from the ground up to provide a solution for this market space and its challenges. Eyeing Informatica's quick success, other vendors quickly jumped in with their transformation engine–based designs in an effort to share in the spoils of this quickly expanding market segment. This segment continues to evolve quickly from its DTEMM roots, with DTEAMM (Design, Transformation, Extract, Access, Monitoring, and Management) environments adding integrated user access and enterprise-scale integrated meta data repositories. Clearly the market is heading toward enterprisewide DTEAMM environments as the preferred solution. DTEAMM solutions will soon own the majority of the market share for data mart construction, monitoring, and maintenance. (See Figure 13.1.)

When considering a data mart tool, demand the following features:

- *Purpose built*
  Go with a purpose-built solution. Don't settle for stitched together Frankenstein technologies or repackaged versions of antiquated tools. A purpose-built tool will be architected from the ground up to provide an effective and sustainable solution to your business challenge. Don't buy into a patchwork of point solutions.

- *True integration*
  Insist on full and seamless integration. Consistent GUI; population, maintenance, and sharing of a logically common meta data repository across the entire data mart process; true multitasking and parallel process execution; and transparent internal

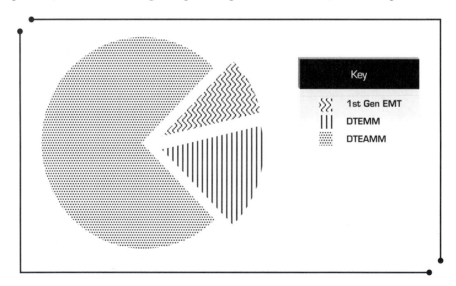

Figure 13.1 Near- to mid-term market share projection

process handoff and scheduling are the elements that mark a fully integrated solution. Manual export and import of meta data between modules; disparate GUIs; multiple meta data repositories; single-threaded sequential processes; and required manual process control and intervention all mark a solution made up of very different underlying modules.

- *Transformation engine based*
  Transformation engine design has proven to be the preferred solution in data mart extraction and transformation processes. It is unique in its ability to minimize object (code, programs, files, scripts) management challenges, to internally leverage parallelism, limit I/O (Input/Output), and to maintain very high throughput rates. Although no industry standard benchmark exists today, anecdotal evidence suggests sustained "end to end" throughput rates much higher than that of first-generation, code generation–based solutions in optimum scenarios.

- *Common, open, and extensible meta data repository*
  A prerequisite for an effective enterprise data mart strategy is a common, open, and extensible meta data repository. There must be one entry point to one logical meta data repository presented to all users of the system, both technical and business. All elements of the data mart system must populate and maintain this common repository. The meta data repository should be open, not a closed proprietary design with limited, structured views. Your individual circumstances and challenges will be unique, so the repository must be extensible, so you can easily modify it to reflect your site.

- *Automatic meta data population and maintenance*
  The tool must support the automatic population and maintenance of the common meta data repository. It must provide sufficient automatic population to reduce the "meta data conundrum" of manual meta population and maintenance. The tool must automatically maintain all pertinent meta data during ongoing operation of the data mart system.

- *Server centric*
  The tool must be server centric. Accept no thick client designs. A server-centric design ensures a smooth path to thin client capability, easy population and maintenance of a common meta data repository, and simplified centralized management.

- *Thin client capable*
  The tool must be capable of supporting thin client access to the meta data by both technical and business users. Primary functions of the data mart system, such as system management and basic query and reporting tasks, must be supported through a thin client interface. If the vendor doesn't have these capabilities now, insist on a presentation outlining their technological road map that will lead to this capability in a reasonable timeframe.

- *Low I/O requirements*
  The tool should limit I/O activity as much as possible. Every disk write and read slows functionality. Avoid solutions that rely on extensive use of temporary

database tables because they require extensive I/O activity for all operations. The goal is to limit I/O to caching operations only.

- *Scaleability*
  The tool must be scaleable. Whatever your current plans are for a nice, little department-specific data mart, you will soon be dealing with the need to either scale up your "nice little data mart" to an enterprise data warehouse or the need to provide every other department with a "nice little data mart." Whichever version of the curse of success befalls you, your choice of tool must support the rapid expansion of your data mart system. Be wary of any tool that is inherently self-limiting, that is, tied to a platform or OS that cannot scale, or that is saddled with an internal architecture that cannot scale.

- *Common extraction and transformation repository*
  Because you will be using this tool to create multiple data marts, you must require a common meta data repository for all extraction, scrubbing, and transformation algorithms and processes. This allows teams working on various data marts to leverage the efforts of each project and avoid needless duplication of effort. This common repository also ensures that consistent business rules will be applied across all data marts.

- *Price/performance*
  You should expect outstanding price/performance ratios in any data mart tool you select. Although the ADP (Average Deal Price) of first-generation tool solutions was often over $400,000, you should expect to implement a complete DTEAMM solution for $35,000 to $100,000.

With the power, performance, and price of modern, purpose-built data mart solutions, it is untenable to build and maintain a data mart system by hand. Choose a tool that meets these criteria and reap the rewards of developer productivity, automatic meta data population and maintenance, integrated processes, parallel execution, common meta data repository, and integrated user access.

Integration Options

Like it or not, eventually someone will most likely be charged with integrating the incremental data marts that you and your teams create. If you develop your incremental data marts under an enterprise architecture, this effort will be smooth and successful. In this section, we examine additional data sourcing options and their impact on data mart integration and what is required to integrate nonarchitected data marts and OLTP (On-Line Transaction Processing) data islands.

Although most incremental data mart efforts begin by extracting the data directly from the OLTP source systems, the curse of success quickly leads to the proliferation of incremental data marts throughout the business, each with its own extraction, scrubbing, and transformation processes and attendant management requirements.

You will probably find that more than two or three incremental data marts running redundant extract jobs will soon overtax your available maintenance and management resources. At the same time, you will probably find that the organization is still not ready to bite off the scope and cost of an enterprise data warehouse, which would provide a wonderfully consistent source of integrated scrubbed historical data for your fast-growing data mart empire. To mitigate this growing horror, most sites turn to two types of common data sources that are each short of a data warehouse, but somewhat better than multiple redundant extract jobs. (See Figure 13.2.)

Staging Area

The first option is to create a data staging area or leverage an existing one in the business. (See Figure 13.3.)

A staging area is simply a replicated copy of the OLTP system's tables, usually in a separate database. The characteristics of a staging area are:

- *Limited/no integration*
  As a replicated copy of the operational system, a staging area has very little or no integration between the OLTP systems. It will be as integrated as the OLTP systems are, and usually no more.

- *Replicated, normalized OLTP model*
  The data model for a staging area is normally a direct copy of the normalized OLTP database.

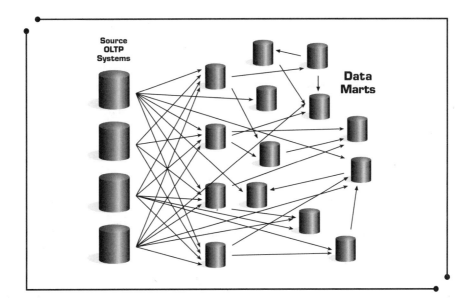

Figure 13.2   Redundant extract jobs

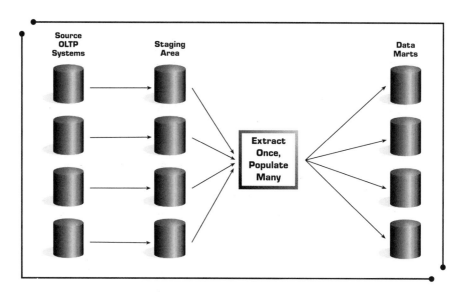

Figure 13.3 Staging area source

- *Variable scrub*
  The data in a staging area may be scrubbed to some extent if the data replication scheme implemented allows for it. Ideally the business will invest the effort to scrub the staging area to create a source of clean data. Otherwise, you must assume that the data will be as dirty as the underlying OLTP system.

- *Detailed*
  The data is fully detailed, with full atomic level of detail available.

- *Volatile*
  The data is volatile and changes in sync with the source OLTP system. Most staging areas mirror the source OLTP system, with changes cascading as soon as the replication technology can deliver them.

- *Little/no history*
  The staging area contains little to no history, just like the source system. Expect no more than a few days to possibly as far back as the last accounting cycle.

- *Varying semantics*
  The staging area contains a wide variety of semantics for common attributes. Unless your OLTP systems are completely integrated, there will be no common semantics.

- *Varying business rules*
  The staging area contains a wide variety of business rules for common metrics unless your source OLTP systems are fully integrated. Do not assume that any metric is calculated consistently across different source OLTP systems.

Most businesses already have a staging area of some kind. If the business has implemented Focus or SAS, there will almost certainly be an entire world of staging area tables driven by a multitude of extraction, scrubbing, and transformation processes. Be very wary of these existing staging area worlds. It is almost certain that nothing is documented; that the many people who built them are long gone, along with their knowledge of how and why they did things along the way; that many hidden business rules are nestled among the extracts, scrubs, and transformations; that these underlying processes will continue to evolve to meet the needs of their existing users; and that you and your data mart team will not be informed of any changes until it is much too late.

If you choose to use an existing staging area, you must own and control all the extraction, scrubbing, and transformation processes exclusively. You must not, under any circumstances, rely on a process that someone else can modify according to their own agenda without your approval or control. At a minimum, you must insist on very rigid service level agreements with the extract owners.

> **REALITY CHECK** Many of you will be faced with a burning business problem and existing extracts that are widely used in the business. This is a classic "rock and a hard place." If you take the quick route to relieve the pain and simply suck the data off the extracts, your entire data mart will be hanging by that tenuous thread. You might want to make sure you pack your own parachute and keep it handy because it is unlikely that you will ever get the chance to go back and build proper data feeds.

In summary, staging areas offer a centralized place to obtain source data for multiple incremental data marts. It is possible for you to create one set of extraction, integration, scrubbing, and transformation jobs that will "extract once, populate many." This allows you to create, monitor, and manage a single set of processes, instead of one for each incremental data mart. These upsides are offset by the requirement for you to exclusively own the extraction and replication processes that populate the staging area. This may be a political challenge in some organizations.

ODS (Operational Data Store)

A better option, albeit at much greater expense and effort, is to construct an ODS (Operational Data Store) to provide source data for your family of integrated data marts. An ODS is basically a read/write data warehouse without the history or aggregation. It provides an integrated, scrubbed, and subject-oriented source for the incremental data marts. (See Figure 13.4.)

The characteristics of an ODS are:

- *Subject based*
  An ODS data model is subject based, in classic data warehouse style. It is not a direct replication of the OLTP normalized design.

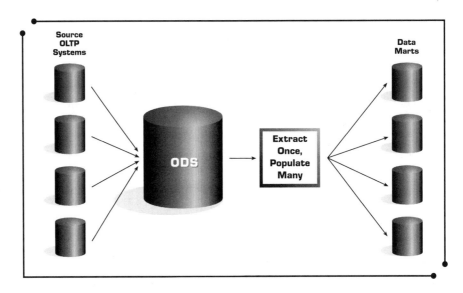

Figure 13.4 ODS architecture

- *Integrated*
  An ODS is fully integrated across all source systems and subject areas.

- *Scrubbed*
  An ODS contains fully scrubbed data.

- *Little/no history*
  Like the source OLTP systems, an ODS contains very little, if any, history. It is operationally oriented and contains none of the long-term history found in a data warehouse or data mart. At most, you can expect to find history back to the last accounting cycle.

- *Detailed*
  An ODS contains fully atomic–level transaction detail from all OLTP source systems.

- *Volatile*
  Unlike a data warehouse or data mart, an ODS is volatile. As the source OLTP systems change, the changes are directly reflected in the ODS.

- *Standardized semantics*
  An ODS reflects common semantics across all subject areas.

- *Standardized business rules*
  An ODS uses consistent business rules to calculate common metrics for all subject areas.

An ODS makes the best source for incremental data mart feeds and is the quickest route to creating and populating incremental data marts in the enterprise. The prospect of constructing an ODS prior to commencement of incremental data mart activities can be troublesome. The ODS can seem daunting if teams make the mistake of assuming that it must be constructed in its entirety before any data marts can be built. The key to success is to not attempt to construct an enterprise ODS to support your initial incremental data marts. Instead, only construct the subject areas in the ODS needed to support each data mart as you construct it. This allows you to build the ODS incrementally along with the step-by-step construction of the incremental data mart system.

A common ODS source for your incremental data marts is the preferred solution, regardless of your long-term plans for an enterprise data warehouse. If you choose to build one, it is a very straightforward process to snapshot the ODS and build the history of the enterprise data warehouse. If you do not choose to implement an enterprise data warehouse, the ODS still provides you with the best possible source of data for any number of incremental data marts you choose to construct.

For a full examination of the design and construction of an ODS, see *Building the Operational Data Store* by Bill Inmon, Claudia Imhoff, and Greg Battas (John Wiley & Sons, 1996).

The Virtual Data Warehouse

Recently a "holy grail" called the "virtual data warehouse" has arisen. This vision takes two forms: direct to OLTP and multiple integrated data marts.

Direct to OLTP

In the first example, users directly access the variety of OLTP systems in the business and miraculously return integrated, scrubbed, transformed, historical data that is perfectly accurate and reliable. (See Figure 13.5.)

The acid test of reality has pretty much quashed this quackery. In the real world, people are fully aware that OLTP systems have:

- No integration
- No history
- Little to no scrubbed data
- No transformations
- Very slow ad hoc response time

No amount of fast I/O or dual port DASD (Direct Access Storage Device) is ever going to change these fundamental facts. Until an organization implements a fully integrated suite of OLTP systems that retains history, uses common and consistent semantics, has perfectly clean data, and automatically provides DSS-oriented transformations, this will

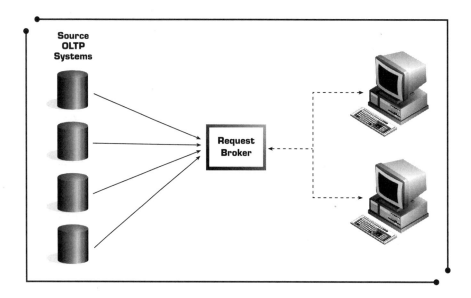

Figure 13.5 Direct to OLTP virtual data warehouse

remain the case. And if they ever solve those challenges, they still must guarantee that the OLTP systems will never suffer any performance degradation due to the DSS activity performed against the transactional tables. I would hazard to guess it will be quite some time before these goals are reached in the majority of business organizations around the globe.

It is safe to say that this version of the "virtual data warehouse" remains an elusive, unlikely answer to the challenges of information resource creation, delivery, and sustenance.

Multiple Integrated Data Marts

An imminently more practical approach is the integration of multiple incremental data marts into a virtual enterprise data warehouse. (See Figure 13.6.)

This vision not only can be accomplished, but it represents the destiny of many incremental data mart systems being built today and in the future. For this vision to become a reality, you must have:

- *Enterprise data mart architecture*
  If you hope to integrate your incremental data marts into a virtual data warehouse, you must build them under the auspices of an enterprise data mart architecture. Each incremental data mart must share common sources, dimensions, semantics, business rules, and metrics.

- *Common meta data repository*
  To provide for coordinated monitoring, management, and access of the "virtual data warehouse" system, you must have a logically common meta data repository.

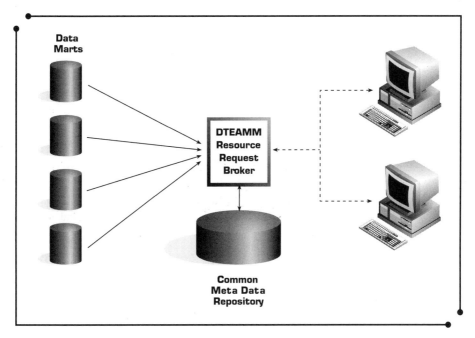

Figure 13.6 Multiple data mart virtual data warehouse

Your tools and technologies may support a physically distributed meta data implementation, but they must present a single logical view to the users, whether technical or business.

- *Request broker*
Most importantly, you must implement a request broker that is capable of taking an incoming request, examining the meta data, and determining the proper source and/or target for the process or information. Currently there is a thin solution set for this capability, but the rapidly growing list of solutions in the market segment will soon answer this need.

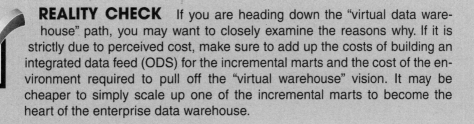

REALITY CHECK If you are heading down the "virtual data warehouse" path, you may want to closely examine the reasons why. If it is strictly due to perceived cost, make sure to add up the costs of building an integrated data feed (ODS) for the incremental marts and the cost of the environment required to pull off the "virtual warehouse" vision. It may be cheaper to simply scale up one of the incremental marts to become the heart of the enterprise data warehouse.

An integrated environment of incremental data marts forming a virtual enterprise data warehouse is a very challenging, if not impossible, retrofit. It is not likely in a LegaMart scenario. It is much more likely that you will allow the existing LegaMarts to die of natural causes and replace them with integrable incremental data marts built under the enterprise data mart architecture.

LegaMart Integration

For many, however, simply letting the LegaMarts of the business wither away on the vine is not an option. They are the unlucky ones sitting in the room when someone farther up the food chain issues the long-dreaded directive to "integrate yon LegaMarts." Thus will begin a long, painful journey. Between the time you are assigned this unenviable task and the last LegaMart is integrated, you will spend many hours disparaging the talents and ancestry of any and all involved in the creation of these nonintegrated monstrosities. LegaMart integration is a difficult, challenging, and often ugly task. Although I cannot offer you much comfort in this effort, I can offer you a road map to success.

1. Identification of Unique LegaMart Elements

The first step is to identify all unique elements in the LegaMarts. These are dimension members, metrics, and calculated aggregations that are unique to that LegaMart and are not integrable with other LegaMarts. For example, a U.S.-based headquarters staff might use a LegaMart with columns labeled "Domestic Sales," "International Sales," and "Canadian Sales." These columns would not be entirely integrable with the Canadian LegaMart's columns labeled "Domestic Sales" and "International Sales." Although the "Canadian Sales" column is common in both LegaMarts (albeit with different semantic terms "Canadian Sales" and "Domestic Sales"), they both have a unique view of "International Sales." Each of the unique attributes you identify need to be relabeled in the post-integration environment. In this example, the Canadian LegaMart's columns would need to be relabeled "Canadian Sales" and "Canadian International Sales," and the U.S. headquarters LegaMart's columns would need to be relabeled "US Domestic Sales" and "US International Sales."

2. Identification of Common Elements

You must identify all common elements across all LegaMarts. Start with the dimensions and then proceed to facts, aggregations, histories, and status tables. Note that you cannot expect to find common semantics across these LegaMarts. You must examine the underlying sources, integrations, and business rules in order to determine if "Gross Sales" in one LegaMart is actually the same thing as "Gross Sales" in another. Welcome to the pain of LegaMart integration. This process is very time and resource intensive and easily sucks all available resources for a very long time. As the days turn to weeks, and the weeks to months, and your team is still slogging through line after line of

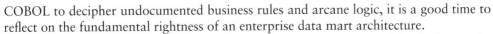

COBOL to decipher undocumented business rules and arcane logic, it is a good time to reflect on the fundamental rightness of an enterprise data mart architecture.

After the seasons have changed, probably more than once, you will finally have a definitive list of all common elements in the enterprise's LegaMarts. At this time, you will most likely need to do a second pass through them because they will have continued to evolve and mutate in the months since you started this effort. The good news is, it goes faster the second time because all you're looking for is delta changes in business rules and transformations since the first pass. About three quarters of the way through the second pass is another excellent time to ponder the righteousness of building incremental data marts under the auspices of an enterprise data mart architecture.

Finally, you will have a current list of all common elements across the entire collection of LegaMarts in the organization.

3. Layback of Common Dimension Keys

Your long journey through the second step will have led to the discovery that dimensions using the same name in multiple LegaMarts have wildly different keys. Your next job is to establish common dimension keys for all LegaMart dimensions and to lay the new key structure back out to the LegaMart dimensions. This is not always as simple as it sounds because at this point you are going to start altering the schema of the LegaMart itself. Up to now, the owners and operators of the LegaMarts have only had to issue you a user ID and password so you could examine the data. Now we begin the part of the process where you actually take control of the destiny of the LegaMart. You can expect some raging turf wars in this stage. The best approach is to minimize the amount of structural change as much as possible. For instance, in the case of the layback of common keys, simply append an additional column to their tables with your new key rather than eliminating their existing structure.

At the conclusion of the process, you should have all LegaMarts with common primary keys in all dimensions. This puts you into the position to perform the next big step of bringing all the dimensions into one place.

4. Integration of Dimensions

Assuming that you have not suffered any mortal wounds at the hands of the protectors of the LegaMarts, you are ready to integrate all the LegaMart dimensions into common dimensions for the enterprise. This involves eliminating redundant dimension members and beginning the semantic battle. You will find that although the sales LegaMart has a dimension called Product, it will be very different from the manufacturing LegaMart dimension also called Product. They will contain different hierarchies, different descriptive attributes, and different metric attributes. It is your job to eliminate the duplicates and build a master product dimension acceptable to the constituencies of all LegaMarts.

To accomplish this, you need to duplicate the hierarchies of each group and include all pertinent dimension metrics from each LegaMart constituency. Expect to end up with many columns containing various flavors of the same basic attribute all labeled with their source LegaMart, for example, "Sales Product Type" and "Manufacturing

Product Type." Build the common dimension masters in a separate RDBMS designated to hold the "enterprise master version of reality," which will become your reference architecture for the integrated data mart environment and the master source for all dimensions to be replicated out to the subsequent independent data marts.

In many cases, you will be unable to gain consensus on a single source system of record for the business dimensions. For example, the Sales group may only consider the order entry system suitable as a source for the customer dimension, whereas the Service organization will only allow the service dispatch system to be the basis for their view of "customer." In this case, you need to turn to one of the available point solutions that perform integration and de-duplication on multiple sources and output a single master file.

5. Establishment of Common Semantics

By far the greatest challenge in any enterprisewide initiative is gaining consensus on common semantics. Your goal is to gain as much conformity as you can. Don't expect to ever get 100% buy-in for all the common semantics across the enterprise. You will always face a small group of users that "have always called total income Net Sales, and that's what we'll always call it, period!" Fight the good fight, and do what you can to get the business to agree that the sky is blue, and that the official term will be blue, not indigo, robin's egg, deep sea, and royal. Best of luck.

If you do happen to get close, don't be afraid to work additional rounds of meetings to drive to consensus. If you can get down to only a few attributes with disparate semantics with only a few hold-out user groups, you can play the "peer pressure" card and force them to play along, however reluctantly.

Once you have done what you can in what will be referred to far into the future as the "great semantic wars," apply the common semantics across all the master dimensions you have built. For all attributes that you were unable to gain consensus on, you must carry duplicate columns, each labeled individually, for instance, Sales Product Type and Manufacturing Product Type.

6. Establishment of Common Business Rules

Now that you have established what the common business dimensions are and have established what the common semantics will be, all that remains is to establish common business rules for the calculation of all metrics in system. And you thought common semantics was tough! Now you get to try to convince the Sales LegaMart constituency that they should adopt the method of calculating "Net Profit" used by their arch enemies in the Marketing group for the marketing LegaMart. You won't win all these battles either, so expect to be carrying multiple columns populated with various forms of the same basic metric. You can expect to end up with "Sales Net Sales" and "Marketing Net Sales" side by side on reports in the future. People become very wedded to their particular method of calculating "the truth" and are loathe to adopt anyone else's definitions. Again, your goal is to gain the greatest level of consensus as possible. Also, don't be afraid to make another pass at consensus when certain bull-headed personalities are removed from the equation, even if it is months or years after your first efforts.

7. Integration of Facts

Once you've established the business rules, you are ready to integrate the various versions of the transaction detail facts found in the collection of LegaMarts in the organization. Again, the process is to create a master integrated environment built from the LegaMarts that is separate from all LegaMart environments. If you don't create this separate system, you will most likely fall prey to internecine political and turf warfare among the competing LegaMart groups. After you are finished with the master integration, you can easily provide integrated versions of each group's LegaMart.

Facts are usually fairly painless to integrate because they are reflections of the base OLTP transactions. Your biggest worry will be variances in scrubbing algorithms and among the various LegaMarts.

8. Re-create Aggregations

Because you have fully integrated dimensions and facts available, it is a fairly straight forward process to re-create the aggregations found in the LegaMarts. This process is very rarely problematic. Your biggest challenge is in consolidating multiple data mart users in one multidimensional aggregation, should you choose to do so.

9. Scrub and Rebuild Histories

Unfortunately this one is more challenging than spinning up the aggregations. You need to recast the existing history tables using any new business rules established in the process and apply the common semantic standards of the integrated environment. For simple relationship histories, such as Product History that tracks Product, Cost, and Price, the effort is very low. For time series snapshots that capture the entire dimension, you have a formidable effort ahead of you if you choose to rebuild the entire history. If you can get buy-in from the user community, it is obviously much easier if you simply start fresh with the new integrated dimensions and begin the historical snapshots at the time of deployment.

Conclusion

If you have made it to this stage of the process with your wits still about you, it is time for a well-deserved celebration. The successful integration of LegaMarts is one of the most challenging tasks you will ever face. It requires high levels of technical, leadership, and political skills—to say nothing of an iron will, boundless determination, endless energy, and very little need for sleep.

The LegaMart integration effort yields a consistent, reliable enterprise data mart environment that shares common sources, dimensions, semantics, business rules, and metrics. As the astute reader will no doubt notice, these are the exact characteristics of an enterprise data mart architecture. Avoid the pain and cost of LegaMart integration—build your data marts using an enterprise architecture. You will never regret the investment.

Integrating Data Islands

Somewhere, in a perfect world in a parallel dimension, there is an incremental data mart system whose sources are all well-defined operational systems. All the data that flows into the system comes from industrial strength, IS (Information Systems) audited and maintained operational systems. Every source field has the integrity of Walter Cronkite and the process rigor of an IRS auditor and is as reliable as 2 AM feedings for a newborn.

Meanwhile, the rest of us get to live in the real world, where nonlegacy data sources are everywhere. The Western division can't live without Bob's Filemaker Pro database of customer nicknames, Purchasing can't imagine a decision support system lacking Susan's Excel spreadsheet of average vendor discounts, and HR (Human Resources) absolutely must have online, click-and-point, integrated access to Mary's organizational charts maintained in WordPerfect.

These sources are all data islands, living off by themselves, cut off from the rest of the data world. They are desert islands with a palm tree or two, producing the coconuts of information that sustain thousands of indigenous workgroups, divisions, and functional users. The data islands are a dark and mysterious place from the IS perspective, filled with buried chests of valuable information, protected by dead applications, missing documentation, creaky systems, blank process maps, and paranoid users.

To attain and maintain high levels of utilization among users, we must find a way to successfully integrate these critical information resources in the data mart environment we design and implement. If we don't, users will marginalize the data mart system, as they continue to run the business off of an unaudited spreadsheet and one column of an obscure green bar report. If your incremental data mart system is not *the* "go to" place in the enterprise for decision support, your system will eventually die. You must have unanimous, homogenous support and validation throughout the organization to sustain the political will necessary for ongoing funding and resources. You can't achieve this without mounting an expedition to discover, map, and integrate the data islands in your enterprise.

This effort is a nontrivial task, at best. If you have an organization in the $600–900 million range, expect to have a couple of people dedicated full time to the data island identification, validation, and integration portion of the data mart project. They will probably need a couple of contractors for the implementation stages, which you can expect to last two to twelve months, depending on the scale of your project.

The first stage, identification, should begin early on in the process. Start listening for signs of data islands in your initial interview process. "We keep that in Lotus" or "John's got that in Access" are the types of side comments between interviewees that

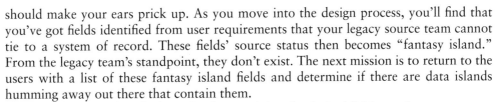

should make your ears prick up. As you move into the design process, you'll find that you've got fields identified from user requirements that your legacy source team cannot tie to a system of record. These fields' source status then becomes "fantasy island." From the legacy team's standpoint, they don't exist. The next mission is to return to the users with a list of these fantasy island fields and determine if there are data islands humming away out there that contain them.

If the users can identify data islands containing the desired fields, you've got a potential source for the data mart system. If not, the fields remain fantasy islands. For the remaining fantasy island fields, you'll need to connect the users with your application development team to gather requirements for an OLTP system that will be used to populate and maintain this new source system.

In many cases, where you identify an existing data island, you may choose to abandon it and move the users to a new OLTP system with enterprise-strength architecture, system design, process rigor, and reliability. It also makes life a lot easier down the road because inevitably IS will inherit the users' data island systems as the people who built them leave or move in the organization. If you establish a standard architecture for these OLTP data island systems, maintaining them is possible. Otherwise, you face a future of dozens of disparate little OLTP data island systems developed in dead products, without documentation, on abandoned platforms that have become mission critical to your incremental data mart system and its users.

If you've successfully identified some data islands out in the User Seas, try passing them through the following validation screen:

1. *Commitment*
   There must be a department/divisional business commitment, in perpetuity, to populate and maintain the data island. This cannot be an individual commitment; people move on. It must be a business commitment from the business owner.

2. *Process rigor*
   The department/division must demonstrate a process with inherent integrity, error checking, and valid process flow.

3. *Openness*
   The data must live in an open and accessible application. Proprietary data structures do not lend themselves to future maintenance and support once this application gets abandoned on your doorstep a few months or years from now.

4. *Scaleability*
   The data must live in an environment that can scale to meet the anticipated needs of the department/division.

5. *Path to standardization*
   The department/division must demonstrate a technological growth path that will facilitate integration and standardization with other data island OLTP processes in the business.

6. *Stability*

   The data must live on a hardware/software platform that is demonstrated to be stable, reliable, and consistent with the strategic computing platforms of the business.

7. *Disaster recovery*

   The department/division must demonstrate a regular backup capability, including off-site storage. Full restoration of the entire computing platform and data in a timely manner is a prerequisite.

8. *Resources*

   The department/division must commit, in perpetuity, the necessary resources to provide and support the above requirements.

Once the data islands pass this screen, and you'll find many that will, it remains to integrate these new sources into the incremental data mart system. The first step is likely to be a link from the incremental data mart or system of record out to the data island to supply it with Cust ID or some other standard key. Next you'll need to get the source feedback from the data island on a regular basis.

Common approaches include:

- Regularly scheduled flat file exports
- Direct ODBC (Open Data Base Connectivity) extraction
- Native middleware connections to merchant databases
- Third-party extraction/replication gateways

Of these, flat files are the most common. They are easy to implement, easy to FTP (File Transfer Protocol), and easy to manage over the WAN (Wide Area Network). Connecting directly to the data island data source via ODBC or a direct middleware connection is the most elegant, but is highly dependent on the strength and reliability of the network infrastructure. Appropriate error handling is essential in this scenario.

As you recall from all the articles, seminars, workshops, brochures, books, and so on that have been inundating you regarding data warehousing and data marts, it is a very iterative process. When you step off into the fantasy island/data island adventure, you are at the heart of an intense, high-frequency iteration loop. Make sure your team members on the data island task force are *very* user focused, desktop tool oriented, and PC/Mac savvy. These team members will be living and breathing pure user data and process for six months or so. It will be challenging and frustrating at times, but in the end their trip to the mysterious and exotic data islands will return to the incremental data mart system some of the most highly prized jewels of data in the users' treasure trove of information.

Summary

Incremental data mart projects have many of the same challenges as an enterprise data warehouse project, along with some very unique challenges of their own. One of the keys to overcoming these challenges is the selection of a robust and scaleable data mart tool to aid in the design, creation, population, monitoring, and maintenance of the data mart system. Many excellent tools are available in the DTEAMM segment for prices from $35,000 to $100,000.

Even these tools cannot fully mitigate the challenges of LegaMart and data island integration. It is almost certain that your data mart projects will include this integration as a requirement. They are both extremely tough endeavors, but rewarding when they are completed and their data is fully integrated into the data mart system.

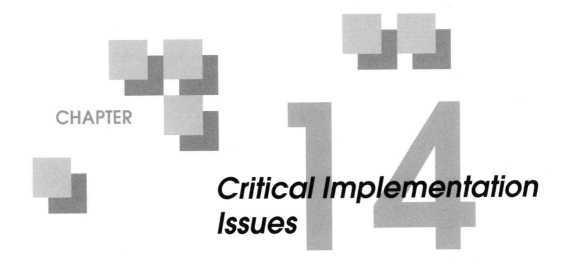

Critical Implementation Issues

Regardless of scale or target user group, your data mart project is likely to fall prey to challenges that are consistent across all industry segments and all data mart projects, be they "top-down" subset data marts or "bottom-up" incremental data marts. It is almost guaranteed that you will need to overcome one or more of these critical implementation issues during the course of your data mart project.

What to Expect

Right out of the gate, you're going to experience some predictable phenomena:

- *Instant heroes*
  You will most likely be delivering integrated, scrubbed, historical information resources to users who have never had access to anything remotely that valuable or usable. You and your team will be instant heroes to the user community. Enjoy this honeymoon period while it lasts because, in most cases, it won't last long. Use this brief period of euphoria to hold celebratory events for the team. Award the team with suitable accolades and forward the congratulatory e-mails from the users to your management.

- *Data integrity*
  Within days of rolling out the system to the user community, you'll start to get calls and e-mail regarding dirty and sparse data. Unfortunately, no matter how many resources you commit to QA (Quality Assurance) during the data mart development process, it is impossible to eliminate all data integrity problems. With dirty data and users, there seems to be some kind of magnetic force involved. Like tornadoes to trailer parks, users are inexorably drawn to dirty data. If you put 200 gigabytes of data out in your data mart, the users will find the five megabytes with integrity problems within days. The upside to this phenomenon is that users will instantly understand the value of data integrity. You will find that they are suddenly more than willing to fund the correction of OLTP (On-Line Transaction Processing) source system data integrity problems that you have been begging for year after year.

- *Additional data points*

  Soon after you begin the iteration loop to correct the data integrity problems the users have uncovered, you will begin to receive requests for additional data points in the data mart. This is especially true for the first few trips around the data mart development methodology iteration loop, when the scope is still very tight and small to facilitate quick development and roll-out. It is a delicate process to maintain iteration speed and momentum, while still answering your user group's requests in a timely manner. Your first pass is to determine if the request falls within your current scope "elevator test." If it is out of scope, the users will have to wait until the next trip around the iteration loop, and the scope can be expanded. If it falls within the scope, you must assign specific resources to sourcing the data and integrating it within the data mart environment. Don't be afraid to do repeated "reality checks" on user requests and make sure you are providing a specific answer to specific pain.

- *Performance issues*

  There is a fundamental law regarding data mart performance: It will never be fast enough. You will be amazed at how quickly users' expectation levels change upon data mart implementation. Even if it used to take 17 days to get an answer under the old system, you can rest assured that 17 minutes will be much, much, much too long for the data mart. Even if you deliver 17-second response time, within weeks you will hear grumblings about how sluggish the system is.

  I always find humorous published performance standards for various types of information systems. Usually the "response time" variations are: OLTP—subsecond response; ODS (Operational Data Store)—seconds to minutes; Data Warehouse/Data Mart—several minutes to hours. Obviously these articles and books are written by people who are somewhat removed from "real life" implementations. Users who have paid $200,000 to $2,000,000 for a data mart are not going to settle for a "many minutes to hours" response time. A realistic goal is response to an average ad hoc query in under a minute. (Now I know that "average ad hoc" is an oxymoron, but I think you understand what I'm driving at.) Do not delude yourself into thinking that the user community is going to continue to fund a data mart that provides response times of 40 minutes to several hours. Even though you will never satisfy the users' lust for speed, you must provide crisp response times to normal use.

- *Additional users*

  The biggest challenge you normally need to deal with upon roll-out is the curse of success. Everyone will want access to the data mart. The more users you add, the greater the data mart system load. Remember the overriding data mart maxim of "scaleability in all things"? This is when it comes home to roost. Your tidy little data mart system that was designed to handle 50 gigabytes of data and 15 users has suddenly exploded to 250 gigabytes and 215 users. Can your tools and technologies scale to meet the demand? If they can't you'd better hope you have kept your résumé polished. You will most likely have immediate opportunities to explore career options in your local metropolitan area.

You can count on additional users almost immediately upon roll-out. Make sure you and your team are prepared for this additional load. Have a process in place for adding new users. Have training classes and orientation sessions scheduled in advance. Have scale-up plans in place with all of your vendors for the data mart system. Make sure your server vendor has additional I/O (Input/Output), memory, and DASD (Direct Access Storage Device) available and in stock prior to roll-out. Ensure that the network infrastructure can handle a two or three order of magnitude increase in users. Have expansion plans in place for the support organizations. In short, it will happen, don't be blind-sided by it. Be like a Boy Scout, "always be prepared."

Known Challenges

Philosophy and Culture

By far the leading cause of death for data mart and data warehouse projects is culture challenges. IT (Information Technology) teams, IT management, and business management are not accustomed to the specific set of cultural changes and challenges that data marts demand of all parties to ensure success.

Systemic Nature of the Data Mart

The first cultural challenge that is often not overcome is the holistic, systemic nature of a data mart system. IT teams are very technology centric. They have a very difficult time adjusting their field of view to encompass the entire data mart system process, from business driver, through extract, to population and access and the solution of business pain. They also have difficulty in considering the human systems that are an integral part of the holistic data mart system. Data mart teams tend to continuously focus in on the technological aspects of the data mart challenge and ignore the political and business issues surrounding the project.

A data mart project crosses a wide range of business processes and functions. It requires an understanding of the organization in detail and on multiple levels. To be successful, the team must navigate the turbulent waters of not only the quickly shifting rapids of ever-changing technology, but also the hazardous shoals and currents of corporate politics, processes, and personalities.

Assuming that the team can overcome those challenges, it must also ensure that the many technical and human processes that make up the data mart system—from the source OLTP systems, to extraction processes, to scrubbing processes, to transformation processes, to load processes, to access processes, to distribution processes, to network infrastructure, to support infrastructure, to user communication processes—are functioning smoothly and reliably, every night of every week of every month of every year. This is the epitome of a nontrivial task, and it is critical that the team understand that this is the scope of the challenge. Successful, sustainable data marts are not about ensuring that one tool or technology works; they are about ensuring that every element of the entire holistic data mart system works, all the time.

Philosophy

At the core of most culture-driven project failures is a fundamental philosophical breakdown. Usually the autopsy reveals that the data mart was built as an example of what technology can do and that the business problems for it to solve were sought out after the fact. Or it shows that the team could not come to terms with a data mart that was built solely and entirely for the user community and was entirely driven by user needs, with little to no consideration for the team's convenience. Or it reveals that the data mart team was comprised of a group of inflexible individuals who could not deal with the constantly shifting requirements of the data mart environment. Or it clearly delineates an IT culture that could not, and would not, accept that any DSS (Decision Support System) could be mission critical. Any one of these attitudes and outlooks will usually prove fatal to a data mart system.

To build and sustain a successful data mart system that will provide a valuable and trusted information asset to the enterprise, you must adopt an entirely business- and user-driven perspective. You must feel comfortable in an ever-changing environment. You must recognize the holistic nature of the system and its inherent mission-critical status to the organization. Do not attempt to proceed with a data mart project if you or your team lacks these characteristics. You will not be happy, and it will show in your efforts.

Data marts are not a data business or a technology business; they are a service business. You and your team must be comfortable being measured on customer satisfaction metrics and working in a service business. Anything short of this commitment guarantees immediate or eventual failure of the data mart system.

REALITY CHECK One of the best things you can do to overcome these challenges is to hold some off-site team-building events with the technical team and the user community. Sharing common experiences and breaking bread is the quickest route to breaking down the barriers between different cultural groups. They are well worth the investment in time and will return a many-fold payback of the financial investment through improved communication and clear understanding of mutual and individual challenges.

Credibility

The data mart lives and dies by its credibility in the organization. As in all things in life, you only have one chance to establish credibility with your audience. The instant the system is made available to the users, they will audit the information they obtain from it with the existing sources they have been using to manage the business. You must document and communicate *all* deltas between the data mart and these existing sources prior to roll-out.

The data mart must have inherent credibility. It must audit to itself on all levels. Any answer derived from a summary table must match exactly to the detail. This is why you must never introduce any feed into a data mart that is not reflected in the detail facts and the business dimensions. All aggregations must be solely derived from the detail facts and the business dimensions.

There will be a very short time line from the data mart's being used and perceived as a point or tactical solution to management's relying on it for strategic use. The information from the data mart will percolate up to the top of the corporate structure at what will seem like light speed. This is especially true in incremental data mart scenarios, where the users have never had access to integrated, scrubbed, historical data before. You do not want data that is not credible to be used for any purpose in the organization, especially strategic decisions by upper management. Thus you must ensure that the data mart has spotless credibility built on solid fundamental design, clear documentation and communication of any known data integrity problems, documented and communicated deltas with previous information resources, and ongoing efforts to constantly improve data quality and reliability.

REALITY CHECK You will find flaws and errors in the data mart system. You must communicate them immediately and openly to the user community. Set up an e-mail list of all users. Use the list to broadcast an immediate message to users when you discover the problem, along with the plan to correct it.

User Tools

Quite simply, you must have a win in this area. You cannot be successful if you deliver a poor choice in user access tools. The tool must be intuitive. It must have an integrated design; must write to and read from the common meta data repository; must support easy, one-click access to the meta data repository; must scale well; must support current and anticipated user requirements; and must have an attractive UI.

Your users will base their judgment of the entire data mart system on the user tools you provide them. It will not matter to the users if you've spent $3,000,000 on the back end processing of the data mart. If you give them an ugly, unproductive interface to the data, they will pronounce the data mart a huge failure.

Meta Data

Your second greatest overall challenge, after culture and philosophy, will be the successful implementation and utilization of meta data. No project can be successful or sustainable without it, yet it is extremely challenging to populate and maintain it in its currently overwhelmingly manual state.

Your meta data must always be available, it must be easily accessible, it must be current, and it must be complete. The meta data must provide all the information necessary for the technical team to monitor and manage the entire data mart system. It also must provide a deep information resource about the data mart system to the user community. It must easily and completely answer the users' primary meta data questions of "where do I?" and "how do I?"

The meta data repository must be open to all tools and technologies; it must be a logically common repository to all tools, technologies, and users; and it must be easily extensible to reflect the uniqueness of your site. The meta data repository must be automatically populated and maintained by every tool and technology used in the data mart system. The meta data repository must present a complete catalog of available information resources to the user community.

This is a tall order, and one that is not easy to come by. Meta data consumes a large portion of the resources expended in the data mart project. No expenditure of resources reaps greater rewards than those invested in meta data.

Training

Where the rubber meets the road in a data mart implementation is the end-user tools used to access, analyze, and distribute information. Your users really don't care if you've got ATM (Asynchronous Transfer Mode) to the desktop and a 128-way SP2 in the basement or a warehouse full of monkeys pulling index cards—they just want answers. They want them fast, they want them accurate, and they want them consistently. Regardless of what you've got behind the screen, the end user's view and perception of your entire multimillion dollar investment is what they see on their monitor when they double click on that DM (Data Mart) icon. If you give them a clunky tool, with a bad UI (User Interface), nonintuitive interface, overly complex operation, and buggy to boot, they will think the entire data mart an abject failure. By the same token, if you give them the latest, greatest, make the coffee in the morning, data access/analysis/slice 'n' dice/distribution/floor wax/dessert topping piece of wonder code from DSS Gods, Inc., but don't train them on what the data is, how to use it, how to access the meta data, and how to effectively use the tool in your environment with your data, you're equally doomed.

One common trait I've witnessed among the tool vendors and those of us who implement their products is a lingering impression that these tools are another form of office automation. From the vendor side, it is reflected in the dearth of practical, how-to guides on building, implementing, and sustaining a successful environment with their products. Almost every DSS software vendor has a flashy evaluation guide that is designed to lead evaluation teams and the press through the features and capabilities of their products. Unfortunately most vendors don't have a companion "cook book" volume for those of us left to implement their products once the evaluation teams make the selection. Instead, we get boxes of software dropped on us and a couple of weeks to figure out the product, build and test an environment, and deliver it to the pilot team of users. There's very little in the way of ongoing resources to help us build and deliver a successful implementation of the chosen tool.

On the customer side, most managers consider these tools to be "just another office automation tool." They tend to lump these tools in the same category as Excel, Word-Perfect, and CC:Mail in terms of required training and training methods. Many sites consider a half day of training to be adequate and a full day to be a waste of users' time and company resources.

Unfortunately these tools are not anywhere near Excel, WordPerfect, and CC:Mail in terms of their training requirements. The reason is that the training challenge is not to communicate the functionality of an isolated tool. The training challenge is to communicate the functionality of a *system*, of which the tool is only a part. It is impossible to prepare a generic training manual or data set for any DSS tool used to access your data mart. To your users, a generic Widget Inc. sales demo database and accompanying examples are irrelevant to their missions of accessing, analyzing, and leveraging the data in your data mart.

It is critical to train users in the entire context and system of the data mart environment. Start by teaching the trainees what is available in the data mart, that is, what subject areas are available. Until the users understand what data is available, how you use it, and what you use it for, any training of the tool(s) is useless.

To greatly increase your chances of success, prepare a custom usage guide for the user community. The best examples are "cook book" in nature. They contain practical how-to examples using the available tools to answer real-world questions pertinent to the target user audience. Most also include hard copies of the table level meta data. If you've got the room, include the field-level meta data as well. For the table-level meta data, estimated size, frequency of update, content description, and known caveats constitute the minimum meta data set required to be useful.

A practical framework for a training/roll-out methodology is:

1. User places request for data mart access.

2. Manager approves request.

3. User's computer system is checked to see if it can support the tools; upgrades are ordered and installed if required.

4. Required network connections are made or upgraded.

5. Network IDs and passwords are established.

6. Database IDs and passwords are established.

7. Tools are ordered or pulled from stock.

8. Tools are installed and tested on the user's system.

9. User attends introductory training (one day minimum).

10. Upon completion of introductory training, user is provided with passwords, documentation, and user guides.

Note that the user is *not* allowed to "play around" on the system prior to training. Letting untrained users out into the data mart playground leads to infinite support costs and an equally infinite supply of queries from hell, bringing your server to its knees.

11. About a week after training, a user coordinator/coach/mentor pays a visit to see how the user is doing with the new tools, offer encouragement, and answer questions.

12. A month or two after introductory training, an advanced class is offered. Power users will snap up this chance to learn advanced querying, analysis, reporting, distribution, and application interoperability methods and techniques.

13. Periodic "brown bag lunches" and seminars are conducted demonstrating practical examples and techniques to use your tools on your data to answer everyday business questions.

The most important point to remember when planning and executing the "tool training and roll-out" element of your project plan is that these tools cannot be viewed as individual elements of technology like a spreadsheet. They are part of a holistic system, and if the user is not trained in that context, all of your efforts to build and deliver the data mart system are likely to come to naught.

Support

Your support element of the data mart system is responsible for 95% of the system's success or failure once you roll out the system to the users. Unfortunately we tend to pay precious little attention to the support infrastructure and human elements until we are ready to hand over the user community to them.

The support system infrastructure must be extremely solid and robust. The support system must be very responsive to user needs and requests. It must demonstrate a high commitment to business goals and customer satisfaction. The support team must know not only the tools, but also the data and the elements of the underlying data mart system.

Obviously these attributes are not going to magically appear the night before you roll out the data mart system. You must work with the support team throughout the data mart project to ensure that when you are ready to toss them the data mart system "ball," they are ready, willing, and able to catch it and run with it.

Disaster Recovery

One critical sustenance issue is a disaster recovery plan for your data mart. If your experience is typical, when it comes time for roll-out, you'll be behind plan, and one of the first things that will slip off the agenda is a test of the disaster recovery plan.

Considering the common characteristics of the many sites I've visited, your project will need a disaster recovery plan at least as detailed, and better rehearsed, than any other mission-critical system of the business. Typically the data mart is one of the business's first forays into client server architecture. It is likely that your team's level of Server OS (Operating System) and RDBMS (Relational Data Base Management System) expertise is relatively low. I find it fairly common for the server OS administrator and the RDBMS administrator to have had little to no previous experience with their relative products prior to the data mart project. This guarantees that your key players are going up a steep learning curve at the same time that you're struggling to understand, design, and implement a new methodology of decision support in the enterprise.

In these low-experience situations, a common recovery plan is "We've installed the RDBMS several times as part of the development of the project, along with the OS a couple of times. We've got a list of the things to do from the RDBMS Vendor/OS Vendor/Consultant in case something bad happens." Don't be seduced by this siren song of readiness for the worst case. As you draw near to roll-out, you'll be under severe pressure from management, users, and your team to get the data mart online. The last thing you'll want to think about is taking the server down to rehearse a recovery. In many cases, you literally won't have a minute to spare because you'll have extracts, loads, and summaries scheduled up to the millisecond you turn on the system for the users.

As dark a prospect as it may seem, you cannot afford not to take the server completely down and completely rebuild it. As you know, circumstance can sometimes be cruel, and if you don't rehearse a recovery, you'll practically guarantee an outage fatefully synchronized with month-end reporting.

Do not believe any assurance of readiness until the team has passed the following test:

- Completely take down the server, including the OS.
- Reformat the drives.
- Reinstall and reconfigure the OS.
- Reinstall and reconfigure the RDBMS, monitors, middleware, and applications.
- Reload and reindex the data.
- Re-create the aggregations.
- Perform the same "from the ground up" process on examples of all client platforms in use in the data mart system.

The first time the team tries this, they will find many, many errors and gaps in those lists left behind by the vendors and consultants. They will probably have to redo many steps. Don't be satisfied until the whole process happens from beginning to end in one continuous, contiguous process. Do not be satisfied with a report of "we found a bunch of stuff wrong with the lists, we fixed it along the way and we're ready now." Make sure that the entire process is fully documented and can be executed even if a key player is not available.

For best results, arrange to take the server down again, unexpectedly, just as when it drops out from under your data mart. This is the true acid test and will guarantee that your team and your data mart are ready for the vagaries of life in the real world.

Summary

These known challenges are based on years of experience at scores of customer sites. It is almost certain that you will experience many of them in your data mart project. You cannot short change any of these factors, especially philosophy, meta data, and support. If you can overcome the challenges outlined in this chapter, you will be well on your way to a successful and sustainable data mart implementation.

CHAPTER

Maintenance and Sustenance

Although 99% of the industry focus has been on the "buy and build" aspects of data warehouse and data mart systems, the real challenges lie in maintenance and sustenance. Given adequate resources, almost anyone can successfully build a data mart, even if by brute force. The true measure of success, however, is not simply in getting the data mart populated and available for end-user access; it is in the ongoing utilization of the data mart and in the reliance in the data mart system for fundamental, mission-critical, tactical, and strategic decisions for the business.

Maintenance

A long-neglected aspect of successful data mart systems is maintenance. With all the money being poured into the "buy and build" segments of the data mart project, it is easy to see why this segment of the process has been neglected. Only now are we seeing dedicated maintenance products enter the market.

Monitoring

A key part of the maintenance aspect of any data mart system is monitoring. It is impossible to maintain what you do not know about, and monitoring provides the mechanism to build a knowledge base about your data mart system. Each monitoring process must seamlessly populate the meta data repository with its results. Your goals are to establish and maintain extensive monitoring capabilities in the areas of usage, process, and infrastructure.

Usage

• *Queries*
  You need to monitor the utilization of existing queries in the resource repositories. This allows you spot unused resources and opportunities for dedicated aggregations. You also need to monitor the stream of ad hoc queries to look for repeated patterns and aggregation opportunities.

- *Reports*
  You should monitor existing report definitions in the resource repository to spot usage patterns and frequent modifications.

- *Indexes*
  Indexes consume a large portion of the system DASD (Direct Access Storage Device) requirements. You will require extensive dedicated index monitoring resources, especially in the early roll-out stages of the project. It is very important to establish the utilization rates of existing indexes and to spot requirements for additional indexes. Expect a lot of change in the required and utilized indexes in the early stages of roll-out.

- *Aggregates*
  Your initial cut at building and providing precalculated aggregations will be a "best guess" based on user interviews. The actual use of the data mart system and the real-world needs of the users rarely match the interviews and the resulting aggregations. You need to closely monitor the utilization of the aggregations you have provided, especially in the early stages of roll-out. You will experience a high rate of change in the aggregation data sets over time, so expect this monitoring requirement to be a permanent part of the data mart system. You will constantly find aggregations that are heavily used and later abandoned.

- *Network bandwidth*
  Data mart systems rely on the LANs (Local Area Networks) and WANs (Wide Area Networks) of the enterprise to survive. If there is no network, there is no data mart. As such, network bandwidth and choke points must be monitored closely. Some types of end-user tools, such as LowLAP (Low-Level Analytical Processing) solutions, can place heavy demands on the network infrastructure. You must pay close attention to saturation rates, especially in your first few month-end and quarter-end periods.

Process

- *Queries*
  The most fundamental business user process you must monitor is the query process. The system will not live for long if there is no way to monitor the ad hoc requests made of the system and an accompanying way to control and eliminate runaway QFHs (Queries From Hell).

- *EMT (Extract, Mapping, and Transformation) /DTEAMM (Design, Transformation, Extract, Access, Monitoring, and Management) processes*
  The entire process of extracting, scrubbing, transforming, and loading the data must be monitored. This monitoring process requires that suitable alarms and triggers be set if a fundamental process fails for any reason.

- *File transfers*
  If you are working with a manual or file-based EMT process, each element must be monitored separately. This starts with monitoring each individual file transfer at each point along the process.

- *Loads*
  Each database table load must also be monitored in a manual or file-based EMT approach. Appropriate alarms and triggers must be set if any load fails to complete.

- *Replication/distribution*
  You will inevitably be dealing with subset data marts, either from parent enterprise data warehouses or parent data marts. In this case, you need to monitor all data replication and distribution processes closely. It is a potentially disastrous situation to have the parent out of synch with the child subset data mart.

- *Index builds*
  After the tables are loaded and replicated, the indexes must be updated or rebuilt. Alarms must be set if these fail because the resulting loss of system performance will render it useless.

Infrastructure

- *Disk fragmentation*
  Core infrastructure factors, such as disk fragmentation, must also be monitored. Disk fragmentation can have very detrimental effects on system response time. As the data mart system tables are appended with incremental delta data, they will begin to fragment. It is important to monitor this situation and reconform the data files when necessary.

- *Table fragmentation*
  To achieve acceptable performance from standard RDBMS (Relational Data Base Management System) products, tables are commonly partitioned across multiple physical and logical devices. As incremental data is added to the data structures in the data mart, attention must be paid to load balancing between these logical and physical boundaries.

- *Index fragmentation*
  Just as the tables are partitioned, the indexes also are spread across multiple logical and physical boundaries. The system must be monitored to determine when it is appropriate to refresh or rebuild the entire index structure.

- *Partitions*
  The logical and physical partitions of the DASD and RDBMS structures must be monitored. Pay particular attention to the temporary RDBMS spaces assigned to user data sets and ad hoc utilization. It takes several month-end and quarter-end periods to establish the optimum configuration of these parameters.

Managing History

Your data mart system will contain a variety of rolling time period tables and data sets. You need to determine what is to be done with the oldest time period when it comes time to add a new layer of history to the data. For instance, you will probably have some detail fact tables that contain a rolling five years of history. Every January 1, you will be starting a fresh new year of detail data in that table. What will you do with the oldest year's data? Are you going to throw it away? This is usually not a wise option.

It is better to make plans prior to roll-out to place the expired history into off-line or near-line storage. Many businesses have periodic needs for extensive history. Near-line optical or off-line magnetic tape may be a perfect strategy if your users only need ten years of detail history once a year for preparing the annual three-year strategic plan.

Managing Growth

Perhaps the greatest ongoing operational challenge of a data mart system is dealing with the explosive growth that so often accompanies success. The key to overcoming this challenge is to define processes before roll-out.

Build and test a process for handling requests for modification and additions from users prior to general roll-out. Ensure that the process includes provisions for both scheduling the work and, more importantly, for communicating the status of the change requests to the users.

Establish a process, technological, and resource road map that will take the data mart system from its initial design size to one to two orders of magnitude larger prior to the pilot phase. This allows you to quickly ramp the system up should the demands of the business rapidly change.

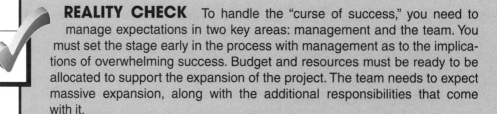

REALITY CHECK To handle the "curse of success," you need to manage expectations in two key areas: management and the team. You must set the stage early in the process with management as to the implications of overwhelming success. Budget and resources must be ready to be allocated to support the expansion of the project. The team needs to expect massive expansion, along with the additional responsibilities that come with it.

Sustenance

Due to the short-term, tactical focus of many data mart efforts, there is often a distorted scale of success. This scale stops at a very short-term focus. Many times, data mart projects achieve initial success, only to fail a few months later. For a data mart to be sustainable and a long-term success, a different scale must be used.

The delta between the short-term focus scale of success and what is required to achieve long-term success is the sustainability gap. (See Figure 15.1.) You must cross this gap in order to achieve long-term, sustainable success for your data mart system. To cross the gap, you must successfully overcome these challenges:

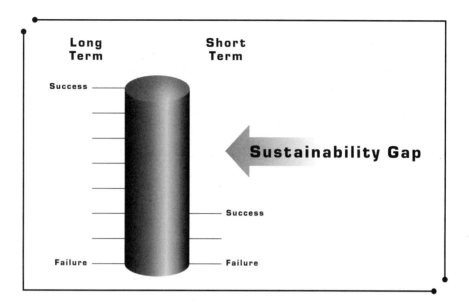

Figure 15.1   Sustainability gap

- Methodology
- Design
- Politics
- Resources
- Technology
- Team metrics

Methodology

As we saw in Chapter 5, a rigid waterfall methodology is not suitable for data mart projects. An iterative methodology that is business driven is the only sustainable process for data mart development. The spiral data mart methodology focuses on business drivers; it packages business drivers with political will and inherent sponsorship. By using a business-driven spiral methodology, the data mart team will always be building solutions for business problems, not building monuments to technology in search of a business problem. (See Figure 15.2.)

The keys to a successful data mart methodology are to be 100% business driver centered and to think incrementally at all times. Keep your scope small and tight for the first few iteration loops. Add to the scope only when there is clear and definable pain in the business that will be solved by the incremental addition. Start small, and build your system incrementally.

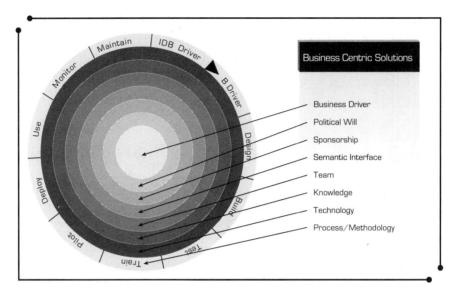

Figure 15.2   Business-driven spiral methodology

Design

A sustainable data mart design has two fundamental design attributes:

- Consumer orientation
- A single metric: ease of use

To be successful and sustainable over the long term, your data mart system must be built on a foundation of user-driven design. The design must reflect a philosophical orientation that is 100% reflective of the ultimate goal of ease of use. A sustainable design is noted for its high degree of denormalization and replication and is almost always a pure star schema. A long-term, successful, and sustainable data mart design includes a wide range of aggregations, as well as dedicated attribute history and status data sets. The design allows users to answer their questions from one to two tables at least 80% of the time. The design incorporates easily accessed and fully maintained meta data. A sustainable data mart design is always constructed under the auspices of an enterprise data mart architecture.

A nonsustainable design is marked by nonarchitected LegaMarts, normalized design, low ease of use, and thin or nonexistent meta data. (See Figure 15.3.)

A sustainable data mart is constructed under an enterprise data mart architecture that identifies:

- Enterprise subject areas
- Common sources

- Common dimensions
- Common semantics
- Common business rules
- Common metrics

The alternative to an architected design is a very painful and expensive integration effort at some point in the future. Regardless of the currently stated goals of the business, it is inevitable that some future management team will seek to reap the possibilities of an integrated set of LegaMarts by forming a "virtual data warehouse." The effort expended to integrate nonarchitected data marts is several orders of magnitude greater than doing the "up front" work to create an enterprise data mart architecture. (See Figure 15.4.)

A sustainable data mart design must deliver and maintain a logically common, open, and extensible meta data repository that is easily accessible from all technical team and business user tools. The meta data repository must deliver the core attributes that technical and business users need. To accomplish this, the team must overcome the meta data conundrum, which states that meta data is both absolutely required for success and is overwhelmingly manual in nature. The data mart project manager must budget sufficient dedicated resources to populate and maintain the meta data repository throughout the entire data mart process.

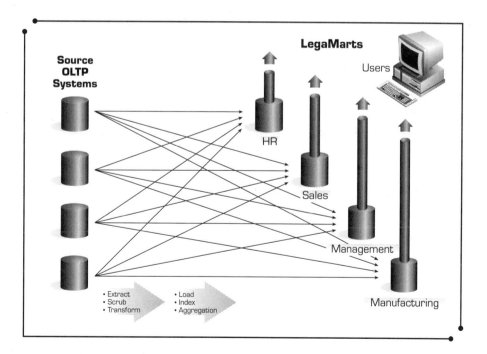

Figure 15.3 LegaMarts

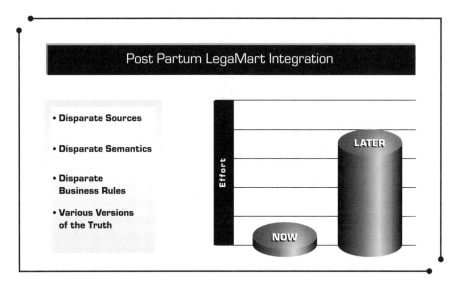

Figure 15.4 Pay me now, pay me later

Politics

No data mart project is sustainable without understanding and leveraging the political context of your organization. Attempting to ignore the political aspects of the project will almost certainly result in the untimely demise of the project and its associated human handlers' careers.

Politics is of particular concern in the following phases of the data mart project:

- Business drivers—identification and ranking
- Sponsorship—selecting individuals
- Subject areas/data marts—selecting and ranking
- Pilots—selecting user groups
- User group support—leveraging success across the organization

The first step in successfully negotiating the murky and ever-changing political waters of your organization is to audit the political relationships in your business. Create a political road map that reflects the relationships of all known players in your data mart world. Identify, rank, and characterize the relationships among organizations, functions, and personalities. This is a delicate task, and you must exhibit both discretion and confidentiality. (See Figure 15.5.)

Once you have established a relationship map, your next goal is to identify "mentor chains" throughout the organization. Mentor chains—from executive to manager to user—form direct communications pathways up, down, and across the organization.

You can use these pathways to your advantage when popularizing success stories about the data mart. Be aware, however, that these high-speed communications corridors are fully bidirectional and carry all types of traffic. Although good news about the data mart will quickly make its way along the path, bad news will travel at light speed. If you've identified a mentor chain that runs from a pilot user to a top executive, you need to head off any bad news at the top if that pilot user has a bad experience in the formative stages of the project. Bad "word of mouth" can kill your data mart as surely as any pure technical failure. Use your knowledge of mentor chains to manage communications regarding the status and health of the data mart project across all layers of the organization's structure.

Your next goal is to identify assassins and vendettas. Assassins will use your data mart project as a way to wreak political revenge upon a rival in the organization. Assassins can be targeted at the IT organization, at your project sponsor, or at a user or user group. Be especially sensitive to potential assassins if your sponsor is a fast-rising "fast tracker" executive or manager. Those who are being passed over while the fast tracker is quickly promoted will often be seething with jealousy and revenge. They won't hesitate to take out the data mart project in any way possible in an effort to tarnish the fast tracker's shiny and spotless reputation.

Vendettas exist on both personal and organizational levels in most businesses. They are usually fairly well known and easily identified. The classic "Sales vs. Marketing" is usually a safe bet. It is also common to find geographical vendettas between regions, especially in sales organizations. You will discover active vendettas along functional lines

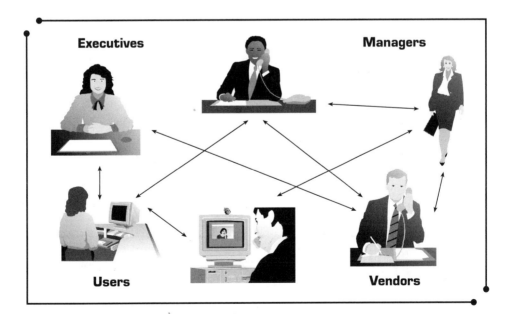

Figure 15.5 Relationship map

and between various levels of management and user groups as well. Your goal is to prevent your data mart project from getting caught in the crossfire between any of these warring groups. It is easy to become a victim of internecine warfare, especially during the selection of initial data marts, subject areas, and pilot groups.

Having established the potential trouble areas of assassins and vendettas, you should now seek to identify internal and external partnerships among all executives and management. Internally, you need to identify partnerships between executives, especially in cross-functional areas. You will find many "marriages of convenience," as executives band together in fast-moving and ever-shifting political alliances in order to advance an agenda or gang up on a threatening rival. Your knowledge of the active vendettas and the agendas of the assassins will greatly assist you in determining the true motives behind the various partnerships and alliances you identify. Your goal is to spot potential opportunities to leverage the success of the data mart cross-functionally across the organization and vertically within specific groups.

External partnerships must be identified between internal executives and managers, and external vendors. You will probably uncover many external vendors with long histories and relationships with executives who are deeply entrenched in the organization. It is critical to not place yourself in a position of competition with an external partner unless you are very confident of your political standing. You are better off aligning yourself with the agendas and goals of the executives and finding a way to partner with a deeply entrenched external vendor than you are to impale yourself and your project on the stake of independence and exclusive internal development.

Finally, you must audit the history and status of the relationships between the IT organization and the business. You must assess all past projects and the state of current projects frankly and honestly. You must also seek out and identify all personality conflicts between members of the IT and business organizations. Your goal is to avoid areas of proven, historical failure; avoid areas of current failure; and eliminate all active personality conflicts from your project and team.

It is not a good strategy to attempt to use a data mart project to heal old wounds from past failures. It is also not a good strategy to use a rapidly developed and deployed data mart to appease a frustrated user group that is enduring a long overdue or disappointing current IT project. Most critically, you must avoid attempting to force two conflicting personalities to work together to develop and implement a data mart system. You cannot afford the risk that a brush fire between individuals will escalate into a full-scale war and consume your data mart project in the conflagration.

REALITY CHECK Political rule of thumb for data marts: Political impact is directly proportional to political risk.

Data mart and data warehouse projects require very high levels of political skill, research, knowledge, and preparation. These projects are not well suited for the political novice. Because they cross functional and organizational lines and involve a very high level of business user involvement and support, data mart projects require very astute political management. Properly managed, there is no better venue for political exposure in the organization; improperly managed, there is no quicker route to political suicide.

Resources

Resource planning and allocation is where many of you will spend the majority of your time in the data mart project. Project management is a well-developed and mature management expertise, and a wide variety of educational and technological support structures exist for these efforts. Paradoxically, given this much history, support, and maturity, project management is where the most fundamentally crippling mistakes are commonly made that doom data mart projects to failure.

Most data mart project managers come from an OLTP (On-Line Transaction Processing) background. In this world, the pattern of resource requirements versus time are well known and understood. (See Figure 15.6.) Data mart projects do not follow this pattern; their time resource curves never come back down as they do in an OLTP project. (See Figure 15.7.)

It is incumbent on the data mart project manager to do two critical things:

1. Effectively communicate to the team and management that extensive ongoing resources will be required for the data mart system.

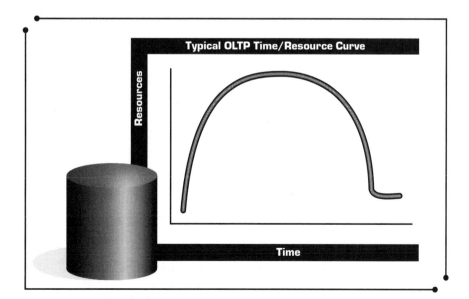

Figure 15.6 OLTP time resource curve

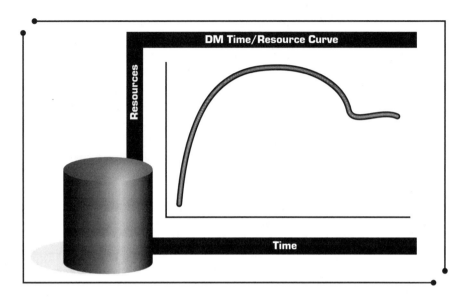

Figure 15.7 Data mart time resource curve

2. Properly budget and allocate sufficient initial and ongoing resources to build *and* sustain the data mart system.

Some rules of thumb that will aid you in these efforts:

• *You will inevitably underestimate the resources required.*
Until you have two or three data marts under your belt, you will underestimate the resources required for your data mart project. You will underallocate resources for meta data population and maintenance, data island integration, new OLTP source system integration, and ongoing data mart system maintenance.

• *Maintain 25% headroom in planning.*
Because of this, you will need to maintain 25% of available resource "headroom" in your resource allocation planning. (See Figure 15.8.) This allows you to have some resource "reserves" that you can assign to trouble areas and still maintain a delivery date as close as possible to your original plans. The alternative is to level load your resources to 100% capacity, get blind-sided by unexpected demands, and then either blow out your budget hiring consultants and subcontractors or be very, very late with your deliverables. Neither of these options are sustainable outcomes.

• *Most of the work is in the integration, scrubbing, and transformation processes.*
If you are building an incremental data mart, you will find that the vast majority of the resources expended are in the area of source system data integration, data scrubbing, and data transformation processes. If you choose to build the system manually, you will expend about 80% of your resources in this area. If you choose

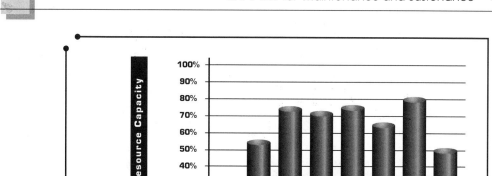

Figure 15.8 25% headroom

a DTEAMM tool, this percentage is significantly lower, but it still represents the majority of the effort of the project. Most of the remainder will be expended overcoming the meta data conundrum.

- *Most initial size estimates are 1/4 to 1/2 the eventual size per subject area/per data mart.*
  The culprit here is aggregations. There is no way to accurately predict what exact form or quantity your aggregation data sets will eventually take. It only requires one multidimensional aggregation of moderate detail to blow most DASD estimates out of the water.

- *Plan for rapid and ongoing expansion.*
  You need to prepare a contingency plan for human and technical resource expansion to support one to two orders of magnitude of expansion of your data mart system within six months. The most common post–roll-out challenge for a data mart system is the curse of success. Everyone will want to add to what you have built, everyone will want to use what you have built, and everyone else will want one of their own. Be prepared for the inevitable.

- *Think scaleability.*
  To be ready, you need to think scaleability from the word go. From organizational structure, to RDBMS design, to server I/O (Input/Output), to network peak capacity, to meta data repository extensibility, the potential and demonstrated scaleability of every data mart system element must be paramount in your evaluation

criteria. Do not, under any circumstances, implement a technology that is not scaleable as a "quick fix" that will be "replaced later as we grow." Once implemented, "quick fixes" become deeply rooted, and you will most likely never have the chance to evolve them into a more suitable solution. Pay the additional price up front to build your data mart system on a very scaleable foundation.

To build and sustain a data mart system, you must lay the groundwork early for the ongoing resource requirements of a data mart system. You must set and manage realistic expectations with management for the ongoing resource requirements for maintenance of the system. If you are just starting out, use a rule of thumb of 60% of the resources required to build the system. After you have created two or three data marts in your environment, you will be able to develop a very clear picture of what the average ongoing requirements are at your unique site. Do not, under any circumstances, allow management to expect that the data mart system will be anywhere close to the low ongoing resource requirements of an average OLTP system.

You must also carefully set the expectations of the data mart team to accurately reflect the high level of ongoing resource requirements in the data mart's very user-driven environment. The data mart system is a world of constant, ongoing change, and the team must know that in advance and be entirely comfortable within that environment. The data mart represents the interface between the available information assets and the needs of the business. Both of these change constantly, and the data mart system will reflect this high rate of change. In particular, the team should expect a high rate of change in the aggregation data sets. (See Figure 15.9.)

From the management standpoint, be particularly wary of resource "tar pits." These resource suckers can quickly consume your planned resources and any additional resources you can throw their way. Heading into the project, you must know that these areas are particularly dangerous:

- *Integrating nonarchitected data marts (LegaMarts)*
  The mother of all resource tar pits, integrating LegaMarts is a project killer for the unwary. This requires extensive dedicated resources and lots and lots of time. Do not attempt this as a key part of your first data mart project. Set it up as an independent, parallel effort.

- *Meta data*
  As you learned in Chapter 7, meta data is predominantly manual in nature. It requires dedicated resources starting at the very beginning of the project and extending for the entire life of the data mart system.

- *New OLTP systems*
  A hidden resource trap often sprung on unsuspecting data mart teams is new OLTP systems. It is very common to build a data mart to replace or supplement reporting and data access capabilities for a new OLTP system. What is not usually taken into consideration is that the requisite source system experts required in any data mart effort will have zero bandwidth to allocate to the data mart effort. You need to

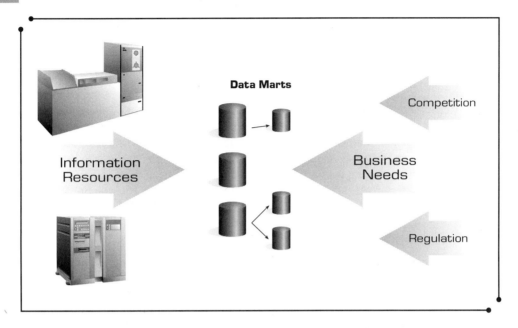

Figure 15.9   Interface between business needs and available information

duplicate the source system experts, either through duplication of their role by "piggybacking" a person onto their OLTP system work, or through hiring external consultants. Do not underestimate the negative impact of little to no access to the OLTP system team. It will cripple your efforts.

- *Data island integration*
Every business has OLTP data islands scattered around the business that users depend on for day-to-day decision making. Naturally they want these data islands incorporated into their data mart system. It requires a dedicated team of data island integrators with very high levels of desktop tool skills and user orientation to successfully integrate data islands into the data mart system. Plan on one to two dedicated people for this effort. If possible, build a solid data island integration team that you can use for the entire series of incremental data marts. If you are working in a subset data mart environment, the data islands must be integrated into the parent enterprise data warehouse or parent data mart.

- *Third-party data sets*
Another hidden resource tar pit is third-party data sets, sometimes called syndicated data. Almost every organization relies on externally provided data for their enterprise data warehouse and data mart systems. Although it is painfully easy to draw a third-party data feed on a white board in your planning sessions, do not

underestimate the initial and ongoing resource requirements of this effort. Not only is there usually significant work in the initial integration, third-party vendors regularly change their schemas and content structures. You must dedicate ongoing resources for this effort. If you have more than a handful of third-party data sets, it will require at least one dedicated person for this effort.

Resource planning and allocation remains one of the most challenging aspects of data mart system project management. Because the market is still very young, there is very little published material on techniques and experiences across various industry segments and data mart types. In this relative vacuum, it remains for you to do your best to set expectations among both management and the team for the significant initial and ongoing resources required for sustainable data mart system construction, implementation, and maintenance.

Technology

Data mart technology consists of both specific point solutions and overarching, all-encompassing environments. (See Figure 15.10.)

Historically, the market has been very focused on the EMT and OLAP (On-Line Analytical Processing)/MQE (Managed Query Environments) technological segments.

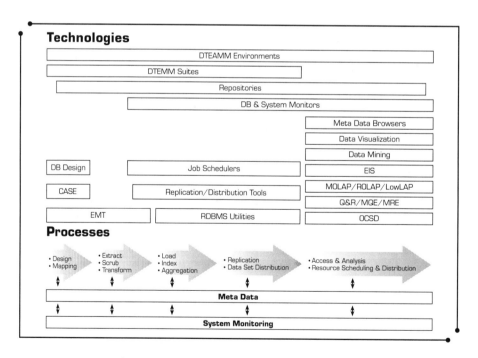

Figure 15.10 Data mart technology

Currently the market focus is moving toward DTEAMM environments. (See Figure 15.11.)

DTEAMM environments offer users the advantages of a fully integrated environment that shares a common UI (User Interface), a logically common and open meta data repository, transformation engine design, integrated user access, and very strong price/performance ratios.

Key Technology Sustainability Issues

From the perspective of sustainability, there are six key features to look for in any data mart technological solution:

- *Integrated environment*
  You will experience much higher productivity and lower support costs with an integrated environment than with a collection of point solutions. Shoot for products that are built from the ground up as an integrated system and built specifically for the data warehouse and data mart market. Avoid Frankenstein patchwork solutions and repackaged "new and improved for data marts" products.

- *Common meta data repository support*
  Regardless of the scale of your current mandate, your organization will soon demand the integration of all the data marts in the business. Ensure that your tools

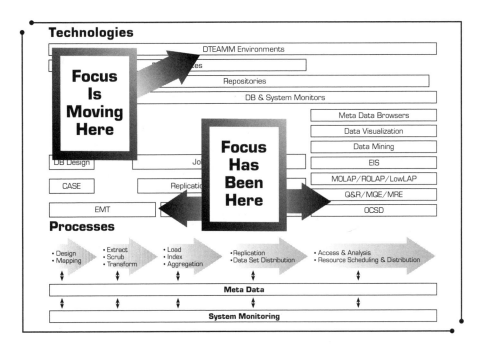

Figure 15.11 Data mart technology movement

and technologies support a logically common meta data repository. You may select a design that has one physical repository or one that has a distributed architecture, but to the technical or business user, the meta data must appear to be one, seamless common repository with a single entry point.

• *Shared resources (algorithms, reports, etc.)*
Due to the curse of success, you will inevitably be tasked with creating multiple data marts for your organization. To maximize productivity, implement tools that allow you to share resources across the organization. You will want to share extract processes, transformation algorithms, reports, analysis data sets, and so on among any authorized users. A logically common meta data repository is a prerequisite for this capability.

REALITY CHECK Currently the area of shared resources is where the industry is weakest. This situation will continue to improve, but solutions are thin at present.

• *Server-centric design*
Buy no thick client solutions. Server-centric technologies provide centralized management and version control and easy migration to intranet and Internet utilization. Carefully examine the underlying architecture of the tools and technologies you are considering purchasing. Pay particular attention to the topology location of critical processes. You do not want your entire system to depend on whether a thick client is up, running properly, and on the network.

• *Thin client support (intranet / Internet)*
Your organization will inevitably require intranet and Internet access and distribution of the data mart information resources. You must be sure that every vendor delivers this capability or communicates a clear technological road map to seamless intranet and Internet support.

• *Scaleability*
Scaleability, scaleability, scaleability. There is nothing more important when considering a technological solution for your data mart system. Whatever you implement must be capable of simple and seamless scaleability to one to two orders of magnitude. Do not implement any nonscaleable tool as a "temporary" solution; you will quickly be overrun by overwhelming success and be trapped with no time or spare resources to implement a properly scaleable solution.

Core Technologies

The core technologies for data mart systems are:

- *Meta data repository*
  No data mart system can survive or sustain without meta data. You must have a logically common meta data repository to provide for the inevitable effort to integrate the data marts.

- *EMT (Extract, Mapping, and Transformation)*
  Given the capabilities and price points of today's solutions, it makes little sense to attempt to build these capabilities by hand. This will be your best investment for a technological solution. You will gain 2–4 times productivity in the development efforts, which is nice, but the greatest payback will be in the automatic population and maintenance of the meta data.

- *End user access and analysis*
  No data mart system has any value if the users cannot easily access and leverage the information. You cannot deliver a "loser" in this area. Given the solid technologies available from multiple vendors, it would be hard to fail to deliver a viable solution. The solution must be intuitive, scaleable, and seamlessly support the meta data repository. These tools have been around for some time, so this segment is much more mature than the EMT/DTEAMM segment, for instance. You should have little trouble in bringing powerful data access and analysis capabilities to every user.

Meta Data Technological Sustainability Issues

Key meta data technological sustainability issues include:

- *Logically common*
  The meta data repository must be logically common to all users, both technical and business users.

- *Open*
  The meta data repository must be open via common industry standards such as ODBC (Open Data Base Connectivity). Avoid proprietary, closed meta data repositories.

- *Extensible*
  The meta data repository must be easily extensible to meet the unique needs of your site.

- *Seamless support from all tools and technologies*
  The meta data repository must be easily directly read and written by all tools in the data mart system. Avoid manual file export and import approaches.

- *Resource browsing, scheduling, delivery*
  The repository must support simple and intuitive browsing of the available data mart system resources. It should also support the scheduling and delivery of any available information resource.

EMT/DTEAMM Technological Sustainability Issues

Regardless of your choice of data mart tools, specific features are required to ensure sustainability.

- *Common, open, extensible meta data repository*
  The EMT/DTEAMM solution must be built on a logically common, open, and extensible meta data repository. Do not accept closed proprietary implementations.

- *Extensive, automated meta data population and maintenance*
  The tool must seamlessly populate and maintain the meta data. Avoid solutions that require the manual export and import of meta data from one tool to another.

- *Shared resources (meta data, algorithms, reports, etc.)*
  The tool must allow multiple project teams to easily share resources such as extraction algorithms and processes, transformation algorithms and processes, and so on. "Check in, check out" management is a very desirable feature.

- *Enterprise scaleability*
  The tool or environment must be scaleable to encompass all enterprise data mart and data warehouse initiatives.

User Access Technological Sustainability Issues

User data access and analysis tools also must pass the following sustainability hurdles:

- *Network load requirements*
  The tools' impact on network bandwidth must be closely examined. You must test the network at projected usage levels for a typical month end and quarter end in order to establish baseline requirements.

- *Server capacity*
  The server capacity required to support all preprocessing of data sets and real-time ad hoc query processing must be established and understood. Again, peak usage level testing is required. Do not wait until the first quarter end to discover that users will experience hour-long waits for query responses.

- *Viable number of users*
  How well will this tool scale? You must be prepared for a very quick expansion in the user base of your data mart system. It is not uncommon for a data mart that was expected to have 15 users to have 300 within six months. Performance and cost/benefit ratios must be taken into consideration.

- *MOLAP (Multidimensional On-Line Analytical Processing) cube size*
  How big will a MOLAP cube be to meet user requirements? How long to load? How long to update? How many users can it really support in real life? These issues must be very clearly understood prior to purchase and implementation. Insist on a "proof of concept" demonstration with your data and server(s) prior to purchase. Pay particular attention to cube size with additional dimensions and lower levels of detail. Vendors tend to demonstrate at high levels of summarization;

your users will immediately want more dimensions and lower levels of detail. The tool must deliver easy and seamless drill through to transactional detail to be sustainable.

- *ROLAP (Relational On-Line Analytical Processing) pipe and server capacities*
ROLAP solutions have high backbone throughput and analysis engine server capacity requirements. Again, insist on a "proof of concept" implementation on your servers, with your data and peak network loads, prior to purchase. Pay particular attention to response times under peak load. Your users will be asking for multidimensional answers at fairly low levels of detail, so do not settle for samples of three dimensions summarized to quarterly levels.

- *ROLAP aggregate awareness*
The ROLAP tool must be very aggregate aware to be sustainable. Your network and server cannot support repeated, unnecessary ad hoc aggregations from low-level detail when precalculated aggregations are available. The ROLAP tool must be capable of automatically accessing the meta data to ascertain the content and structure of the available aggregations, and of populating the meta data with recommended aggregations based on utilization patterns.

- *Support of shared resources (queries, reports, analysis, etc.)*
The tools selected must support the sharing of information resources such as queries, reports, analysis data sets, and so on via the common meta data repository. The tools should support the simple and easy scheduling and delivery of any available information asset in a variety of standard formats.

- *Server-centric design*
The tools must reflect a server-centric design. Analysis engines, data cubes, and repositories must be server resident. Accept no thick client solutions.

- *Thin client model*
The tools must have robust thin client support. The tools must allow any user with a browser to perform any needed ad hoc query, report design, analysis, or resource browsing and delivery function.

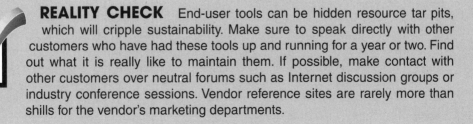

REALITY CHECK End-user tools can be hidden resource tar pits, which will cripple sustainability. Make sure to speak directly with other customers who have had these tools up and running for a year or two. Find out what it is really like to maintain them. If possible, make contact with other customers over neutral forums such as Internet discussion groups or industry conference sessions. Vendor reference sites are rarely more than shills for the vendor's marketing departments.

Technology—Key to Sustainability

The proper choice of technological solutions largely determines the overall sustainability of the data mart system. You must make educated, well-researched selections from the variety of solutions offered. To succeed, you must resist being swayed by a flashy demo and dig deep to determine the sustainability and scaleability of each offering.

Team Metrics

The majority of the eventual success or failure of a data mart hinges on fundamental cultural and philosophical issues among the individuals, groups, and teams involved with the project. It is impossible to simply mandate that such cultural or philosophical change take place. The organization must establish specific metrics to measure, monitor, and reward individuals. Without metrics, and their associated impacts and implications, any culture shift becomes pure rhetoric, destined to quickly fade away in the face of the ongoing stream of corporate initiatives and directives. Without a foundation of metrics, your organization cannot effect the shift in cultural and philosophical outlook required to achieve a sustainable data mart system.

Metric Goals

The overall goals of the metrics are to establish the fact that data marts are a service business, *not* a data business and *not* a technology business. In the data mart business, customer satisfaction is the only metric.

Customer Service Metrics

Data mart teams tend to become focused on technological metrics, such as "how many gigabytes does the system have?" and "how many processors does the server have?" These metrics are meaningless in a sustainable data mart system. Customer service metrics are the only metrics that matter, and they are measured in customer satisfaction.

Customer satisfaction metrics are segmented into the following areas:

- *Meta data*
  Meta data customer satisfaction metrics include population rates, currency and frequency of maintenance, quality, and ease of access. It is much easier to dedicate specific human resources to the meta data population and maintenance tasks and measure their efforts than it is to spread the workload across the entire team and monitor each member's contributions.

- *Ease of use*
  Ease-of-use customer satisfaction metrics include measuring the entire data mart process—from the point of a business user ordering access to the system, the system training, the tools installation process, the system support, the business user tools, and the meta data environment. These metrics are distributed to the appropriate roles in the data mart team. For instance, the system designer is measured on the ease of use of the data design.

- *Response time*
  Response-time customer satisfaction metrics apply to every element of the system. This includes the business user system ordering process, the installation process, system change requests, system addition requests, support calls, query response, and resource distribution. These metrics are distributed to the appropriate process owner, such as making the system support manager responsible for average response time to a business user support call.

- *Validity of data*
  The validity of system data metric includes the accuracy, timeliness, reliability, and confidence level of the data mart system's data resources. These metrics are specifically assigned to process and data owners.

- *Up time*
  System up-time customer satisfaction metrics include the up time of the client systems, the WAN and LAN, the data and application servers, and all other system elements such as wireless data links. These metrics are specifically assigned to each respective system owner. Many large-scale data mart systems have a specific role assigned to disaster recovery. In this case, the up-time metric is closely aligned with this role.

- *Quality of support*
  In real-world data mart system implementations, customer satisfaction is heavily influenced by the quality of the support the business users receive. The specific metrics include the overall system knowledge of the support staff, data knowledge, and tool knowledge. Metrics are also based on the attitude of the staff, both in phone support and on-site support situations. These metrics are assigned to each individual support team member.

The monitoring, collection, and analysis of customer satisfaction metrics is worthless unless there is a financial impact on the individual responsible for the metric. Unless and until the career opportunities and the paycheck of each individual responsible for a customer satisfaction metric are directly affected by that metric, nothing will change. Executives can spout as much as they want about cultural shift and user orientation, but until there is a direct dollar impact, it remains simply empty rhetoric.

Each team member must have performance reviews and resulting promotion, demotion, and remuneration adjustments directly tied to customer satisfaction metrics. Until you reach this point, your data mart system will lack the foundation it requires to be sustainable.

Summary

It is fairly easy to deliver a short-term, high-impact data mart to the business. However, this is a shallow and short-sighted goal. The data mart system can become one of the most valuable assets of the entire enterprise. To do so, it must be sustainable. To achieve sustainability, you must execute each of these factors, especially remuneration-dependent customer service metrics.

If you take only one message from this book, take the fact that data marts are not a data business; they are not a technology business. Data marts are a service business.

Glossary

20/20 hindsight
The perfect, error-free perception available after the fact. Usually implemented by those uninvolved in a project to offer suggestions on how the project could have been done better.

24x7
A schedule of operation that is 24 hours a day, seven days a week.

28.8/33/56k dial up
A connection made by modem from a remote computer to a network or host computer at a transmission speed of 28.8kbs (kilobits per second), 33kbs or 56 kbs.

3270 terminals
Character-based display terminals and keyboards that are directly connected to a host computer, usually a mainframe. Terminals have no internal computing capability; all processing is accomplished on the host.

64/56k
A dedicated, leased digital phone line connection between a remote location and a network or host computer. 64k and 56k refer to the transmission speed of the connection, 64kbs (kilobits per second) and 56kbs, respectively.

Aberdeen Group
A consulting and analyst firm.

Acronyms
Combinations of letters used to represent a series of words or phrases.

ActiveX
A Microsoft standard for computer application components.

Ad hoc
A nonrecurring, one-time, or random query or analysis.

ADE (Application Development Environment)
A programming language or environment used to develop applications to solve business problems.

ADP (Average Deal Price)
The average purchase price of software, hardware, and associated required consulting and training necessary for a complete installation and successful utilization.

Aggregation
Also commonly called a summary, an aggregation is a collection of data calculated from detail transactions. An aggregation is usually a sum, count, or average of the underlying detail, and often is calculated along several business dimensions, i.e., total sales by customer by product.

AI (Artificial Intelligence)
Computer technology that seeks to provide human-like knowledge and decision capabilities to non-human processes and functions.

Alpha geek
The member of a workgroup most conversant with technology and tools. Also known as "power user."

API (Application Programming Interface)
A reference provided by software developers to facilitate other computer applications in communicating with their application.

Applets
Small applications that provide specific functions, such as calculation or modem operation. Applets are usually loaded and unloaded dynamically as required. When used in an Internet browser or other thin client scenario, they may be cached to disk to speed loading.

Application
A computer program developed to provide a specific function or answer a specific business need.

Architecture
A definition of the interconnection of computer components, network components, or system components.

ASCII (American Standard for Computer Information Interchange)
A format for data storage and transmission, commonly referred to as "text" format.

ATM (Asynchronous Transfer Mode)
A packet-based, switched, point-to-point data transmission protocol capable of transmitting data, voice, video, and audio simultaneously at very high speeds.

Backbone
A high-speed network used to connect servers, mainframes, storage devices, and network routing and switching equipment.

Backflush

The process of replicating the scrubbed and integrated data from a data mart or data warehouse system back into one or more OLTP systems.

Bandwidth

A measurement of throughput rates. Usually used in conjunction with measuring network transmission speed, although colloquial use has extended the term to human resources, as in: "He doesn't have the bandwidth to be responsible for data island integration."

Basic/Visual Basic/VBA (Visual Basic for Applications)

A programming language sold by Microsoft.

Batch

A computer process that runs in a sequential series of processing steps.

Bill Inmon

Author of many books on data warehousing and other computing topics. Popularly known as the "father of data warehousing."

Bit

One unit of binary information. A bit is either a one or a zero.

Black hole

An area of a project that sucks resources away from other priorities, never to be seen again. Black holes have limitless appetites for resources.

BOB (Best Of Breed)

A computing and technology strategy based on finding and implementing the best product in each category required to solve a business problem.

Bottom up

A data warehouse strategy based on building incremental architected data marts to test products, methodologies, and designs first, then using these data marts to justify the construction of the enterprise data warehouse.

BPR (Business Process Reengineering)

The analysis and redesign of business processes and associated technology systems.

Browsers

A thin client application that is used to navigate, investigate, and select information. Browsers are used to navigate and access the world wide web (WWW) and are also commonly used to navigate and access meta data.

Business case

A presentation of the justifications for the pursuit of a technology project.

Business driver

A problem in the business that can be solved by technology.

Business rules
The logic applied to calculate or otherwise derive a value.

Business scope
The measurement of how widespread the impact of a technological solution is upon the overall business operations.

Byte
Eight bits of information.

C/C++
Compiled programming languages used to develop computer applications.

C/S (Client/Server)
A computing architecture in which a client computer communicates over a network to exchange data with a server computer.

Cache
A copy of program code or data that is kept in memory or on a local hard drive to provide quick access by a CPU or computer application.

CASE (Computer Aided Software Engineering)
A computer application that automates some aspects of database and application design and implementation.

CDC (Change Data Capture)
The process of identifying and/or segmenting the incremental data generated from an OLTP system over a given time period.

CEO (Chief Executive Officer)
The top management position in a corporation.

CEO table
A database table or series of tables or data sets created and maintained to meet the needs of the senior management team.

CFO (Chief Financial Officer)
The top management position in the finance functional area of a corporation.

CGI (Common Gateway Interface)
A standard protocol for communication between a web server and a database server.

CIO (Chief Information Officer)
The top management position in the information technology area of a corporation.

CISC (Complex Instruction Set Computer)
A CPU that is designed to support the direct execution of very complex operations in one (or very few) CPU cycles.

Clients
Computer systems operated directly by users to interface with computer applications.

CLM (Career Limiting Move)

A strategic or tactical error that ends or limits one's career.

COBOL (Common Business-Oriented Language)

A third-generation compiled language used to develop computer applications.

Compromise creep

The expansion of a project's stated or implied goals.

Computer

An electronic device allowing the controllable, programmable execution of calculation logic.

Confidence level

A business meta data attribute used to measure the organization's faith in a specific data field. Usually expressed in a three-level scale (poor, moderate, high).

CPUs (Central Processing Units)

The logic engines of computers responsible for interpreting and executing instructions contained in computer programs.

CRT (Cathode Ray Tube)

Monitors attached to computers used to display images formed by a scanning electron beam.

CYPY (Current Year & Prior Year)

A collection of data containing only information from the prior year and the current year. Popularly used to answer the primary needs of business that focus on measuring current year performance versus prior year results. By implementing a CYPY table, designers limit the utilization of the full set of historical detail, which often yields poor response times compared to the much smaller CYPY table.

DA (Data Architect)

The person responsible for designing the logical and physical data models.

DASD (Direct Access Storage Device)

Commonly used to refer to "hard" disk drives, which are data storage devices that digitally record information on spinning platters coated with magnetic material.

DASD fear

The fear often expressed and manifested by those who are uncomfortable with the prospect of storing and managing many gigabytes or terabytes of data.

Data Base Associates International

A consulting and analyst firm.

Data cube

A proprietary data structure used to store data for a MOLAP end-user data access and analysis tool.

Data integrity
The requirement to provide data that is free of errors and omissions.

Data islands
Stand-alone OLTP systems that are usually operated outside the influence and/or control of a central IS organization.

Data mart
An architected set of data designed and constructed for decision support purposes, reflecting the design principles of a data warehouse provided to serve the needs of a homogenous user group.

Data mining
The process of examining large sets of detail data to arrive at relationships, trends, and projections of future outcomes.

Data visualization
The process of displaying data in visual form, such as in charts.

Data warehouse
An enterprisewide collection of data that is subject oriented, integrated, scrubbed, involatile, easy to access and use, and contains historical data and summarizations.

Database
A computer application that stores data and allows access and manipulation of the data.

DB2
A database sold by IBM that runs on a variety of computer platforms.

DBA (Data Base Administrator)
The person responsible for the operation and management of a database.

DCI (Digital Consulting Incorporated)
An organization that organizes and executes computer industry trade shows and events.

Delta
The difference between two values.

Denormalized
A data storage design that combines all pertinent data in as few tables as possible.

Detail fact table
A table used in a star schema to store the detail transaction level data.

Dimension tables
A table used in a star schema to store descriptive, hierarchical, and metric information about an aspect of the business that is used for an analytical perspective. Common examples include product, customer, geography, and time.

Disaster recovery
The policies and plans used to restore a computer system from system failure.

Disk drives
See DASD.

DisposaMarts
A form of data mart that is created to support limited-term programs in the business.

DM (Data Mart)
See Data mart.

Domain
In business, a sphere of common influence or function. On the Internet, a domain name is a label for a specific address, e.g., egltd.com.

DSS (Decision Support System)
A system of computer applications and specifically designed data sets used to provide answers and analysis for business managers.

DTEAMM (Design, Transformation, Extract, Access, Monitoring, and Management)
A transformation engine–based client server computer application that provides for most aspects of data warehouse and data mart system design, construction, utilization, monitoring, and management.

DTEMM (Design, Transformation, Extract, Monitoring, and Management)
Similar to a DTEAMM application, but lacking any data access and/or analysis capabilities.

DW (Data Warehouse)
See Data warehouse.

EDI (Electronic Data Interchange)
A standard for exchanging information electronically between computer systems. Commonly used to pass order, billing, and shipping information between corporations.

EIS (Executive Information System)
A computer application and specifically designed data sets used to provide answers and analysis to executive business management.

EMT (Extract, Mapping, and Transformation)
Computer applications that generate compiled computer language programs for the purposes of extracting and transforming data from source OLTP systems and populating data warehouse and data mart systems.

Enterprise data mart architecture
A high-level enterprise wide framework that describes the subject areas, sources, business dimensions, metrics, business rules, and semantics of an organization. It is used to identify shared sources, dimensions, metrics, and semantics in an iterative data mart or iterative subject area development methodology.

Enterprise data warehouse
See Data warehouse.

Enterprise server
A term used to describe a mainframe computer without attracting the negative connotations of "mainframe" in today's market.

ER (Entity Relationship)
A type of database design used to identify the topics of interest (entities) and their connections to each other (relationships). An ER design is more normalized than a star schema and is often used when the DSS database is used primarily as a parent for star schema data marts directly accessed by users.

Extensibility
The ability to easily modify an application, repository, or schema to reflect the unique attributes of a specific business.

Extract
The program used to pull data from a source OLTP system or other data source.

Extranet
An intranet open to specific outside parties via a firewall gateway. Usually used to allow intranet access by customers or suppliers.

FDDI (Fiber Distributed Data Interface)
A standard for lightwave network physical topology devices using fiber optic connections for high-speed data transmission.

Feed
A computer program or process that supplies data from a source OLTP system or other data source.

Firewall
A computer, router, or system that insulates an internal computer network from the Internet. The firewall allows only specifically qualified traffic to pass into and out of the internal network.

Flat file
A computer data file that contains information in text format (ASCII on non-mainframe platforms).

FOC masters
People who are very familiar with FOCUS, a reporting and system development computer application.

Focus
A reporting and system development computer application sold by Information Builders, Inc. (IBI). Focus operates on over 50 different computer systems and is a popular system

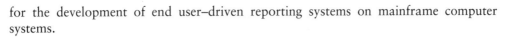

for the development of end user–driven reporting systems on mainframe computer systems.

Footprint
The amount of processing power, disk storage, and RAM required by a computer application.

Foreign key
A unique identifier used to connect a table in a relational database to another external or "foreign" table.

Fractional T1
A type of dedicated connection used to connect networks or computer systems that allows for various data transmission rates, usually in 56kbs (kilobits per second) or 128kbs increments.

Fragmentation
The dispersing of data segments in noncontiguous blocks on a DASD device caused by operational processing or incremental update.

Frame relay
A data communication standard that allows packet switching of small data packets over a WAN.

Frequency of update
The time period between updates of data sets in a data mart or data warehouse, e.g., daily, weekly, or monthly.

FTP (File Transfer Protocol)
A protocol for the transfer of data files across TCP/IP networks, including the Internet and intranets.

Gartner Group
A consulting and analyst company.

Gigabyte (GB)
2^{30} bytes or 1,073,741,800 bytes.

Glass house
The computer center used to house mainframe and other computer systems. So named because mainframes and other early computer systems required specifically designed rooms to support their power and cooling requirements. These rooms often had glass walls to allow viewing of the multi-million-dollar computer systems.

GUI (Graphical User Interface)
A computer system interface that uses visual pictures, graphics, controls, and icons to provide control and interaction with users.

Green bar reports
Reports printed on tractor feed paper with alternating green and white horizontal bands. Commonly produced by mainframe computer systems on high-speed line printers.

Hard disk drive
See DASD.

Hardware
The mechanical components of a computer or network system.

History table
A table used to capture changing relationships in a decision support system. Usually used to capture slowly changing elements of a dimension table.

HTML (Hyper Text Markup Language)
A subset of SGML (Standard Generalized Markup Language), HTML is an interpreted text-tagging protocol to provide for uniform display of fonts, tables, and other WWW (World Wide Web) page elements on any compatible WWW browser computer application.

HTTP (Hyper Text Transfer Protocol)
A standard for transmitting and exchanging HTML pages.

Hypercube
See Data cube.

I/O (Input/Output)
The reading and writing of data internally and externally of a computer system.

IBI (Information Builders Incorporated)
A computer software vendor most widely known for its information reporting product Focus.

IBM (International Business Machines)
A company that sells a wide variety of computer hardware and software systems. Most widely known for its mainframe computer systems.

IDC (International Data Corporation)
A technology consulting and analysis company most widely known in the data warehouse industry for its survey on ROIs of successful data warehouses.

Impact reports
A technical meta data report that illustrates the impact on the target data warehouse and/or data marts if a field is changed in the source system(s).

Incremental data mart
A data mart constructed as part of an incremental strategy to achieve the goal of an enterprise data warehouse. Usually constructed to test and prove technologies, vendors, methodologies, and designs, and to demonstrate ROI.

Index
A feature of databases that allows quick access to stored data.

Informix
A database vendor primarily known for its parallel database performance and its design approach to providing storage and retrieval of nontabular data types such as video, text, and audio.

InstaMart
A very short life span data mart usually created, accessed, and deleted by an end-user access and analysis tool.

Integration
The process of combining data from multiple, nonintegrated OLTP systems to provide a unified data resource via a data warehouse or data mart.

Internet
A worldwide system of interconnected computer networks. The Internet is built on a series of low-level protocols (HTTP, HTML, FTP) and provides easy and powerful exchange of data and information.

Intranet
An internal system of connected networks built on Internet standard protocols and usually connected to the Internet via a firewall.

IS (Information Systems)
The functional division of an organization responsible for the design, implementation, and maintenance of the systems that create, store, and allow access and analysis of the data and resulting information of the enterprise. Also commonly called IT (Information Technology), Information Services, and other variations.

ISDN (Integrated Services Digital Network)
A nonleased digital phone line. ISDN is provided by RBOCs (Regional Bell Operating Companies) in the U.S. and various phone services in other areas of the world. It is a digital standard that allows data transmission of up to 128kbs (kilobits per second) over standard copper, twisted-pair wiring using BRI (Basic Rate Interface) service. ISDN is currently the primary way to deliver relatively high-speed data service to remote offices and homes, although it will most likely be surpassed by various quickly emerging XDSL (Digital Subscriber Line) services that offer much higher transmission rates over the same copper wire transmission medium.

IT (Information Technology)
The functional division of an organization responsible for the design, implementation, and maintenance of the systems that create, store, and allow access and analysis of the

data and resulting information of the enterprise. Also commonly called IS (Information Systems), Information Services, and other variations.

Java

Java is a development language for building computer applications. It was developed as a subset of the C language by Sun Microsystems and has quickly become the industry's primary cross-platform development language. Java is used extensively for WWW, applet, and thin client application development. Java's strength is its ability to run on any computer, provided the computer has a JVM (Java Virtual Machine) available. Its greatest weakness has been that it is an interpreted language, meaning that the JVM must translate the universal Java code to the native computer's operating code as the application executes. This leads to slow performance. This weakness has been mitigated by Java compilers, which generate machine-specific code allowing quick performance, albeit at the cost of the universal cross-platform nature of Java code.

JCL (Job Control Language)

A mainframe programming language used to control the execution of applications.

JVM (Java Virtual Machine)

A computer application that dynamically interprets the Java code contained in an application written in the Java computer development language and translates it to Java byte code, which executes on the local OS and CPU.

Kilobyte

Although commonly expressed as 1,000 bytes, a kilobyte is actually 2^{10} or 1024 bytes.

Knowledge workers

Individuals in an organization tasked with information retrieval and analysis. Historically, the primary customers of IS DSS services.

Kudzu

A nonnative plant introduced into the American South in an attempt to control soil erosion that is renowned for its ability to crowd out other plant life and dominate a local ecosystem.

LAN (Local Area Network)

A connection of computers and servers, usually targeted to providing shared print and file storage services.

Legacy systems

Existing OLTP systems in an organization, usually used to refer to mainframe-based applications.

LegaMart

A nonarchitected data mart that has become entrenched in the business and is relied on by a user constituency.

Load
The insertion of data into a database.

LOB (Line Of Business)
A description of functional organizations in a business, e.g., sales, marketing, manufacturing.

Lotus Notes
A text/document database computer application sold by IBM's Lotus division.

LowLAP (Low-Level Analytical Processing)
Thick client OLAP functionality provided by Q&R/MQE tools.

Magnetic tape
A strip of plastic that has been coated with metal oxide allowing the recording of patterns of magnetic flux, which are interpreted as the 1s and 0s that form the bits of the computing world.

Mainframe
A large-capacity computer that offers high levels of security and stability. Mainframe computers are the traditional domain of the IS professional and provide the environment that modern business computing was built on. Their traditional stability and strength have been offset by their high purchase/lease and operating costs in light of lower cost, high performance server technologies.

Mbs (megabits per second)
1,000 kilobits per second. Usually used to measure network bandwidth, or throughput rates.

MDDBMS (Multi-Dimensional Data Base Management System)
A database system that optimizes the storage, retrieval, and recalculation of multiple dimension data sets. MDDBMSs are commonly used to support MOLAP applications. They provide lightning fast response at the price of limited scaleability and significant management overhead.

Megabyte (MB)
2^{20} bytes, or 1,048,576 bytes.

Mentor
A person who provides guidance, leadership, and coaching.

Meta data
Information about the data warehouse or data mart system. Meta data encompasses all aspects of the data warehouse or data mart system, including technical, human, and data resources.

Meta Group
A consulting and analysis firm best known in the data warehouse industry for its co-sponsorship of the DCI Data Warehousing industry trade shows and conferences.

Methodology
A procedural documentation of the steps required for a successful design, implementation, and maintenance of a data warehouse or data mart system.

Metric
A discernible measurement, e.g., dollars, units, hours.

MF (Mainframe)
See **Mainframe.**

Microsoft
A company that sells a wide variety of computer software and some hardware elements. Most widely known for the MS-DOS and Windows operating systems.

MIPS (Millions of Instructions Per Second)
A measurement of computing power, it is the measurement of the number of instructions executed by a CPU within one second.

Mission statement
A succinct statement of the purpose for an organization, project, or system.

MOLAP (Multidimensional On-Line Analytical Processing)
OLAP analysis provided by a system relying on dedicated, precalculated data sets.

MPP (Massively Parallel Processing)
A computing architecture that combines many CPUs, each with dedicated RAM and DASD resources.

MQE (Managed Query Environment)
An end-user access application that uses a semantic layer to insulate the users from the underlying database structure.

MRE (Managed Reporting Environment)
An end-user application that allows users to access, share, and schedule the delivery of preformatted reports. Some MRE tools allow the users limited ability to modify and/or create reports.

MTD (month to date)
The aggregation of a metric from all activity from the beginning of the month to the current time slice.

Multidimensional aggregation tables
An aggregation that contains metrics calculated along multiple business dimensions, e.g., sales by product by customer.

Multidimensional tables
See **Multidimensional aggregation tables.**

NC (Network Computer)

A thin client computer platform that relies on server resident computation, resources, data, and applications to provide computing services to users.

NDA (Non-Disclosure Agreement)

A legal agreement that binds the recipient of proprietary information to keep all such information confidential.

Network

A system of interconnected computing resources (computers, servers, printers, etc.)

Network bandwidth

A measurement of the transmission speed of the interconnection medium of a network. Usually expressed in Mbs (megabits per second), e.g., 10bms, 100mbs.

Network PC

A thin client computer platform that relies on client-resident computation, resources, data, and applications to provide computing services to users. Sponsored by Microsoft and Intel, Network PCs are basically sealed computers running a low-maintenance version of Microsoft Windows.

Newbie

A person who is new to an area of technology.

Normalized

A type of database design that spreads data into tables that contain only unique and pertinent attributes of the subject of the table.

Novell

A network operating system vendor widely known for its distributed directory services, file, and printer sharing technologies.

NT

A multitasking, multiprocessing server operating system sold by Microsoft.

OC3

An optical data communication standard that allows transmission rates of 155.52 mbs (megabits per second).

OCSD (On-Line Content Scheduling and Delivery)

A set of server-resident applications that allow users to select and schedule delivery of information resources such as reports.

ODS (Operational Data Store)

A set of integrated, scrubbed data without history or summarization provided for tactical decision support. ODSs are also commonly used to populate data warehouses and data marts.

OLAP (On-Line Analytical Processing)
A computer application that allows multidimensional manipulation, display, and visualization of data.

OLTP (On-Line Transaction Processing)
A computer application that automates one or more business processes, e.g., order entry.

OODBs (Object Oriented Data Bases)
A database that allows the storage and retrieval of multiple data types, e.g., text, video, audio, and tabular data.

Optimizer
An element of database systems that seeks to optimize the use of the database resources and speed the retrieval of data by controlling the order of processing and the use of internal resources.

Oracle
A vendor of database systems widely known for its relational database product that dominates the "merchant" database market.

OS (Operating System)
A computer program that controls the operation of the basic elements of the computer (CPU, I/O, memory) and the application programs that are executed.

Partitions
A virtual or physical separation of data in memory or on DASD.

Patricia Seybold Group
A consulting and analyst organization.

PC (Personal Computer)
A computer used by an individual user, usually characterized by a floppy disk, a local hard disk drive, an industry standard CPU, and an industry standard OS.

PERL (Practical Extraction and Report Language)
An interpreted programming language popular in the UNIX environment.

Pilot
An initial test release of a new computer application or system to a small, controlled user group.

Platform
A type of computer system, e.g., mainframe, UNIX, NT.

Political will
The collective support of an initiative, project, or program by an organization.

POTS (Plain Old Telephone Service)
Standard, analog telephone service connected to the public switched phone network.

Primary key

The unique identifier(s) used as unique members of a relational database table.

PSRC (Project Status Report Card)

A hierarchical, collapsible reporting document used to track the status of the primary activities and technologies of a data warehouse or data mart project.

PYMTD (prior year month to date)

A calculated aggregation containing values from the prior year from month beginning to current time slice.

PYTD (prior year to date)

A calculated aggregation containing values from the prior year from the beginning of the year to current time slice.

Q&R (Query and Reporting)

A type of data access and analysis computer application that allows users to build queries of the database and construct reports via a GUI.

QA (Quality Assurance)

A functional group within the IS organization that provides quality standards and audits computer programs and systems for compliance.

QFHs (Queries From Hell)

Queries that overload the database system.

RAID (Redundant Array of Inexpensive Disks)

A DASD hardware/software system that uses a series of interconnected disk drives to provide storage. RAID 1 and RAID 5 are the two most common RAID implementations in data warehousing and data marts. RAID 1 is a mirroring standard, where data is written to two identical disk arrays, providing full backup of information. RAID 5 involves at least one parity disk drive, which facilitates the re-creation of data if a primary data storage disk fails. RAID 1 is quick, but more expensive; RAID 5 requires fewer drives, but is much slower to write information to.

RAM (Random Access Memory)

An electronic component of computers that allows the storage of data in a very fast, read/write environment. OSs and applications are loaded into memory from disk, where they are sequentially executed by the CPU.

RDBMS (Relational Data Base Management System)

A computer application that allows the storage and retrieval of data. Relational databases store data in a series of joined tables.

Red Brick

A vendor of a specialized DSS database which offers very high performance for DSS applications.

Replication
The duplication and distribution of data from one database to one or more additional databases or other target(s).

Replication server
A dedicated computer system that executes a replication application.

Repository
A database system used to store information. In data warehousing and data marts, repositories are most commonly used to store meta data.

Resource tar pits
Areas of a data warehouse or data mart project that consume unexpectedly large amounts of resources for unexpectedly inordinate amounts of time.

RI (Referential Integrity)
A feature of database systems that ensures that any record recorded into the database will be supported by proper primary and foreign keys.

RISC (Reduced Instruction Set Computer)
A CPU that is designed to execute a very limited set of instructions at very high speeds.

ROI (Return On Investment)
The direct attributable value an organization realizes from an investment.

ROLAP (Relational On-Line Analytical Processing)
A computer application that provides OLAP functionality from data stored in a relational database.

Sales engineer (SE)
A technically qualified person who aids in the demonstration and implementation of a product during and after the sales process.

SAS (SAS Institute)
A vendor of computer applications most widely known for its statistical application, SAS, which runs on a variety of computer platforms.

SAS "heads"
People who are very familiar with the design, construction, and operation of applications using the SAS system.

Scaleability
The capability of a hardware or software system to expand to accommodate additional requirements.

Schema
The diagrammatic representation of the data storage aspects of a database system.

Scope

The definition of the extent of a project. There are two aspects to scope, business scope and technical scope.

Scope creep

The slow expansion of scope during a project.

Scrubbing

The correction of errors, omissions, and flaws in the data.

SE (Sales Engineer)

See Sales engineer.

Semantic layer (SL)

A GUI abstraction layer placed between the user and the technical structure of the database.

Server centric

A computer application that stores its data, and optionally its primary application execution, on a server.

Servers

Computer systems connected to one or more clients that provide file storage, printer sharing, data storage, and application execution.

SFA (Sales Force Automation)

A computer application that is designed to support the activities of the sales function, e.g., activity scheduling, contact management.

Slice 'n' dice

The capability to quickly and easily view data along multiple dimensions. The most commonly used feature of OLAP applications.

SL (Semantic Layer)

See Semantic layer.

SMP (Symmetrical Multi-Processing)

A computer system design that uses multiple CPUs that share memory and DASD resources.

Snowflake schema

A variation of the star schema that uses some normalized elements in the dimensions.

Software

Computer code that provides instructions to computer hardware.

Source field

The database field that data is extracted from to be populated into a data warehouse or data mart system.

SP2

An IBM MPP computer system.

Spiral methodology
A methodology that mandates a series of steps that are repeatedly executed sequentially, with an expanding scope for each iteration.

Sponsorship
A person or group within an organization that funds, provides rationale, and takes responsibility for a project.

Spreadsheets
Computer applications that allow for the easy manipulation of numerical calculations.

SQL (Structured Query Language)
A computer programming language used to communicate with database systems.

Staging area
A collection of data extracted from OLTP systems and provided for population into DSS systems.

Star schema
A database design that is based on a central detail fact table linked to surrounding dimension tables. Star schemas allow access to data using business terms and perspectives.

State
The status of a user in a computer application or system.

Subject area
A set of data that is organized to reflect a business perspective and area of interest, e.g., finance, human resources, sales.

Subject oriented
A DSS system that uses subject areas to organize data.

Subset data mart
A data mart that is created by extracting data from a parent data warehouse or parent data mart.

Summarization
See **Aggregation.**

Sustainability Gap
The delta between a short term scale of success for data mart projects (usually restricted to simply delivering some data to users), and a long-term scale of success measured in the sustained success of the entire data mart system.

Sybase
A vendor that sells computer applications. Best known for its RDBMS product and its application development environment, PowerSoft.

Syndicated data
See **Third-party data.**

System of record

An OLTP system that has been identified as the sole or primary source for a target data warehouse or data mart field.

T1/DS1

A dedicated, leased, digital phone line capable of speeds of 1.544 mbs (megabits per second).

T3/DS3

A dedicated, leased, digital phone line capable of speeds of 45 mbs (megabits per second).

Target field

A field in a data warehouse or data mart system that is to be populated with data from a source system.

Terabyte

2^{40} bytes, or 1,099,511,627,776 bytes.

Terminal

See 3270 terminal.

TCP/IP (Transmission Control Protocol/Internet Protocol)

A networking standard that forms the basis for the Internet. Most commonly used in broadcast network systems such as Ethernet.

Thick client

A computer application in which all of the application processing and execution happens on the client.

Thin client

A computer application in which all or most of the application processing and execution happens on the server.

Third-party data

Data sets that are purchased or obtained from sources outside the organization. Census data, industry sales, and market share are common examples.

Time slice

A segment of time, e.g., daily, weekly, monthly.

Top down

A data warehousing and data mart strategy in which the enterprise data warehouse is constructed first, then all subset data marts are created from it.

Topology

A description or representation of the physical devices and connections in a computer or network system.

TPC (Two Phase Commit)
A database standard for OLTP systems that allows multiple databases to be updated with the same data point.

Transformation
The modification of source data prior to its insertion into the target.

Transformation engine
A computer application that transforms data dynamically via a direct connection to the source system and a direct load of the target system.

UI (User Interface)
The portion of a computer application or OS that users interact with in order to control the application or OS.

UNIX
A multiuser, multitasking, multiprocessing operating system originally developed by AT&T.

Up time
A measurement of the availability of computer systems.

UPC (Universal Product Code)
A standard bar code marking and numeric unique identifier applied to products.

URLs (Uniform Resource Locator)
An Internet standard for providing addressing information for WWW pages.

UTP (Unshielded Twisted Pair)
A networking physical topology consisting of twisted pairs of copper wire, such as those used in standard phone wiring.

VEL (Vendor Evaluation Leader)
A person responsible for leading the evaluation and selection of vendors of computer applications in a data warehouse or data mart project.

Virtual enterprise data warehouse
An enterprise data warehouse constructed of multiple data marts and a request broker computer application.

VLDB (Very Large Data Base)
A database containing a vary large collection of data. VLDBs were once considered to be anything more than 200 gigabytes; today the standard is usually any database more than 1 terabyte.

WAN (Wide Area Network)
A network system that connects LANs.

Waterfall methodology

A methodology that mandates that every step of the process must be fully completed before moving on to the subsequent step. Waterfall methodologies are not appropriate for data warehouse or data mart projects due to their very slow speed.

Where clause

A portion of a SQL statement that specifies which qualifications should be applied to determine which rows should be retrieved by the database.

WWW (World Wide Web)

A global selection of HTML pages made available by the Internet.

WYSIWYG (What You See Is What You Get)

A marketing term used to describe computer applications that produce printed versions that exactly match what is displayed on the computer display.

YTD (year to date)

A calculated aggregation containing values from the beginning of the year to the current time slice.

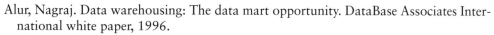

Bibliography

Alur, Nagraj. Data warehousing: The data mart opportunity. DataBase Associates International white paper, 1996.

Appleton, Elaine. Use your data warehouse to compete! *Datamation,* May 1996, pp. 34–38.

Barquin, Ramon, and Edelstein, Herb. Planning and designing the data warehouse. Prentice-Hall, Upper Saddle River, NJ, 1997.

Brackett, Michael H. The data warehouse challenge, taming data chaos. Wiley, New York, 1996.

Comaford, Christine. Attention: Data mart shoppers! *PC Week,* September 23, 1996.

Darling, Charles. How to integrate your data warehouse. *Datamation,* May 15, 1996.

DBMS interview—February 1996: Meta Group's Karen Rubenstrunk. *DBMS,* February 1996.

Dorshkind, Brent. Warehouses ride NT to workgroup. *LAN Times,* October 10, 1996.

Eckerson, Wayne. Understanding data marts, research report. Patricia Seybold Group, 1996.

Fadlalla, Adam. Data warehousing technologies. *Enterprise Systems Journal,* October 1996.

Fisher, Lawrence M. Along the Infobahn: Data warehouses. *Strategy & Business,* Q3/96, 4, pp. 76–83.

Fosdick, Howard. Moving data between servers. *Enterprise Systems Journal,* June 1996, pp. 49–52.

Gambon, Jill. Best medicine: Data warehouses—Pharmaceutical. *Information Week,* September 9, 1996.

Gill, Harjinder S., and Rao, Prakash C. The official guide to data warehousing. QUE, Indianapolis, IN, 1996.

Graham, Stephen. The financial impact of data warehousing. *DM Review,* Vol. 6, No. 6, June 1996, pp. 39–41.

Haber, Lynn. Data mart decisions. *Client/Server Computing,* September 1996.

Haris, Alexander. Window of opportunity. *Individual Investor,* July 1996, pp. 54–55.

Harmon, Tim. Getting data mart smart. Meta Group presentation, 1996.

Hufford, Duane. Data warehouse quality, Part 1. *DM Review,* Vol. 6, No. 1, January 1996, pp. 51–52.

Hufford, Duane. Data warehouse quality, Part 2. *DM Review,* Vol. 6, No. 2, February 1996, pp. 31–34.

Hurd, Mark. Data warehouse business case. *DM Review,* Vol. 6, No. 8, September 1996, pp. 16–20.

Imhoff, Claudia. End users, Use 'em or lose 'em. *DM Review,* Vol. 6, No. 10, November 1996, pp. 54–56.

Imhoff, Claudia. Migrating from data marts to the architected data warehouse environment. Presentation at the 1997 Second Annual Implementation Conference. The Data Warehousing Institute, 1997.

Inmon, W. H., and Hackathorn, Richard D. Using the data warehouse. Wiley, New York, 1994.

Inmon, W. H. Building the data warehouse. Wiley, New York, 1992.

Inmon, W. H. Refreshment strategies in the data warehouse environment. *Enterprise Systems Journal,* September 1996.

Inmon, W. H. Virtual data warehouses: The snake oil of the '90s. *DM Review,* Vol. 6, No. 4, April 1996, pp. 50–54.

Inmon, W. H., Imhoff, Claudia, and Battas, Greg. Building the operational data store. Wiley, New York, 1996.

Kay, Emily. Business analysis: Decisions, decisions. *Information Week,* June 17, 1996, pp. 73–77.

Kelly, Sean. Data warehousing, The route to mass customization. Wiley, West Sussex, England, 1996.

Kimball, Ralph. Dangerous preconceptions. *DBMS,* August 1996.

Kimball, Ralph. Factless fact tables. *DBMS,* September 1996.

Kimball, Ralph. The data warehouse toolkit. Wiley, New York, 1996.

Lambert, Bob. Break old habits to define data warehousing requirements. *DM Review,* Vol. 5, No. 11, December 1995, pp. 50–51.

Leon, Mark. Meta data standards vie for spotlight. *InfoWorld,* September 30, 1996.

Lovelace, Herbert. Dining at the paradigm. *Information Week,* September 23, 1996.

Meredith, Mary Edie, and Khader, Aslam. Designing large warehouses. *Database Programming & Design,* June 1996, pp. 25–30.

Newman, David. Data warehouse architecture. *DM Review,* Vol. 6, No. 9, October 1996, pp. 34–38.

Osterfelt, Sue. Glitz vs. punch line. *DM Review,* Vol. 6, No. 10, November 1996, p. 26.

Poe, Vidette. Building a data warehouse for decision support. Prentice-Hall PTR, Upper Saddle River, NJ, 1996.

Read, Jeffrey. Power is but six rules away. *Computing Canada,* September 29, 1996.

Scherr, Jay. How to budget a warehouse. *Computing Canada,* September 26, 1996.

Sidhu, Ranbir. Enterprise computing: Nynex data mart. *InfoWorld,* August 19, 1996.

Stedman, Craig. No mart is an island. *ComputerWorld,* October 7, 1996.

Stedman, Craig. Warehouse costs scare up changes. *ComputerWorld,* September 23, 1996.

Tanler, Richard. Data warehouses & data marts: Choose your weapon. *DM Review,* Vol. 6, No. 2, February 1996, pp. 14–17.

Tholemeir, Robert, Thomas, David M., and Kappel, Richard W. Data Warehousing—a competitive necessity, *First Albany Corporation research report,* 1997.

Thomas, David M., and Kappel, Richard. Relational database management systems (RDBMS) research report. First Albany, 1996.

Varney, Sarah. Datamarts: Coming to an IT mall near you! *Datamation,* June 1996, pp. 44–46.

Waterson, Karen. Database replication explained. *Datamation,* September 1, 1996.

Watson, Hugh J., and Haley, Barbara J. Data warehousing: A framework and survey of current practices. *Journal of Data Warehousing,* Vol. 2, No. 1, January 1997, pp. 10–17.

Weldon, Jay-Louise. Queries plus. *Database Programming & Design,* March 1996, pp. 25–27.

White, Colin. Data warehouse: What's in a name? *Database Programming & Design,* March 1996, pp. 53–54.

Winter, Richard. Birds, bees, and bitmaps. *Database Programming & Design,* June 1996, pp. 55–57.

Index